# Market Segmentation

# Market Segmentation

How to do it
How to profit from it

Malcolm McDonald and Ian Dunbar

ELSEVIER
BUTTERWORTH
HEINEMANN

AMSTERDAM • BOSTON • HEIDELBERG • LONDON • NEW YORK • OXFORD • PARIS
SAN DIEGO • SAN FRANCISCO • SINGAPORE • SYDNEY • TOKYO

Elsevier Butterworth-Heinemann
Linacre House, Jordan Hill, Oxford OX2 8DP
30 Corporate Drive, Burlington, MA 01803

First published 2004

**British Library Cataloguing in Publication Data**
McDonald, Malcolm, 1938–
   Market segmentation : how to do it, how to profit from it
   1. Market segmentation
   I. Title II. Dunbar, Ian, 1951–
   658.8'02

   ISBN 0 7506 5981 5

**Library of Congress Cataloguing in Publication Data**
A catalogue record for this book is available from the Library of Congress

For information on all Elsevier Butterworth-Heinemann publications visit our website at http://books.elsevier.com

Printed and bound in The Netherlands

# Contents

# Foreword

One of the abiding principles of sound business practice is: 'Know your customer; know your market.'

The objective, of course, is to gain competitive advantage by building sustained customer loyalty, with products and services meeting, quite precisely, the demands of closely defined markets.

As markets have become more complex, so has this essentially basic process of market segmentation. It is the view of many that, in both the manufacturing and service sectors, the art of defining target markets rarely progresses beyond the assembly of somewhat dull demographics. The logical conclusion is that, if everybody is doing the same, differential advantage is difficult to attain.

Now, Professor Malcolm McDonald and Ian Dunbar have peeled away the layers of complexity and confusion to produce a step-by-step guide through the difficult terrain of market segmentation. The value of their book to business people everywhere is that it offers the kind of practical applications needed in today's intensely competitive marketplace.

Lord Marshall of Knightsbridge
Chairman, British Airways

# Preface and acknowledgements

This book has its origins in a painstaking process of research into the practical difficulties that organizations experience in segmenting their markets, research which we initiated in 1992. We discovered that most of the academic work in this domain is prescriptive, with virtually no pragmatic guidelines provided to enable managers to make sense of the confusing array of data and information available to them.

So we developed a process, which we worked through with some of the best-known companies in the world, amending the process until it was sufficiently robust to share with a wider audience. The result was the first edition of this book which was launched in 1995.

Since its launch, the extensive adoption of our market segmentation process by companies ranging from world leaders in their fields to smaller domestic companies has continuously broadened our knowledge base substantially. This has enabled us to refine the process, improve the guidelines for its implementation, identify where more detailed explanation is required and, at the same time, develop a quick route through the process for those readers who are familiar with the detail and require only a summary of how to implement each step.

The result is this third edition of the book in which we have not only advanced the improvements introduced into the second edition (1998) with respect to the segmentation process, supporting examples, worked-through case study and worksheets, but have also introduced new practical approaches to its implementation, exercises to help with learning and a 'Fast track' for each step in the process.

Our presentation of the process in this book enables the segmentation practitioner to follow each step manually, utilizing data already held by the company. We recognize, however, that in many markets the range and complexity of data the practitioner may have to address and then manage can become a distraction, the time and effort required to extract the maximum value from the analysis diverting their attention away from the marketing issues they need to concentrate on and carefully consider. For such markets we have provided the required help in a PC-based software package. This package, called *Market Segment Master*®, has now been substantially upgraded to a state of the art software tool that not only supports the process as it appears in this book but also provides a practical tool to marketers for running cluster routines on appropriate data from other sources, such as externally commissioned segmentation research projects. Readers who would like the help of software in segmenting their markets can obtain details and order their copies at www.marketsegmentation.co.uk. Alternatively, contact Ian Dunbar at The Market Segmentation Company, 22 The Platt, Haywards Heath, West Sussex, RH16 2SY, United Kingdom (tel. +44 (0) 1444 441110, fax +44 (0) 1444 441011, e-mail info@marketsegmentation. co.uk), or contact Professor Malcolm McDonald at Cranfield University School of Management, Cranfield, Bedford, MK43 0AL, United Kingdom (e-mail m.mcdonald@cranfield.ac.uk).

Returning to this book, we would like to stress that it is most definitely a practical book which, if used properly, will result in actionable market segments. To achieve this result will require time and resources. It is not a book just for reading. It is for reading and doing, and is best used by a team, rather than an individual.

Finally, to name everyone who should appear in this acknowledgements section is impossible, because so many clients we have had the privilege of working with and the many colleagues who have been interested in our work have influenced our education, thinking and practical development of the process presented here over the years until it became 'watertight'. Two particular colleagues we would like to mention, however, are Dr Hugh Wilson, whose work in 'e-marketing' has enhanced our understanding of the issues to be addressed by market segmentation in this modern, electronic, fast-changing world, and Marcus Clark who, along with his team, has invested a substantial amount of time and resources over the last few years in developing our new software.

We both wish you a happy and profitable segmentation.

Malcolm McDonald and Ian Dunbar

# An important note to the reader from the authors

```
   ┌──────────┐
  ╱            ╲
 ╱     STOP     ╲
 ╲              ╱
  ╲            ╱
   └──────────┘
```

**1**

Successful segmentation is the product of a detailed understanding of your market and will therefore take time.

**2**

Segmentation is appropriate for those markets where it is essential to combine individual customers or consumers into larger buying 'units' to ensure your marketing activity is both cost-effective and manageable.

**3**

The process as presented in this book is aimed primarily at defining segments in terms of the particular marketing mix each requires. Segmentation at higher levels is, of course, possible and many of the principles contained in this book would apply, although in a less detailed form.

For those who need a quick route through
the segmentation process, the 'Fast track'
sections at the beginning of Chapters 4 to
10 will help you. Be careful however:

A little learning is a dangerous thing.
Drink deep, or taste not the Pierian Spring.

Alexander Pope

Refer to the main body of the chapter
whenever this is required to complete its
particular step in the process successfully.

# Deciding on which track you need

It is important that you complete the questionnaire on the page opposite
before you decide on which track you need.

# ARE YOU GETTING THESE ESSENTIAL DELIVERABLES FROM YOUR MARKET SEGMENTATION?

**Score out of 10**
0 = not at all
## Market structure and segmentation
10 = totally

Q1     Is there a clear and unambiguous definition
of the market you are interested in serving,
with the definition based on a specific purpose
or intended use, not on a product or service?      [     ]

Q2     Is the market clearly mapped, showing
product/service flows, volumes/values
in total, where decisions are made and
the quantities they account for?      [     ]

Q3     Are the segments clearly described and sized?
These must be groups of customers
with the same, or comparable, set of needs,
not demographics or sectors.      [     ]

Q4     Are the real needs of these segments properly
quantified, with the relative importance of these
needs clearly identified?      [     ]

Q5     Are the segments clearly linked to a set of
characteristics that identify the customers
found within them?      [     ]

## Target segments

Q6     Are all the segments classified according to
their relative attractiveness to the company
over the next three years based on clear,
unambiguous criteria?      [     ]

Q7     Is there a clear and quantified analysis of how
well your company satisfies the needs of these
segments compared to competitors, as perceived
by the customers found within them?      [     ]

## Segment-based marketing

Q8     Are your marketing objectives set by segment
and consistent with their position in the portfolio?   [     ]

Q9     Are the strategies for these segments (including
products, price, place and service) consistent
with these objectives?      [     ]

Q10    Is there a structure, information and decision-
making system which enables you to serve
these segments effectively?      [     ]

                                   **Total score**      [     ]

## Interpretation

In our experience, not many readers are able to score above five on many of these questions. This is not the point, however. The purpose of the questionnaire is to focus your attention at the beginning of the book on what essential deliverables market segmentation should produce. You can then determine the extent to which you need to focus on the detailed contents of this book.

If you work carefully through this book and implement it in your organization, you will be able to give yourself high scores in all boxes. Then, you will be a truly market-focused organization!

Malcolm McDonald and Ian Dunbar

# List of figures

# List of tables

# Chapter 1
# **The state of marketing**

# Summary

This chapter provides a brief review of the state of the marketing domain. It provides some reflections on why, following the white heat of excitement about the future of marketing in the early 1960s, it has today lost much of its influence in the corporate world, in spite of all our best efforts. The purpose of focusing on the many things that have gone wrong with marketing is to emphasize the pivotal importance of this book, since it is the failure to get to grips with market segmentation that lies at the heart of much of this failure. Little of what is best in marketing theory and practice works without correct market segmentation.

This chapter is immediately followed by a chapter that sets out a model designed to put marketing back at the heart of organizational strategy-making and, in doing so, bring about its recovery. At the core of this model is market segmentation.

This chapter is organized as follows:

- A review of marketing practice
- Consultants and fads
- The distancing of academics from the real world
- A brief summary of how marketing can recover
- A review of the chapter

# Achievements

Perhaps there is some point to all the recent concerns that have been raised about the state of marketing. So, before suggesting a way forward, let us make a very brief review of what we have achieved after over fifty years of marketing. Let us look at the three main constituent parts: practitioners; consultants; and academics.

## Practitioners

As for practitioners, what better place to start than with the 43 companies featured in the famous book by Peters and Waterman, *In Search of Excellence* (1982), of which, according to Richard Pascale (1990), only six were still excellent eight years later on.

A review of Britain's best performing companies over the period 1979–2000 reveals that, since the year they were at the top, over 25 per cent of them have subsequently collapsed, nearly 33 per cent have been acquired and of those that survive, many have not had the smoothest of rides.

Table 1.1 shows the profitability and defection rate of a real company by segment (particularly note the company's performance in the least and most profitable segments), whilst Figure 1.1 (from a Cranfield University School of Management database of leading European companies using an anonymous Audience Response System) shows that, in spite of the famous article on customer retention by Reicheld and Sasser (Jnr.) (1990), very few companies measure customer retention by segment.

For 'customer' also read 'consumer'. A discussion about these two terms appears in Chapter 4.

In spite of its importance, very few companies measure customer retention by segment.

**Table 1.1** Measurement of segment profitability and defection

| | Total market | Segment | | | | | |
|---|---|---|---|---|---|---|---|
| | | 1 | 2 | 3 | 4 | 5 | 6 |
| Percentage of market represented by segment | 100.0 | 14.8 | 9.5 | 27.1 | 18.8 | 18.8 | 11.0 |
| Percentage of all profits in total market produced by segment | 100.0 | 7.1 | 4.9 | 14.7 | 21.8 | 28.5 | 23.0 |
| Ratio of profit produced by segment to weight of segment in total population | 1.0 | 0.48 | 0.52 | 0.54 | 1.16 | 1.52 | 2.09 |
| Defection rate (percentage) | 23.0 | 20.0 | 17.0 | 15.0 | 28.0 | 30.0 | 35.0 |

*Source:* Payne, A. (1999). Cranfield University School of Management database.

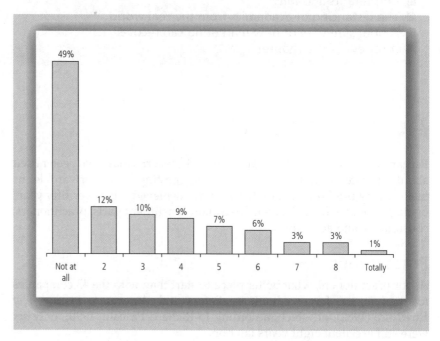

**Figure 1.1**
Companies measuring customer retention by market segment
(*Source:* Cranfield University School of Management (April 2002). Marketing Value Added conference.)
(*Note:* The scale ranges from 1, 'Not at all', to 9, 'Totally'.)

In spite of the fact that it always has been the cost of dealing with customers after the product or service leaves the 'factory' that determines profitability, very few organizations measure segment or customer profitability.

Figures 1.2 and 1.3, also from a Cranfield University School of Management database of over 500 leading European companies over a five year period, show clearly that very few organizations measure segment or customer profitability, in spite of the fact that it always has been the cost of dealing with customers after the product or service leaves the 'factory' that determines profitability.

Figure 1.4 indicates what marketing information the financial community needs to make sensible investment decisions. It also shows very clearly that very little of this is reported in annual accounts.

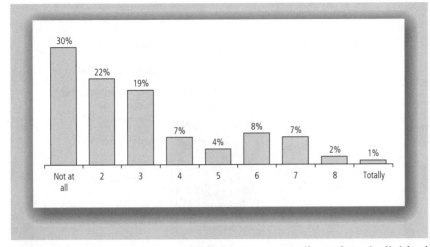

**Figure 1.2**   The extent to which costs are attributed to individual accounts
(*Source:* Cranfield University School of Management (2002).
Key Account Management Research Club.)
(*Note:* The question asked was, 'To what extent do you allocate attributable costs (interface costs) to individual accounts (not marmalading costs across the whole customer base)?' The scale ranges from 1, 'Not at all', to 9, 'Totally'. Figures represent the average for the years 1998 to 2002 inclusive.)

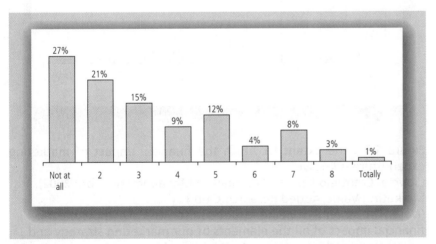

**Figure 1.3**   The extent to which the real profitability of the top ten accounts is known
(*Source:* Cranfield University School of Management (2002).
Key Account Management Research Club.)
(*Note:* The question asked was, 'How well do you know the real profitability of the top ten accounts?' The scale ranges from 1, 'Not at all', to 9, 'Totally'. Figures represent the average for the years 1998 to 2002 inclusive.)

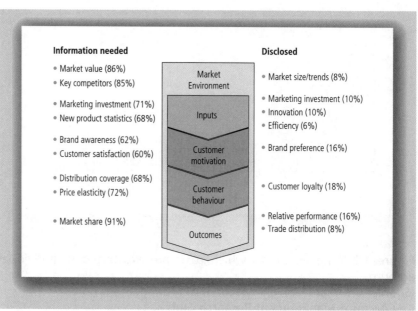

**Figure 1.4**
External investor marketing disclosure (*Source:* 'Information needed', Brand Finance plc (1999); 'Disclosed', Davidson, H., Cranfield University School of Management visiting professor. Used with kind permission.)

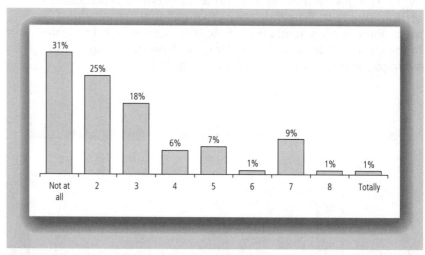

**Figure 1.5** The extent to which the financial impact of marketing expenditure is known
(*Source:* Cranfield University School of Management (April 2002). Marketing Value Added Research Club.)
(*Note:* The statement being responded to was, 'We know the financial impact of all the elements of our marketing strategy and we measure and report them to the board.' The scale ranges from 1, 'Not at all', to 9, 'Totally'.)

From yet another Cranfield University School of Management database which captures the attitudes of senior non-marketing managers to marketing practitioners, we find that marketing practitioners are seen as 'unaccountable, untouchable, expensive and slippery'. This leaves us in little doubt about the current state of marketing practice.

Finally, and also from a Cranfield University School of Management database, Figure 1.5 reveals a depressing honesty amongst senior marketing practitioners about their lack of knowledge about the financial impact of marketing expenditure.

In short, notwithstanding that the above represents a somewhat random and biased selection of examples of the state of practitioner marketing, most readers will recognize that they are not far from the truth.

## Consultants

Turning secondly to consultants, which includes the likes of advertising agencies, they appear to have fared little better.

The authors have painstakingly listed over three hundred consultant fads developed during the past thirty years, a small selection of which are listed in Table 1.2.

**Table 1.2** A selection from some 300 fads – 1970 to date

| *Fad* |
| --- |
| In Search of Excellence |
| Marketing Warfare |
| One Minute Manager |
| Managing by Walking About (MBWA) |
| Skunk Works |
| 7 Ss |

During the past 10 years, many companies have sought a remedy for their declining fortunes by retreating into faddism, hungrily adopting one fad after another as they were peddled by eager consultants. In most cases these initiatives have failed, because organizations have treated them as a quick-fix bolt-on without addressing their underlying problems.

One such fad has been business process re-engineering (BPR). This has been an outstanding success in those companies which have used it to redesign their processes to create value for customers. But in those organizations which have not grasped the nettle of customer satisfaction, it has achieved merely cosmetic productivity improvements (Edwards and Peppard, 1997). Yet another has been balanced scorecards. This too, for CEOs who understand the need to balance the requirements of all the stakeholders in a company delivering customer value, has been very successful. It is a strategy used with great success by BAA (British Airports Authority plc), for example, for managing its complex web of stakeholder relationships. But for those CEOs who do not understand the importance of being market driven, it has proved to be just another fad.

Of course all of these initiatives are fabulous and do work, but only when they are seen in the context of providing superior customer value as a means of providing superior shareholder value. Alas, even in those organizations committed to 'relationship' and 'one-to-one' marketing, too

*All of these initiatives are fabulous and do work, but only when they are seen in the context of providing superior customer value.*

often customers remain the Cinderellas. As Harvard Business School's Susan Fournier has pointed out (Fournier, Dobscha and Mick, 1998), rapid development of relationship techniques in the USA has been accompanied by growing customer dissatisfaction. The much vaunted relationship that companies were so eager to forge with their customers involved not so much delighting them as abusing them, suggested Fournier.

The problem is that companies have become so internally focused they have got carried away with supply-side issues and taken their eye off the customer ball. *Until organizations make a serious effort to lift their heads above the parapet and understand their markets and their customers better, all the great initiatives referred to above will amount to expensive, time-consuming mistakes.* Most boards are spending too much of their valuable time on internal operational efficiency (doing things right) at the expense of external operational effectiveness (doing the right things).

In conclusion, whilst consultants have not surprisingly fared somewhat better than the marketing practitioner community, they could hardly be adjudged to have had a big impact on practice.

## Academics

Finally, of course, there is the academic community. Table 1.3 lists a small selection of quotations from well-known academics. Most damning of all is the last one.

**Table 1.3** Quotations from well-known academics

| Quote and author |
| --- |
| 'Much research is directed at technical refinement, which produces low risk, quick win publications that are largely irrelevant or incomprehensible to practitioners. The voice of academics is becoming weaker.'<br>Hugh Wilmott<br>Manchester Business School |
| Robin Wensley said that marketing academics have had little impact.<br>'A much wider understanding of the nature of the competitive market place is required, given that it is such a central phenomenon.' |
| 'Of the ten issues most concerning practitioners (confirmed by three academic papers and the Marketing Science Institute of America), the number of papers that addressed them in the two top, five-star rated academic journals was a derisory 4 per cent.'<br>Malcolm McDonald<br>Cranfield University School of Management |

*Source:* McDonald, M. (2000). Academy of Marketing Debate, University of Derby.

Academics are being increasingly encouraged to write for a narrow, esoteric audience in media which are of little relevance to the real world.

One wonders whether there is a grain of truth in the assertion that academics are being increasingly encouraged to write for a narrow, esoteric audience in media which are of little relevance to the real world.

Whilst academic journals clearly have relevance to academics and whilst their role is fully appreciated, the influence and prestige afforded to them in university business schools is out of all proportion to the problems facing the global marketing community and only succeeds in diverting the abundant genius in our academic community into a cul-de-sac. Furthermore, the style of such pieces is also becoming increasingly dense, impenetrable and irrelevant.

# Recapturing the high ground

The net impact of this sad neglect by the academic, consultant and practitioner communities is that marketing as a function has been increasingly relegated away from the core strategy-making engine of organizations to become a sales support department, in charge of T-shirts and promotion.

So, what can be done to begin to recover from the sorry state the marketing community finds itself in?

First, we have to work hard to recapture the high ground – the strategy domain – and firmly establish it as a key, strategic function with a clearly defined purpose which can be measured, researched, developed, protected and examined. This, however, means reaching some kind of consensus about what marketing is.

> The marketing community will have to work hard to recapture the high ground – the strategy domain – and firmly establish it as a key, strategic function.

Let us be unequivocal about marketing. Marketing is a process for:

- defining markets;
- quantifying the needs of the customer groups (segments) within these markets;
- determining the value propositions to meet these needs;
- communicating these value propositions to all those people in the organization responsible for delivering them and getting their buy-in to their role;
- playing an appropriate part in delivering these value propositions (usually only communications);
- monitoring the value actually delivered.

For this process to be effective, organizations need to be consumer/customer driven, which is the main purpose of this book. Above all, organizations need to understand that, without correct market definition and correct market segmentation, marketing will never occupy a central role in strategy-making.

## Chapter 1 review

This chapter provided evidence of the failure of marketing to have a major influence in boardrooms. In arriving at this conclusion, we briefly reviewed what had been achieved over the past fifty years of marketing with respect to practitioners, consultants and academics.

We concluded that much of this failure can be attributed to a lack of understanding of the pivotal importance of market segmentation in successful marketing. This is where this book now takes us in the next chapter.

# References

Edwards, C. and Peppard, J. (1997). 'Operationalising strategy through processes'. *Long Range Planning*, Vol. 30. No. 5, 753–6.

Fournier, S., Dobscha, S. and Mick, D. G. (1998). 'Preventing the premature death of relationship marketing'. *Harvard Business Review*, January–February, 42–50.

Pascale, R. T. (1990). *Managing on the Edge*. New York: Simon and Schuster.

Peters, T. J. and Waterman, R. H. (1982). *In Search of Excellence*. New York: Warner Books.

Reicheld, F. F. and Sasser, W. E. (Jnr.) (1990). 'Zero defections: Quality comes to service'. *Harvard Business Review*, September–October, 105–11.

Chapter 2

# The central role of market segmentation in profitable growth

# Summary

Although marketing may have currently fallen behind other business disciplines in its race for the strategy stakes, it is the firm belief of the authors that it has only temporarily stumbled. Marketing's epitaph is far from being written, as proved by the dedicated, professional marketers in numerous companies around the world who are making major contributions to the financial success of their companies through their detailed understanding of the markets they are in, in-depth insights into the needs of their customers and the development and delivery of carefully targeted value propositions.

This chapter outlines what marketing should actually entail if it is to regain its rightful place at the heart of organizational strategy-making. At the core of this model of best practice is market segmentation.

This chapter is organized as follows:

- A review of the definition of 'Marketing' and what it actually entails
- The central role of defining markets and segments, and understanding value
- A summary of the processes involved in determining the value proposition to the customer
- The challenge of integrated marketing communications
- A look at delivering and communicating the value proposition
- How to monitor the value delivered to the customer, and received from the customer
- The role of marketing in value creation
- A review of the chapter

# From tactics to strategy

The marketing process introduced at the end of Chapter 1 is shown diagrammatically in Figure 2.1.

Before expanding on each box, it will be seen that boxes 1 and 2 are clearly about strategy determination, whilst boxes 3 and 4 are about tactical implementation and measurement. It is these latter two that have come to represent marketing as a function, which is still principally seen as sales support and promotion.

> One of the authors recently drove through a new housing estate, where a neon sign above an upmarket prefab blasted out the following words: *'The Marketing Suite'*, loosely translated as: *'This is where you come to get sold to'*. And when government bodies, charities and the like say *'we need marketing'*, what they mostly mean is *'we need some promotion'*.

The options, then, are clear. We either stop this pretence at strategy and concentrate on where the marketing community actually is, which is sales support, or take marketing centre stage, with a major impact on corporate strategy development.

● Definition: Marketing is a process for: defining markets; quantifying the needs of the customer groups (segments) within these markets; determining the value propositions to meet these needs; communicating these value propositions to all those people in the organization responsible for delivering them and getting their buy-in to their role; playing an appropriate part in delivering these value propositions (usually only communications); monitoring the value actually delivered. For this process to be effective, organizations need to be consumer/customer driven.

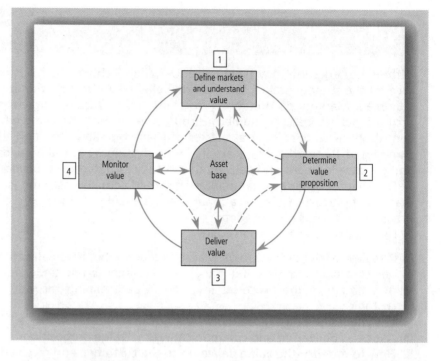

**Figure 2.1**
The marketing domain (*Source:* McDonald, M. (2002). *Marketing Plans: How to Prepare Them, How to Use Them*. Oxford: Butterworth-Heinemann.)

There is more than enough evidence that three of the fundamental determinants of corporate success, namely, correct market definition, market segmentation and positioning, are poorly understood in the corporate world at large.

There is more than enough evidence that three of the fundamental determinants of corporate success, namely, correct market definition, market segmentation and positioning, are poorly understood in the corporate world at large. So, let us begin by looking in a little more detail at each of the boxes in Figure 2.1.

The process is clearly cyclical, in that monitoring the value delivered will update the organization's understanding of the value that is required by its customers. The cycle may be predominantly an annual one, with a marketing plan documenting the output from the 'Understand value' and 'Determine value proposition' processes, but equally changes throughout the year may involve fast iterations around the cycle to respond to particular opportunities or problems.

We have used the term 'Determine value proposition', to make plain that we are here referring to the decision-making process of deciding what the offering to the customer is to be – what value the customer will receive, and what value (typically the purchase price and ongoing revenues) the organization will receive in return. The process of delivering this value proposition, such as by making and delivering a physical product or by delivering a service, is covered by 'Deliver value'.

We use the word 'proposition' to indicate the nature of the offer from the organization to the market.

Thus, it can be seen that the first two boxes are concerned with strategic planning processes (in other words, developing market strategies), whilst the third and fourth boxes are concerned with the actual delivery in the market of what was planned and then measuring the effect. Throughout, we use the word 'proposition' to indicate the nature of the offer from the organization to the market.

It is well known that not all of the value proposition delivering processes will be under the control of the marketing department, whose role varies considerably between organizations. The marketing department should be responsible for and central to the first two processes, 'Understand value' and 'Determine value proposition', although even these need to involve numerous functions, albeit co-ordinated by specialist marketing personnel. The 'Deliver value' process is the role of the whole company, including for example product development, manufacturing, purchasing, sales promotion, direct mail, distribution, sales and customer service.

The various choices made during this marketing process are constrained and informed not just by the outside world, but also by the organization's asset base. Whereas an efficient new factory with much spare capacity might underpin a growth strategy in a particular market, a factory running at full capacity would cause more reflection on whether price should be used to control demand, unless the potential demand warranted further capital investment. As well as physical assets, choices may be influenced by financial, human resources, brand and information technology assets, to name just a few.

## Define markets and segments, and understand value

Whilst the fundamental purpose of this book is about market definition and segmentation, the purpose of this section in this chapter is to position the segmentation process as being central to every corporate function.

Inputs to this stage of the process will commonly include:

- the corporate mission and objectives, which will determine which markets are of interest;
- external data such as market research;
- internal data which flows from ongoing operations.

The process involves four major sub-processes, shown in Figure 2.2.

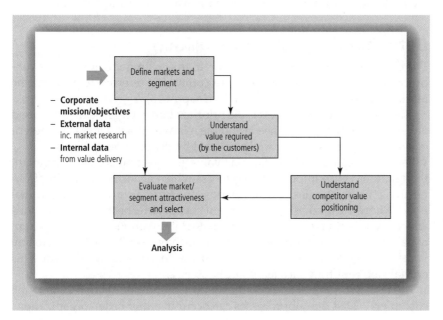

**Figure 2.2**
Define markets and segments, and understand value

First, it is necessary to define the markets the organization is in, or wishes to be in, and how these divide into segments of customers with similar needs. The details of how this can be done are the core of this book. The choice of markets will be influenced by the corporate objectives as well as the asset base. Information will be collected about the markets, such as the markets' size and growth, with estimates for the future.

Once each market has been defined, it is necessary to understand what value the customers within each of the segments it divides into are looking for. This value is most simply thought of as the benefits gained from the product or service, but it can also encompass the value to the customer of surrounding services such as maintenance or information. This step also encompasses what the customer is prepared to give in exchange, in terms of price and other criteria, such as loyalty. Expressing customer value requirements is dealt with in detail in Chapter 7. This step of 'Understand value required' also includes predicting the value which will be required in the future.

'Understand competitor value positioning' refers to the process of establishing how well the organization and its competitors currently deliver the value that the customers seek. Again it involves looking into the future to predict how competitors might improve, clearly a factor in planning how the organization is to respond.

From these three processes, the relative attractiveness of the different markets and, within each of them, their different segments can be evaluated. One tool of relevance here is Porter's five forces model (1985), showing the forces which shape industry competition and hence the attractiveness of a given market, or of a given segment.

The output will be some form of analysis, and one way of summing up much of the key information is in a portfolio matrix. Such a matrix provides a sensible basis for prioritization amongst the many possible product/ segment combinations which the organization could address. A detailed methodology for doing this is outlined in Chapters 9 and 10.

## Determine the value proposition

The definition of the value proposition to the customer contains five sub-processes, shown in Figure 2.3 (more commonly referred to as 'strategic marketing planning' and looked at in Chapter 13).

The key input to this process is the prioritization of target segments, based on an analysis of customer needs and the relative attractiveness of different customer segments, which was produced by the previous process.

Before we can begin to plan our value proposition for each segment, though, there is an important subprocess which is normally missing from planning methodologies: 'Predict market structure'. This deals with the vital issue of how the market structure might change, irrespective of any actions which we might take, as a result of channel innovations. Clearly if we are to be bypassed by our suppliers, or if our customers are likely to wish to buy via an e-hub rather than directly from us, we need to know about it. This crucial step is outlined in detail in Chapter 12.

The next two subprocesses define the core of the value proposition to the customer. Whilst the subprocesses can occur in either order, organizations

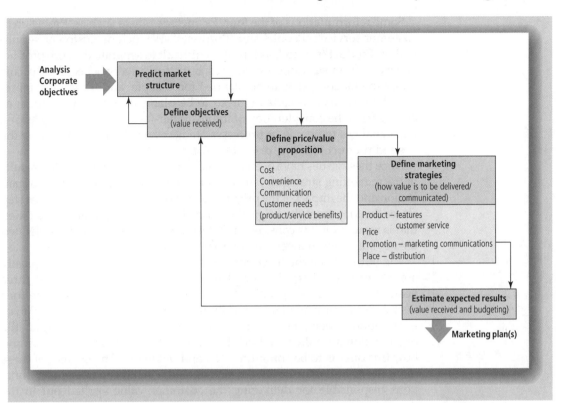

**Figure 2.3**
Determine value proposition

typically start by defining the value they hope to receive from the segment: 'Define objectives'. This involves defining marketing objectives in terms, for example, of market share, volume, value or contribution by segment.

The other half of the equation is defining the value to be delivered to the customer in return. This price/value proposition can be thought of using the four 'Cs': 'Cost', 'Convenience', 'Communications' and 'Consumer wants and needs' (Lauterborn, 1990). These translate the four 'Ps' of marketing from what the organization does to what the customer cares about. For example, the customer is concerned with 'convenience' of purchase, which influences how the organization will 'place' the product through distribution channels. Similarly, instead of 'product', we have 'consumer wants and needs' which are met by the product. The customer is interested in the total 'cost' to them, not necessarily just the upfront 'price'. And finally, 'promotion' translates into the two-way 'communications' in which customers declare their requirements and learn about the organization's offerings.

The fourth subprocess may involve iterations with the third one since, in defining the marketing strategies – how the value is to be delivered and communicated – it may be necessary to reconsider what that value can actually be. We have listed the four major aspects of this process using the four 'Ps'. While separate plans, or plan sections, may be produced for each of these, the decisions are closely intertwined: for example, the choice of distribution channel will impact what communications are feasible, what surrounding services can be delivered, and what price can be charged.

Some reformulations of the four 'Ps' include others such as 'Provision of customer service', 'People' and 'Processes'. We include customer service within 'Product/service', as it is often difficult to separate the core product or service from surrounding services, but clearly every aspect for the customer interaction needs to be planned for. 'People' and 'Processes' represent dimensions that certainly need to be planned, but we view them as arising from the consideration of the customer-focused four 'Ps', by asking what changes to people or processes are necessary in order to achieve the desired product offering, price, place or promotions.

Once these issues have been resolved, an estimate of the expected results of the marketing strategies can be made, in terms of the costs to the organization and the impact of the price/value proposition on sales. This final step closes the loop from the original setting of objectives, as it may be iteration that is required if it is considered that the strategies that have been defined are not sufficient to meet the financial objectives.

The output from the 'Determine value proposition' process is typically a strategic marketing plan, or plans, covering a period of at least three years. In some cases, specific plans are produced for aspects of the four 'Ps', such as a pricing plan, a distribution plan, a customer service plan or a promotions plan. However, even when no plans are produced, the organization is implicitly taking decisions on the offer to the customer and how this offer is to be communicated and delivered. The content of these plans has to be communicated to and agreed with all departments or functions responsible for delivering the customer value spelled out in the plans.

> The output from the 'Determine value proposition' process is typically a strategic marketing plan, or plans, covering a period of at least three years.

## Integrated marketing communications

Before considering the delivery of value, we will give some further attention to promotion, as this is ultimately crucial in creating value for stakeholders. Promotion is changing in a number of respects. New channels such as the internet are emphasizing an already growing trend from mass media such as advertising through addressable media such as direct mail to interactive media such as call centres and the Web. Integrating these channels within a coherent strategy is not an easy task.

Writers in the field of Integrated Marketing Communications emphasize that before engaging on detailed planning for each medium – writing sales plans or promotions plans, for example – it is necessary to choose which medium to use for which customer interactions. This is illustrated in Figure 2.4.

The choice of channel/medium is generally a complex one, involving different media for different communications with the same customer. The organization will also frequently wish to leave some options in the hands of the customer. For example, a Dell customer may find out about Dell from colleagues or from press advertising; investigate which product to buy, what the price is and what configuration is required using the Web; print out order details and pass them to the purchasing department to place the order via fax; check on the delivery time via telephone; take delivery via a parcels service; and obtain customer service using e-mail. Customers are no longer content to have the medium dictated by the supplier.

> Customers are no longer content to have the medium dictated by the supplier.

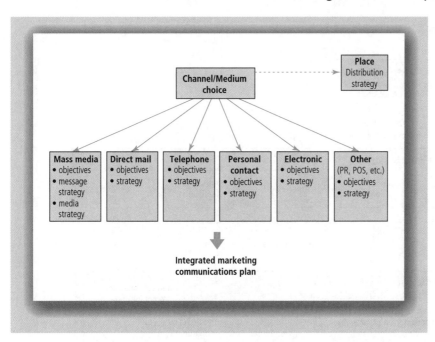

**Figure 2.4**
Define marketing strategies – promotion

Having chosen the most appropriate medium for given customer contacts with particular segments, the traditional planning by medium can then be conducted.

The choice of medium is clearly closely intertwined with the distribution strategy. Distribution channels often have a mix of purposes, providing both a means of conveying a physical product to the customer, and a medium for information exchange. A car showroom, for example, provides information on the vehicle, an opportunity for a test drive, a location where price negotiations can occur, and a step in the physical delivery of the car to the customer. A clothes shop provides a location where the information exchange of trying on a garment and feeling it can occur, in a way which is difficult to replicate using direct marketing approaches. So the focus of promotion on information exchange is closely linked to the physical issues of distribution. However, considering the two separately can result in new solutions, such as direct banking, Web shopping for CDs (which may need to be sampled but will not need to be felt physically), and complementing the sales force with telemarketing and websites for minor transactions or less important customers in business-to-business markets.

## Delivering the value proposition

The third major process is to deliver the value proposition. This is illustrated in Figure 2.5.

The major input to this process is the strategic marketing plan(s) derived from the previous stage.

The starting point for our analysis of this process was Porter's value chain (1980). This is reflected in the tasks we have listed within 'Deliver the product/service' in the top half of the figure: research and development,

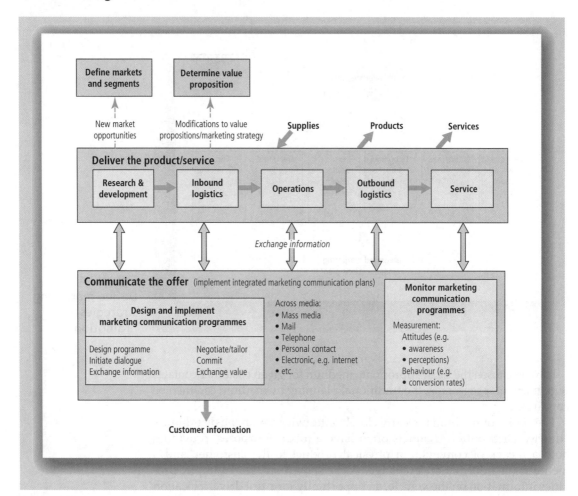

**Figure 2.5**
Deliver value
proposition

leading to inbound logistics, then through operations to outbound logistics
and finally to service.

However, we suggest that there are a number of marketing activities
which shadow these value chain activities, under the general heading of
'Communicate the offer'. Porter placed 'Marketing' after 'Operations' in the
value chain, but in today's one-to-one world, these communications can
occur in parallel with all the tasks involved in value delivery. One might, for
example, check a product with customers at the research and development
stage. The product may be tailored by the customer, resulting in different
components being bought in, assembled and delivered, and so on.

Communicating the offer is typically managed by designing, implementing and monitoring a number of marketing communication programmes. A communication programme could be, for example, a direct
mail campaign; an advertising campaign; a series of sales seminars; an
in-store promotion; and so on. We have also stretched the term 'marketing
communication programmes' to include management of such media as the
sales force, which may be managed in a more continuous way, with annual
targets broken down by quarter or month.

Communicating the
offer is typically
managed by designing,
implementing and
monitoring a number of
marketing
communication
programmes.

**Table 2.1** Rethinking the sales process

| Supplier perspective | | Interaction perspective | | Buyer perspective | |
|---|---|---|---|---|---|
| *Advertising* | *Selling* | *Marketing activity* | *Interaction* | *Decision theory* | *Customer behaviour* |
| | | Define markets and understand value | | | |
| | | Create value proposition | **Recognize exchange potential** | Problem recognition | Category need |
| Brand awareness | | | | | Awareness |
| | Prospecting | **Initiate dialogue** | | | |
| | | | | | Attitude |
| | | | | Information search | |
| Brand attitude – benefits info. – brand image – feelings – peer influence | Provide information | **Exchange information** | | | Information gathering and judgement |
| | Persuade | **Negotiate/tailor** | | Evaluation of alternatives | |
| Trial inducement | | | | | Purchase process |
| | Close sale | **Commit** | | Choice/ purchase | |
| | Deliver | **Exchange value** | | | |
| Reduce cognitive dissonance | Post-sales service | ↓ | **Monitor** | Post-purchase behaviour | Post-purchase experience |

Whatever the medium, the campaign will be aiming to contribute to one or more of the tasks listed in Figure 2.5 within the 'Design and implement marketing communication programmes' box. The tasks may have an unfamiliar look: in order to represent the interactive, one-to-one nature of today's marketing, we have renamed the classic steps in the sales process. Table 2.1 illustrates traditional views of the sales and purchasing process, with this revised, interaction perspective between the two.

Traditional 'push-based' models of marketing, in which after the product is made prospects are found and persuaded to buy the product, are illustrated on the left of the table. The delivery and service that follow are operational functions with little relationship to marketing.

Traditional models of buyer behaviour, illustrated on the right of the table, assume more rationality on the part of buyers but underplay the importance of what the buyer says back to the seller. The seller's offer is assumed to be predetermined, rather than developed in conjunction with the buyer.

The stages of the process of communicating value are therefore re-described as follows:

- 'Recognize exchange potential' replaces 'Category need' or 'Problem recognition'. Both sides need to recognize the potential for a mutual exchange of value.
- 'Initiate dialogue' replaces creating 'Awareness' or 'Prospecting'. The dialogue with an individual customer may be begun by either party. One feature of the Web, for example, is that on many occasions new customers will approach the supplier rather than vice versa.
- 'Exchange information' replaces 'Provide information'. If we are to serve the customer effectively, tailor our offerings and build a long-term relationship, we need to learn about the customer as much as the customer needs to learn about our products.
- 'Negotiate/tailor' replaces 'Persuade'. Negotiation is a two-way process which may involve us modifying our offer in order better to meet the customer's needs. Persuading the customer instead that the square peg we happen to have in stock will fit their round hole is not likely to lead to a long and profitable relationship.
- 'Commit' replaces 'Close sale'. Both sides need to commit to the transaction, or to a series of transactions forming the next stage in a relationship, a decision with implications for both sides.
- 'Exchange value' replaces 'Deliver' and 'Post-sales service'. The 'Post-sales service' may be an inherent part of the value being delivered, not simply a cost centre, as it is often still managed.

One-to-one communications and principles of relationship marketing, then, demand a radically different sales process from that traditionally practised. This point is far from academic, as an example will illustrate.

---

The company in question provides business-to-business financial services. Its marketing managers relayed to us their early experience with a website which was enabling them to reach new customers considerably more cost-effectively than their traditional sales force. When the website was first launched, potential customers were finding the company on the Web, deciding the products were appropriate on the basis of the website, and sending an e-mail to ask to buy. So far, so good.

But stuck in a traditional model of the sales process, the company would allocate the 'lead' to a salesperson, who would phone up and make an appointment, perhaps three weeks hence. The customer would by now probably have moved on to another online supplier who could sell the product today, but those who remained were subjected to a sales pitch, complete with glossy materials, which was totally unnecessary, the customer having already decided to buy. Those who were not put off would proceed to be registered as able to buy over the Web, but the company had lost the opportunity to improve its margins by using the sales force more judiciously.

> In time, the company realized its mistake, and changed its sales model and reward systems to something close to our 'interaction perspective' model. Unlike those prospects which the company proactively identified and contacted, which might indeed need 'selling' to, many new Web customers were initiating the dialogue themselves, and simply required the company to respond effectively and rapidly. The sales force were increasingly freed up to concentrate on major clients and on relationship building.

The changing nature of the sales process clearly raises questions for the design of marketing communications, such as: who initiates the dialogue, and how we measure the effectiveness of our attempts to do so across multiple channels; how we monitor the effectiveness not just of what we say to customers, but what they say back; and about the role of marketing communications as part of the value that is being delivered and paid for, not just as part of the sales cost.

The effectiveness of any organization's channel and communications plan will clearly depend on determining the appropriate medium for the different stages outlined in the centre of Table 2.1. The principles involved are spelled out in Table 2.2.

**Table 2.2** The communications mix and the sales force

| Channel/ Medium | Purchase phase | | | | |
| --- | --- | --- | --- | --- | --- |
| | Initiate dialogue (%) | Exchange information (%) | Negotiate/ tailor (%) | Commit (%) | Exchange value (%) |
| Offline advertising (TV, press, etc.) | 15 | 0 | 0 | 0 | 0 |
| Direct mail | 45 | 30 | 10 | 10 | 0 |
| Sales force/ face-to-face contact | 10 | 20 | 35 | 30 | 90 |
| Telephone | 20 | 35 | 50 | 60 | 0 |
| Website | 5 | 10 | 5 | 0 | 10 |
| Other (state: e.g. e-mail) | 5 | 5 | 0 | 0 | 0 |

*Note:* The figures indicate what percentage of each purchase phase is completed using the listed communication channel/medium.

Two examples follow of an attempt by a major global travel company to understand the information seeking and purchasing processes of different segments. These are given as Figures 2.6 and 2.7. From these two of seven different segments, it can be seen that the behaviour of each is totally different. The remainder of this book is about the process of market segmentation. It is, however, crucial to understand that without such segmentation knowledge an integrated communications plan would be impossible as, indeed, would *any* marketing programme.

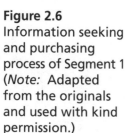

**Figure 2.6**
Information seeking and purchasing process of Segment 1 (*Note:* Adapted from the originals and used with kind permission.)

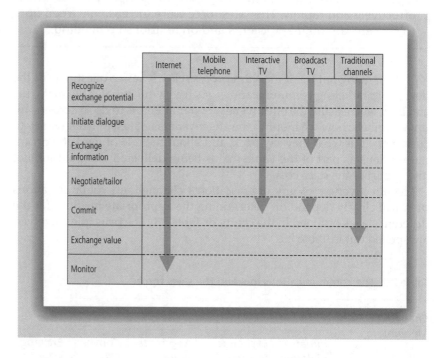

**Figure 2.7**
Information seeking and purchasing process of Segment 2 (*Note:* Adapted from the originals and used with kind permission.)

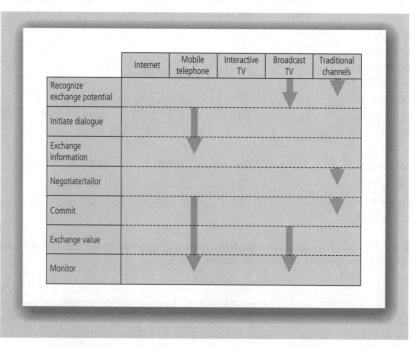

The programmes will then need monitoring. We distinguish the monitoring of the effectiveness of particular programmes, measured in such terms as response rates to a direct mail campaign or awareness and attitudes arising from advertising, from monitoring of the overall value delivered to the customer, which forms the next major process.

Outputs which come from the value chain activities are products and services. An important output from the communication subprocesses is customer information: what the customer's problems or issues are, the particular needs arising from these, what products and services are purchased, what complaints have been made, and so on.

Today, this 'Deliver value' stage involves IT at every turn – sales force automation, call centres, the internet and the front-office CRM systems that underpin them.

## Monitor value

Monitoring the value delivered to the customer, and received from the customer, is the purpose of 'Monitor value', illustrated in Figure 2.8.

There are four main areas where monitoring can occur, corresponding to the main types of information dealt with in the planning processes of 'Understand value' and 'Determine value proposition'.

First, the organization can monitor whether the value the customers actually require corresponds to the previous analysis of customer requirements carried out as part of 'Understand value'. The information for this may be gained partly from the information gained in the 'Deliver value' process, or it may require special activity such as market research.

Second, the value delivered can be monitored against the value proposition which was defined during the 'Determine value proposition' process. As all aspects of value are as measured by the customer's perception, this will again involve asking the customer by some means.

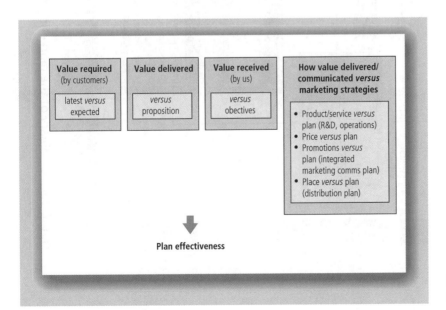

**Figure 2.8**
Monitor value

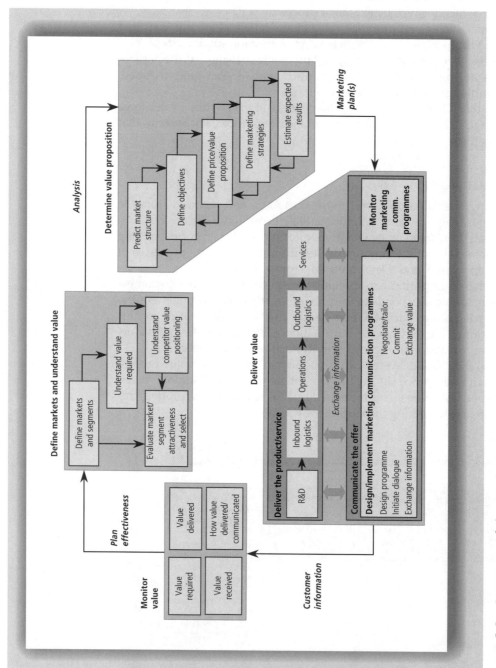

**Figure 2.9** Summary of the marketing process

The organization will also wish to monitor the value it receives against the marketing objectives defined during 'Determine value proposition'. This is the area that most organizations are best at, through monthly analysis of sales by product, channel and so on (though analysis by segment or customer is often poorer than analysis by product, with customer profitability or lifetime value generally difficult to obtain). But as the financial results are a result of customer satisfaction, monitoring the value delivered to the customer is equally important, and for many organizations one of the simplest ways of improving performance.

Finally, the overall effectiveness of the marketing strategies by which the value was delivered may be evaluated.

Figure 2.9 shows a consolidated summary of the marketing process.

## Marketing's role in value creation

There is, however, one final but crucial piece of the jigsaw to put in place. Table 2.3 states clearly that marketing can and should have a central role to play in creating sustainable competitive advantage.

**Table 2.3** The purpose of strategic marketing planning

The overall purpose of strategic marketing, and its principal focus, is the identification and creation of sustainable competitive advantage.

*Source:* McDonald, M. Cranfield University School of Management.

Figure 2.10 shows a typical array from any stock exchange of the relationship between risk and return, the diagonal line being the Beta.

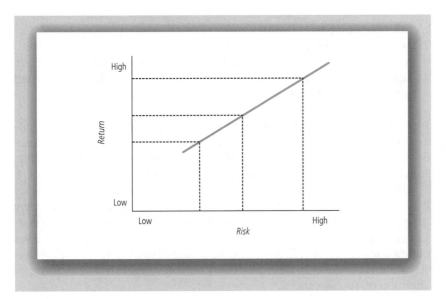

**Figure 2.10**
Financial risk and return
(*Source:* Adapted from Srikanthan, S. Cranfield University School of Management. Used with kind permission.)

Any firm on the line will normally be making industry average returns for its shareholders – in other words, making returns equal to the weighted average cost of capital (WACC). Firms making consistent returns greater then the WACC are creating shareholder wealth, known generally as shareholder value added, economic value added, positive net present value (NPV), super profits, sustainable competitive advantage and so on. Figure 2.11 shows diagrammatically how sustainable competitive advantage can be achieved.

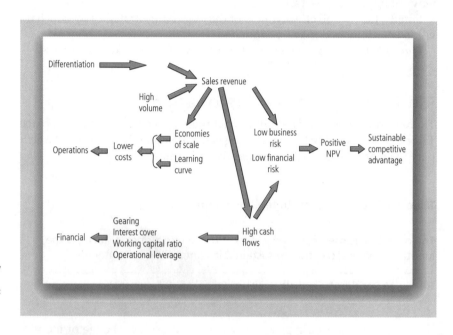

**Figure 2.11**
The route to sustainable competitive advantage
(*Source:* McDonald, M. Cranfield University School of Management.)

As Peter Doyle (2000) has pointed out, modern finance is based on four principles:

1  cash flow (the basis of value);
2  the true value of money;
3  the opportunity cost of capital (other investments of a similar risk);
4  the concept of net present value (the sum of the net cash flows discounted by the opportunity cost of capital).

Also, he pointed out that whilst accountants do not measure intangible assets the discrepancy between market and book values shows that investors do. Hence, expenditures to develop marketing assets make sense if the sum of the discounted cash flow they generate is positive.

A little thought will indicate that every single corporate activity, whether it be research and development, IT, purchasing or logistics, is ultimately reflected in the relative value put on a firm's offer by its customers. The marketing function, as defined in Figure 2.1 (but particularly the strategic roles outlined in boxes 1 and 2) is central to this, as every one of the four (or five, six or seven Ps) can only be improved by the *whole* organization focusing its attention on its customers.

A little thought will indicate that every single corporate activity, whether it be research and development, IT, purchasing or logistics, is ultimately reflected in the relative value put on a firm's offer by its customers.

# Chapter 2 review

In this chapter we looked at what marketing actually entails if it is to have a major impact on corporate strategy development.

After briefly reviewing the definition of marketing we looked at each stage of the process it involves.

First, we discussed the importance of defining the markets an organization was in, or wished to be in, and the importance of understanding the values different groups of customers in each of these markets were looking for, based on an analysis of their needs. Here, we also identified the significance of establishing an organization's competitiveness by segment and determining the attractiveness of segments to the organization.

We then looked at what was involved in putting together the value propositions designed to meet the needs of each segment, the output from which is commonly referred to as a strategic marketing plan. A particular point we made about this stage of the process when reviewing the definition of marketing was the necessity of reaching agreement with all those in the organization who contribute to delivering the value propositions.

Before considering the next stage in the marketing process, delivering the value proposition, we gave some additional attention to promotion, a key component of delivering value (and all too often the only responsibility of marketing executives). Here, we not only made the point that the promotional plan should be based around segments, but that the choice of medium should also take account of the different interactions that take place with customers. We also made a link between the choice of medium and the distribution strategy, given that distribution channels are often a medium for information exchange.

Our review of what was included in delivering the value proposition illustrated that this was a role for the whole company. In addition to communicating the offer, which we suggest should be looked at as an interaction between customers and the organization, we also included research and development, inbound logistics, operations, outbound logistics and services in this stage of the process. The changing nature of the sales process and its impact on the design of marketing communications was also covered.

We then discussed the final stage of the marketing process in which companies monitor the value delivered to the customer and the value received from the customer. Out of this, we can evaluate the overall effectiveness of the marketing strategies by which the value was delivered.

Finally, we briefly reviewed the role of marketing in value creation where we identified that marketing had a central role to play in creating sustainable competitive advantage.

It is clear from this that the crucial stage in the marketing process is the first one, defining markets, market segmentation and understanding the needs of customers in each of the segments. If this is not done correctly, the other stages in the marketing process will be ineffective.

# References

Doyle, P. (2000). 'How shareholder value analysis re-defines marketing'. *Market Leader*, Spring.

Lauterborn, R. (1990). 'New marketing litany: 4Ps passé, C words take over'. *Advertising Age*, Vol. 61, Is. 41, October.

McDonald, M. (2002). *Marketing Plans: How to Prepare Them, How to Use Them*. Oxford: Butterworth-Heinemann.

Porter, M. E. (1980). *Competitive Strategy: Techniques for Analysing Industries and Competitors*. New York: Free Press.

Porter, M. E. (1985). *Competitive Advantage – Creating and Sustaining Superior Performance*. New York: Free Press.

# Chapter 3
# Preparing for segmentation – avoiding the big mistakes

# Summary

Before starting any project, let alone one as strategically critical as segmentation, it is always useful to know such things as where you are heading, what you need to get there and what the route map looks like. The main purpose of this chapter is to provide you with this information for your segmentation project.

At the very outset, you should know that the segmentation process in this book is presented primarily in a format designed to utilize information already held by your company. It also provides a structured approach for the collection and use of information in segmentation research projects.

This chapter is organized as follows:

- A review of different approaches to market segmentation and why the customer's perspective defines the approach that delivers the best results
- A look at the bases for international market segmentation
- A brief discussion about the objective of this book and the need to ensure that internal company structures relate to external market segments
- How companies vary on being customer driven and organizationally committed to segmentation
- Considerations for effective market segmentation
- A brief review of the impact on companies of the 'postmodern' customer and where the three main issues this identifies are covered in this book
- Views on who should be involved in the segmentation team
- A summary of the data required for segmentation
- The rules for segmentation
- A summary of the advantages of segmentation and the additional benefits of the approach detailed in this book
- A summary of the two phases and seven steps in the segmentation process
- The importance of setting marketing objectives for segments and implementing appropriate strategies
- Three short case histories illustrating the impact of market segmentation
- A review of the chapter

# Definition of market segmentation

In the previous chapter we clearly positioned the segmentation process as central to every corporate function. We then went on to describe segments as consisting of customers[1] with similar needs. Acknowledging that a market is not homogeneous and divides into segments is, of course, recognition

---

[1] We discuss the difference between 'customers' and 'consumers' in the next chapter. For the purposes of the current discussion we will subsume those who decide which product or service will be bought under the title of 'customer', though, quite clearly, for some companies they will be referred to as 'consumers'.

Definition: ●
Market segmentation is
the process of splitting
customers, or potential
customers, in a market
into different groups, or
segments.

that not all customers are the same, with market segmentation being the process of splitting customers, or potential customers, within a market into different groups, or segments. But why have we defined segments as consisting of customers with similar *needs*?

To answer this question, let us first consider who is the *final* arbiter of whether or not a company achieves its corporate financial objectives. (In the not-for-profit sector, 'customer satisfaction' is obviously a proxy for 'financial objectives'.)

Quite simply, for the overwhelming majority of companies in the world, especially those operating in competitive markets, the final arbiter is the customer. In these markets the customers no longer see themselves as playing 'second fiddle' in the marketing stakes; they are becoming more marketing literate, more knowledgeable about the options that are available and are increasingly demanding what they want, where they want it, when they want it and how they want it. Customers choose between competing products and services based on their assessment of superior value: in other words, they choose the proposition that consists of the benefits they are looking for at a price they perceive as providing superior value for money, which, we would add, does not necessarily mean it has to be the 'cheapest'. The challenge for every company is to be able to deliver the winning propositions, profitably. But first, of course, the company has to understand from a customer's perspective what these propositions need to be.

## Marketing insight

For some companies, experiencing and then having to accede to the views of their customers is a lesson learnt many years ago. For example, the launch in 1985 by the Coca-Cola Company of 'New Coke' to replace 'Coke' with the claim that it was offering a better taste, is a 'classic' example. 'New Coke' did not meet the needs of their customers, particularly the emotional tie they had with the original brand, and the Coca-Cola Company finally bowed to customer pressure and relaunched 'Coke' as 'Coke Classic' not long after their attempt to replace it.[2]

Customers, therefore, segment themselves and what the company must focus on and understand are the needs that customers are seeking to satisfy and, in doing so, understand the motivations that drive the choices made by customers.

Despite this fundamental truth about market segmentation, supported by the fact that all of us, as customers ourselves, choose between competing products and services on this basis, many companies still predetermine how their market divides into segments based on, for example, such criteria as the products or services offered, or on demographics (sometimes referred to as 'firmographics' in business-to-business markets), and organize their marketing effort principally around these dimensions. The reason for this is that, whereas market segmentation seems comparatively simple as a concept, it is viewed as extremely difficult to implement in practice, requiring, as it does, a *market-based* approach.

[2] 'Coke', 'New Coke' and 'Coke Classic' are all registered trade marks of the Coca-Cola Company.

The following is a brief review of the 'predetermined' approaches frequently used in market segmentation. In this review we also highlight the part that they can play in a market-based approach to segmentation.

*Products and services*  The problem with segmenting markets according only to the products or services offered, or the technology type, is that in most markets, many *different* types of customers buy or use the same products or services. For example, if a mail company organizes itself around express packages, or around mail sorting, it is unlikely that the company will ever get to understand fully the real and different needs of, say, universities, banks, advertising companies, direct mail houses, manufacturing companies, retailers and so on.

However, by understanding which particular features of the product or service appeal to different customers, along with features associated with all the other aspects of a purchase, such as the channel, we have a route for understanding the motivations behind the choices that are made. This is because it is through these features that customers seek to attain the benefits they are looking for. Once this is understood, the needs-based propositions required for different segments can be developed.

*Demographics*  Variables such as sex, age, lifestyle and so on, when used to define segments, are by implication claiming, for example, that every 30–35-year-old will respond to the same proposition. Just reflect for a moment on the students in your year at school; would you expect them all to be wearing the same clothes, taking the same types of holidays, pursuing the same interests and driving the same cars? When someone wakes up on their birthday, do they become a stereotype associated with that age? For administrative convenience we would like the answer to be 'yes', but the answer is 'no'.

In business-to-business markets, customers are frequently segmented around business classification lines, which implies that all the companies in a particular sector, such as financial services, have exactly the same requirements and will respond to a single proposition. This approach could well be ignoring one or more of the following:

- different divisions and departments existing behind the business descriptor may have different applications for the product or service you supply. For example, would the mail company mentioned earlier find that the advertising and promotions department has the same requirements and specifications for mail services as the sales ledger department?
- the requirements of, say, advertising and promotions departments may well be the same regardless of business type;

- even within a single division of a company, there may well be different applications for the product or service you supply which, in turn, may have different specifications attached to them;
- segmentation along business classification lines assumes all the companies within the classification employ identical people with identical values. Businesses, of course, don't buy anything; it's their employees you have to sell to!

Although demographics on their own cannot define a segment because they do not define the proposition a segment requires, they have an important role to play in a segmentation project. This background information about customers can be used to identify the particular profiling characteristics associated with the customers found in each segment. In other words, demographics helps identify who is found in each segment which, in turn, will help you determine how to reach them.

*Geography*   Rather like demographics, segments based on geographic areas, however tightly defined, assume that everyone in a predetermined area can be expected to react to a particular offer in exactly the same way. Even at the postcode level this does not appear to work; simply look along your own street. Has everyone got the same furniture, do they buy from the same shops, eat the same food?

Once again, however, although geographic areas on their own cannot define the propositions required by segments and, therefore, cannot define segments, they, too, have a useful role to play in a segmentation project. This particular type of background information about customers can be used to identify the most likely locations the customers in each of the segments may be found and, therefore, further help you determine how to reach them.

A further consideration with respect to 'geography' is its use in international market segmentation. We look at this topic in the next section.

*Channel*   Routes to market are becoming more sophisticated and complex, a topic we look at in a later chapter in this book, and are also becoming an increasingly important component of many winning customer propositions. Channels in themselves, however, do not define segments as they are simply the means by which customers and companies connect with each other. It is only when you understand the motives behind the channel choices made by customers that the channel component of a needs-based proposition can be developed.

However, even if channel does not feature as a key component of a winning proposition, it is, along with demographics and geography, background information about customers that should be tracked during a segmentation project. It could well be that some segments can be associated with particular routes to market, therefore it is the channel(s) they use that provides the means for reaching them with their specific proposition.

*Psychographics*     Here we have another customer insight that can contribute to a segmentation project but, on its own, cannot define the entirety of a winning customer proposition. However, by identifying internal drivers of customer behaviour that can be associated with specific segments, psychographics can help define the most appropriate promotional stance to take. This not only provides the means of catching the attention of target groups in an ever cluttered world of communication, it can also provide the means by which you isolate and reach particular segments.

What we conclude from this discussion is that, while each of the above approaches to forming customer segments may be administratively convenient, they do not on their own define segments but provide insights that are *contributors* to a successful segmentation project.

---

Customers segment themselves, they do not slot themselves into predetermined categories, and the propositions that appeal to them are those that satisfy their needs by delivering the benefits they are looking for at a price they perceive as providing superior value for money.

**Marketing insight**

---

We can therefore extend the definition of market segmentation so that it captures both its focus and its purpose; market segmentation, therefore, is the process of splitting customers, or potential customers, within a market into different groups, or segments, within which customers share a similar level of interest in the same, or comparable, set of needs satisfied by a distinct marketing proposition.

Extended definition: Market segmentation is the process of splitting customers, or potential customers, in a market into different groups, or segments, within which customers share a similar level of interest in the same, or comparable, set of needs satisfied by a distinct marketing proposition.

---

For companies fully to realize the opportunities available to them in their markets, segmentation projects should focus on customers and their needs.

**Marketing insight**

---

# International market segmentation

Segmentation models in international marketing tend to consist of geographical groups, such as Western Europe, Eastern Europe, North America,

ASEAN, Australasia and so on. Unfortunately, however, such groupings are of very limited value as actionable marketing propositions, since they bear little relationship to actual consumption or usage patterns.

| Marketing insight | Segmentation models based on geographical groups bear little resemblance to actual international markets. |
| --- | --- |

Taking Europe as an example, there are typically three discrete groupings: European Union (EU); European Free Trade Association (EFTA); and Eastern Europe. Within Eastern Europe, however, there are at least three subgroups: the 'strong' group (the former Czechoslovakia and Hungary); the 'middle' group (Poland, Bulgaria, Romania and the former Yugoslavia); and the 'poor' group (the former Soviet republics). Even within Western Europe, there are significant differences arising from natural phenomena. For example, Scandinavia has short summers and long winters; Greece, Portugal, Italy and Spain have long summers and short winters; the Netherlands has low plains; and Switzerland has mountains.

Again, the per capita gross domestic product of Switzerland is seven times that of Portugal and, at the same time, there are significant communication and distribution differences. As examples: there is virtually no domestic television in Norway, whereas in Italy television has very high levels of penetration; retail channel concentration is very dense in Northern Europe, whereas there is a preponderance of small, independent outlets in Southern Europe; there are also significant cultural and linguistic differences, and so on. If, therefore, geography is to be relevant, it is more sensible to think in terms of: the Anglo Saxon North; the Latin South; North-east France, Benelux and North-west Germany; and so on. Even this, however, is simplistic, in the sense that there are basically three kinds of 'products' which have to be considered when looking at such segmentations.

1 *Truly global products*
  These are either products or services that are inherently global, such as international services, world-standard industrial products, high-technology products and so on, or they are fashion or national products that have become global, such as Chivas Regal, Coca-Cola, Rolls-Royce, McDonald's and Dunhill,[3] and so on. These have become global because their national appeal is replicated in other countries, though this has not precluded the need for some local variations.
2 *National products*
  These typically exist where the market thrives on supplier responsiveness, client relationships and national preferences, and where global efficiencies are less critical.

[3]'Chivas Regal', 'Rolls-Royce', 'McDonald's and 'Dunhill' are all registered trade marks of their respective organizations.

3 *Hybrid products*

Here, adaptation across countries is possible and this requires a rethinking of simple geographical segmentation bases to ones based on customer groups with similar needs across national boundaries. In advertising, for example, J. Walter Thompson discovered:

- Three broad breakfast types across Europe.
- A fashion lager segment across Europe.
- Commonalities in computer software applications across Europe.

There are, as a result, significant legal, regulatory, linguistic, communication media and distribution channel differences across Western Europe and even throughout the world. There are, consequently, few truly global products and many traditional habits that remain deep-rooted, militating against international segmentation. On the other hand (and this applies particularly to Western Europe), there are a number of growing trends that suggest that the need for international market segmentation will become increasingly important. These include:

- The desire for monetary union, social affairs union, foreign affairs union and defence policy union.
- Increasing product and technical standardization.
- Deregulation of transportation, telecommunications, pharmaceuticals and others.
- Attitude convergence relating to areas such as work, individuality, materialism and the environment.
- Pan-European buying.
- International mergers, acquisitions and joint ventures.
- Increased international travel, education, media exposure, fashion, and so on.

The bases for international market segmentation are, therefore, likely to be specific groupings of countries such as the new 'Euro Regions' outlined earlier, or customer groups across selected countries.

Thereafter, the normal rules of market segmentation apply.

# Objective of this book

The objective of this book is to provide a logical process by which managers can explore whether there is any potential for new business opportunities as a result of re-examining the way in which they define their market segments. It then moves on to identifying the appropriate objectives and strategies for these segments and how segmentation fits into the marketing plan.

Segmentation is a creative and iterative process, the purpose of which is to satisfy customer needs more closely and, in doing so, deliver sustainable competitive advantage for the company. It is defined by the *customers'* needs, not the company's, and should be revisited periodically.

The process is as applicable to business-to-business markets as it is to business-to-consumer markets. Both these markets consist of customers looking for the proposition that best meets their needs at a price they perceive as providing superior value for money. The process is designed to uncover exactly what these needs are and, therefore, what value proposition each segment is looking for.

The process of segmentation also helps identify new opportunities, for products, services and markets.

The importance of segmentation to any business should not be underestimated: market segmentation is the basic building block for effective marketing planning, as discussed in the previous chapter and illustrated in Figure 3.1, and should reflect a market/customer orientation rather than a product or service orientation.

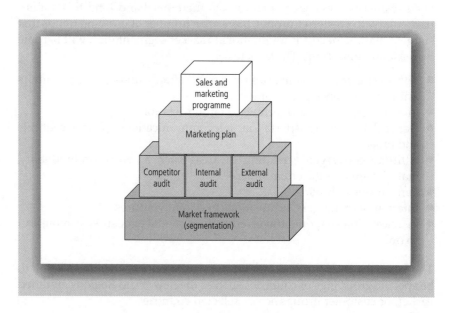

**Figure 3.1**
The building blocks of effective marketing planning

Most organizations will need to use more than one level of segmentation criteria to identify the customer types and to categorize their specific needs. Organizations are also likely to find that the process of segmentation has to be carried out at more than one stage in the overall distribution and value-added chain, different stages having distinct customer types with their own specific needs. (The distribution and value-added chain is looked at in Chapter 5.)

Market segments offering the greatest opportunities will be those that are growing and profitable, in which companies can effectively meet their customers' needs of today, or for which companies can develop their products or services to meet the needs of tomorrow.

Following the selection of market segments to be targeted, companies can then develop focused marketing strategies. This planned approach to meeting the needs of customers helps companies to be proactive instead of reactive, enabling them to take advantage of market opportunities and gain competitive advantage.

It should be noted, however, that, whilst the segmentation process itself is externally focused in its consideration of the market 'out there', companies looking to 'meet their customers' needs effectively', should also consider how the company's own departmental structure and staff relate to the chosen target segments. For example, when a customer from a particular segment contacts your company in the course of doing business with you, it could well negate the company's segmented approach in its external marketing activity if, in dealing with this customer's requirements, the applicable internal department subsumes the customer under one, all-embracing procedure, and fails to match up to the external activity.

No computer program, let alone a book, however advanced, could ever cover all possible market segmentation outcomes. This particular book does not claim to provide the definitive answer to any organization's segmentation problems. What it will do is provide a logical process for you to follow. Above all else, however, it requires you to be creative and flexible in your thinking and asks you not to be hidebound by your current market segmentation definitions.

# Segmentation archetypes in companies

The 'internal' (company) and 'external' (market) matching required for effective segmentation provides a convenient framework for looking at how companies currently define and segment their markets.

Piercy and Morgan (1993) provide a conceptual framework for viewing market segmentation which acknowledges the distinction between 'explicit' and 'implicit' aspects of the market. An 'explicit' perspective refers to the view that markets are 'out there' and are essentially groups of customers. The 'implicit' perspective relates to the role of a company's perceptions, culture, processes and structure in determining the company's view of the market.

By assessing a number of companies on the basis of their framework, a series of archetypes which represent differing approaches and emphases in segmenting the marketplace have been developed by Jenkins and McDonald (1997). These archetypes help demonstrate how companies actually relate to their target markets and the potential implications of these differing positions.

## Company archetypes

In order to develop a clearer picture as to how different approaches to explicit and implicit segmentation may appear in companies, four case studies are described.

### Case 1 – The international airline

Many of the major international airlines of today have, on the whole, traditionally segmented their global market on the basis of geographic territories.

Before the development of products and brands in British Airways, the airline's marketing was driven by powerful territorial line managers with revenue responsibility for specific routes and the geographic areas served by these routes. The only exception was the country manager for the UK who, primarily because of the size of revenue generated in the UK, operated autonomously and was equivalent in status to a 'route general manager'.

Although its markets were discussed in terms of 'business', 'leisure' and 'visiting friends and relatives' (VFR), even, at times, having campaigns focused into these travel sectors, marketing expenditure budgets were set by territory and were often judged in terms of the revenue generated by that territory. The route general managers, however, were judged both by territory and by route, with route revenue coming from all over the world. A prime function for the routes, therefore, was the allocation of seats and cargo space to the different territorial markets around the world. Obtaining such capacity, however, was particularly difficult on services operated by a route division other than the one in which a territory was located.

With an aircraft fleet and crew traversing all geographic boundaries, product design was primarily a corporate task and was kept fairly simple by looking at the world in terms of different classes of travel, such as first and economy. Schedules were rarely designed around customer requirements and were governed by:

- the drive to keep aircraft in the air for as much time as possible, as this was when they were earning revenue;
- night time restrictions at airports;
- agreements between governments and airlines themselves.

Tweaking the in-flight offer was, however, available to the route offices. They could request menus to suit the palates of the geographical areas through which the aircraft flew, and they could employ extra cabin crew members from their overseas territories to bring a 'local flavour' to their services for the indigenous traveller. Essentially, however, the company was sales orientated, the emphases being to fill capacity and thereby requiring seats to be sold. Customers were those who happened to sit in the seats. There was no strategic perspective as to how particular groups of customers should be managed.

## Case 2 – The chemical company

In 1924, Brunner Mond and Company began to manufacture nitrogen fertilizer from ammonia at a site in Billingham on the north bank of the River Tees. Nitrogen, however, is not the only element likely to be depleted in the soil on commercial farms and by 1930 the company was producing 'complete' fertilizers containing nitrogen and two further important soil nutrients, phosphate and potash, in compound form. This extension of the product range suited the company, as it meant its nitrogen was being used in a greater number of products.

Usage of fertilizers tends to fall into three distinct product groups; nitrogen on its own; nitrogen with phosphate and potash; and a third group consisting of just phosphate and potash. To ensure the company had a complete range, the third group of products, those containing just phosphate and potash, were also sold, primarily because it was believed that offering the full range pulled through sales of the separate product lines (later proved to be largely a myth). The principal focus of the business, however, was around the ammonia production technology. This was the most complex chemical process for the fertilizer business, and the company's greatest margins came from products containing the most nitrogen. The production of compounds was fairly simple in comparison (once the nitrogen had been produced) and was carried out in a separate plant on the site.

Given the origin of the business, the source of its margins and distinct manufacturing plants, it could only appear logical to structure the management of the business and its information flows around the three product lines. This is exactly what happened and the three product lines were represented in the marketing function by product managers. The product management teams not only liaised with the manufacturing plant on product specifications and production volumes, they also drove the promotional campaigns of the business and set the sales targets, though only for their products. This was perfectly acceptable, of course, because the market, on the whole, bought these three product types largely at different times of the year.

It was readily accepted in the company that, broadly speaking, the market was split between fertilizers for growing grass and fertilizers for the growing of arable crops. There were even products specifically manufactured for each of these two sectors, distinct services offered to each of them, and dedicated specialist advisers based at headquarters. Despite this, the thrust of the business was based around product lines, each of which eventually fell under the control of its own business team. Lying over this split was the sales force, divided, for management purposes, into geographical territories. Their sales targets were, as already mentioned, presented to them along product lines, and any sales support literature was similarly divided, as all the budgets were allocated along product lines.

## Case 3 – The bank

Some years ago, the senior customer services representative of one of the UK's largest banks was being interviewed on the radio. The main area of discussion centred around opening times (usually 10.00 a.m. to 3.30 p.m. at that time) and the limited number of cashiers (tellers) on duty during the peak, lunchtime period. The reason given for the opening times was that the public forgot that the transactions which the bank undertook on their behalf took time, and if they were open to their customers from 9.00 a.m. to 5.30 p.m. during the week, never mind at weekends, the staff at the bank would probably need to work from 8.00 a.m. to 7.00 p.m. The bank's public hours were the most it could offer when its staff worked from 9.00 a.m. to 5.30 p.m., which seemed fair, of course, because these were the hours worked by most of their customers! With regard to the lunchtime queues, the reasons for these were equally straightforward and reasonable: the bank's cashiers also had to have lunch breaks.

These issues, rather than humbling the customer into acceptance, fuelled the growth of the building societies. Marketing arrived in the financial world in a big way during the 1980s and attractive salaries and extra financial benefits tempted some of the best. They had found a gold mine waiting to be developed. Unlike many businesses, banks clearly know who their customers are. The switching costs for these customers are high when compared to other industries. This means the banks have traditionally enjoyed a high level of customer retention. Here, therefore, was a great opportunity for developing financial products and selling the variety of services available from the bank into a known customer base. Here, also, was the opportunity to develop products suited to the different stages of life and put them in front of the customer progressively as they travelled along life's highway.

The large, in-house databases could also be profiled by matching them up against externally held databases containing psychographic information. This would help in the better targeting of new product offers into the banks' own customer bases, and enable the banks to specify target customer profiles from externally held lists when prospecting for new customers. Inevitably complex segmentation structures were devised and numerous new products developed, and the banks became portrayed more as centres for financial services.

However, the purpose of these segments was to find ways of selling internally or competitively-defined products, these segments being variable according to the different projects for which they were devised. The majority of banks still opened at the times the customers were in work and the cashiers still went to lunch during the peak period. If anyone wanted to talk about any of the new services, the unmanned enquiry desk always had a welcome for them, once someone had responded to the bell!

## Case 4 – The retailing group

There is a very large retailing group in the UK which became a prime example of an organization that structured itself around its chosen segments.

The different high street brands of the group were targeted into specific segments and were not just fronts. Behind each lay a complete infrastructure with its own marketing group, buyers, financial controllers, administration and so on, all focused into the survival of the brand in its segment. Some brands eventually tired, but that was due, in part, to 'time out' being called on the segment. At the same time, however, the company introduced new brands to exploit the opportunities available in newly emerging segments.

## Case study conclusion

These cases are presented as illustrations of the potential alignment of the organization to market segments. In the international airline, segmentation is driven by internal structures and processes. The power of the territory manager defines the way the organization aligns itself to the market. This perspective does not begin with the customer, but with the structure of the sales organization. This view of the market is also limited to particular functions and activities within the organization and does not appear to operate across functions or at a strategic level.

In contrast, the chemical company represents an organization whose entire structure and mode of operation represents a particular view of the market. This view is clearly process-led or product-led and is not a customer driven view of the market place. Unlike the international airline, it is a view which is embedded throughout the organization.

The bank presents a different type of situation. Here, the organization has a customer-based approach as to how it segments the marketplace. This view, however, is restricted to the functional marketing activities of the organization. It does not permeate the way in which the organization, as a whole, sees the external world and does not appear to influence many of the processes and procedures which do impact on the customer.

The retailing group provides an organizational view which is centred on customer groups. This form of segmentation is deeply embedded in the operations and perspective of the employees as it forms the basis for the organizational structure.

All of the above examples reflect different approaches as to how an organization may align itself to the segments within the marketplace and it appears that there are two principal dimensions which differentiate between these examples:

1 customer driven;
2 organizational integration.

1 *Customer driven*

The examples of the bank and the retailing group are both approaches which are clearly centred on the customer. In these situations, a market and its segments are customer groups as defined by, amongst others, Kotler (1991). In the case of the bank, the customer focus is limited to particular initiatives which are task-specific and function-specific. In the case of the retailing group, customer focus permeates and defines the separate business units. In contrast, the approach taken by the international airline and the chemical company is not centred on the customer. This is not to imply that at some point they were not customer driven. The issue is that these approaches for defining and segmenting the market no longer begin with the customer. They have become internalized and are thereby driven by internal factors such as sales force territories, budgets and organizational structures. These are implicit views of the marketplace which have become part of the organization's culture and perspective on its environment.

2 *Organizational integration*

The international airline and the bank both exhibit low levels of organizational integration. The way in which the market is segmented is the domain of particular groups, or functions within the organization. In these situations, segmentation is very much an operational, as opposed to a strategic, process. It is concerned with a particular media campaign or for establishing particular sales objectives. Outside these particular groups, these segments are not understood or recognized. In contrast, the chemical company and the retailing group both illustrate a high level of organizational integration. In these situations, segmentation is not just a way of targeting potential customers, but an intrinsic part of the structure and culture of the organization. All parts of the organization recognize that the market is segmented in this particular way, these segments providing a strategic basis for how the organization understands its interaction with the business environment.

## Classifying market segmentation in organizations

These two dimensions for considering the organizational aspects of segmentation, customer driven and organizational integration, can be incorporated into a matrix as shown in Figure 3.2.

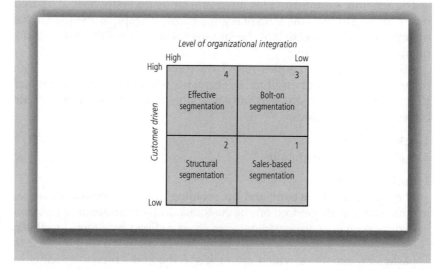

**Figure 3.2**
Segmentation archetypes in companies (*Source:* Jenkins, M. and McDonald, M. (1997). 'Market segmentation: Organizational archetypes and research agendas'. *European Journal of Marketing*, Vol. 31, No. 1, 17–32.)

1 *Sales-based segmentation*
The first cell (bottom right), sales-based segmentation, describes an organizational archetype where the market is segmented on the basis of how the sales function is organized, which does not necessarily reflect clusters of particular customer characteristics or needs. In addition, these approaches are relatively superficial, and they are not embedded in the way the organization, as a whole, is structured, or the way it operates. This archetype represents segmentation which is driven by, and is largely exclusive to, the sales operations of an organization. The international airline is an example of this particular archetype. Here, the approach to segmentation operates at a territory level where some adjustment of the offer is permitted (use of local menus and cabin staff). However, this view of the market is not embedded in the way the organization as a whole is driven. The organizational priorities are represented by the need to maximize the capacity of the fleet of aircraft and the fact that this capacity resource is allocated through the management of routes rather than particular territories. The international airline, therefore, provides an example of an approach to segmentation which is internally (sales territories), as opposed to being externally (customer) driven and which does not reflect the priorities and focus of the organization as a whole.

2 *Structural segmentation*
The second cell, structural segmentation, represents a further archetype where there is little emphasis on segments as groups of customers.

Segments are defined by how the organization is structured. However, in contrast to the sales-based archetype, this approach to the market is deeply embedded in the organization as a whole. The chemical company is an example of this situation. The organization described in this case uses product management teams, who are responsible for marketing activity at both the strategic and operational levels. These groups are also working with sales territories which are allocated on a geographical basis. At this level, therefore, the segmentation is not explicitly customer driven, although the sales territories may reflect differing patterns of agriculture, and the differing product types may be applied at different times of the year. However, the product divisions which are fronted by the product management teams are embedded in the structure and nature of the organization. The requirements of a complex and capital-intensive process (producing ammonium nitrate) have meant that the product divisions which represent different aspects of this process are highly integrated into the fabric of the organization. This cell, therefore, presents an approach which is both production and sales driven and which is embedded in all the structures and processes of the organization.

3 *Bolt-on segmentation*
The third cell, bolt-on segmentation, presents an archetype where a high level of customer focus is brought into the defining of market segments. In this case, the organization applies customer data which are often available within the organization, such as location, purchase patterns and product preference. These data are combined with external classification systems which align the customer base to particular socio-economic profiles. In contrast to the previous archetypes, this segmentation approach is driven by the information held on the customer base as opposed to the structure of sales operations. However, this archetype is close to sales-based segmentation, as it is limited to a number of functional areas within the organization and is not integrated into the organization as a whole. In this case, the purpose of the segmentation exercise is to assist in selling existing products and targeting promotional campaigns, which are essentially operational, as opposed to strategic issues. In this archetype the segmentation framework does not guide new product development, nor does it affect the core processes and power base of business. The bank is presented as an example of this particular archetype. In this example, a high level of customer information already exists within the business. In many situations this is applied simply to target mail shots or other promotions, aimed at selling existing products. These segments do not provide a focus for redefining the business processes, a basis for new service concepts or the removal of existing products. A customer focus exists, but this does not permeate the whole operation of the business, as it is not considered at a strategic level.

4 *Effective segmentation*
The fourth cell, effective segmentation, combines both a customer focus and a high level of organizational integration. In this cell, the organization is able to apply customer-based data in order to develop a set of defined segments. In contrast to the bolt-on segmentation approach, the organization has integrated these segments across the key functional activities. They provide a basis not only for the promotional activity,

but also for strategic decision-making and internal marketing; in the case of the latter, this clarity of particular market segments provides a powerful basis for bringing the customer into the organization: see Levitt (1960). They also provide a focus for the entire processes and operations of the organization on these market segments. The large retailing group is suggested as an example for this cell. This group has a set of retailing concepts which are driven by clearly defined market segments. These segments have been defined around customer groups, but are also deeply embedded in the organization through their own operations and processes, which are tailored to the needs of their respective segments. In this case, all those in the organization can picture the target segment and have a basic appreciation of how the segment can be served most effectively.

## Classification conclusion

The four case studies indicate that it must surely be better to be more customer focused and organizationally committed to a particular form of segmentation. The international airline concerned made massive losses for a sustained period and only survived through this period because of its state-owned status. The chemical company experienced enormous losses during the 1980s and only escaped closure by the narrowest of margins. Likewise, banks made substantial losses. The aim of this framework is, therefore, to provide a basis for beginning to assess segmentation, not only as an external clustering of customers, but also in terms of the strategic and internal implications for an organization.

# Effective market segmentation

There are a number of factors to be considered before proceeding to specify the step-by-step process for effective market segmentation.

1 *Proposition flexibility*
   This is the degree to which a proposition can be tailored to the needs of different groups of customers. It can range from a fixed product offering to one in which the offer is almost completely specific to an individual customer. The first category could be pharmaceuticals. An example of the second could be consultancy. Another consideration is the degree of resource flexibility of the organization. For example, organizations with large fixed/capital assets are limited in the degree to which they can be adjusted around customer needs. By contrast, an organization mainly dependent on human resources could be almost infinitely flexible.
2 *Market granularity*
   Market granularity is the degree to which customer needs and motivations differ within a defined market. It can range from near homogeneous, in

which all customers share very similar needs and motivations, to heterogeneous, when the opposite applies. Basic commodities may be in the first category, whilst technically complex product/service amalgams may be in the second. Customer heterogeneity can range from very low to very high.

Figure 3.3 below shows the area of potential for market segmentation.

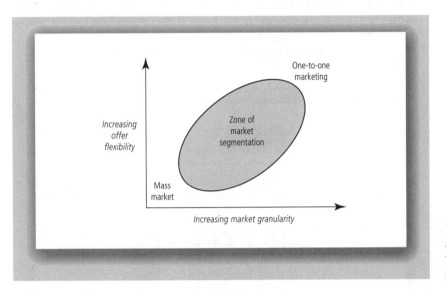

**Figure 3.3**
Area of potential
for market
segmentation

Thus, it can be seen that market segmentation applies to most situations and there will be few exceptions when it is not central to commercial success. Indeed, even at the extremities, effective market segmentation can often make the difference between success and failure.

This raises the question of the number of segments that an organization can deal with effectively, which could be between five and ten if *all* the segments in a market are to be targeted (most markets tend to divide into between five and ten segments). Depending on data available, organizations may then be able to personalize approaches to customers in their selected segments on a 'one-to-one' basis, but this is usually only possible if the strategy for the segment to which they belong is effective.

3 *Organizational considerations*

The most important point about organizational structure is that there are a number of issues that *all* firms have to address. These are:

- geographic location;
- functions (such as finance, research and development, marketing and so on);
- products;
- markets;
- channels.

Of these, increasing competition has forced organizations to agree that the two main issues are *products* and *markets*, which is why many organizations have 'product/technology managers' and/or 'market managers'.

A product manager orientated system will ensure strong technical competence, but can easily lead to superficial market knowledge, whereas a market manager orientated system can lead to poor overall product development.

Consider, for example, Northern Sealants, who manufacture a broad range of adhesives that fall into two broad categories: seals and sealants. They supply these products to a large number of markets internationally, with the main users coming from: gas, oil and petrochemical refineries; automotive; electrical; and original equipment manufacturers (OEM).

Their organizational structure is as shown in Figure 3.4.

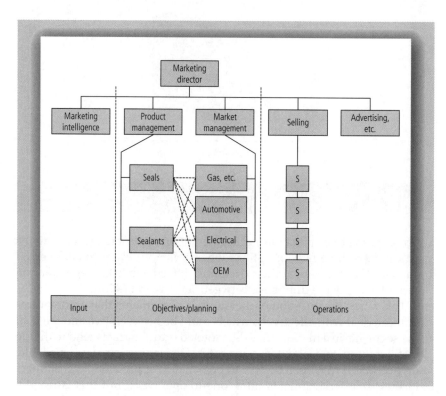

**Figure 3.4**
Organizational
structure of
Northern Sealants

It can be seen that Northern Sealants have both a product management and market management structure. Market segmentation is clearly the role of the market managers and close liaison between the two functions is crucial. However, it is becoming increasingly clear that in the new climate of customer power that the major authority has to be vested in market managers. In the case of Northern Sealants, the market management structure was repeated in major geographic territories, which took account of differences in local conditions, such as routes to market.

In this case, segmentation, as described in this book, took place at the 'gas', 'automotive', 'electrical' and 'OEM' levels, as each of these sectors was sufficiently different to justify separate approaches. It was also possible in this instance to have an in-depth knowledge of and an international focus on these vertical markets, rather than allowing territory 'barons' to dictate the product/market mix.

There is a more detailed discussion of this topic in Chapter 14. For now, all that is necessary to appreciate is that all organizations have to have an organizational structure for the purpose of management and control. It is obvious that segmentation should take place as near to the final customer as possible, but segmentation will also take place at other points, as necessary, in organizations with complex routes to market (see Chapter 5).

The point to be made here is that the process detailed in this book is universally applicable, so readers should concentrate on the process rather than worrying about organizational considerations.

From the case studies discussed in the previous section, it can be seen that for three of them the organizational structures took precedence over market considerations with disastrous consequences and whilst it is not always possible to organize internationally around segments as opposed to markets or products, it should nonetheless be segments that are the ultimate drivers of corporate strategy.

# The 'postmodern' customer

A great deal of discussion at the time of writing is about the impact on companies of what is being referred to as the 'postmodern' customer or, put more simply, the 'new' customer. This debate has been generated largely because of the rapid developments in IT and communications, with such prospects as the kitchen oven communicating with a potato on how long it should be cooked, and the realization that previously convenient classifications of 'markets' no longer appear to work.

Putting the potato and oven to one side for the moment, the observation with respect to 'markets' is that individual customers appear to differ in the propositions they are looking for within what were once seen as single markets. For example, when buying a bottle of wine, the wine bought when an individual has been invited round to dinner with friends can be different from the wine bought when the same individual is looking for a drink to take home for a quiet night in, even when both types of wine are available at both purchasing opportunities. As another example, when an individual is looking for a savings plan, their requirements are often different from those when they are looking for car insurance, though both are financial services products and may even be bought from the same company. And, as a final example, the individual who on Tuesday travels business class when flying to a meeting in Europe, is found in the economy section when flying on a family holiday the following Saturday.

All this, of course, requires there to be a correct definition of 'market', an issue we first raised in the original edition of this book in 1995, extended to a number of pages in the second edition in 1998 and, as you will shortly see, now occupies a full chapter on its own and forms the first step in the segmentation process. We will, therefore, leave further discussion on this aspect of the postmodern customer to the next chapter.

The main outcome of the debate about the postmodern customer is that the implication for business is that they must now drive their internal processes from the demand side of the business equation rather than purely from the supply side. In other words, drive these processes from an understanding of the needs of customers in terms of the product or service they require, its price, how it is promoted and from where it can be acquired. At the same time, the business has to ensure that they can supply these customers with what they need at a price the customer is willing to pay, and do all of this profitably. Understanding the demand side of the business equation has always been at the heart of our segmentation process and is comprehensively covered in this book.

Regarding the impact of IT, in particular the impact of the internet, what this has achieved for customers is a breaking down of the physical barriers to a more 'perfect' market, thereby enabling customers to find out about and source more of the various alternative offers available. It has also introduced an additional delivery channel for non-physical products such as those found in financial services, along with music and videos; provided an additional medium for promotional messages; and presented an additional route to market. With respect to the latter, this additional route to market presented by the internet can, in many respects, be regarded as an evolution in direct marketing. Not only has it improved the efficiency of direct marketing, it has also introduced new dimensions to this method of doing business. From the customer's perspective, it has, for example, put them in control of the sales process and removed the challenge of fighting off unwelcome sales pitches from the telesales operatives. In doing so, it has attracted new customers to direct marketing. We look at the impact of the internet on channels in Chapter 12.

# Segmentation team

Before embarking on a segmentation project, a key question to answer concerns who should be involved in the segmentation team.

Whilst it is not unusual for short-term sales and profit pressures to prevent the allocation of time and resources to carry out market segmentation, it should be the primary responsibility of the general manager to ensure that it is done.

Ideally, a mixed team of representatives from the main functions of the company is required, because segmentation is central to corporate strategy and affects all areas of the business, and because each function has different contributions to make to the process. Within the team, a core group consisting of two to three individuals should be established. The function of this core group is to carry out all the detailed work required in the segmentation process, the core group reporting back to the full team for consultation, comment and guidance.

Team members from the functional disciplines should have had customer contact and have a good knowledge of the products, markets, customers and the company.

In some circumstances, there should also be an outsider, who is not involved in the industry, but has experience in *market* segmentation, to act as a facilitator for the process and to offer an objective and alternative viewpoint to the discussion. Segmentation, however, is not a project to be contracted out to an external consultancy from whom you eventually receive a report and presentation. Complete ownership of the project and its conclusions is essential if the company intends to commit itself to implementing the findings.

Segmentation can be carried out at all levels of the organization. Strategically, there needs to be a corporate segmentation which will fit within, or help companies develop their mission statement. At lower levels within the organization, there will be segmentation within the strategic business units (SBUs), and, finally, segmentation at a lower level, such as at customer group, product, or at geographic level. This book principally concerns segmentation at SBU and lower levels.

Segmentation is also a subject that should be periodically revisited, as markets are dynamic, segments can alter over time and changes in the macro-economy and the markets can alter the attractiveness of different market segments, especially in fast-changing markets. Also, there are benefits in being creative and innovative and developing new alternative approaches in order to gain and then sustain a competitive advantage.

As your selected team progresses through the process, you will need to answer the following questions:

- How should you segment the market?
- How detailed should your segmentation be?
- How do you define segments in the best possible way?
- Which segments offer the greatest opportunities?

# Data for segmentation

The process in this book is primarily presented in a format designed to utilize data already held by your company, and segmentation, when carried out thoroughly, often requires a broad range of data. The segmentation team will therefore require access to sales and financial data and market research findings in order to provide extra information to help the decision-making process. Inevitably, the quality of the input will have a large impact on the quality of the output.

The data required for segmentation can be summarized as follows:

- the customers' underlying intentions for entering the market;
- an understanding of how the market works;
- the size of the market and how this divides between the competing products and services (approximations at least);
- characteristics that can be used to identify the different customers found within the market (customer profiling);
- the key product and service requirements, and key channel, frequency and method of purchase requirements, from the customer's point of view;

The process in this book is primarily presented in a format designed to utilize data already held by your company.

Definition:
Market research is concerned specifically with research about markets and involves the collection, organization, analysis and dissemination of facts and opinions from existing or potential customers about themselves and about organizations and/or their products and services. (Marketing research is concerned with research about marketing processes.)

- the benefits delivered by these requirements, also from the customer's point of view;
- the relative importance of these benefits to the different customers found within the market.

As you progress through the various steps in the process you may identify information shortfalls which you will need to address. In many instances, the most appropriate method of addressing these shortfalls will be by commissioning market research. Guidelines on how to incorporate market research findings can be found in the text. The segmentation process in this book also provides a structured approach for the collection and use of information in segmentation research projects.

## Marketing insight

Standard segmentation schemes available from external agencies rarely provide the insights required by individual companies to achieve significant competitive advantage. Even if you gain advantage from them today, your competitors can buy them tomorrow and rapidly catch up with you.

A particularly useful exercise at the end of the project is to consider what changes are required to the current information systems in your company to support segmentation.

It is because of the data required for segmentation that the larger, in-company projects benefit from the support of specifically designed PC-based software packages, as briefly mentioned in the Preface. These packages will certainly be required for analysing the quantitative stage of a segmentation research project. Having such a resource enables the segmentation team to concentrate on the marketing issues they are addressing.

# Rules for segmentation

The criteria used for segmentation must have the following characteristics:

- each segment should consist of customers who are relevant to the purchase situation in that they are responsible for making the decision or can affect buying behaviour;
- each segment should have sufficient potential size to justify the time and effort involved in planning specifically for this business opportunity;
- each segment should be distinguishable from other segments, such that each has a distinctive set of requirements and can be served by an equally distinctive marketing strategy;
- each segment should be reachable by sales and distribution channels currently being used or which could be used;

- each segment should be capable of being identified by a set of characteristics, such that the customers in that segment can be reached by a distinctive and cost effective communications strategy;
- the company must be capable of making the necessary changes to its structure, information and decision-making systems so that they become focused on to the new segments.

---

The biggest obstacle to implementing a segmented approach to marketing successfully can often be the company itself because of a reluctance to change. Early anticipation of potential difficulties, along with the development and implementation of counter-measures designed to win over the hearts and minds of key decision-makers in the organization, will be time well spent. In most cases this can often be achieved by engaging them in the project, preferably as a member of the overall team, or at least by seeking their views and keeping them up to date with progress.

**Marketing insight**

---

# The advantages of segmentation

These can be summarized as follows:

- recognizing customers' differences is the key to successful marketing, as it can lead to a closer matching of customers' needs with the company's products or services;
- segmentation can lead to niche marketing, where appropriate, where the company can meet the needs of customers in that niche segment resulting in segment domination, something which is often not possible in the total market;
- segmentation can lead to the concentration of resources in markets where competitive advantage is greatest and returns are high;
- segmentation can be used to gain competitive advantage by enabling you to consider the market in different ways from your competitors;
- by means of segmentation, you can market your company as a specialist in your chosen segments, with a better understanding of customers' needs, thus giving your products or services advantages over those of your competitors.

The additional benefits of the approach to segmentation detailed in this book are:

- it checks your logic and your basic assumptions about your market;
- it helps with your team-building approach;
- it goes across vertical structures, often uncovering hitherto undiscovered customer needs.

# Segmentation process summary

The segmentation process consists of two phases:

**Phase 1**   Developing segments
**Phase 2**   Prioritizing and selecting segments

The first phase of the process, which covers the essential steps you should follow to develop a segmented structure for your market, is applied to the whole market your business is operating in, not just to that bit of the market you are currently successful in. It therefore includes the customers of your competitors, as well as your own, along with the products and/or services bought by these customers.

The second phase of the process then looks at how to select those segments your business should be operating in.

## Developing segments

This first phase of the process contains three stages, broken down into five steps and is summarized in Figure 3.5.

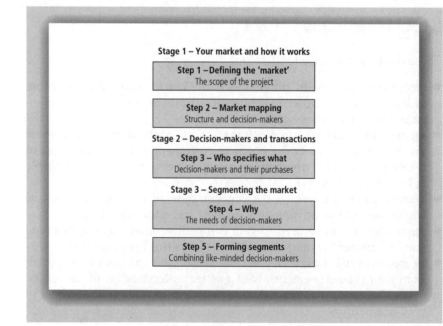

**Figure 3.5**
The segmentation process: Phase 1 – developing segments

## Stage 1: Your market and how it works

The first step, defining the 'market', establishes the scope of the segmentation project by specifying the geographic area covered by the project and by clearly understanding from a customer's perspective their underlying intentions for entering the market in terms of the use, or purpose they have for the purchase of your products or services or those of your competitors. Where necessary, the scope is modified to take into account the realistic capabilities of your organization.

The second step, market mapping, requires you to present the market you have defined as a diagram. It is rather like a flow chart along which cash from the final users flows to you and your competitors, the suppliers, and the products and services from the suppliers flow to the final users. In many markets, however, a flow chart simply tracking the physical stages of the distribution chain is inadequate in covering the role played by 'influencers' on the purchase decision, and/or the purchase decision routines encountered by companies in the market.

From the supplier's perspective, the market map, in truth, is probably better described as the obstacle course they have to overcome in order to get through to the final user.

Once the market map is complete, you are then required to determine at which points along it decisions are made about competing products or services, as it is at these points that segmentation should occur.

This step also enables you to introduce into the process any current segmentation structure you may have for the market being segmented and to test its validity.

## Stage 2: Decision-makers and transactions

Step 3 enables you to look at any of the decision-making points on the market map and construct a model of the market based on the different customers found within it and the transactions they make. It requires you to record the key features sought by the market when deciding between competing offers. These are selected from the actual products and services on offer (what is bought) and from the options presented by where it can be bought, when it is bought and how.

It is during this step that information is recorded about the decision-makers which can be used to identify them in the market.

## Stage 3: Segmenting the market

Step 4 moves from the transactional look at the market covered in the previous step to looking at the reasons why the features sought by the decision-makers when deciding between alternative offers are important to them. Once the real needs, the real benefits, have been understood, their relative value to each 'cell' in the model generated by Step 3 is assessed. The importance of price in each purchase is also recorded.

Step 5 then describes techniques for grouping these cells together in order to obtain the best fit. Cells similar to each other in terms of the relative importance of the needs they are looking to have satisfied are therefore combined to form 'segments'.

In most markets the number of concluding segments is between five and ten.

This step then subjects each 'segment' to a reality check based on the size of each segment, the differentiation between the offers they require, your ability to identify and reach the different customers found in each segment, and the compatibility of these segments with your company.

To help explain the process of developing segments, a case study is used. This not only helps illustrate each step in turn, it also demonstrates how each step relates to the other steps. Further examples are also included where appropriate, both alongside the case and throughout the text.

## Prioritizing and selecting segments

The second phase of the process looks at how to select those segments in which your company should be operating and for which it should be developing marketing strategies. There is a single stage in this second phase, broken down into two steps, and summarized in Figure 3.6.

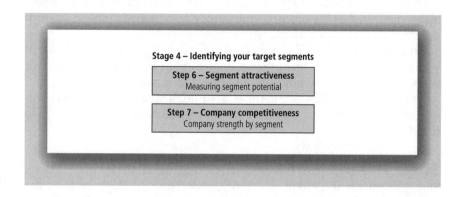

**Figure 3.6**
The segmentation process: Phase 2 – prioritizing and selecting segments

## Stage 4: Identifying your target segments

Step 6 in the overall process of segmentation first defines the criteria your company would use in order to determine the attractiveness to the company of any segment. The relative importance of these criteria to each other is then established, followed by a means of quantifying each of them.

An overall attractiveness score is then calculated for each concluding segment based on how well each of them satisfies your company's requirements.

The final step in the segmentation process then establishes your company's ability to meet the requirements of each concluding segment, compared with the ability of the competition to meet these requirements, from the *segment's* point of view.

By combining segment attractiveness and relative company competitiveness, you can construct a strategic picture of your market which can be used to select those segments which will enable your company to achieve its corporate objectives.

# Marketing objectives and strategies

Segmentation is not an end in itself. Only by developing and implementing the appropriate strategies for each of your chosen segments will your company be able to reap the benefits of segmentation. It is because of this that a chapter has been set aside in this book to discuss the setting of marketing objectives and strategies for segments (Chapter 13).

# Segmentation case histories

This chapter concludes with three short case histories, the first two of which illustrate how superior profitability results from successful market segmentation. The third case history illustrates how failure to recognize that past successes were segment-based nearly ended up in disaster.

## Case 1 – A national off-licence chain[4]

In the mid-1980s, a national off-licence chain, with retail units in major shopping centres and local shopping parades, was experiencing both a decline in customer numbers and a decline in average spend. The original formula for success of design, product range and merchandising, meticulously copied in each outlet, no longer appeared to be working.

The chain had become a classic example of a business comfortably sat in the middle ground, attempting to be all things to all people, but managing to satisfy very few of them.

Rather than sit back in the belief that the business was just passing through a difficult patch, and what worked yesterday was bound to work again, the company embarked on a project designed to understand both their actual and potential customer base.

The first stage of this study turned to one of the more sophisticated geodemographic packages in order to understand the residential profiles of each shop's catchment area. Not unexpectedly, many geodemographic differences were found, and the business quickly accepted that it was unlikely that the same retail formula would appeal to the different target markets found in them.

Rather than look at each shop separately, the catchment area profiles for each shop were subjected to a clustering routine in order to place similar catchment areas together. This resulted in 21 different groupings, each of which was then profiled in terms of their potential to buy different off-licence products using purchasing data from national surveys. (The company's own in-house retailing data would, of course, only reflect the purchasing pattern of their existing customers or, at worst, only a proportion of their requirements if this was limited by the company's current product range.)

However, stocking the requisite range of products in their correct geographical location would not necessarily attract their respective target markets. The chain was already associated with one type of offer which, in addition to including a particular range of drinks, also included the basic design of the shops and overall merchandising.

The project, therefore, moved into a second stage, in which the market's attitudes and motivations to drinking were explored and relative values

[4]Based on Thornton (1993).

attached to the various dimensions uncovered. This was achieved through an independently commissioned piece of market research and resulted in the market being categorized into a number of psychographic groups. This included, amongst others, 'happy and impulsive' shoppers, 'anxious and muddled' shoppers, 'reluctant but organized' shoppers, and the 'disorganized, extravagant' shoppers.

By ensuring this stage of the project linked the attitude and motivational findings to demographic data, the two stages could be brought together. This enabled the original 21 clusters to be reduced to five distinct segments, each of which required a different offer.

The company now had to decide between two alternative strategies:

1  to focus into one segment using one brand and relocate its retail outlets accordingly through a closure and opening programme; or,
2  to develop a manageable portfolio of retailing brands, leave the estate relatively intact, and re-brand, re-fit and re-stock as necessary.

They decided to pursue the second.

Realizing that demographic profiles in geographic areas can change over time, and that customer needs and attitudes can also evolve, the company began to monitor its market quite carefully and was quite prepared to modify its brand portfolio to suit changing circumstances. In the early 1990s, however, the five retail brands of 'Bottoms Up', 'Wine Rack', 'Threshers Wine Shop', 'Drinks Store from Threshers' and 'Food and Drinks Store' sat comfortably within the five segments. They also sat comfortably together in the same shopping centre, enabling the group to meet effectively the different requirements of the segments found within that centre's catchment area.

Perhaps more importantly, this strategy sat comfortably alongside the financial targets for the business.

## Case 2 – Sodium tri-poly phosphate!

Sodium tri-poly phosphate (STPP) was once a simple, unexciting, white chemical cleaning agent. Today, one of its uses is as the major ingredient of a sophisticated and profitable operation, appearing under many different brand names, all competing for a share of what has become a cleverly segmented market.

Have you ever wondered how the toothpaste marketers classify you in their segmentation of the market? Much simplified and for illustrative purposes only, Table 3.1, based on Haley (1968), which presents an overview of the main segments, may assist you.

## Case 3 – Amber nectar

A privately owned brewery in the UK was enjoying exceptional profitability for its industrial sector. In terms of output, it was by no means the largest brewery in the UK, and in terms of geographic cover, it operated only within a particular metropolitan area.

At one of the regular meetings of the board, it was agreed that the company had clearly developed a very successful range of beers and it was time to expand into new geographic areas.

**Table 3.1** Segments in the market for toothpaste

| | | Segment name | | | |
|---|---|---|---|---|---|
| | | *Worrier* | *Sociable* | *Sensory* | *Independent* |
| *Profile* | *Demographic* | C1 C2 25–40 Large families | B C1 C2 Teens Young smokers | C1 C2 D Children | A B 35–40 Male |
| | *Psychographic* | conservative: hypochondriacs | high sociability: active | high self-involvement: hedonists | high autonomy: value orientated |
| *What is bought, where, when and how* | *Product examples* | Signal Mentadent P | Macleans Ultrabrite | Colgate Aquafresh | own label |
| | *Product features* | large canisters health properties | large tubes whitening properties | medium tubes flavouring | small tubes |
| | *Outlet* | supermarket | supermarket | supermarket | independent |
| | *Purchase frequency* | weekly | monthly | monthly | quarterly |
| *Why it is bought* | *Benefits sought* | stop decay | attract attention | taste | functionality |
| *Price paid* | | medium | high | medium | low |
| *Percentage of market* | | 50% | 30% | 15% | 5% |
| *Potential for growth* | | low | high | medium | nil |

*Note:* 'C1', 'C2' and so on appearing in the demographic profiles of each segment represent socio-economic groups which were in use in the UK until 2001, now replaced by eight analytic classes numbered from 1 through to 8. 'Signal' and 'Mentadent P' are trade marks of Lever Fabergé; 'Macleans' and 'Aquafresh' are trade marks of GlaxoSmithKline; 'Ultrabrite' and 'Colgate' are trade marks of Colgate-Palmolive.

The expansion programme met with aggressive opposition from other brewers, particularly the very large brewers. This came as no great surprise to the board who, before setting on the expansion path, had built up a large 'war chest', largely made up of past profits, to finance the plan. The board knew the competition would react in this way because they were being challenged by a very successful range of beers, a 'success' that would ensure product trial, then customer loyalty, in the new areas.

As with all good marketing-focused companies, the progress of the marketing plan was regularly monitored against its target by a specially appointed task force headed by the chief executive. In addition, the sales and marketing director, a key member of the task force, held regular meetings with his own key staff to ensure continuous evaluation of the sales and marketing strategies being followed.

The plan badly underperformed and was eventually abandoned.

In the post-mortem that followed, the brewery discovered why it had been so successful in the past, and why this success could not be extended to other areas of the UK. To its loyal customers, a key attraction of the beers manufactured by this brewery was the 'local' flavour. The 'market' for this company was the metropolitan area it already operated in, its competitors being other local brewers in the same area. Exporting this success was clearly, therefore, not going to work. Expansion could only be achieved by setting up new local breweries in other areas, or by acquiring already established local breweries.

Without this brewery realizing it, the customers for beer in the UK had already segmented themselves. This brewer's segment was the 'regional chauvinist', and in the particular region it operated in the company already had an overwhelming market share: hence its profitability.

With an earlier understanding of this segmentation structure, the company would have spent its war chest more effectively and achieved its growth objectives.

## Case history conclusion

These three case histories illustrate the importance of intelligent segmentation in guiding companies towards successful marketing strategies. However, it is easy to understand this success *after* the event, as occurred in one of the cases! The problem, for most of us, is how to arrive at market segments that will enable us to create differential advantage. That is the purpose of this book.

# Chapter 3 review

This chapter provides essential guidelines for a successful segmentation project.

We began by discussing different approaches to market segmentation and concluded that understanding customers by their needs was the most appropriate approach to adopt, particularly as this was how customers segmented themselves. This approach also provides companies with the insights they need to produce winning propositions.

This was followed by a review of the bases for international market segmentation where we observed that many of the models based on geographic groups had little value as actionable marketing propositions. We concluded that different groupings of countries, or customer groups across selected countries, may prove to be more useful, after which the normal rules for segmentation would apply.

We then went on to present the objectives of this book and, while doing so, pointed out that the segmentation process contained within the book is as applicable to business-to-business markets as it is to business-to-consumer markets. The relationship between segmentation and marketing planning was highlighted along with the importance of ensuring that internal company structures relate to external market segments.

A suggested framework for looking at how companies currently define and segment their markets was then put forward which matched the degree of customer focus in their segmentation to the extent to which they organize their structures around these segments. Four company archetypes were suggested based on their approach to segmentation: sales-based segmentation, structural segmentation, bolt-on segmentation and effective segmentation.

Next, we discussed the factors that have to be considered with respect to effective market segmentation. Here, we looked at the degree to which an offer could be tailored to meet the needs of different customers along with the degree to which customer needs and motivations differed within the defined market. We also raised the issues that organizations have to address regarding their own internal structures and concluded that, in those situations where it is not possible to organize around segments, it should nonetheless be segments that are the ultimate drivers of corporate strategy.

The impact of what is being referred to as the 'postmodern' customer was then briefly reviewed in which three main issues were identified. These were: the importance of correct 'market' definition; that companies should understand customer needs and take more account of them in their internal processes; and the changes brought about by recent developments in IT. All three are covered in this book.

We then moved on to discuss who should be involved in the segmentation team and suggested that this should consist of representatives from the main functions of the company in which resides a smaller, core team who undertake the project. We also suggested that an independent outsider experienced in market segmentation, but not involved in the industry, would be a useful addition to the team. The point was made, however, that segmentation was not a project to be contracted out.

In discussing the segmentation team, we also emphasized that segmentation was a subject that had to be periodically revisited as markets change over time.

The data requirements for segmentation were looked at next. Here we pointed out that the process in this book is presented primarily in a format designed to utilize data already held by the company, and this may identify information shortfalls that require market research. If research is required, it, too, can follow the structure of this segmentation process.

We then presented the characteristics that each segment was required to have, such as having sufficient size to justify the expending of business resources on them, being sufficiently different from all the other segments in terms of their requirements and being reachable in some way. We also emphasized the importance of ensuring that companies focused on these segments and were prepared to make the changes this required to their current processes.

After briefly summarizing the advantages of segmentation we then presented an overview of the segmentation process. This has been broken down into two phases, 'Developing segments' and 'Prioritizing and selecting segments' in which there are seven steps, five in the first phase and two in the second phase.

Next we pointed out that segmentation was not an end in itself and that once the segments had been identified, marketing objectives and strategies had to be developed for each segment the company wished to target. Only by implementing these strategies would the benefits from the segmentation project be realized. A chapter on setting marketing objectives and strategies is included in this book.

Finally, we presented three short case histories that illustrate the importance of *market*-based segmentation.

# References

Haley, R. I. (1968). 'Benefit segmentation: A decision-oriented research tool'. *Journal of Marketing*, Vol. 32, July.

Jenkins, M. and McDonald, M. (1997). 'Market segmentation: Organisational archetypes and research agendas'. *European Journal of Marketing*, Vol. 31, No. 1, 17–32.

Kotler, P. (1991). *Marketing Management: Analysis Planning and Control*. Englewood Cliffs, NJ: Prentice-Hall.

Levitt, T. (1960). 'Marketing myopia'. *Harvard Business Review*, July–August, 45–56.

Piercy, N. F. and Morgan, N. A. (1993). 'Strategic and operational market segmentation: A managerial analysis'. *Journal of Strategic Marketing*, Vol. 1, No. 1, 123–40.

Thornton, J. (1993). Market segmentation from Bottoms Up. *ResearchPlus, the Market Research Society*, December.

# Chapter 4

# Determining the scope of a segmentation project

# Summary

This chapter looks at the most crucial and complex issue in marketing, namely, how a market is defined. Until this is clearly understood, issues such as market share, the identification of target customers and their needs, and even the recognition of competitors, will continuously cause difficulty. It is the essential first step of your segmentation project, as illustrated in Figure 4.1.

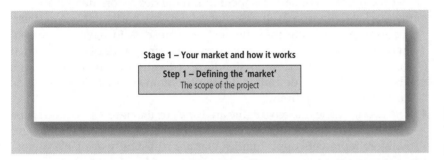

**Figure 4.1**
The segmentation process – Step 1

This chapter is organized as follows:

A 'fast track' for those looking for a quick route through the key points
A discussion about the geographic scope
Using the needs-based approach to define the market being segmented
The difference between wants and needs
■ Care in using products and product categories to define markets
Striking a meaningful balance between a broad definition and a narrow definition
Using distinct price bands and using different end-uses or applications of the product to make projects more manageable
■ A discussion about whose needs are being defined
The difference between consumers and customers
Making the market definition appropriate to your company and its capabilities
■ Allowing for limitations imposed by corporate structure
■ Sizing the market being segmented
A review of this step in the segmentation process
Background to the case study being used to illustrate Steps 1 to 5 of the segmentation process, the definition of its market and further examples
Exercises further to help you determine the scope of your project

# Fast track

● Describe the geographic area covered by the project. Keeping it within the borders of a single country is a manageable starting point. If you want to include other countries ensure that the stage of market development, the available routes to market and the pattern of marketing activity are all the same, or at least very similar to each other.

This book refers to those whose needs are being defined as 'customers'.

- Describe the 'market' being segmented in terms of a *customer need* in a way which covers the aggregation of all the alternative products or services which *customers* regard as being capable of satisfying that same need. Capture this description by completing the following sentence with a phrase that identifies *the* specific purpose or intended use *customers* have in mind for the products or services *they* see as being in a competitive set, along with any relevant circumstances.

The customer *need* is to …

List the products or services included in the definition, but ensure that the market definition itself does not refer to any particular one of them. For example, to state that the customer need is to have a 'pension' ignores the fact that customers can choose from a range of options when looking to 'secure a desired standard of living for when they retire'. Also ensure that the definition does not contain any meaningless words such as 'quality' or 'brand'.

- *If necessary*, refine the geographic area and/or the need so that the scope of your project is meaningful in terms of your company's capabilities and therefore represents opportunities that are realistically available to you. *If absolutely necessary*, further refine the scope to take into account any internal company 'boundaries', such as those imposed by SBUs, as initially it may be more pragmatic to segment that part of the market currently satisfied by your product line.

We use the word 'product' to avoid unnecessary references to 'services', 'not-for-profit services', 'capital goods' and 'retail'. The text is equally relevant to these.

  It is important, however, that you monitor the trends in the use of the products or services you have elected not to include within the scope of your segmentation project but which satisfy the same need. This is because you may need to consider moving into these products or services in the future in order to meet corporate objectives. In the meantime, continue this project for your specified market.
- Size the defined market in the specified geographic area in terms of the volume or value that is available to you and your competitors. Approximate figures are acceptable.

Readers who are sure that they have a clear and appropriate description of the geographic and 'market' boundaries for their segmentation project may go straight to Chapter 5.

This concludes the fast track for Step 1 of the segmentation process.

# Geographic scope

A segmentation project clearly requires a geographic boundary as this will enable the project team to size the market, identify the localities in which the market dynamics have to be understood and, once the segments have been identified, develop the appropriate marketing objectives and strategies for those localities. This can be as much of an issue for local companies as for global companies.

Keeping the project within the borders of a single country is a manageable starting point because the stage of market development, the available routes to market and the pattern of marketing activity will probably be the same throughout the country. Even this, however, may be too broad for some companies, simply because their geographic reach is limited by physical and/or economic considerations, or even because their appeal has a strong local sentiment attached to it. For example, a local medical practice will find it difficult to offer an effective service beyond a certain distance, a regional distribution company will find it difficult to provide a viable home delivery service around the country and in Chapter 3 we saw how a privately owned brewery struggled to 'export' its product to other localities because its beer had a strong 'local' appeal.

For companies trading in numerous countries around the world there is clearly an enormous attraction in finding a single global segmentation model that can be applied to every country. However, the experience of 'globalization' has highlighted for many of these companies that they have to 'act local' in order to succeed in their market. This does not mean that every country is completely unique in respect of the segments found within it. What the international company may find is that the global picture for their market can be captured by one of the following:

1 to all intents and purposes there is a single global segmentation model which at the local level simply requires a series of small changes to the segment details to make the global model applicable; or,
2 although different segmentation structures exist in many countries, individual segments are found in more than one country the total of which can be brought together into a global model consisting of a manageable pool of segments; or,
3 a combination of 1 and 2 with not every segment found in each country, as in 2, and various segments requiring small changes to their details to make them applicable at the local level, as in 1.

To get to this point will require a progressive series of segmentation projects with each project based on a sensible geographic boundary. As experience builds up with each project it is likely to reach the point where no additional segments are being uncovered and patterns emerge which associate external dimensions, such as the stage of market development and socio-economic factors, with specific segments. Once this occurs, subsequent projects can be reliably scaled back to exercises that simply test the existence of various segments.

As a guide to predetermining which countries can be included in a single segmentation project, ensure that in each of these countries the stage of market development, the available routes to market and the pattern of marketing activity are the same, or at least very similar.

The advent of e-commerce appears to add another dimension to this discussion both for those companies who once served only a local market but now, thanks to the internet, serve a global customer base, and for start-up companies looking to the internet for a wide geographic reach. It is unlikely that many (if any) of these companies can afford a global segmentation project, so the most sensible starting point would be the geographic area that is key to the business with a progressive roll out of the project as already described. Guidelines as to which geographic areas the segmentation project should be extended into could, of course, be based on the areas from where enquiries to the company website originate and where sales are made.

# Defining markets

Let us start the discussion about 'markets' by referring to that well-known (and often abused) concept of market share.

Most business people already understand that there is a direct relationship between relatively high share of any market and high returns on investment, as shown in Figure 4.2.

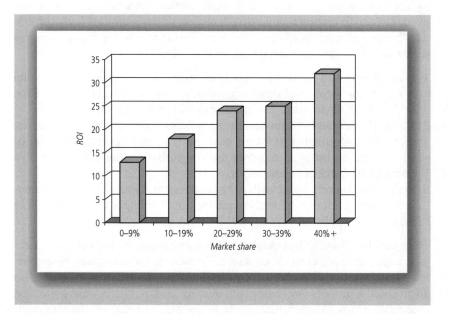

**Figure 4.2**
The relationship between market share and return on investment (ROI) (*Source:* Strategic Planning Institute's 'Profit Impact of Market Strategies' (PIMS) database.)

Clearly, however, since BMW branded cars are not in the same market as Ford branded cars, for example, it is important to be most careful about how 'market' is defined. Correct market definition is crucial for:

1 measuring market share and market growth;
2 the specification of target customers;
3 recognition of relevant competitors; and, most important of all,
4 the formulation of marketing strategy, for it is this, above all else, that delivers differential advantage.

One of the most frequent mistakes made by people who do not understand what market share really means is to assume that their company has only a small share of some market, whereas, if the company is commercially successful, it probably has a much larger share of a smaller market.

## Developing the market definition

The general rule for 'market' definition is that it should be described in terms of a *customer need* in a way which covers the aggregation of all the alternative products or services which *customers* regard as being capable of satisfying that same need. It is not, therefore, defined in terms of what a company sells,[1] but in terms of what customers are setting out to achieve. For example, we would regard the in-company caterer as only one option when it came to satisfying lunchtime hunger. This particular need could also be satisfied at external restaurants, public houses, fast-food specialists and sandwich bars. The emphasis in the definition of 'market', therefore, is clearly on the word *'need'*.

> ● Definition:
> A market is the aggregation of all the products or services which customers regard as being capable of satisfying the same need.

**Marketing insight**

An important distinction to note at this point is that, while a 'market' describes a customer need in a way which covers the aggregation of all the alternative products or services customers regard as capable of satisfying that need, 'segments' focus on specific products or services, their characteristics and properties, along with other components of the total marketing proposition, that different groups of customers are looking for in order to satisfy their particular needs within a market.

A key difference, therefore, between a 'market' and a 'segment' is that a specific marketing strategy can be defined for a segment, whereas for a market, we can only list the alternative products or services. It is simply a different level of aggregation of customer needs.

Aggregating currently available products or services regarded by users as alternatives is, however, simply an aid to arriving at the definition, as it is important to recognize that new products, yet to be developed, could better satisfy the users' need. For example, the button manufacturer who believed its market was the 'button market' would have been very disappointed when zips and Velcro began to satisfy the need for garment fastenings! A needs-based definition for such a company would have enabled the management to recognize the fickleness of current products, and to accept that one of their principal tasks is to seek out better ways of satisfying their market's needs and to evolve their product offer accordingly. Other examples would include the manufacturer of video cassette recorders (VCRs) who believed its market was the 'VCR market' and now sees the facility to record and play TV broadcasts and films on demand being satisfied by Digital Versatile Disks (DVDs). The manufacturer of fax machines who believed its market was the 'fax market' has seen e-mails and the internet replace the fax machine as the preferred method for the immediate transfer of documents, data and images to another location. The supplier of board games who believed that 'board games' defined their market has seen it eroded by PlayStations, X Boxes, Game Cubes and

---

[1] For companies that do not sell products or services, such as suppliers of public services, simply substitute the word 'sells' with 'supplies' as the rule is applicable to all types of companies.

interactive TV.[2] There are many more examples of myopic market definitions which generate their short-sighted views of the market by focusing
the definition on today's products.

| | |
|---|---|
| **Marketing insight** | It is crucial that the market definition should avoid the inclusion within it of specific products or services, as this can lead to a narrow and blinkered understanding of the real market. |

Table 4.1 contrasts some product-specific definitions with their possible
needs-based definitions.

**Table 4.1** Defining markets

| Definition based on the product | Definition based on the need |
|---|---|
| Car insurance (personal) | … to cover the unexpected financial costs of accidents and losses associated with a motor vehicle |
| X-ray equipment (medical) | … to have visual images of the inner parts of a body (as an aid to diagnosis) |
| Business books | … to have accessible information about business |
| Fertilizers | … to provide nutrients to plants |
| Potato crisps | … to have a savoury snack |
| Lubrication oil | … to increase the working life of mechanical parts by reducing the negative impact of friction |

Closely aligned to specific products are 'product categories' which were
primarily created from a production and sales perspective by the suppliers to capture what they saw as a competitive set. These industry-defined
categories, therefore, became convenient boundaries in which marketers
could measure the market share of their brand. Customers, however, do
not confine themselves to industry-imposed definitions and look for products which fall within what they perceive as 'needs categories'. Measuring
market share in a category that customers do not recognize either provides delusions of adequacy that could be masking a terminal decline, or
delusions of inadequacy that hold you back from realizing your true competitive strength.

> In the early twentieth century a number of companies became
> household names for travel across the Atlantic. These companies
> operated some of the finest ships found anywhere in the world

---

[2] 'PlayStation' is a registered trade mark of Sony Computer Entertainment Inc. 'X Box' is a
registered trade mark of the Microsoft Corporation. 'Game Cube' is a registered trade mark
of Nintendo.

and provided the only means of passenger transportation across the Atlantic. 'We're in shipping', they said, 'and that's what our customers want' and between them they had a 100 per cent share of the 'market'.

Later in the same century some enterprising engineers made flying a commercial proposition and it didn't take long before a number of new companies became household names for travel across the Atlantic. What was really annoying (to the shipping companies) was that these new companies not only attracted new passengers to transatlantic travel but also took passengers away from the shipping companies, initially from the premium end of the market and eventually across every category of passenger.

Interestingly, not one of these airlines had ever operated a ship!

By focusing on their product and defining the market along product lines the shipping companies had become blinded to the true market their customers were in. Their transatlantic customers didn't need a ship; they were looking for transportation in order to be on the other side of the Atlantic. Today, the shipping companies that still provide passenger services across the Atlantic have little presence in the market they were originally in. The passengers they now carry across the Atlantic primarily travel by sea in order to satisfy needs other than that of pure travel.

Had the shipping companies recognized the market their customers were in they could have considered developing an air travel product. This would have enabled them to avoid the trauma they went through in the second half of the twentieth century.

The transatlantic travel example highlights the danger of relying on industry-defined 'categories' of products or services to define a 'market', especially for long-term planning and survival. Measuring your share of passengers travelling on ships was useful during the time that ships provided the only means of transport across the Atlantic, but useless when airlines appeared on the scene and began to compete with the shipping companies. Where a 'market' begins and ends is defined by the competitive set as perceived by the customers in that market and described in terms of the need that they are satisfying. Any other definition of a market will endanger the long-term survival of your company.

**Marketing insight**

The above example also highlights what is possibly one of the greatest areas for misunderstanding in marketing, namely the distinction between customer wants and needs. This is therefore an opportune moment to turn our attention briefly to the subject of customer wants.

Companies are often accused of manipulating their customers by making them want things they do not really need. If this were so, we would not have a situation in which a very high proportion of all new products launched actually fail! The fact is that people have always had needs, such as, say, for getting to one place from another, be it across land or across water. What changes in the course of time is the way people satisfy this need, as was witnessed by the transatlantic shipping companies.

What customers *want* are the products and services that best meet their *need* at the price they are prepared to pay.

What customers want is the product or service that they perceive best meets their need at whatever price they are prepared to pay. They may have wanted to travel by sea between the old and the new world in the first half of the twentieth century, but once the airlines could provide the desired service at an acceptable price, customers headed for the airport rather than the seaport. The airlines themselves, of course, only became commercially viable because people needed a means of getting to one place from another. Without the existence of this need, both the shipping companies and the airlines would have found themselves launching products that actually failed.

It is necessary to strike a meaningful balance between a narrow definition and a broad definition to arrive at a market definition customers would recognize.

In addition to avoiding a market definition that is too narrow, it is also important to avoid arriving at a market definition that is too broad. For example, 'financial services' embraces a vast range of very different products and services, far too many to be regarded as a single market. Besides, has anyone actually bought a product or service called 'financial services'? The carbonated drinks company that believes its products should be measured in terms of their share of the total human liquid intake, which therefore includes tea, coffee, water and so on, is clearly defining a 'market' few if any customers actually operate in. Perhaps the individual emerging from the Sahara desert after having nothing to drink for days on end could view this vast product range as representing a realistic breadth of options, but even then they tend to ask only for water.

The outcome for a project which is attempting to segment a market which is too broadly defined is usually one of the following:

1 the segmentation project becomes unmanageable because of the broad range of products and services being looked at and because of the very diverse needs the different ranges of products and services are actually satisfying; or,

2 the concluding segments (markets often divide into between five and ten segments) can only be described in vague terms, making it very difficult, if not impossible, to define clearly the specific marketing mix (product/service, price, promotion and place) each segment requires, therefore defeating the whole object of segmentation.

---

A UK company which had originally started as a supplier of home mortgages and savings products was looking to extend its portfolio of products in order to compete with banks and insurance companies. To help develop products and services targeted at specific customer groups the company commissioned a single segmentation project looking at 'financial services'. After months of detailed discussions with numerous customers costing well over £60 000 the project ground to a confused halt. Individual customers were being 'inconsistent' because they were seen to change their buying criteria across the product range. For example, when customers were being asked about holiday insurance and pensions, they had quite different views as to what criteria they would use to choose between different products and suppliers. This, as far as the company in question was concerned, made the project unmanageable.

The company concluded that it was impossible to segment their market and the project was abandoned.

If only they had listened to how their customers categorized the product range and how their customers defined the markets this company was trying to sell into, the project would have worked.

The only true arbiters of what constitutes a market are customers, though they are unlikely to be able to answer the question, 'what is the market?' However, by understanding how they categorize products and services in terms of the specific use or purpose they are putting the products or services to will enable the marketer to define correctly the market(s) they have to segment.

**Marketing insight**

If you are a company with a range of products and services that you suspect may fit into more than one market, Exercise 4.4 at the end of this chapter provides a series of steps you can follow which will help define the market(s) you are in.

Another possibility that may refine the scope of a market definition can be the circumstance or the mindset in which the customer is operating. For example, a customer may be looking to buy clothing that is suitable for work at one moment, then looking to buy clothing for a fun evening out at another moment, and all during the same shopping trip. In choosing a venue for an evening out, a customer may be looking for a quiet relaxing venue one evening and for a themed and fun venue the next evening. The busy worker trekking home after a hard day in the office or on the factory floor faced with squeezing in a meal for the family before setting off for their Pilates[3] session at the local gym would possibly turn to a ready-made meal for that evening, but would not be seen dead serving the same meal when hosting a dinner for friends. In all three of these examples the competitive sets and buying criteria will differ according to the circumstance, purpose or objective the customer has in mind. Therefore, they should all be treated as separate markets. Do not be surprised, however, if you find a particular product appearing in more than one market.

'Market hopping', which is what the above examples illustrate, generates a great deal of confusion for marketers who have failed to understand the market(s) they serve from the customer's perspective. This is particularly the case for companies that serve a number of different 'needs sets' and see their customers being inconsistent in the criteria they use to choose between alternative products or services.

But there is nothing new in this. Take the basic human requirement of food and drink; providing for guests and the everyday household has been different for thousands of years. What has happened, however, especially since the middle of the twentieth century, is that the choices available to customers have increased, the socio-economic environment has changed and acceptable social norms have evolved. This has resulted in markets fragmenting into a number of sub-markets which are now large enough to be segmented in their own right.

**Marketing insight**

[3] Pilates is an exercise regime currently in vogue which increases core strength and suppleness.

In 2002 the British spent a total of £1900 million on ready-made meals and nearly one in three British adults now eats a ready-made meal more than once a week (compared with one in six in France). 'Convenience' is certainly one of the attractions (a MORI poll in the UK found that 77 per cent of purchasers claimed that they only bought these meals when they did not have time to cook) but they have also become the mainstay meal for those who are generally time-poor and/or have no inclination to cook (often replacing Indian and Chinese takeaways). In addition, some of the higher quality chilled foods, such as Café Culture from Marks & Spencer,[4] are now promoted as equivalent to your favourite restaurant (and claimed to 'make dining in feel as though you are dining out').

Any suppliers who still consider that ready-made meals serve a single market are clearly misleading themselves.

The following is a further example of a business striking a meaningful balance between a broad market definition and a manageable market definition:

Television broadcasting companies could be described as being in the 'entertainment' market, which also consists of theatres, cinemas and theme parks, to name but a few. This is a fairly broad definition. It may, therefore, be more manageable and productive for the television broadcasters, when looking at segmenting their market, to define their market as being the 'home entertainment' market. This could then be further refined into the pre-school, child, teenager, family, or adult home entertainment market.

If the 'market' you have defined for your segmentation project still appears to be too broad, there are two further refinements which you may be able to apply in order to break the market down into more manageable units:

1 by using distinct price ranges within which customers appear to operate; or,
2 by using distinct end-uses or applications of the product or service as market boundaries.

The first of these two refinements may be appropriate to competitive sets which span a wide price range, such as exists for many types of motor vehicle. As we pointed out in our opening comments for this section, BMW branded cars are not in the same market as Ford branded cars, even though they both manufacture what could be regarded as similar categories of cars, such as family saloons and multi-purpose vehicles (MPVs). The BMW marque is, however, competing with the likes of Mercedes, Jaguar and Lexus, all of which fall into a particular price range, a price range

---

[4] 'Café Culture' is a trade mark of Marks & Spencer plc.

within which a customer group clearly operates. The question now becomes; is this customer group large enough to be regarded as a 'market' which can be further broken down into economically viable segments? For the car example the answer is clearly 'yes' and the criteria used by customers to choose between alternative cars in each of the price ranges is quite different.

If you believe that breaking down your market into price ranges is an appropriate step to take, check out the following two questions before adopting this refinement:

1 Do they represent price ranges within which customers clearly operate? The clue obviously comes from the customers themselves and the alternatives that they consider fall into a particular competitive set.
2 Is the amount of business in each price range large enough to justify a separate segmentation project, leading to segments that can produce an acceptable return on the investment each of them will require?

You need to answer 'yes' to both questions in order to have the case for splitting a market into distinct price ranges with each of them treated as separate segmentation projects.

---

Most markets consist of products at different price points, usually reflecting a variation of some sort around the core product. In addition, most markets have some customers who always look for the cheapest and others for the most expensive. This does not mean that these markets should be split into different price ranges. The two check questions we have provided should help you decide, but if you are still unsure regard it as one market in your first pass.

**Marketing insight**

---

Turning now to the second suggested refinement: Companies supplying, for example, industrial lubricants may find segmentation more manageable and productive if their market is defined in terms of the particular application of the product, such as heavy industrial use or precision engineering. Likewise, the manufacturer of paint may find it useful to break down the market for paint according to whether it is for external use or internal use. Interestingly, some research among domestic users of paint has even highlighted that the selection process for paint differs according to the type of room it is being bought for (the buying criteria for paint in the 'public rooms' being different from the buying criteria for paint in the 'private rooms'). It would, however, really depend on how widespread this practice is before it could be concluded that differentiating between 'private room' decoration and 'public room' decoration at the market definition stage would be a sensible starting point.

---

Whenever there are different end-uses, or applications, for a product or service, this often indicates that more than one market is being served.

**Marketing insight**

---

With the above considerations in mind, how should the market(s) you serve be defined? As a reminder, the general rule for 'market' definition is that it should be described in terms of a *customer need* in a way which covers the aggregation of all the alternative products or services which *customers* regard as being capable of satisfying that same need. To help, try and capture this description by completing one or the other of the following sentences with a phrase that identifies *the* specific purpose or intended use *customers* have in mind for the products or services *they* see as being in a competitive set, along with any relevant circumstances.

1 When choosing between these alternative products/services the *need* that each customer is looking to satisfy is to...
2 Customers acquire these products/services because they have a *need* to ...

Or, more simply:

3 The customer *need* is to ...

Ensure that the market definition does not refer to any particular product or service, or contains any meaningless words such as 'quality' or 'brand'. It is, however, useful to list the products or services covered by the definition.

## Whose needs are being defined?

A question that sometimes occurs when developing a market definition, particularly in complex markets, concerns the use of the word 'customer'. Specifically, who is the customer and, therefore, whose needs are being defined?

Definition:
The consumer is the final user of goods or services. Customers are intermediate people or organizations who buy directly from us.

Let us start with the difference between customers and consumers. The term 'consumer' is interpreted by most to mean the final user of the product or service, who is not necessarily the customer. Take the example of the parent who is buying breakfast cereals. The chances are that they are intermediate customers, acting as agents on behalf of the eventual consumers (their family) and, in order to market cereals effectively, it is clearly necessary to understand the needs of the end-consumer, as well as the needs of the parents.

The point here is that it is necessary to be aware of the needs of eventual consumers down the buying chain.

Consider the case of the industrial purchasing officer buying raw materials such as wool tops for conversion into semi-finished cloths, which are then sold to other companies for incorporation into the final product, say a suit, or a dress, for sale in consumer markets. Here, we can see that the requirements of those various intermediaries and the end-user are eventually translated into the specifications of the purchasing officer to the raw materials manufacturer. Consequently, the market needs that this manufacturing company is attempting to satisfy must in the last analysis be defined in terms of the requirements of the ultimate users – the consumer – even though our direct customer is quite clearly the purchasing officer.

Given that we can appreciate the distinction between customers and consumers and the need constantly to be alert to any changes in the ultimate consumption patterns of the products or services to which our own contributes, the next question to face is: who are our customers?

Direct customers are those people or organizations who actually buy direct from us. They could, therefore, be distributors, retailers and the like. However, as intimated in the previous paragraph, there is a tendency for organizations to confine their interest, hence their marketing, only to those who actually place orders. This can be a major mistake, as can be seen from the following case history.

---

A fertilizer company that had grown and prospered during the 1970s and early 1980s, because of the superior nature of its products, reached its farmer consumers through agricultural merchants (wholesalers). However, as other companies copied their technology, the merchants began to stock competitive products and drove prices and margins down. Had the fertilizer company paid more attention to the needs of its different farmer groups and developed products especially for them, based on farmer segmentation, it would have continued to create demand pull through differentiation.

As it was, their products became commodities and the power shifted almost entirely to the merchants. At the eleventh hour this fertilizer company recognized whose needs it truly had to serve, those of the farmers, and rescued itself from an untimely death by redefining its product range and targeting its products accordingly.

---

There are countless other examples of companies which, because they did not pay sufficient attention to the needs of users further along the value chain, gradually ceased to provide any real value to their direct customers and eventually went out of business.

**Marketing insight**

In summary, therefore, the term 'customer' for many practitioners of marketing refers to the distribution channel and the term 'consumer' refers to the final user, which means that every company has consumers ('consumption is the sole end and purpose of production', Adam Smith, 1776, *The Wealth of Nations*). However, companies whose final users are found in other businesses do not see themselves as selling to consumers; they are in business-to-business marketing, the terms 'consumers' and 'consumer marketing' being associated with selling to the general public. But just to confuse matters even further, companies who see themselves as being in consumer markets deal with consumer queries through their 'customer' service department.

As a general rule, the definition for a market should focus around the needs of the final user, the consumer, and in many markets this also happens to be the one who has to find the money which pays everyone else

*As a general rule, the definition for a market should focus round the needs of the final user.*

along the distribution chain, though there are exceptions to this latter point, as already highlighted earlier. However, given the association of 'consumers' with particular types of markets, that segmentation is applicable to both consumer and business-to-business markets, and that there is not a general consensus on the distinction between customers and consumers, this book will subsume both under the title of 'customer'. As a general rule, therefore, the definition for a market should focus around the needs of the final customer, in other words, the final user.

The exception to this general rule is when the product or service in question has little if any perceived value to the final user, a situation that can occur when the product or service is incorporated into another. For example, the manufacturer of small electronic components for cars is unlikely to find that the drivers of cars have a great deal of interest in their particular product. Defining the market in terms which describe the needs of car drivers with respect to this product is therefore unlikely to be very useful. In such circumstances the 'customer' for market definition purposes would be the final individual who attributes value to the product or service in question. On the other hand, the chemical company that uses environmentally-friendly manufacturing processes may find that extending their understanding of a market to the final users, even with products that completely lose their identity in their final form, can provide the company with a competitive edge.

## Marketing insight

One of the recent, and apparently successful, examples of a company that spent resources on both understanding and marketing to its final users, even though its product becomes incorporated into another, is the Intel Corporation. The success of the 'intel inside'[5] campaign, however, was dependent on customers accepting that a value proposition could be attributed to a computer's microprocessor. Once this had become established, manufacturers of computers became compelled to include these microprocessors in their products which, in turn, limited their price negotiation powers.

A point to note here is that a product which is perceived by customers to have little 'value' today may be seen in a completely different light in the future, and there is a great deal of value in having customers specify your product.

Finally, let us return to the parents buying breakfast cereals for their family. The manufacturers of breakfast cereals have to segment the final users of these products in order to produce successful product lines. These manufacturers also have to ensure that the retailers stock their products. To do this the manufacturers have to understand the needs of retailers and ensure that their business practices meet the requirements of their retailers. In turn, the retailers have to ensure that the parents who buy breakfast cereals choose to shop at their outlets. The retailers therefore have to understand the needs of these intermediate customers and ensure that their outlets meet the preferred shopping experiences of different parents. The breakfast cereal manufacturer would, therefore, benefit from segmenting

*Margin notes:*

*Because there is not a general consensus on the distinction between customers and consumers, this book will subsume both under the title of 'customer'.*

*An exception to the general rule for market definition is when the product or service has little, if any, perceived value to the final user.*

---

[5] 'intel inside' is a registered trade mark of Intel Corporation.

both the final users of their products and the retailers of their products in two quite distinct projects.

An excellent example of a company that has developed detailed insights into both its consumers and intermediaries is Procter & Gamble (P&G). As can be seen from the simple diagram in Figure 4.3, P&G create demand pull (hence high turnover and high margins) by paying detailed attention to the needs of consumers. But they also pay detailed attention to the needs of their direct customers: in this instance Wal-Mart, the giant food retailer in the USA. Wal-Mart are able to operate on very low margins because, as the bar code goes across the till, this triggers P&G to invoice them, produce another and activate the distribution chain, all of this being done by means of integrated IT processes. In this way, P&G have reduced Wal-Mart's costs by hundreds of millions of dollars.

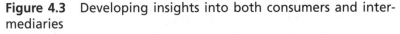

**Figure 4.3**  Developing insights into both consumers and inter-mediaries

## Ensuring the definition is meaningful to your company

In some instances the sequences discussed in this chapter so far still result in a market definition that is not as meaningful as it could be to your company, particularly if you are a company focused into a particular part of an overall market. The following example may therefore provide further help in defining the market your business is in:

A company manufacturing nylon carpet for the commercial sector wanted to check that it had a realistic definition of the 'market' it was in. The first step was to sketch out the total available market for all floor covering. This is summarized in Figure 4.4.

Clearly, it would be wrong to include the first group, namely those used in the industrial sector, in the company's market defin-ition. The qualities required from such flooring cannot hope to be matched in a carpet made from any currently known type of fibre; they are, therefore, not seen as alternative products to the industrial sector. Similarly, in both the commercial and domestic sectors, nylon carpet is not a competitor for the luxury end of the market. This luxury part of the market buys carpet made from natural fibres, particularly wool.

This leaves the non-luxury commercial and domestic sectors which, in total, represented the company's potential available market. It was potentially available because the company could,

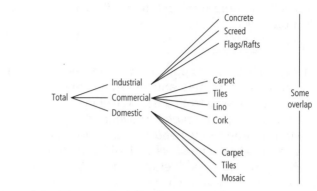

**Figure 4.4** The market for floor covering

for example, produce nylon carpet for the domestic sector and extend its market this way. Similarly, the company could move into manufacturing nylon carpet tiles and extend its operation into this product for both the domestic and commercial sectors. There was also no reason why the company should not look at replacing lino, cork or mosaic flooring with nylon carpet.

Many of the opportunities in the potentially available market, however, represent possible strategies for the future. They would be considered during the marketing planning process when the future plans for the current business activity did not achieve the required financial targets (see McDonald, 2002). The question now, therefore, is, what is the company's realistically available market?

To assist the company in this final stage of arriving at a market definition, the 'needs' being met by the current products, as highlighted by the current customers, were first listed. This revealed that the company's nylon carpet was bought because:

- it fell into a particular price range;
- it was quiet underfoot;
- it had a life expectancy of fifteen years;
- it was available in pleasant colours and textures;
- the manufacturing plant was within a sixty-mile radius.

In addition to the obvious, this list removed lino, cork and mosaic from the company's available market.

Finally, the company looked at the applicability of its current distribution and selling methods to the potentially available market, ruling out those sections of the market which required different selling and distribution approaches. This meant that it was unrealistic to include the domestic sector in the market definition.

Products and manufacturers which met all the criteria were then listed, along with their end-users. The company had now arrived at both a market definition and a current market size.

This example once again illustrates the need to arrive at a meaningful balance between a broad market definition and a manageable market definition. Too narrow a definition has the pitfall of restricting the range of new opportunities segmentation could open up for your business. On the other hand, too broad a definition has the potential of not only overwhelming the segmentation exercise, but also producing results which lead the company into areas it simply is not suited to serve.

The market definition sequence highlighted in the example of the nylon carpet manufacturer can be summarized as follows:

1 First, define the totally available market (TAM) by expressing it as 'a need that can be satisfied by *all* the alternative products or services'. For the carpet manufacturer this meant *all* floor coverings. To take another example, for the canner of dog food this would include *all* dog food. This would ensure that the canner had an overview of what was happening in the market as a whole, as some of the trends may be of great interest (including trends in buying meat from the butcher). However, to segment the whole market when it includes alternatives your company could not hope to offer is not very helpful.

2 Now define the potentially available market (PAM) by taking into account what your company's products or services and their directly competitive products or services *could* be used for within the TAM. For the carpet manufacturer this excluded industrial floor coverings but included, for example, the domestic sector, a sector they did not currently sell into but could serve with the products they had. For the canner, this would exclude meat from the butcher and dried dog food. For the button manufacturer it would exclude zips and Velcro. These exclusions, however, represent possible strategies for the future. PAM is therefore expressed as 'the need that could be satisfied by products and services supplied by your company along with their competing products or services'. However, to segment a 'possible' market before segmenting your current market could result in your company missing growth opportunities which offered quick rewards and carried very little risk.

3 Finally, therefore, define the realistically available market (RAM), as this will become the market to be segmented. This refines the market further by taking into account the requirements of the company's customers and prospects and the current distribution channels used by the company, along with any realistic alternatives. This really focused the carpet manufacturer on to a particular fibre, texture and geographic selling area; it would focus the dog food canner to any similar requirements associated with their customers; and would focus the button manufacturer onto buttons. RAM is therefore expressed as 'the need that is currently satisfied by the products and services supplied by your company along with all their competing products or services'.

Whilst it is tempting to think that the examples given above amount to 'rigging' the definition of market and that there is the danger of fooling ourselves, we must never lose sight of the purpose of market segmentation, which is to create competitive advantage for ourselves by creating greater value for customers.

> It is necessary to arrive at a meaningful balance between a broad market definition and a manageable market definition.

| **Marketing insight** | Thus, for the carpet manufacturer – or for a London orchestra that defines its market in terms of the need that is satisfied by the aggregation of all London classical orchestras rather than by all entertainment – as long as its market definition enables it to outperform its competitors and grow profitably,[6] this is the key. Obviously, however, the definition needs to be kept under review and revised as and when necessary. |
|---|---|

Although great care is needed in making the decision to exclude products or services from the market you are segmenting, great care is also needed in making sure that the market definition is meaningful to your company.

| **Marketing insight** | It is important, however, that you monitor the trends in the use of the products or services you have elected not to include within the scope of your segmentation project but which satisfy the same need. The purpose in doing this is to help you decide the extent to which you may need to consider moving into these products or services in the future in order to secure the company's desired position in this market and meet its corporate objectives. |
|---|---|
| | What you must avoid is the trap that the Gestetner company and their duplicators fell into in the 1960s, and IBM and the mainframes fell into in the 1990s. Both companies ignored the trends in their markets towards the use of alternative products. |
| | In the meantime, continue this project for the market you have specified. |

Whatever definition you finally arrive at, ensure it can be directly related to the products or services in question. General 'motherhood' statements, such as defining the customer need as 'maximizing profit', tend to lose sight of their origins. Only a specialist area of financial services would be able to obtain meaningful benefits from a market defined as 'maximizing profit'.

| **Market research note** | Whenever in doubt about customers and their needs, ask them! To help arrive at a market definition, it may be necessary to undertake some qualitative research either as one-to-one discussions, or with groups of customers. Understanding the alternative products and services as the customers see them, listening to how they discuss their needs along with their likes and frustrations with the alternatives on offer today can save hours of hypothetical discussions and lead you to a truly market-focused definition. |
|---|---|

## Markets and SBUs

In addition to ensuring that the market definition is meaningful to your company, another issue you may need to address is associated with corporate structure.

In many companies, the market being segmented will fall within the responsibilities of one strategic business unit (SBU) and progressing with the project is therefore quite straightforward.

---

[6] A reminder: In the not-for-profit sector, customer satisfaction is obviously a proxy for financial objectives such as 'profitability'.

An SBU will:

1  have common customers and competitors for most of its products;
2  be a competitor in an external market;
3  be a discrete, separate identifiable unit;
4  have a manager who has control over most of the areas critical to success.

As a general rule, therefore, a segmentation project can be conducted within the confines of a single SBU. If, however, some products or services managed by a single SBU meet the needs of totally different markets, there will have to be more than one segmentation project.

For some companies, the market being segmented does not sit so neatly within their current structure and straddles two or more divisions. This can occur when a business is structured along product lines and these products are seen to compete with each other in one, or more, of their markets. For example, in a market defined in terms of 'being able to secure a desired standard of living from a planned date of retirement', both pension plans and investment plans are used by customers to achieve this goal, yet these two lines are often found within two different business units.

The preferred solution is to segment the market as defined and therefore include the competing product lines. However, it may be that in the first instance it is more pragmatic to start with your current SBU structure and segment that part of the market currently satisfied by your product line, not forgetting to monitor the trends in the use of the products or services you have excluded.

> Company structure considerations may require you initially to exclude certain product lines from your 'market'.

---

In companies consisting of a number of SBUs, it is recommended that you start segmenting markets at the lowest level of disaggregation within the organization's current structure.

Later on, it should be possible to use the same process for higher and higher levels of aggregation to check whether it may be possible to merge any of your current SBUs. Indeed, it may even be possible, eventually, to reorganize the whole company around 'new' groupings of either customers or products. This is covered in Chapter 7 in the section titled, 'Addendum for those intending to test the validity of a current SBU structure'.

**Marketing insight**

---

To conclude this section on defining markets, it is worth reflecting on the comments made by one of the co-founders of Revlon, Charles Revson, as he is credited with one of the more famous needs-based definitions of a market. When he drew the distinction between products and needs for his company, he captured it by describing the factory as being the place where the company made chemicals, 'but in the store', he sold 'hope'. Clearly, this is not an adequate market definition, but it does illustrate a needs-based approach to the process described in this chapter.

# Sizing the defined market

Now that the market you are segmenting has been clearly defined a volume or value figure is required in order to size it as it is today, with estimates for the future. In most cases the annual figure for the market would be used. Being able to size the defined market is particularly important for later stages in the process, especially when sizing segments. The size of a segment is used to determine whether or not a segment represents a viable business proposition and therefore worth the time and resources required for the development of a specific offer for that segment.

With market definitions that step outside established product categories, attributing a size to this newly defined market may well present a number of challenges. Sizing markets in countries where even established category figures are simply not available is clearly going to present some quite major challenges. As marketers, however, we are accountable to the business and to its shareholders for the financial impact of our decisions and our marketing expenditure. It is therefore essential that we find data sources and techniques that enable us to arrive at an approximate but intelligent figure for the market in which we want to spend the company's resources.

Government and government agency publications often provide high-level statistical summaries of many industries, as do many trade and professional associations. Periodic research by commercial agencies and consultancies is also often published as books of tabulated tables and is either generally available to all or restricted to those companies who contributed to a syndicated study. Data for these reports is obtained by traditional survey methods, by Electronic Point of Sale (EPOS) data, by industry sales data and so on. A potentially useful source of information about individual firms in the UK is the data held at Companies House, though only registered companies are included and data can be out of date and incomplete. Private agencies offer alternative sources of data, sometimes with added details on specific characteristics.

Census data and electoral roll data are the two main sources of information about individuals and can be bought from agencies that collect such data. 'Lifestyle' survey databases built from millions of questionnaires collected from the public over several years also provide useful insights for determining the size of a specific market. More detailed census data is not available at the individual level, but is available for 100 000 Enumeration Districts (EDs) in the UK. Each ED has hundreds of geo-demographic characteristics, which may be of relevance in calculating a market size.

For markets that have been established for a number of years which have rich and detailed data sources along with large sample sizes, sophisticated statistical techniques can be used to infer market size. However, for markets falling outside established definitions, data will be comparatively scarce and extrapolations from surveys will often be the main source. Carefully designed analysis methods may need to be employed to resolve uncertainties introduced by small sample sizes, and models based on limited data and plausible assumptions will have to be used to infer market size.

Where limited or simply no market data exists, assumptions about our own sales will have to be used for the initial approximation of market size. Ad-hoc research will then have to be commissioned to provide more substantive figures, with statistical techniques and modelling used to project the sample into a 'market' figure.

*Finding data sources and techniques to size markets is essential; an intelligent approximation is acceptable.*

**Marketing insight**

If research is your chosen method of determining market size, defer commissioning the research until later in the project. It is best left until you are ready to determine the size of each segment in the market. Although it is stating the obvious, the sum total of all the segments will equate to the size of the market, so leaving the research until this point will 'kill two birds with one stone', making better use of your marketing spend.

Companies occasionally indicate a preference to quantify a market in terms of profitability. As profitability is often a reflection of the efficiency or inefficiency of individual companies, it is not an appropriate measure of market size. The ability to generate profit, however, is a consideration when looking at how to prioritize and select segments (see Chapter 9).

# Process check

Defining the scope of a segmentation project is a critical first step and requires a great deal of considered thought.

We have discussed the issues to be borne in mind when defining the geographic scope of a segmentation project. This highlighted the need for the area to be within your geographic reach as a business and, if this area goes beyond a single country, the criteria that should be considered when determining which countries can be included in a single project.

We then moved on to the most interesting part of the discussion, namely how to define the 'market' being segmented. Where a 'market' begins and ends is defined by the competitive set as perceived by the customers in that market and is described in terms of the need that they are looking to satisfy. Specific products or product categories, therefore, do not necessarily define the scope of a market as far as customers are concerned. We have identified how the 'need' may be influenced by the circumstance or the mindset in which the customer is operating or even by the specific end-use or application they have in mind for the product. We have also discussed the importance of striking a meaningful balance between a definition that is too narrow and one that is too broad and how to refine the definition to ensure it is meaningful in terms of the capabilities of your organization. This then led us to consider the impact of corporate structures on the practical scope of a project, a consideration that is often required when a market straddles more than one SBU. The opportunity to address internal structures that are out of line with markets occurs later.

In the discussion about market definitions we looked at the difference between consumers and customers and concluded that whenever a final user (the consumer) has the purchase made for them by an intermediary (the customer), marketers need to know about both if they are to develop the best 'package' to meet their needs. The starting point, however, is the final user but because there is not a general consensus on the distinction between customers and consumers, this book subsumes both under the title of 'customer'.

Finally, the market to be segmented has to be sized and where figures are not readily available it is essential that we use whatever means we can in order to arrive at an intelligent approximation. This may need to wait until research is commissioned for the project as a whole.

# Case study – Agrofertilizer Supplies

As briefly mentioned in Chapter 3, a case study is used to illustrate each step in the process for developing segments (Steps 1 to 5). The case study is based on a real company which began operating in the 1920s and picks up on the story as it stood in 1988. For reasons of commercial confidentiality, however, as well as to assist in demonstrating the process in practice, the case study has been modified. Due to these changes the company in the case study is renamed 'Agrofertilizer Supplies'.

Full details about the company featured in this case study, which includes the important contribution made by segmentation to a business plan that proved to be a critical turning point in the company's fortunes, can be found at www.marketsegmentation.co.uk.

To summarize briefly the background to the case: Agrofertilizer Supplies is an independent business within a large, international chemical company, though its sales of fertilizers are predominantly in the UK. Within the larger group there exists a company which produces seeds for the agricultural sector and an agrochemical company, both of which also operate as independent businesses. Unfortunately, Agrofertilizer Supplies are losing market share and making financial losses in a line of business which is becoming increasingly competitive, a situation not helped by a steady fall in the level of overall demand. Cost-cutting measures have helped stem the losses but more needs to be done. The board are now looking to the marketing group for some answers.

To provide a basis for these answers, a small team within the marketing group has been charged with developing a detailed understanding of the UK market in order to determine where the most profitable opportunities exist for Agrofertilizer Supplies. Supporting the team is a group drawn from across the business including finance, distribution, sales and manufacturing.

A segmentation project is about to start and the team recognize that the first step is to define clearly the scope of the project.

The geographical scope is quite straightforward, simply because the company is highly dependent on sales of their product in the UK. However, defining the 'market' in terms of the customer need requires a little more thought.

The first issue is to be clear on who the customer is, and therefore whose needs are being defined. To all intents and purposes the final users of the product are farmers and they usually buy their fertilizers through agricultural merchants. The 'customer' for the project is therefore the farmer, though at a later stage it will be essential for the team to understand the needs of the agricultural merchants. A potential complication that was quickly resolved came out of the fact that on some farms the individual who spread the fertilizer was an employee of the farmer, which could be taken as meaning that these individuals were the focus for the project. However, they only spread what the farmer specified, so the final user for definition purposes is clearly the farmer.

Fertilizers represent one of the components required for growing commercial crops,[7] the others (under the control of the farmer) being seeds and, in most cases, agrochemicals. The question to be addressed, therefore, is whether the market should be defined in terms of 'commercial crop growing' or focused around 'commercial crop nutrients'.

The arguments put forward in favour of 'commercial crop growing' could be summarized as follows:

- the three products have similar distribution channels;
- the three products are complementary to each other;
- dealing with one sales representative would appeal to farmers;
- it would offer greater cross-selling opportunities.

On the other hand, the arguments put forward in favour of focusing the definition around 'commercial crop nutrients' included:

- they have a distinct contribution to the growing of commercial crops;
- there is a practical limitation on the technical knowledge of the sales force;
- the realistic timescale for putting together a combined offer was too long;
- farmers appeared to regard the three products as distinct product lines.

Two particular observations became pivotal to the final decision:

1 The final users, the farmers, did consider fertilizers to be a distinct group of products and, in fact, 'compartmentalized' the products required for growing crops into their three distinct categories. The three product lines were, therefore, not seen as alternatives.
2 The only market Agrofertilizers could serve in the foreseeable future was that of commercial crop nutrients. The technology and skills required to produce and sell seeds and/or agrochemicals was outside the scope of the company.

The market to be segmented, therefore, was the 'commercial crop nutrients' market. This does not mean to say that as time moves on this definition will continue to be the right one. It was just the most pragmatic definition at the time of the project.

Within this market, however, were customers whom Agrofertilizer Supplies could never hope to serve, namely the farmers who only ever applied organic nutrients to their crops. The realistically available market to the company and, therefore, the market to be segmented excluded these farmers.

Finally, the team had to size the market they were about to segment. Fortunately this was pretty straightforward as there were both government statistics and their own trade association's statistics. The annual total UK tonnage came to 3750 kilotonnes, which was forecast to decline during their planning horizon.

To conclude this stage of the process for Agrofertilizer Supplies, it is worth noting that although the output from farms continues along a further distribution and value added chain to the point where it is consumed as food, there was no evidence at the time of the project that these customers had an interest in the choice of fertilizer used by the farmer. There were certainly final consumers looking for organically grown food, but beyond this distinction there was no further interest.

This case study is continued in the following chapters.

---

[7] 'Crops' refers to both arable crops and the production of grass for feeding livestock.

# Further examples

Two examples are included here, with further examples appearing in Exercise 4.2. The first example is of a company developing a realistic definition for its market and the second is of a company that discovers it is in two markets, whereas it had thought it was only in one.

## Example 4.1

The first example is of a publishing company specializing in producing magazines for a selection of interests based around the home, such as gardening, cooking, do-it-yourself and so on. Its sole method of selling and distributing its product is through direct marketing, with customers making regular payments direct to the company for their subscription to these magazines.

The company defined its market along the lines of, 'the customer need is to have access to information in their specific area(s) of interest as and when they require it'. Clearly, however, this need can be met by more than magazines and the list of competing products included books, videos, CDs, DVDs, websites and recorded television programmes ('recorded' to make them accessible 'as and when' required). In order to arrive at a definition of a market they could realistically compete in and, therefore, the market they should be segmenting, they drew up a hierarchy of operational requirements along the following lines:

1 customers who accept direct marketing (the company's only operational model);
2 customers who will commit to a number of issues (having to sell each individual issue separately by direct marketing was uneconomic);
3 customers who take printed magazines.

For their segmentation project, they principally focused on customers who fell into the defined market and, therefore, fitted the company's operational requirements as this was the market realistically available to them at that time. However, when they commissioned research to help them in their project, they included questions about alternative formats as they wanted to track the trends towards their use. The company believed that they might well have to consider other formats in the future if they were to achieve their long-term corporate objectives. After all, they were not a printing company.

## Example 4.2

The second example is of a credit insurance company who believed that the only market they were in was that of providing customers with debt protection, though for the customer it was seen as protecting their sales revenue. However, when they began to talk to their customers they found that a number of them were using the product as 'virtual capital' to improve their cash-flow management. What these customers were doing was using the guarantee of debt payment provided by the credit insurance company as an asset which they could then use to increase their borrowings, a market in which invoice discounting and factoring were competing.

The company discovered that it was, in fact, operating in two markets, both of which they had to segment. What is also worth noting is that, whereas their original market was fairly static, this 'new' market was growing at around 20 per cent per annum and was 25 times larger than their original market. They also discovered that they had an extremely competitive product for this 'new' market, something their customers in this market had already worked out.

# Reference

McDonald, M. (2002). 'Setting marketing objectives and strategies'. In *Marketing Plans: How to Prepare Them, How to Use Them*, pp. 255–310. Oxford: Butterworth-Heinemann.

# Exercises

Often there is confusion regarding what constitutes a market. Unless such confusion is dispelled from the outset, the whole marketing edifice will be built on sand. However, as so often is the case, what on the surface appears to be a relatively simple task can prove to be extremely testing, especially when it challenges current assumptions and corporate structure.

---

**Exercise 4.1**

This exercise vastly simplifies the problem some companies face when addressing 'market' definition.

Alpha Ltd has five major products, A, B, C, D and E, which are sold to five different customer groups, as represented in Figure 4.5. Virtually all sales are achieved in the darker shaded areas.

Is this company's market:

(a) the darker shaded areas?
(b) the intersection of products A, B and C and customer groups 2, 3 and 4?
(c) products A, B and C for all customer groups?
(d) customer groups 2, 3 and 4 for all products?
(e) the entire matrix?

Possible interpretations for Exercise 4.1 are as follows:

1  It would be possible to define our market as the darker shaded area ((a) in the exercise), i.e. the product/customer group area currently served. The problem with this is that it might tend to close our eyes to other potential opportunities for profitable growth and expansion, especially if there is a danger that our current customer groups may become mature.
2  It is also possible to define our market as the intersection of products A, B and C and customer groups 2, 3 and 4 ((b) in the exercise). The problem with this is that while we now have a broader vision, there may be developments in product areas D and E and customer groups 1 and 5 that we should be aware of.
3  To a large extent, this problem would be overcome by defining our market as products A, B and C for *all* customer groups ((c) in the exercise). The problem

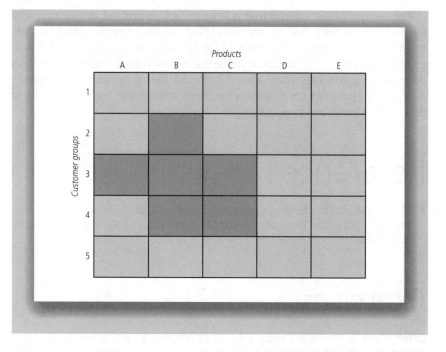

**Figure 4.5**
Market definition for
Exercise 4.1

here is that markets 1 and 5 may not require products A, B and C, so perhaps we need to consider product development (products D and E).

4 It is certainly possible to consider our market as all products for customer groups 2, 3 and 4 ((d) in the exercise). The potential problem here is that we still do not have any interest in customer groups 1 and 5.

5 Finally, it is clearly possible to call the whole matrix our market ((e) in the exercise), with customer groups 1 to 5 on the vertical axis and each of products A to E on the horizontal axis. The problem with this is that we would almost certainly have too many distinct product and customer groups and this could lead to a costly dissipation of effort.

In addition, any combinations of (a) to (e) above could be used as long as there is a sensible rationale to justify the choice.

The answer to the conundrum is possibly found in the definition of 'market': 'A market is the aggregation of all the products or services which customers regard as being capable of satisfying the same customer need.' The first part of the clue therefore comes from the five customer groups and whether or not they see any of the five products as competing with each other in terms of the need that they are seen to be satisfying. Once this has been understood we would then look at the company's realistic capabilities in order to determine what, if any modifications to these conclusions would be required in order to exclude those areas the company was simply not suited to serve. This would be a matter of management judgement.

## Exercise 4.2

Here, we present some possible market definitions along with a few comments. Which of the following are 'market' definitions?

1 The pensions market: No; simply on the grounds that it is describing a product, a product designed to satisfy a need, and there are other products

that can also satisfy this need. Try and describe what it is most customers are attempting to achieve when considering whether or not to invest in a pension.

2  The conveyance of individuals over long distances: Understanding a customer need in these terms would have probably enabled the train companies of Europe to have emerged as the successful European airlines of today, but they preferred to see themselves as train operators. Many of today's airline companies see themselves as 'airlines', but how many passengers would switch to a teleporter if, and when, it ever came into being? Beam me up Scotty! Yes or No?

3  The ball bearings market: Another product description. If you were to ask customers what they were looking for and attempted to capture it by completing the sentence, 'The customer need is to …' the sentence could well be completed by the phrase, '… support rotation'. Ball bearings are therefore competing against other products and technologies that also support rotation, such as magnetic levitation. Rather than the manufacturers thinking about improving their ball bearings, it would be better for them to think about how to improve methods of supporting rotation because it is this particular functionality that customers are seeking to achieve from their purchase.

4  To communicate verbally, remotely and in real time with anyone I choose: Yes or No? It may benefit from adding, 'whenever I choose'.

5  Portable sources of energy for powering equipment: Yes or No? It could be improved by refining it as there are clear differences between a consumer market and an industrial market, not only in the energy capacity being sought but also in the appropriate distribution channels.

6  The luxury chocolate market: Yes or No? Probably better thought of as the 'treat' market for some purchasing motivations, which is attractively insensitive to price.

7  The market for central heating: Yes or No? What the customer is really looking for is a means of maintaining an ambient temperature of their choosing.

8  The air freight market: Yes or No? This is too product focused. What the customer really cares about is having their goods delivered to where they want within their time-frame constraints.

9  To have access to a variety of experiences out of the ordinary: Suggested as the market definition for theme parks, before the imagination starts to run away with itself!

---

This exercise turns to your own company. Often, the way a market was selected in the first instance can provide clues regarding how it can be defined. Consider one of your current markets and explain:

1  How it came to be chosen.
2  How you would define it, so that it is clearly distinct from any other market, and capture this by completing the sentence appearing below.

### Exercise 4.3

The customer *need* is to …

And add to the definition a list of the products or services it covers.

**Exercise 4.4**

This is for companies with a range of products or services looking for a series of steps to follow which will help define the market(s) they should be segmenting. This is the exercise referred to in the main text.

1 Allocate your company's products into their competitive sets, preferably as viewed by the customer. Please note that it is possible to have the same product appearing in more than one competitive set if it can be put to more than one use. For example, pensions can be used to provide retirement income or to finance a loan for a house purchase. An airline seat can be used for business travel or for leisure travel. A beach holiday can be used by sun worshippers or by parents with young children looking for kids' activities (or should that be 'distractions'?). A corporate charge card can be used for business expenses or to obtain a short-term injection of cash.

2 Add to each competitive set all the appropriate products supplied by competitors along with any additional products the customers are known to consider and, in some cases, use as alternatives. Once again, a single product can appear in more than one list.

3 For each resulting competitive set, describe the use the customer puts the products to, in other words, the *need* customers are seeking to satisfy. Avoid using any of the product names in this description. If necessary, split product groups if this is the only way you are able to arrive at a meaningful description of their use.

4 Merge those competitive sets which appear to be put to the same use and therefore meet the same or similar customer need. For each concluding list, refine the words describing the use the competing products are put to, such that the description conveys the need they are meeting. These can now be viewed as 'needs sets' and are possible 'market' definitions.

5 For each 'market', assess the total value (or volume) of business the competing products represent for the geographic area being looked at. In deciding on the geographic area, take into account any known geographic limits customers impose on the location of suppliers they will consider. For example, suppliers of office equipment may need to be within a certain drive time.

6 Try the following reality check which is designed to ensure that segmenting the market you have now defined will produce segments that are worth investing your company's resources in.

   As markets tend to divide into between five and ten segments, divide the value (or volume) figure for each 'market' by five:

   (a) If the resulting figure represents sufficient value (or volume) to justify a distinct marketing mix, your market definitions are probably correct. However, if the resulting figure can be divided by five again and still justify a distinct marketing mix, the 'market' definition is probably too broad and requires more focus.

   (b) If the resulting figure is too small to justify a distinct marketing mix, redivide the 'market' figure by four (to allow for some segments being small and others being an acceptable size) and if this figure is still too small your 'market' definition is possibly too narrow and may benefit from being merged with another.

Ensure that any revised definition makes sense in terms of a 'needs set' which customers would recognize and in which they make transactions.

Chapter 5
# Portraying how a market works and identifying decision-makers

# Summary

This chapter takes a detailed look at the way a market works in order to identify where decisions are made about competing products and services. It is these decision-makers who then proceed to the next stage of the segmentation project as it is their requirements you must understand in order to develop successful marketing propositions. *Successful segmentation* is based on a detailed understanding of decision-makers and their needs.

This is the second step in the segmentation process, as illustrated in Figure 5.1.

This book refers to those whose needs you must understand (if you are to develop successful marketing propositions) under the title of 'decision-maker'. You may find it more appropriate in your market to refer to them as 'specifiers'.

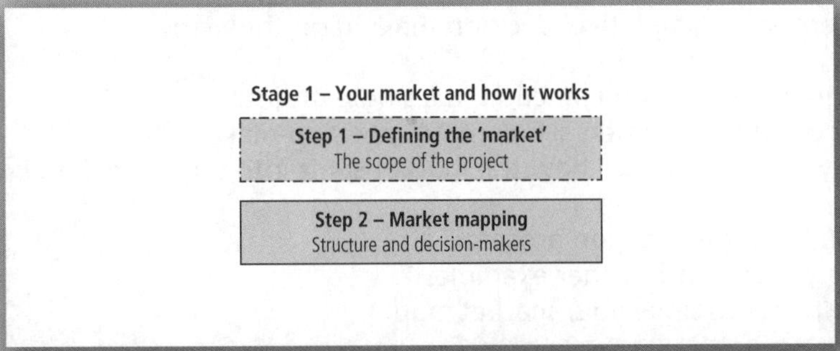

Stage 1 – Your market and how it works

Step 1 – Defining the 'market'
The scope of the project

Step 2 – Market mapping
Structure and decision-makers

**Figure 5.1**
The segmentation process – Step 2

In many markets, especially business-to-consumer markets, drawing a 'market map' and identifying decision-makers has been quite a simple exercise. However, even in these markets, the emergence of alternative routes to market has made market mapping an essential exercise, an exercise that should be revisited and updated on a regular basis.

Although in structurally very simple markets you may feel it is possible to skip this step of the segmentation process, it is strongly recommended that you at least review the 'Fast track' section of this chapter and give it most careful thought before deciding that market mapping is not relevant. *In our experience, market mapping is relevant to all organizations.*

This chapter aims to provide you with a practical guide to market mapping so that your first market map(s) can be constructed using information already held by your company. This information can come from departments such as sales, customer services, distribution, accounts and so on. Past market surveys and industry statistics can also be useful sources of information, assuming you have any. Verification, if required, can be included in any follow-up work you commission for your segmentation project as a whole.

In addition to segmenting those you target with your products and services, it is sometimes necessary to conduct a separate segmentation project for intermediaries, such as retailers, so that you have a detailed understanding of how to win shelf space. This is to ensure that once you have got your products aligned to segments, the segments can then access these products through the channels they prefer to use.

This chapter is organized as follows:

■ A 'fast track' for those looking for a quick route through the key points
■ Presenting the stages ('junctions') along the distribution and value-added chain as a map
■ Showing the 'routes' that connect final users with suppliers
■ Approaching the map from the suppliers' perspective, instead of the final users' perspective
■ Where to end the map for a company that is not a supplier
■ Ensuring your map includes any 'hidden' final users
■ Covering the different stages a purchase has to go through within organizations
■ Capturing the role of influencers in a market, including the role of consultants
■ Attaching quantities to the market map
■ Expanding the detail of a junction to highlight any differences found there ('junction types')
■ Market maps in the tabular form
■ Identifying where decisions are made in the market ('market leverage points')
■ Accommodating 'shared' and 'cumulative' decision-making on the map
■ Selecting the junction to be segmented
■ Guidelines for including more than one junction in a single project
■ Whether to include or exclude customers who are not decision-makers
■ Taking the opportunity to test views on how the market splits into segments ('preliminary segments')
■ A review of this step in the segmentation process
■ Market map for the case study and further examples
■ Exercises further to help you compile your market map

'Market mapping' as defined and developed by the authors has become an increasingly important part of the toolkit for marketers. In addition to providing an informative picture of the distribution and value-added chain that exists between final users and suppliers, it can also be used to present your own company's performance on these routes to market and to illustrate where your sales and marketing resources are allocated. This provides a useful check when evaluating your sales and marketing strategies, especially when looking at predicted changes to the market's structure and when comparing yourself with your key competitors on where resources are committed.

This book refers to those who produce the products or services supplied to a market as 'suppliers'.

A separate chapter which looks at market mapping in more detail and how to capture the above refinements follows the conclusion of the segmentation process. This is also a useful stage at which to plot your chosen segments onto the market map. A further chapter then takes a look at future market mapping and predicting market transformation. These are Chapters 11 and 12 respectively.

# ⬤ Fast track

● Starting with the final users of the products or services included within the scope of your segmentation project, note what proportion of the total market they actually decide on: that is, make the decision on which of the competing products or services will be purchased. If this is not 100 per cent, note who the final users turn to next for the decision and then record what proportion of the total market this group decide on. Approximate percentages are acceptable.

● List the alternative decision-makers in a sequential order according to how close they are to the final users. Continue until you have accounted for 100 per cent of the market. If it is showing signs of getting complicated and you have already found where, say, 80 per cent of the decisions are made, that should be sufficient to progress with your project. Each stage along the 'market map' (represented by a cube in Figure 5.2) is called a 'junction' and a junction where decisions are made is known as a 'market leverage point'.

● Use the decision-making percentages and the market size (from Chapter 4) to determine the quantity decided at each leverage point.

● It helps if you sketch out the market map and capture the decision-making along the lines suggested in Figure 5.2.

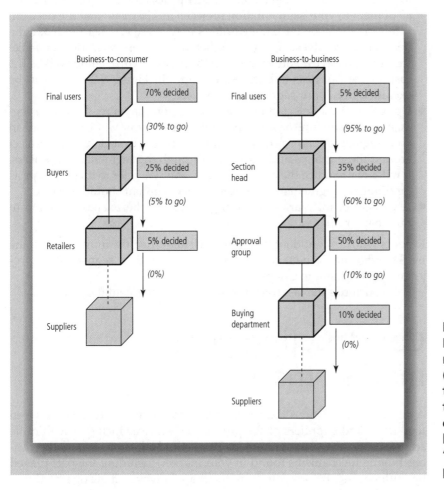

**Figure 5.2**
Fast track – market mapping
(*Note:* In a business-to-consumer market the 'final user' could, for example, be a child with the 'buyer' being a parent.)

Clearly some final users will also be buyers. What we are trying to establish on the market map are buyers who make the decision on behalf of final users.

Do not overlook the possible role of advisers, buying guides or consultants on your map.

- Select the junction with leverage to be taken through to the next stage. It is usually easier to progress the segmentation project a single junction at a time. As a normal rule it is best to start with the final users. This would work with the business-to-consumer example in Figure 5.2 but appears to be nonsense in the business-to-business example. The next guideline would be to start at the junction nearest the final user where significant leverage occurs. In the business-to-business example, starting with the 'Approval group' would make sense as they account for the highest proportion of the decisions. However, working through the segmentation project for both the 'Section heads' and 'Approval groups' in parallel may be manageable; try it and see.

- When the junction you are segmenting consists of some who make the decision and others who do not, and it is a junction where it would be to your advantage to have them make the decision themselves, include *all* of them in your segmentation project *if it is by choice* that the decision is left to others. Better targeted offers may persuade them to make the decision themselves. If, on the other hand, those who do not make the decision have no other choice in the matter (which could well be the case in the business-to-business example in Figure 5.2), they can be excluded from your segmentation project.

- Optional: At the selected leverage point, you may already have a segmentation structure or see a natural division you want to test out in your segmentation project. It is quite acceptable to structure the project around these groups and take them through the segmentation process. It will not prejudice the outcome in any way. We refer to these groups as 'preliminary segments'. Each preliminary segment should be sized.

- A worksheet for market mapping appears in the Exercises section of this chapter.

Readers who are confident that they have identified the individuals in the market who should be taken to the next stage of their segmentation project may go straight to Chapter 6.

This concludes the fast track for Step 2 of the segmentation process.

# Constructing your market map

**Definition:**
A market map defines the distribution and value added chain between final users and suppliers, which takes into account the various buying mechanisms found in a market, including the part played by 'influencers'.

A 'market map' defines the distribution and value added chain between final users and suppliers of the products or services included within the scope of your segmentation project. This should take into account the various buying mechanisms found in your market, including the part played by 'influencers'. Before you draw the map, however, it is suggested that you read the whole of this chapter.

*This is a key step in the market segmentation process and you should spend as much time as necessary to ensure you correctly identify the individuals or groups to be taken into the next stage of the segmentation project.*

Although an organization may be serving different markets, it is possible that the products or services in these markets go through the same distribution and value added chain to similar end-users. In such cases a template can be drawn for the market maps and used across the organization.

A company in the financial services sector, for example, may be able to do this.

**Marketing insight**

The series of figures which follow progressively incorporate various points made in the text about market maps. Although the diagrams in these figures are a useful first stage in constructing market maps, you may find that the diagrammatic approach to market mapping is not to your liking. The alternative is to construct your market map in a tabular form. This chapter contains guidelines designed to assist you in constructing your market map this way. It is recommended, however, that you first read all of this section, using diagrams as a means of observing how the various steps in market mapping help develop a detailed picture of your market. Then, if you wish, you can change to the tabular form and construct your market map this way.

Finally, you may find that for particularly critical and/or complex parts of your map it often helps if the detail for these areas is captured in a separate diagram or table away from the composite map in order to emphasise their importance and/or portray them more clearly.

If the products or services in the market you are segmenting have little, if any, perceived value to the final users and this has been recognized in the definition of your market (as discussed in the previous chapter), your market map need only cover the distribution and value added chain between the final individuals who attribute value to these products or services and the suppliers.

We will, however, refer to them as 'final users' in the text.

Ensure, however, that you are not overlooking an opportunity to improve your sales and profitability. If in any doubt, include the ultimate final users in the market map.

**Marketing insight**

## Getting started

It is useful to start your market map by plotting the various stages that occur along the distribution and value added chain between the final users and all the suppliers of products or services competing with each other in the defined market. At the same time, indicate the particular routes to market the products are sourced through, as not all of them will necessarily involve all of these stages. An example of this starting point for market mapping is shown in Figure 5.3.

These stages (represented by the cubes in Figure 5.3) are referred to as 'junctions', with each junction on a market map positioned hierarchically,

*Be sure to draw a market map for the whole of the defined market rather than just the part you currently deal with. This is to ensure that you understand your market dynamics properly.*

according to how close it is to the final user. The first junction along the market map would, therefore, be the final user.

*It is not essential to draw the map starting from the final user.* You may prefer to draw the map starting with the supplier, progressing towards the final user, followed by adding the particular routes to market the products pass through. *Neither is it essential to draw the map down the page.* You may prefer to draw the map across the page starting with either the final user or the supplier as in Figure 5.4. Do whatever you feel most comfortable in doing.

**Figure 5.3**
Starting a market map and adding the routes between the transaction stages (*Note:* This market map consists of four stages, one each for final users, retailers, distributors and suppliers. This map illustrates that products are also acquired by the final users direct from the suppliers, as well as from retailers. Some retailers also bypass distributors and acquire their stocks direct from the suppliers.)

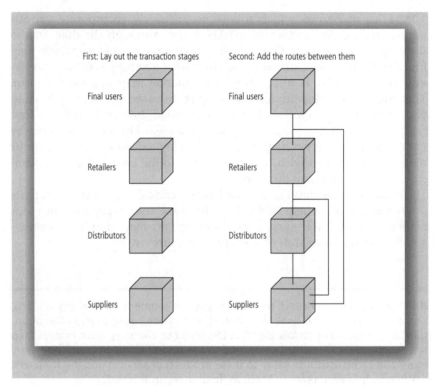

As we progressively add junctions to the market map and attach the details we cover in this chapter, we will continue with the format in Figure 5.3. When we move to the next stages of market mapping later on in the book we will adopt the format in Figure 5.4. We find it is easier to attach the next levels of detail when the market map is in the horizontal format.

**Marketing insight**

If you have elected to draw your map starting with the final users, think of it as tracking all the various 'stages' that occur from when the intention to acquire a product is initiated through to the product's place of origin, in other words, to the supplier.

If you are drawing your map starting with the suppliers, think of it as tracking all the various 'stages' a product has to pass through before it arrives at its final destination, in other words, with the final user.

In either case, not all the stages necessarily consist of a transaction or an actual transfer of the product itself. This is a point we cover later.

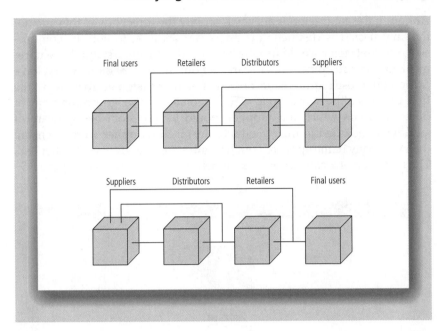

**Figure 5.4**
Starting a market
map – alternative
layouts

For those of you segmenting markets in which your company is not at the extreme of the map you should give it careful thought before deciding to exclude the stages between you and the suppliers. For example, if you were a distributor in the market depicted in Figure 5.3, it would be important to capture the fact that some product was sourced direct from the suppliers. Capturing this fact would be particularly important if this route to market was growing at your expense, as you would need to understand why it was taking place and what strategic changes were required to secure the future of your business.

*It is very important that your market map extends all the way through to the final user, even though you may not actually conduct transactions with them directly.*

Market maps sometimes overlook the final user when one of the following occurs:

1 a contractor or agency is engaged to carry out the work on behalf of the final user; or,
2 the product is purchased on behalf of the final user.

Taking the first of the above two possibilities: in some markets, the direct customer/purchaser will not always be the final user, even though they may even appear to consume the product, as is illustrated in the following set of circumstances:

A company (or household) may commission a third party contractor to carry out some redecoration, or an advertising agency to develop and conduct a promotional campaign, or a financial adviser to produce and implement a financial programme.

For all of us, the doctor we visit when seeking treatment is, in many respects, a contractor when it comes to prescribing medicine.

**Marketing insight**

Although the contractor or agency is strictly the direct buyer, they are not the final user. The distinction is important because, to win the commission, the contractor would usually have needed to understand the requirements of their customer and, in carrying out the commission, would have carried out those requirements on behalf of their customer. To miss out the final user from the market map would, therefore, have ignored an array of different needs which the supplier would benefit from being aware of (and have included in their product offer) if the supplier were to ensure their company name appeared on the contractor's 'preferred supplier list'. The inclusion of a contractor on a market map is illustrated in Figure 5.5.

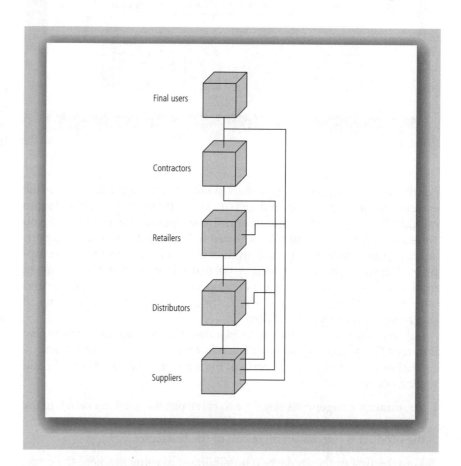

**Figure 5.5**
Market map with
contractor

Secondly, ensuring your market map continues right the way through to the final user is also appropriate in those situations where final users have their products purchased for them: for example, by their parents or by their company's purchasing department. Here we would be looking to capture the decision-making and/or order-placing hierarchy that exists between the final user and whoever places the order; which is a particularly important understanding for any company's sales and marketing programme. This may simply require a small change to the market map already presented in Figure 5.5, such as replacing 'Contractors' with 'Parents'. In other markets, however, especially in business-to-business markets, this will require further junctions to be added to the market map as illustrated in Figure 5.6.

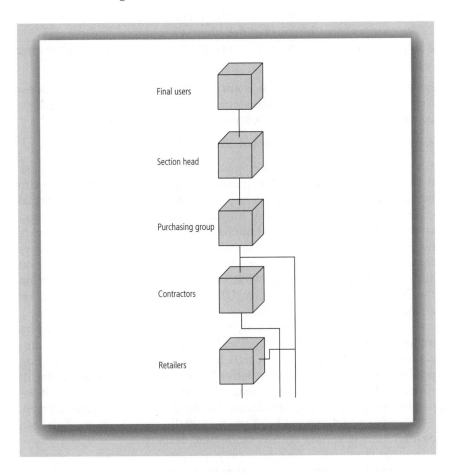

Final users

Section head

Purchasing group

Contractors

Retailers

**Figure 5.6**
Market map with final users 'hidden' from the suppliers

A further addition to the market map in Figure 5.6, particularly in business-to-business markets, could be the inclusion of a distinct junction for the purchasing procedures that are known to take place between, say, a department's intention to buy and placing the order. For example, once the marketing group have agreed with IT on the new technology they want to install in their call centre, it may first need to be approved by a capital sanctions committee and then by the board before it is passed to purchasing. Although purchasing procedures are likely to differ between companies, capture it in a single junction at this stage of constructing your market map. An opportunity to expand the detail occurs later on when we add junction types.

In many markets the final user is often represented by the last individual in the chain who has to dig into their pocket, or budget, to pay everyone else in the chain. There are, inevitably, some exceptions, such as, for example, food and clothes for children, most office staff, workers on the shop floor, nurses and radiographers, and so on.

**Marketing insight**

As the figures have illustrated, most market maps will have at least three principal components:

A discussion about the difference between 'consumers' and 'customers' appeared in Chapter 4.

1 Final users (often referred to as 'consumers')
2 The channel (distribution channel, often referred to as 'customers')
3 Suppliers (originators of goods and services, namely the manufacturing and service industries)

Ensure your market map includes the stages where influence and/or advice occurs about which products to use.

For many markets, however, it is also essential that their maps include a fourth component, namely the stage(s) where influence and/or advice occurs (not necessarily a transaction) about which products to use:

4 Influence and advice (sources of 'information')

For example, an individual looking at investment opportunities may seek the advice of an independent financial adviser, though they may choose to transact the investment themselves rather than through their financial adviser. Alternatively, they may turn to specialist financial publications, specialist reports in the general media, or visit websites set up to provide investment information and even the opportunity to exchange views through their chat room. Similar sources of information are available on all sorts of products, some of which, such as the *Which?* publications from the Consumers' Association in the UK, can have a powerful influence on an individual's choice of product.

In business-to-business markets, publications and reports produced by industry associations, professional bodies and others are available to companies looking for information to help them decide between competing products and services. An alternative to reading through the reports, of course, is for the company to engage the consultancy services of an independent expert, adding yet another, but important, layer to the market map.

Independent influencers need not necessarily be consultants. They can be final users who have already made their decision.

## Marketing insight

For some technically sophisticated and expensive products, it is crucial in any sales strategy to get the equipment installed in what are sometimes referred to as 'luminary' or 'reference' sites. These are businesses and institutions, and sometimes particular individuals who work there, known to be respected among their peer group. The influence generated by these sites on the choice of equipment made by others can be quite substantial. Such sites should therefore appear on the market map.

There are also many business-to-consumer markets in which the choice of product by some final users is influenced by the choice of product made by other final users, individuals whom they turn to for information and recommendations. They, too, should appear on the market map.

When referring to 'influencers' it is important to note that we are *not* referring to the power, or otherwise, of advertising or any other type of promotion. We are referring more to the influence of what are perceived as authoritative and independent sources of information that are *deliberately* sought out by some customers as part of their buying process. The important point here is that in many instances we are seeing an 'influencer' not directly featuring in any transaction. These influencers should appear on the market map, as shown in Figure 5.7, just as if they were a transaction stage.

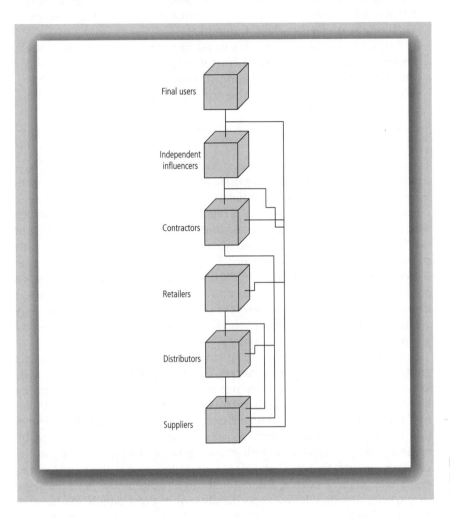

**Figure 5.7**
Market map with influencers

*Overlooking the role of independent influencers in a market can result in lost sales opportunities.*

In the early 1990s a company supplying expensive capital goods put together a detailed sales and marketing programme targeted at key decision-makers in the top corporations. Each corporation was allocated to a specific salesperson and every decision-maker was to be carefully tracked down and relentlessly pursued in the quest for ever-increasing sales.

What the strategy overlooked, however, was that nearly 40 per cent of their market was in fact not determined by the corporations themselves, but by independent consultants who not only evaluated the company's requirements, but also produced the specification and, to all intents and purposes, controlled the tender list. Although the final decision was generally made by the corporation, it was more often than not a done deal by that stage, with one supplier clearly in the lead.

Rather than limit their sales to 60 per cent of the market, the company in question added consultants to its market map and amended its sales and marketing strategy. By including this other 40 per cent of the market the company had increased its sales opportunities by two-thirds.

For most market maps, the decision on which junction a particular activity should be placed in will be very clear. However, there will be instances where the decision is not immediately apparent. For example, a farmer's co-operative may simply replace a retail outlet or a wholesaler, in which case it could just as easily be placed in the same junction as the retailer or wholesaler, as appropriate. Alternatively, a co-operative may source its products from either a wholesaler, or direct from the manufacturer, in which case it is clearer to position the co-operative on the market map at a stage which is nearest to the final user. Following the same guidelines, a consultant who advises the farmers on which specific product to buy would clearly be placed in a junction one stage below the farmers and ahead of any retailers or wholesalers.

*When companies perform two roles in a market, these two roles should appear as two junctions on the market map.*

A confusion that sometimes occurs in market mapping is when a single entity performs two roles in a market. For example, numerous supermarkets and small confectioners are not just retailers of bread produced by large bakeries; they also bake bread on their own premises. Are they therefore a retailer or a supplier of bread, or should there be an additional junction on the map to cover both roles? This dual role is best tackled by retaining the junctions of 'supplier' and 'retailer' and then noting at the supplier junction that this consists of supermarkets and small confectioners as well as large bakers, a detail that can be added now or at the stage in market mapping when we specifically look at these details. We have, of course, already come across customers with two roles in a market when we were discussing final users as 'influencers'. In these circumstances, it should be noted at the 'influencer' junction that, along with other types of influencer, final users are also found at this junction.

## Marketing insight

Referring, again, to the farmer's co-operative example, a co-operative could have its own consultants to provide technical advice to farmers as well as distribute goods and services to the farmers. This is a clear example of a single entity performing two roles. However, even if *every* consultant in this market worked for one of the distributors, it would still be important to recognize these different roles as two distinct junctions on your market map.

Not every farmer wants to use a consultant.

Finally, it may even be appropriate for your market to identify the field sales force as a separate junction, particularly if business is conducted either through a field sales team or direct without reference to field sales, such as by telephone sales or the internet. This situation is captured in Figure 5.8.

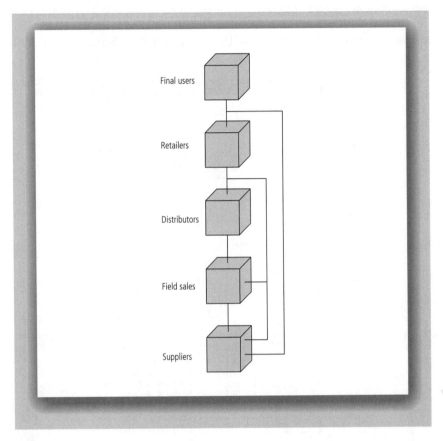

**Figure 5.8**
Market map with field sales identified separately
(*Note:* In this market map, field sales are not contacted by any of the final users and only by some of the retailers. All the distributors have their business conducted through field sales.)

In implementing these directions and those which follow, you may find that you have to redraw or amend your market map a number of times. All you are doing at this stage is progressively creating a preliminary form of macro market segmentation. Later on, you will proceed to do more detailed segmentation.

A worksheet for market mapping appears in the Exercises section of this chapter.

---

It is clearly useful to verify the routes to market and the role of influencers along with the decision-making and purchasing procedures in any market research you commission for your segmentation project.

**Market research note**

---

## Initial quantification of the market map

With quantification playing an important part later on in the process, mark at each junction and along each route the volumes or values dealt with by each of them. The figure used to size the market in Chapter 4 is the base for this allocation, which in most cases will be the annual figure for the market. Where figures for this detailed breakdown of the market are not available, guesstimates should be made in order to scale the role of each junction and the different routes between them. You may find it easier to start with percentages and then, when satisfied with the allocation, convert the percentages to figures. This is illustrated in Figures 5.9 and 5.10.

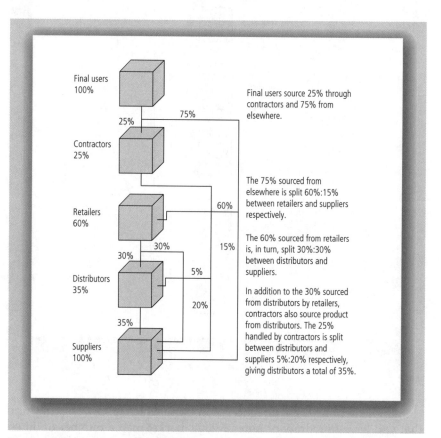

**Figure 5.9** Initial quantification of a market map – percentages (*Note:* The number of units 'consumed' by the final users usually equates to the number of units entering the market. Please take some time to follow the routes through the map and you will observe that, like the work of an accountant, it all 'balances'. As the explanatory notes in the figure indicate, each percentage appearing on the map is based on the market total. So, for example, the 60 per cent of product sourced by the final users from retailers is 60 per cent of the market total. The balance of the 75 per cent sourced by final users other than through contractors, i.e. 15 per cent, which, is the above example, is sourced direct from the suppliers, is the figure that appears on the market map (though you may have arrived at this figure by determining that the split of the 75 per cent between retailers and suppliers is 80:20).)

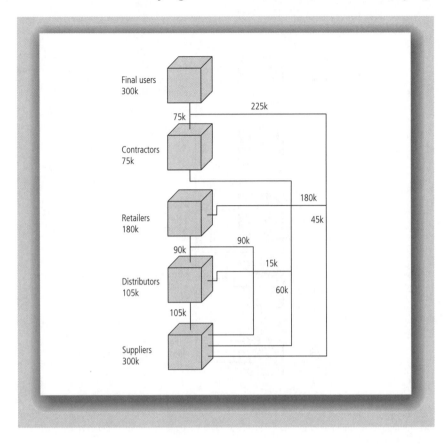

**Figure 5.10**
Initial quantification
of a market map –
figures
(*Note:* The
quantities are
thousands (k) of
units. The total
number of units in
this market is
300 000 (300k).)

If 'influencers' feature on your market map and some of them are also final users, it is only the quantity they advise others on that is included at the 'influencer' junction.

One of the objectives of any quantitative research commissioned for your seg-mentation project should be to provide you with useful statistics about your market to reduce the amount of guesswork.

**Market research note**

## Adding junction types

This next stage for your market map is to expand the detail it contains, as the 'top line' picture developed so far is possibly hiding some important differences between customers. These differences could provide useful information for your segmentation project.

Note at each junction on your market map, if applicable, all the different types of companies/customers that are found there, as illustrated in Figure 5.11. If you have included a junction for 'Purchase procedures', your list for this junction would consist of the different procedures that are

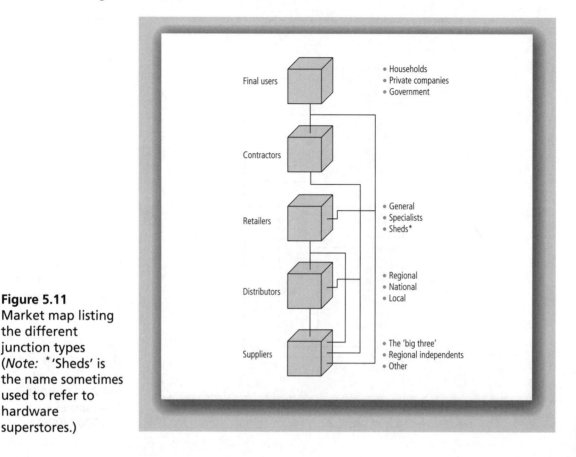

**Figure 5.11**
Market map listing the different junction types (*Note:* \* 'Sheds' is the name sometimes used to refer to hardware superstores.)

found at this junction, such as 'Financial director and Purchasing', 'Main board and Purchasing' and so on.

If you already have a segmentation structure for any of these junctions and you are using this process to test its validity, you can use this structure to define the respective junction types. This will be useful when we are looking at preliminary segments a little later in this chapter. The market mapping routine you have followed so far could, of course, be challenging the traditional structures you have been applying to your market. In such instances, you may prefer to replace what now appears to be the out-of-date list with the new list.

What may now become apparent is that the 'top line' picture of the market hides the fact that some customer types do not use all the routes to market shown at their junction. For example, it may be the case that 'Households' never use 'Contractors' in this particular market. Redrawing the market map to show this detail is looked at in a later chapter. It is not required at this stage of the process.

A refinement which is useful at this point is to split the volume or value quantity dealt with by each junction between the junction types. Figure 5.12 illustrates how to record this for the 'Final user' types appearing in Figure 5.11. Guesstimate these figures if they are not known and note this as a requirement for any follow-up work.

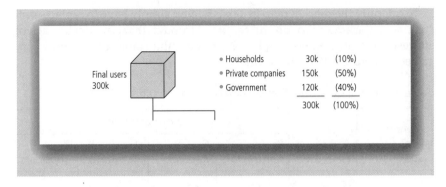

**Figure 5.12**
Quantities split
between junction
types

If easier, you can limit this level of detail to the groups you take through
to the next stage of your segmentation project. This is discussed a little
later in this chapter.

## Market maps in the tabular form

If you would prefer to present your market map in the tabular form, Table
5.1 presents the market map in Figure 5.5 using this format. To arrive at
the layout appearing in Table 5.1:

1 First, list the junctions down the right-hand side starting from the final
user, and then repeat the list across the top.
2 Now indicate which junctions the final users source their products
through and repeat this for each junction.

As already stated, it is not essential to start from the final user. You can
start with the suppliers if you find this easier.

**Table 5.1** Market map with contractor presented in tabular form

|  | Sourced through | | | | |
|---|---|---|---|---|---|
|  | A<br>Final users | B<br>Contractors | C<br>Retailers | D<br>Distributors | E<br>Suppliers |
| A<br>Final users |  | ✓ | ✓ | X | ✓ |
| B<br>Contractors |  |  | X | ✓ | ✓ |
| C<br>Retailers |  |  |  | ✓ | ✓ |
| D<br>Distributors |  |  |  |  | ✓ |
| E<br>Suppliers |  |  |  |  |  |

*Note:* For ease of reference each junction is identified by a letter from the alphabet.

To quantify the market map in Table 5.1 you simply have to replace each 'tick' with the amount of product sourced through that junction by each of its respective customers. Table 5.2 presents the same information contained in Figure 5.10 in this format.

**Table 5.2** Initial quantification of a market map in tabular form

| Market size: 300k | A Final users | Sourced through | | | |
|---|---|---|---|---|---|
| | | B Contractors | C Retailers | D Distributors | E Suppliers |
| A Final users | 300k | 75k | 180k | X | 45k |
| B Contractors | | 75k | X | 15k | 60k |
| C Retailers | | | 180k | 90k | 90k |
| D Distributors | | | | 105k | 105k |
| E Suppliers | | | | | 300k |

*Note:* Using 'Retailers' (junction 'C') as an example and reading across the table (left to right): 180k units are sourced through retailers by final users and the retailers, in turn, source 90k of this 180k through distributors (junction 'D') and the remaining 90k through suppliers (junction 'E').

Different junction types can be listed under their respective columns along with the volume or value figures dealt with by each of them by the addition of an extra row for 'Junction types' at the bottom of the table.

# Market leverage points

A reminder: Because there is not a general consensus on the distinction between customers and consumers, this book subsumes both under the title of 'customer'.

Now, *highlight* those junctions where decisions are made about which of the competing products or services will be purchased. These are known as 'market leverage points'. It is not necessary for *all* the customers at a junction to make this decision for the junction to become a leverage point.

Locating where leverage occurs in a market identifies the customer group(s) who will proceed to the next stage of your segmentation project. It is therefore a critical output of market mapping and should be worked through carefully.

The easiest junction at which to start this stage of market mapping is at the final users' junction. This applies to all market maps whether or not you started your map from the final users. The approach to use is as follows:

1 First, list the proportion of the total market of competing products which final users decide will be purchased.

If this is 100 per cent you can move straight on to the next section. If this is not 100 per cent –

2 Take the junction that the final users turn to next and note what proportion of the total market they decide on. If the cumulative total is still not 100 per cent, repeat this exercise for each subsequent junction until you have accounted for 100 per cent of the market.

Approximate best guess percentages are acceptable and note that this needs to be verified in any follow-up work.

You can track this through using your market map as illustrated in Figure 5.13 (based on Figure 5.10).

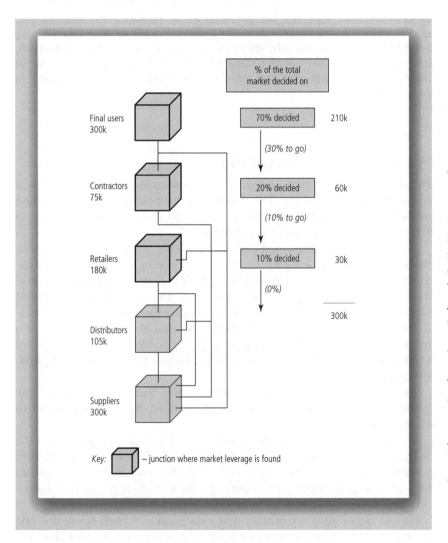

**Figure 5.13**
Market leverage points on a market map
(*Note:* If you are using the tabular format for your market map, the leverage information can be added to the 'grid squares' in Table 5.2 containing the unit totals for each junction. Alternatively, either insert an extra column for 'Market leverage' next to the list of junctions and use this for recording the leverage, or add a further row at the bottom of the table and note the leverage information in their respective columns.)

In Figure 5.13 we have a market in which 30 per cent of annual sales are decided at junctions other than the final user junction. Rather than make the decision themselves between the competing products and services, some final users are turning to their first point of contact and letting them make the decision on their behalf. In the example given, this is a role filled by contractors and retailers, though in other markets it could well be parents, consultants, section heads, the purchasing group and so on.

Once again, if 'influencers' feature on your market map and some of them are also final users, it is only the quantity they decide on behalf of others that is included at the 'influencer' junction. The quantity they decide on for their own use is included in the 'final user' figures.

| | |
|---|---|
| **Marketing insight** | In addition to showing the amounts decided at each junction you may also wish to note the amounts influenced by various junctions. Your market map would then illustrate the full role of each junction in the market. This is not, however, a requirement at this stage of the process and you may prefer to leave this refinement until the more detailed look at market mapping in Chapter 11. |

## 'Shared' decision-making

Figure 5.13 assumes that each junction operates independently when it comes to decision-making. This enables us to make a straight allocation of decision-making between the junctions so that the total adds up to 100 per cent. But this is not always the case.

Take the example presented earlier in this chapter which talked about a marketing group looking to install new technology in their call centre. There will clearly be instances where drawing up the specification and deciding on which supplier is to be given the contract will be shared between marketing and IT. It may well include others, such as the purchasing group. When this occurs, a straight allocation of decision-making on a market map that has 'marketing' and 'IT' as separate junctions will not work, but showing them separately is important for understanding how the market operates.

To cover this situation, simply note at the 'marketing' junction the amount they share with IT. This could be along the lines suggested in Figure 5.14.

The above situation will also be seen in business-to-consumer markets. For example, when looking for a new car, the final user, the driver, will certainly have their own requirements but they may also feel obliged to take into account the requirements of others in their household before deciding which car to buy.

*Before concluding that decision-making is shared, apply the 'one phone call test'.*

However, before you conclude that a decision is shared, apply the 'one phone call test'. This assumes you have sufficient funds only for one final phone call in order to swing the sale in your favour. You therefore have to make this call to the most important decision-maker (or influencer). Who would you call? If making this choice is not too difficult, it suggests that the decision really belongs to one junction.

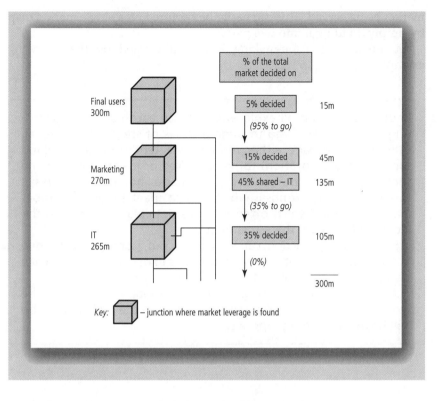

**Figure 5.14**
Shared market leverage points on a market map (*Note:* The quantities are monetary and in millions (m).)

A customer seeking advice before making a purchase does not mean they are sharing their decision with the source of the advice. The information they collect is usually evaluated against their own requirements. All that has happened is that their choice is now better informed.

For example, a parent deciding that a mobile phone is in fact a 'must have' item could well turn to the younger members of their family for help and advice in deciding which model and network they should choose. They then evaluate this information and make their own decision.

**Marketing insight**

## 'Cumulative' decision-making

By 'cumulative' decision-making we are referring to markets which consist of one or more junctions which act as 'gateways' through which you and all your competitors have to pass before making a successful sale. A company that fails at a gateway junction does not make a sale. In terms of decision-making, therefore, allocating 100 per cent between the junctions does not correctly portray how this market works.

Pharmaceutical companies clearly come across this situation when looking to launch a new drug. They need approval for the drug by the licensing authority before it can be sold. In terms of decision-making, 100 per cent rests with the licensing authority and, once approved, a further 100 per cent will be distributed between the different junctions in the market being served. This can easily be captured on a single market map by simply dividing it into two parts.

'Cumulative' decision-making is also illustrated by the following example:

> In order to win an oil exploration licence each company submitting a tender has to go through a series of stages for approval. Failure at any stage either requires the tender document (and supporting presentation) to be reworked or it simply knocks the company out of the contest. Each stage, however, requires a totally different proposal which has to meet its own decision-making criteria (which often requires detailed insights into the individuals making the assessment).
>
> Each stage, or junction, can be mapped out, just as we have done in this chapter, except that when it comes to decision-making, each stage is given 100 per cent.
>
> A strategy for each stage is then developed based on the requirements of the invitation to tender and the individuals who will be assessing the proposals.

# Selecting the junction to be segmented

*In most markets, segmentation should first take place at the final users' junction, if this is sufficiently important.*

For most markets it is recommended that segmentation should first take place at the final users' junction, provided it is a junction where there are decision-makers and that the quantity decided at that leverage point justifies it. Once the segmentation process has been completed for this particular junction, the process can then be repeated for each successive junction where decisions are made. It is often the case that these subsequent projects benefit from having the segmentation process completed for earlier junctions if they are sufficiently important.

Not all markets, however, are suited to this guideline, as illustrated in Figure 5.15 (a repeat of Figure 5.2 in the 'Fast track' section).

Basing a segmentation project on the final users in the business-to-consumer example in Figure 5.15 would clearly make sense as they account for 70 per cent of the quantity decided in that particular market. However, segmenting the final users in the business-to-business example in Figure 5.15 would appear to make no sense at all. To have such a low percentage of final users with leverage could be either because they have little choice in the matter, or because the products or services in question are of little interest to them, which may apply, for example, to the supplier of telephone services.

The next guideline would be to start at the junction nearest to the final users where significant leverage occurs. In the business-to-business example

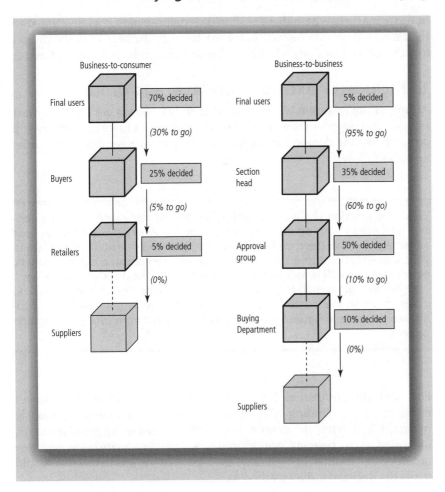

**Figure 5.15**
Selecting the junction to be segmented

this could be the 'Section heads', though starting with the 'Approval group' would appear to make more sense as they account for the highest proportion of the decisions. Although as a general rule it is easier to progress your segmentation project a single junction at a time, in the business-to-business example in Figure 5.15, working through the segmentation project for both the 'Section heads' and 'Approval groups' in parallel may be manageable; try it and see.

*As a general rule it is easier to progress your segmentation project a single junction at a time, providing it accounts for a significant amount of the purchase decision.*

If you elect to work with more than one junction at a time, it is advisable that they are found within one of the following categories:

1 users, or those who stand in for the users and 'represent' them; or,
2 those who play a part in the distribution chain; or,
3 those who take a product or service and add to it in some way before selling it on.

What each of these categories intend to do with a product is clearly quite different, and this will be reflected in their requirements. Therefore, to include junctions from more than one category in a single project is likely to make the project unmanageable and, in turn, unproductive.

*If more than one junction is to be included in the project, ensure they perform a similar role in the market.*

In those markets where there is shared decision-making, as illustrated in Figure 5.14, it usually helps if you work through the segmentation project for each of the junctions who share this responsibility at the same time.

## To include or exclude non-leverage groups

An important question we need to address before moving on to the next stage of your segmentation project is whether or not to include those who do not make the decision at the junction you are segmenting. Our guideline is as follows:

**Marketing insight**

When the junction you are segmenting consists of some who make the decision and others who do not, and it is a junction where it would be to your advantage to have them make the decision themselves, include *all* of them in your segmentation project *if it is by choice* that the decision is left to others. Better targeted offers may persuade them to make the decision themselves.

If, on the other hand, those who do not make the decision have no other choice in the matter (which could well be the case in the business-to-business example in Figure 5.15), they can be excluded from your segmentation project.

For both the companies below, a better understanding of customer requirements, including the requirements of customers previously regarded as having no interest in selecting between alternative offers, identified extra revenue opportunities and higher margins with these non-leverage groups. In both cases the customer groups in question could make the decision if they wanted to.

A market research project, commissioned by a manufacturing company to help them with their segmentation project, identified that 11 per cent of the total market went to final users who simply bought whatever their local retailer stocked. This same research project, however, also identified that if a manufacturer were to put together a product range specifically targeted at this group (a group previously ignored by all the manufacturers), the group would specify this product range, thereby shifting the leverage away from powerful retail buyers.

Another manufacturing company, whose products were installed in domestic, industrial and commercial premises by trade professionals, conducted an analysis of the total UK market for their product line. This analysis illustrated that around half the total volume went to customers who, they believed, were not leverage points. Key in this group were the domestic users who were heavily dependent on a very diverse group of installers who, in turn, were heavily dependent on the purchasing policies of powerful distributors. In looking for opportunities to develop 'pull-through' for their product, this company researched both the non-leveraging domestic and non-leveraging installer groups. The findings of the research identified new opportunities with some, though not all, the customers in these two groups. This led to some important strategic changes for the company, and to have ignored these two non-leveraging groups in their project would clearly have been very short-sighted.

The company in the following example, however, excluded the non-leveraging groups from their segmentation project. This was because the decision had been taken away from them and they had no choice in the matter.

A manufacturer of expensive medical equipment found that in many hospitals the decision on what equipment was to be bought had moved away from the final users and their departmental heads to the senior management. In fact, these departments, who historically had controlled the decision for virtually all equipment purchases and with whom the manufacturer had developed a competitive edge, were now responsible for little over half of what was bought.

A key component of their segmentation project, therefore, was to understand where the decision-making had moved to and on what criteria these decisions were based. Anyone who did not have decision-making authority was excluded from the project.

The findings had major implications for their sales strategies and required the addition of support packages, such as financing, which they had never considered in the past and had little experience with. What the company found particularly difficult with these 'new' leverage groups was that they could no longer depend on the technical leadership of their equipment to win the contract. It did, however, explain why they were losing market share to a manufacturer whose equipment they rated as inferior, but who had a financing division.

If it is appropriate that only those with leverage go through to the next stage of your segmentation project, a further refinement you could add to your market map is to split the quantity leveraged between the junction types at each junction to be segmented. Figure 5.16 illustrates how to record this for the 'Final users' appearing in Figure 5.11.

Guesstimates for these figures may, of course, be required. They can be verified in any follow-up work.

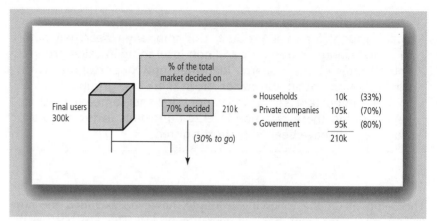

**Figure 5.16**  Quantities decided on split between junction types
(*Note:*  A useful preparatory step is to split the volume or value
quantity dealt with by the junction between the junction types (as in
Figure 5.12). The percentages appearing in the above figure for each
junction type relate to what they individually decide on. These
percentages are applied to the quantities listed in Figure 5.12.)

| **Market research note** | The market map provides important guidelines for any market research commissioned to improve your understanding of the market your business is in. It identifies the different target groups to be included in the sample frame for both the qualitative and quantitative stages of the research. |
|---|---|

# Testing current views about segments: preliminary segments

Because many companies already hold views about how their market
splits into segments, with these views based either on previous segmentation work, natural divisions that have been observed or on ideas that may
have been developed while constructing the market map, it is clearly useful if the validity of these views can be tested in some way and, in doing
so, be able to track them through the segmentation process. This can be
achieved by introducing these views into the project as 'preliminary segments'. Preliminary segments are optional, but before deciding whether
or not they are relevant to your project, we suggest you first read through
this section.

'Preliminary segments' are optional.

We should emphasize that structuring your project around these groups
and taking them through the segmentation process is quite acceptable. It
will not prejudice the outcome in any way. The process you are following

will break these preliminary segments down into a number of smaller decision-making groups and then look across *all* of them for similarities in their requirements, regardless of which preliminary segment they came from. *Preliminary segments simply form a base from which to work.*

If you decide to introduce preliminary segments into the project, it is recommended that you keep the number low, preferably five or less and certainly no more than ten. This is particularly important when working through the segmentation process using information already held by your company.

Preliminary segments could consist of any of the following:

- a current segmentation structure;
- junctions (if more than one junction is included in a project);
- junction types;
- leverage and non-leverage groups (if both are to be included);
- standard approaches to dividing customers in your industry, for example, using demographics for individuals and firmographics for companies (discussed in the next chapter);
- extent of experience in the market, separating out, for example, first-time buyers and experienced buyers.

A particularly useful option for preliminary segments is to differentiate between customers according to the particular end-use, or application, they have for the product or service, assuming this possibility exists within the confines of the market definition for your project.[1] It is highly likely that these different applications will have an important input into how the market splits into segments. For example, take your own company and the cleaning services you require; the requirements for the general office areas, customer areas and the manufacturing plant (particularly if the manufacturing process involves precision instruments) could very well be different. It would clearly help the company segmenting a market that covered all of these end-uses to regard each application as a distinct preliminary segment.

*Preliminary segments based on different end-uses (applications) for the product can be particularly helpful.*

In business-to-business markets, different applications can often be associated with different industries or with different departments. Likewise, the different rooms in a house can be considered as being different 'departments' when the products or services for these rooms are being bought with a different 'application' in mind, such as, for example, items bought for the guest's bedroom and your own family's bedrooms. A further option for preliminary segments, therefore, is:

- Different end-uses (applications) for the product.

Finally, two distinct groups you may want to consider in your project are lapsed customers who appear to have opted out of the market completely and prospects who, on the face of it, appear to have the 'need' captured in the market definition but are not buying anything as yet. In both cases, a better understanding of their requirements and the development of appropriate offers could lead to new and profitable sales opportunities.

---

[1] A discussion about using distinct end-uses or applications as market boundaries can be found in 'Developing the market definition' in Chapter 4.

As your project will refer to the preliminary segments on a number of occasions, it is easier if each of them is identified by using a name that describes *who* it represents. This helps emphasize that segmentation is about customers and it will also contribute to the next step in the process where we take a more detailed look at describing who the decision-makers are.

## Sizing preliminary segments

To help you in later steps in the process, attempt to allocate to each preliminary segment the quantity they account for. As before, come up with your best guess.

# Process check

The primary purpose of market mapping in segmentation is to identify which customers should proceed to the next stage of the project. It is a key step and requires to be worked through carefully.

We have progressively built a market map by tracking the distribution and value added chain found between final users and suppliers, and shown the various routes that are taken through the map to link the two together. While doing this we highlighted the need to ensure that the map does not overlook any 'hidden' final users. We also highlighted the importance of including influencers and/or advisers on the map, even though they may not feature in any transaction.

We then moved on to quantifying the map based on the volume or value figure used to size the market in the previous chapter. We noted that guesstimates would probably be required to complete the allocation of this figure to the various stages ('junctions') and routes along the map, particularly for a first look at market mapping. Any subsequent quantitative research should then be used to improve the accuracy of this allocation.

The details on the market map were then extended to show the different types of companies/customers found at each junction on the map and these were also quantified.

We then highlighted where decisions were made about the competing products or services ('market leverage points') and illustrated their decision-making importance by showing how much of the market their decision accounted for, with further guesstimates being used when required. We also discussed how to accommodate 'shared' and 'cumulative' decision-making on the map.

This then led us to consider which of the decision-makers should be taken to the next stage of the segmentation project, the guideline being to segment the final users first before moving on to look at other decision-makers. For markets in which the final users only account for a small proportion of the decision-making, other options were discussed. We also identified the criteria to follow when electing to combine a number of junctions on the market map into a single project, though the guideline is to work with one junction at a time. We followed this by considering the circumstances in which it is appropriate to include in the project those who leave the decision-making to someone else. New propositions based around the needs of these customers could persuade them to regain control of the decision, assuming their circumstances allow them to do this.

Finally, we presented the opportunity to introduce into the project and test any currently held views about how the market splits into segments ('preliminary segments'). These could be long-held views or new ideas that have been developed while building the market map. This is purely optional and will not prejudice the outcome in any way.

## Case study

The segmentation team at Agrofertilizers have clearly defined the scope of their project and have been able to size the market using government statistics and their own trade association's statistics. It was now time to identify which group of customers should be the focus for their project. The preference within the company was to start with the agricultural merchants, as they were key in getting fertilizers to the farmers and the group on which they spent most of their sales and marketing resources. However, the team weren't so sure that this was the best place to start, even though a detailed understanding of merchants and their requirements would certainly be helpful.

The market map put together by the team is summarized in Figure 5.17.

From the information available, the team concluded that around 60 per cent of the market was decided by farmers, with a small percentage attributable to the specialist publications and the rest split between consultants and distributors. It was therefore agreed by the full segmentation team that their first segmentation project had to focus on the farmers. It was also agreed that the project should include the farmers who currently did not make the decision for themselves. An understanding of why these farmers chose not to make their own decision was of great interest to the company as they were keen to explore if there were opportunities for moving the balance of power in the market firmly back into the hands of the farmers. It was shifting, uncomfortably, into the hands of powerful merchants. Besides, it had become very apparent to the team that the company did not really understand the buying priorities of farmers in the market for commercial crop nutrients. The company basically told farmers what was best for their crops and, as one of the sales team commented, 'we have never really "sold" anything to a *farmer*'.

Although not essential, the team considered it would be helpful if the farmers were identified as either 'arable' farmers, 'grassland' farmers (keeping dairy animals, beef and/or sheep) or as farmers running a 'mixed' enterprise. These were the three principal categories the company referred to when describing farmers and became the preliminary segments for the project. They sized these three preliminary segments as follows:

- arable – 950 ktn;
- grassland – 1450 ktn;
- mixed – 1350 ktn.

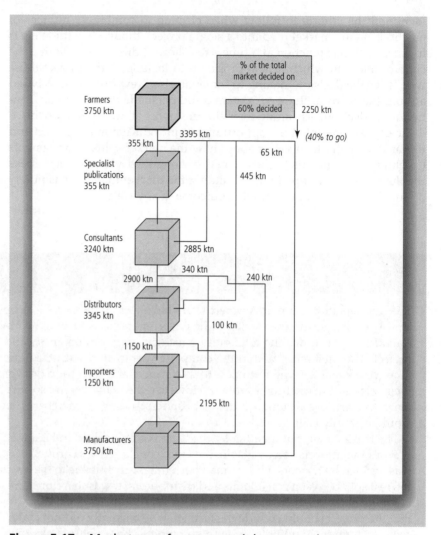

**Figure 5.17** Market map for commercial crop nutrients
(*Note:* Only the leverage figures for the final users are illustrated on this market map. There were three types of consultants operating in the market, independent consultants, a number working for distributors and a number working for the manufacturers (the largest of the three types). Only the independent consultants charged for their services at the time of the project, the others providing their services as part of their company's offer. This was why such a high proportion of the market went through consultants. Three types of distributors were also identified: national; independents; co-operatives and clubs (grouped as a single type). A more detailed map for this market appears in Chapter 11. The quantities are kilotonnes (ktn) of fertilizers.)

It is worth noting that in classifying a farmer, for example, as an 'arable' farmer, this did not always mean the farmer was exclusively growing arable crops. It also included farms which had, for example, grassland for beef cattle, but for whom that part of their overall business was less important than the arable crops. Conversely, some of the farmers classified as 'grassland' farmers could also be growing some arable crops but, once again, their focus would be on the grassland part of their business.

A summary of the project's status so far is illustrated in Figure 5.18.

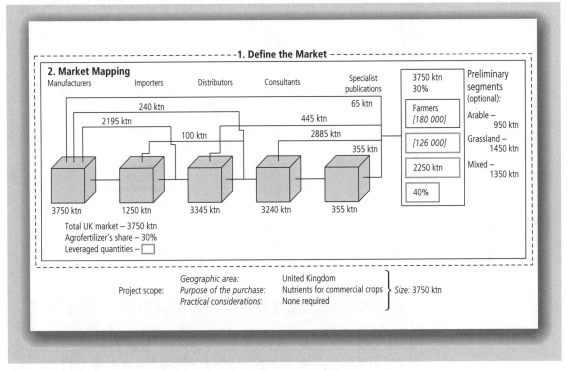

**Figure 5.18** The segmentation process – Steps 1 and 2
(*Note:* The market map is now in a horizontal format with the suppliers (manufacturers) on the left. The company's share of the market is included in this map, as is their estimated share of the quantity specified by the final users. A figure representing the number of farmers in the UK also appears [180 000], along with an estimate of the number who decide on which fertilizer will be bought. The inclusion of market share and the number of customers with leverage is covered in Chapter 11, 'Realizing the full potential of market mapping', and is not required at this stage.)

# Further examples

The following are a selection of market maps pulled together by various companies as part of their segmentation projects. The level of information they contain is varied. All have been edited for reasons of commercial confidentiality.

The example in Figure 5.19 is for a market whose needs are met by a particular type of internal wall covering which, although principally targeted at the professional trade, is also bought by home owners who wish to do-it-themselves (DIY).

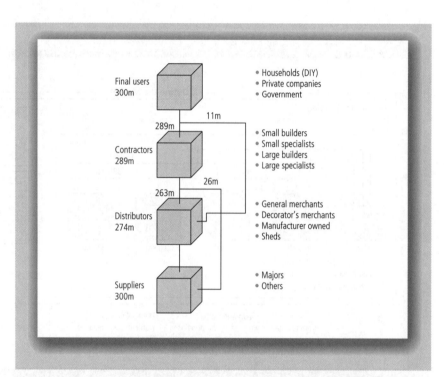

**Figure 5.19** Market map example – internal wall covering
(*Note:* The particular company undertaking the segmentation project for the market represented in this figure was, in fact, located in the distributors' junction. They were particularly interested in understanding the motivations behind final users dealing direct with the suppliers and the trends in this particular route to market. The quantities are monetary and in millions (m).)

The second example, Figure 5.20, is for a company publishing educational books and support materials in a particular field.

Figure 5.21 is for a market whose needs are currently met through the use of very expensive, specialized technical equipment. This equipment is found both in large companies and in smaller, specialist companies.

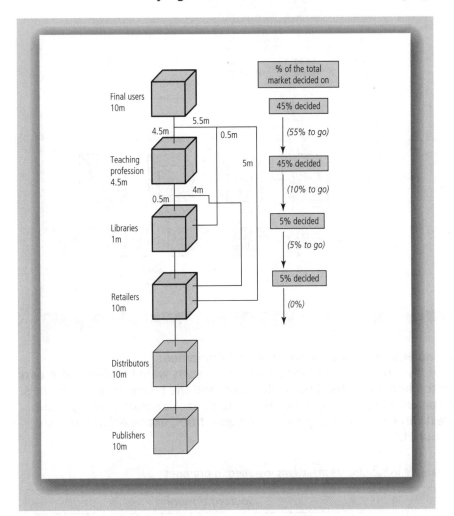

**Figure 5.20** Market map example – acquiring knowledge
(*Note:* Although material would be borrowed from libraries and used by many individuals, the quantities relate to sales, are monetary and in millions (m). Five types of final users were identified for this market map, including working professionals, postgraduate and undergraduate students. With respect to the teaching profession there were three types and libraries were basically split between public libraries and those in academic institutions. At the retailers' junction the project team identified eight junction types, including bookseller chains, specialist booksellers, library suppliers, book clubs and internet booksellers.)

The final example is for a company manufacturing items that are installed both in commercial and domestic premises. This company preferred to use the tabular format and their first look at the map for their market appears in Table 5.3.

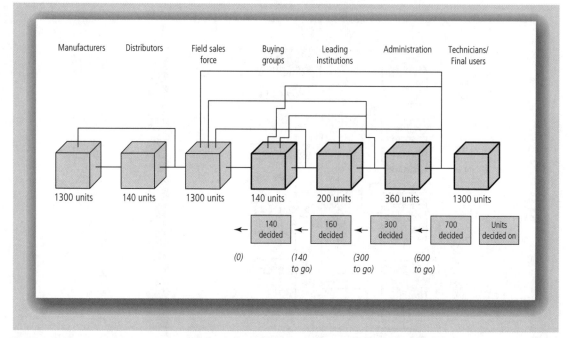

**Figure 5.21** Market map example – specialized technical equipment
(*Note:* In later stages of this project the technicians and final users were separated into two distinct junctions with the final users deciding on 460 units and the technicians on 240 units. To progress the development of segments, the company took each decision-making group in turn through the next three steps of the process. The quantities, expressed as units, are pieces of equipment bought.)

**Table 5.3** Market map example in tabular form – items installed in premises

| Market size: 3275 | A *Final users* | Sourced through | | | |
| | | B *Consultants* | C *Installers* | D *Distributors* | E *Suppliers* |
|---|---|---|---|---|---|
| A *Final users* | **3275** | 330 | 2900 | 45 | X |
| B *Consultants* | | **330** | 330 | X | X |
| C *Installers* | | | **3230** | 3230 | X |
| D *Distributors* | | | | **3275** | 3275 |
| E *Suppliers* | | | | | **3275** |
| *Junction types* | Residential Public Commercial | Consultants | In-house engineering National fitters Local independent Contractors | National Large independent Small independent Sheds | Domestic manufacturers Importers |
| *Leverage* | 64% | 5% | 30% | 1% | – |

*Note:* The market information accessible to this company was limited. The above table was produced by using well-informed guesstimates, linked into data that were available. As in many companies, the nearer this company came to the final users, the less they actually knew about them. The quantities are in thousands of units.

# Exercises

For this exercise, take a product or service that you use at work or at home and capture all the stages that occur from when your intention to acquire the product is initiated through to the product's place of origin, in other words, to the supplier, if you can take it that far. Start with a fairly straightforward acquisition and progress to a more complex one, such as an acquisition which involves seeking advice and/or obtaining the approval of others. A worksheet for this, and the following exercise, appears in Figure 5.22. Make as many copies as you need.

**Exercise 5.1**

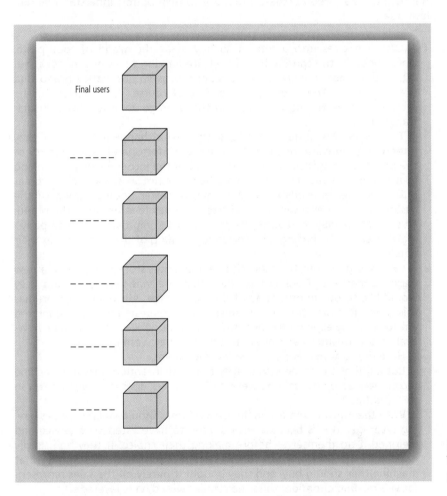

**Figure 5.22**
Worksheet – market map

Once you have completed all the stages for your acquisition, consider what other customers in the same markets would do. Add any additional stages this uncovers to the market map and include the various routes that occur between the junctions.

Finally, highlight those junctions where decisions are made about which of the competing products or services will be purchased and indicate, as best as you can, the proportions decided at the various leverage points.

**Exercise 5.2**

Now apply the above to your market. You may need to conduct a few trial runs before drawing your final market map.

Once you have completed the map as best you can, consider discussing it with others in the company to see if they can add any further details to what you have drawn up.

How does this first look at the distribution of leverage compare with your company's allocation of its sales and marketing resources in the market?

How do you think this map may change in the next few years?

---

**Exercise 5.3**

Here we discuss three purchase situations to help better understand market leverage.

1 A customer goes into a retailer to buy a specific brand of toothpaste. Unfortunately, the specific brand they are looking for is not in stock, but rather than look elsewhere, the customer buys an alternative brand that is on the shelf. The alternative brand is, of course, one selected by the retailer, so does this make the retailer the leverage point for this particular transaction?

   The customer still has leverage, despite what happened, because they intended to purchase one particular brand. Unfortunately, the strength of the brand is not sufficient enough to counter the inconvenience of looking in a number of retailers for it, so when it is not in stock, the customer buys whatever is available at the time. A better understanding of the customer's preferences may reveal opportunities to strengthen the brand. This situation may, of course, be remedied by improving the company's logistics and/or by having a better understanding of the retailers and their needs.

2 A customer goes into their local home appliances store to purchase a new washing machine. Their last washing machine was very good and they would like to buy another one of the same make. Although the store has this brand in stock, the sales representative suggests another model and enthusiastically explains the benefits of the alternative. The customer, however, is not convinced and buys the machine they went in to buy.

   Here the customer is clearly the leverage point.

   But another customer with exactly the same intention buys the machine recommended by the sales representative. Where does the leverage rest in this situation?

   With the information available, the customer should still be seen as having leverage. This is because they appear to have listened to advice and weighed it up themselves before making their choice. If they had simply gone into the shop and asked the sales representative to suggest what machine they should buy, and they bought it purely on the sales representative's recommendation, then the retailer would have leverage.

3 A buying group set up to act on behalf of a number of businesses is purchasing laptop computers. Some of the businesses have provided the buying group with the model and the brand they require while others have given a broad indication of the specification they require but, apart from that, have left it in the hands of the buying group. What is the leverage position here?

   For the businesses who have specified both the brand and the model, the leverage, quite clearly, rests with them. For the others, the fact that they have at least provided a broad specification means that the leverage is shared between the buying group and these particular businesses. If, on the other hand, these businesses had simply instructed the buying group to purchase laptop computers and left it at that, the leverage would rest with the buying group.

It is worth concluding this exercise by adding that it is usually advantageous to segment the final users in a market first, provided they are either:

1  sufficiently important with respect to decision-making; or,
2  they could be encouraged to become an important group of decision-makers if only the right offers were made available.

Chapter 6

# Developing a representative sample of different decision-makers

# Summary

For the vast majority of markets it simply is not feasible, or even necessary, to include all the decision-makers who are now the focus of your segmentation project. The concluding segments are therefore derived from a sample of decision-makers who, between them, represent the market as a whole.

For projects which include current decision-makers and potential decision-makers, this book now uses the term 'decision-maker' to refer to both.

This chapter provides the guidelines you require in order to develop a representative sample of different decision-makers when conducting a segmentation project using internal resources. In building your model of the market, this, the third step in the segmentation process, as illustrated in Figure 6.1, also identifies the characteristics and properties of a purchase on which decisions are made along with the customer attributes that will be used to describe the decision-makers.

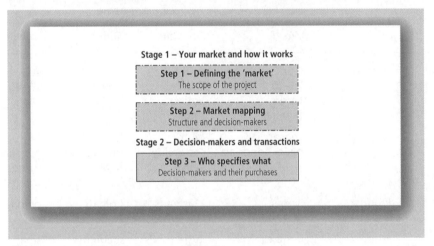

**Figure 6.1**   The segmentation process – Step 3
(*Note:* 'What' refers to all aspects of a purchase and therefore includes 'where' products are bought, 'when' they are bought and 'how' they are bought in addition to what the actual product or service itself is, consists of, or is made from.)

Information for this step potentially can be found in a number of areas and may require you to talk with a cross-section of representatives from sales, marketing, customer services, customer enquiries and ordering, as well as from distribution. Revisiting appropriate past market surveys may also provide valuable input. It is important to remember, however, that the project is looking at the market as a whole, not just your own customers.

The principle behind this step is that by observing the purchase behaviour of decision-makers and understanding the key constituents of this behaviour, we have a platform for developing a detailed understanding of their motivations. It is, therefore, a critical link with the next step of the segmentation process, which looks at why decision-makers select the particular products and services they specify. This, in turn, becomes the basis on which the segments are formed.

An alternative approach to developing your own model of the market is to commission an external market research agency to take over your segmentation project at this point,

Defer any external
market research until
the internal
segmentation project
has completed the
phase of developing
segments.

and an agency which fully understands what *market* segmentation involves will deliver a good project. However, it is our experience that this is best deferred until your internal segmentation project has completed the phase of developing segments, after which you will be able to compile a better informed and much more product-ive brief. Justifying the expense of a market research project may also have to depend on the strategic implications which emerge from the findings of the internal segmentation project.

The crucial role of this step in the segmentation process, and of the step that follows it, is clearly illustrated in the much simplified example of a completed segmentation project in the market for toothpaste, originally presented in Chapter 3 and, for ease of reference, repeated in Table 6.1.

**Table 6.1** Segments in the market for toothpaste

| | | Segment name | | | |
|---|---|---|---|---|---|
| | | *Worrier* | *Sociable* | *Sensory* | *Independent* |
| *Profile* | *Demographic* | C1 C2<br>25–40<br>Large families | B C1 C2<br>Teens<br>Young smokers | C1 C2 D<br>Children | A B<br>35–40<br>Male |
| | *Psychographic* | conservative: hypochondriacs | high sociability: active | high self-involvement: hedonists | high autonomy: value orientated |
| *What is bought, where, when and how* | *Product examples* | Signal Mentadent P | Macleans Ultrabrite | Colgate Aquafresh | own label |
| | *Product features* | large canisters<br><br>health properties | large tubes<br><br>whitening properties | medium tubes<br>flavouring | small tubes |
| | *Outlet* | supermarket | supermarket | supermarket | independent |
| | *Purchase frequency* | weekly | monthly | monthly | quarterly |
| *Why it is bought* | *Benefits sought* | stop decay | attract attention | taste | functionality |
| *Price paid* | | medium | high | medium | low |
| *Percentage of market* | | 50% | 30% | 15% | 5% |
| *Potential for growth* | | low | high | medium | nil |

*Note:* 'C1', 'C2' and so on appearing in the demographic profiles of each segment represent socio-economic groups which were in use in the UK until 2001, now replaced by eight analytic classes num-bered from 1 through to 8.

The details captured for each segment in Table 6.1 include a series of attributes describing who they are, the key constituents of their purchase, and the principal motivation underpinning their behaviour, all of which we carefully consider in the segmentation process. However, before arriving at these concluding segments, it will have been essential for the project to have first developed a representative sample of decision-makers, to have understood their purchase behaviour and, in turn, their motivations, and to have recorded information about each of them that describes who they are, with the principal reasons for their purchase used as the basis for consolidating the sample into meaningful segments. The step you are about to follow, along with the next two steps, progressively takes you through this sequence.

This chapter is organized as follows:

■ A 'fast track' for those looking for a quick route through the key points
■ An introduction to 'micro-segments' and how they represent distinct groups of customers, along with an overview of their key components
■ Identifying the features that are used by decision-makers to differentiate between competing offers ('Key Discriminating Features') – one of the key components of a micro-segment
■ Guidelines to consider when selecting features for the micro-segments
■ A brief review of the four categories from which the Key Discriminating Features are selected (what, where, when and how)
■ A brief comment about the role of price at this stage of the project
■ Using personal and, if appropriate, company characteristics to profile decision-makers – another key component of a micro-segment
■ A brief review of the four standard categories used in profiling (demographic, geographic, geodemographic and psychographic)
■ Using outlets and channels, along with other interests and product usage as possible profiling categories
■ Ensuring that the profiling attributes are practical
■ The procedure to follow when developing micro-segments, including the sizing of micro-segments – the third and final key component of a micro-segment
■ Keeping control on the number of micro-segments
■ A review of this step in the segmentation process
■ A selection of micro-segments for the case study and further examples of the components of micro-segments
■ Exercises further to help you develop micro-segments

# Fast track

● To start this step, and to ensure that it is driven from a customer's perspective, divide the market into identifiable groups of customers you can visualize and talk about. This equips you with useful points of reference for developing the sample for your project (referred to as 'micro-segments'). Working with such 'reference groups' is far better than starting from an entity called 'the market'. Base each reference group on criteria that clearly link it to a particular set of individuals, such as, age, lifestyle, income, turnover, size, occupation, type of company, location and so on. Preliminary segments are a good starting point here, though you may want to break them down further if this helps associate them with particular groups of customers. Size each reference group as best you can.

- Take one reference group at a time, familiarize yourself with the customers it represents and develop it into a micro-segment by carefully listing the features that the individuals in this group particularly look for and use to discriminate between competing propositions in your market, with any differences within the group captured as separate micro-segments. These features are referred to as 'Key Discriminating Features' (KDFs) and are selected from 'what' is bought, 'where' it is bought, 'when' and 'how' it is bought. Features describe what it is, consists of, or is made from as opposed to an advantage or benefit (a 'benefit' describes what the customer gets that they explicitly need). A suggested layout for recording micro-segments and their KDFs appears in Table 6.2 (used to illustrate a grading structure for KDFs), but at this stage use only a single star to indicate a micro-segment's KDFs. Using a spreadsheet or database package on a PC is particularly helpful for this part of the process.

  Ensure the features are market differentiators and not market qualifiers (what all competitors must have simply to enter the market and be seen as a contender), that they reflect the customer's perspective and exclude meaningless feature descriptions such as 'brand', 'quality' and 'service' that tell you nothing about what is being bought. It is *not* appropriate at this stage of the process to associate customers with the degree of focus they may have on 'price'.

- Now attempt to indicate the relative importance of the KDFs to each other for the micro-segment using a simple grading structure initially based on, for example, one to three stars as illustrated in Table 6.2. A micro-segment is defined as consisting of a group of decision-makers who share a similar level of interest in a specific set of features.

  If you do not feel able to indicate the relative importance of KDFs for micro-segments, simply leave them with a single star, thereby implying that they have the same level of interest in their specific set of features.

- Consider a cross-section of customers included in the micro-segment to confirm if they would all *generally* agree with the list of KDFs and their grading, and if they would not, develop additional micro-segments to cover any meaningful differences.

- Verify each micro-segment by checking that it is based on actual decision-makers, its reality check, by confirming who it is representing. This can be further verified by simply looking through a micro-segment's KDFs to check that such a combination is either known to occur, and therefore represents an existing transaction, or actually makes sense.

- Attach profiling characteristics to each micro-segment to describe who is found within it, including, if appropriate, their company's characteristics. These tend to be demographic, geographic, geodemographic and/or psychographic descriptors. Also add details about the outlets and channels they use as this may provide the vital link between a specific proposition and its target segment. Ensure the profiling descriptors

**Table 6.2** Fast track – recording micro-segments and indicating the relative importance of their KDFs

| Feature category | Group | Specification | Micro-segments | | | | |
|---|---|---|---|---|---|---|---|
| | | | 1 | 2 | 3 | 4 | 5 |
| 'What' | Style | Slipstream | | *** | | | |
| | | Medium cover | | | | * | ** |
| | | Full cover | | | ** | | |
| | | Latest fashion | *** | | | | |
| | Colour | Bright | | | | ** | |
| | | Subdued | | | * | | * |
| | | 'This year's' | *** | | | | |
| | Brand | Sports – general | | | | * | |
| | | Olympic link | | *** | | | |
| | | Fashion label | *** | | | | |
| 'Where' | Retailer | Sports specialist | | ** | | * | |
| | | Department store | | | ** | | |
| | | Fashion house | *** | | | | |
| | | Catalogue co. | | | | | ** |

*Note:* The most important KDFs are identified by three stars (***) in this table. Note the structure of features into 'Categories', then 'Groups' and finally the 'Specification' of the feature itself. In addition to numbering the micro-segments (1, 2 and so on) they can be given names to describe who they represent and/or a 'label' that illustrates the reference group they came from, such as H1 (the 'H' referring to its originating reference group). These labels provide a quick and easy way of identifying for each concluding segment the source of its customers. As you will see in the above, micro-segment 2 has no KDF related to colour and micro-segments 3 and 5 have no KDF related to brand.

are of practical use to your sales and marketing activity in identifying customers. Use a simple grading structure to indicate what proportion of a micro-segment's customers each characteristic applies to with, for example, three or four tick marks indicating the characteristics applicable to all of them, as illustrated in Table 6.3. If you are not sure about the proportions, just indicate each profiling attribute that is applicable to a micro-segment with a single tick mark.

It is also possible to use other interests and product usage as part of the profiling if they are known, or suspected to correlate with different needs (please refer to 'Profiling – additional categories' later in this chapter for guidelines).

- Size each micro-segment as best as you can, by referring back to the group it originated from and utilizing any market figures that may be available. Remember that it is better to be approximately right than precisely wrong.
- Once all the reference groups have been converted into micro-segments, review each micro-segment against the complete list of KDFs and make any appropriate additions to the KDFs that have been listed for them.

**Table 6.3** Fast track – adding profiling characteristics to micro-segments

| Feature category | Group | Specification | Micro-segments | | | | |
|---|---|---|---|---|---|---|---|
| | | | 1 | 2 | 3 | 4 | 5 |
| 'What' | Style | Slipstream | | *** | | | |
| | | Medium cover | | | | * | ** |
| | | Full cover | | | ** | | |
| | | Latest fashion | *** | | | | |
| ... *and so on* | | ... *and so on* | | | | | |

| Profiling category | Group | Specification | | | | | |
|---|---|---|---|---|---|---|---|
| Demographic | Age | Up to 15 | | ✓ | | | |
| | | 16 to 29 | ✓✓ | ✓ | ✓ | ✓ | |
| | | 30 to 45 | ✓ | ✓ | ✓ | ✓✓ | ✓ |
| | | 46 and over | | | ✓ | | ✓✓ |
| Psychographic | Personality | Socialite | ✓✓✓ | | | | |
| | | Sports enthusiast | | ✓✓✓ | | | |
| | | Sports interested | | | | ✓✓✓ | |
| | | Traditionalist | | | ✓✓✓ | | ✓✓✓ |
| Acquisition routes | Outlet | Sports specialist | | ✓✓✓ | | ✓✓✓ | |
| | | Department store | | | ✓✓✓ | | |
| | | Fashion house | ✓✓✓ | | | | |
| | | Catalogue co. | | | | | ✓✓✓ |
| | Channel | Face-to-face | ✓✓✓ | ✓✓ | ✓✓✓ | ✓✓ | |
| | | Direct – tel. & mail | | | | | ✓✓✓ |
| | | Direct – internet | | ✓ | | ✓ | |

*Note:* The distribution of a micro-segment between the alternative characteristics in each profiling group has to be looked at separately. Three tick marks (✓✓✓) are used in this table to indicate characteristics applicable to all the customers represented by a micro-segment.

- Finally, review and compare the finished micro-segments with each other and increase or decrease the importance of appropriate KDFs if this better reflects the differences between individual micro-segments. Use no more than five stars (or tick marks) to highlight the most important KDFs as this will ensure that the final picture remains visually comprehensible.

  If you come across duplicate micro-segments, the duplicates can be merged only if their intended end-use is the same and you believe the benefits they are looking for are the same (which may require you to wait until the next step).
- You should develop as many micro-segments as necessary to represent the market, which could be around twenty or around thirty. If the number becomes unmanageable, refer to 'Managing micro-segments – keeping control' later in this chapter.

- While developing micro-segments it is crucial to remind yourself and the team that:
  - micro-segments are based on actual decision-makers, not fictional individuals;
  - they represent the defined market as a whole, not just your own customers;
  - their KDFs are from the market as a whole, not simply limited to the features you and your particular intermediaries offer; and,
  - their KDFs are what they see as important, not what you would prefer them to see as important.

  Micro-segments therefore represent the customer's view of the market.
- A worksheet for developing micro-segments appears in the Exercises section of this chapter.

Readers who are reasonably confident that they have developed a representative sample of different decision-makers in the defined market may go straight to Chapter 7.

This concludes the fast track for Step 3 of the segmentation process.

# The components of a 'micro-segment'

By the end of this chapter you will have developed a number of 'micro-segments', each of which will represent a distinct group of decision-makers in your market and form the sample for your project. The uniqueness of a micro-segment is that when determining which of the alternative offers is to be bought, the decision-makers it represents demonstrate a similar level of interest in a specific set of features, with these features being the characteristics or properties of 'what' is bought, 'where' it is bought, 'when' it is bought and 'how' it is bought, as appropriate for the micro-segment. Recording the behaviour of customers this way provides the project with a vital link to understanding the real needs of customers. It is essential, therefore, that it is approached from the customer's perspective. The principle built into this segmentation process is that customers only seek out the features they regard as key because of the benefit(s) these features, either individually or in conjunction with other features, are seen to offer them.

> ● Definition:
> A micro-segment is a group of decision-makers who share a similar level of interest in a specific set of features.

> ● Definition:
> A feature refers to a characteristic or property of a product or service, distribution channel, purchasing frequency and purchasing method.

The first component of a micro-segment is, therefore, the list of features that the individuals in that micro-segment regard as important to them when selecting which competing offer to buy.

Because micro-segments are based on actual decision-makers and not fictional individuals, it is possible to associate characteristics with each micro-segment that describe who is found in it. These descriptions are generally made up of the demographic, geographic, geodemographic and/or psychographic profiles of customers. Their purpose is to help find some way of identifying who is likely to be found in each of the concluding segments so that we can communicate with them. For, clearly, however sophisticated we might be in isolating segments, unless we can find some way of describing them such that we can address them through our communication programme, difficulties will be encountered when implementing strategies targeted at specific segments. Profiling is tackled at this stage of the process, as opposed to the stage where we have our concluding segments, because this is the point at which we refer to individuals and it is therefore the more appropriate stage at which to record 'who' they are.

The second component of a micro-segment is, therefore, the profiling attributes of its decision-makers.

With quantification playing an important part later on in the process when we assess whether or not a segment is big enough to justify the expense of developing a specific offer for it, each micro-segment should include a volume or value figure to indicate what proportion of the total market the micro-segment accounts for. This may, of course, have to be a best guess at this stage of the project. The figures used for the market map are the base for this allocation.

The third and final component of a micro-segment is, therefore, its size. In summary, each micro-segment consists of:

1 the features regarded as important by the decision-makers it represents;
2 characteristics that tell us who these decision-makers are;
3 a volume or value figure.

---

**Marketing insight**

At this stage of the process we use the term 'micro-segment' because its size may be insufficient to justify the development of a distinct offer for the decision-makers it represents. In addition, micro-segments are based on features but features do not define a segment. Segments are based on the needs customers are seeking to have satisfied by the features. This is looked at later in the process and micro-segments reviewed in terms of their needs, with like-minded micro-segments merged to form segments.

---

Before developing micro-segments for your market, it is important to consider what features should be used to define a micro-segment and to discuss customer profiling and its practical dimension. This will ensure that the micro-segments you develop are of value to your project. While this is the recommended route through this crucial step in the segmentation process, you may prefer to go straight to the section on 'Developing micro-segments' that appears later in this chapter. You can then refer back to the section which looks at the features to be used in the project, 'Key Discriminating Features (KDFs)', and the section on profiling, 'Profiling and ensuring it is practical', as and when required.

# Key Discriminating Features (KDFs)

The features that are of interest to a segmentation project are those which the decision-makers focus on and regard as important when they are determining which of the competing products will be bought. These features are referred to in this book as 'Key Discriminating Features' (KDFs). They are sometimes referred to as 'determiners' or 'differentiators'. Clearly, it is essential that these features are looked at from the customer's perspective, not your own, even if this means that they include features you would prefer not to be there.

At this point, you may find it useful to refer to Table 6.8 that appears later in this chapter so that you can see the format for recording micro-segments and their KDFs.

As a first step towards identifying the KDFs, you may find it a helpful exercise to draw up a list of *all* the features available across the full range of products or services competing with each other in the defined market, whether or not you supply all of them, along with *all* the distribution channels used, purchasing frequencies and available purchasing methods. Features can then be selected for the various micro-segments by reference to this list, with all the features appearing in the micro-segments becoming the KDFs.

● Definition:
Key Discriminating Features are the characteristics and properties of a purchase which customers regard as decisive when making a distinction between alternative offers.

---

If you elect to draw up a list of all the features available before developing your micro-segments you may find it easier to build the list by referring to each of your preliminary segments in turn, using them as reference points, assuming you have introduced them into your project. Alternatively, draw up your list by referring to the market as a whole. Do whatever you feel most comfortable in doing.

Building this list using a spreadsheet package on a PC is particularly useful. It can also be used later when developing micro-segments.

**Marketing insight**

---

In many markets, however, beginning with a list of features results in quite an extensive catalogue and although such lists provide a convenient reference, it is possible that only a small selection of these features are influential as far as the customers are concerned. If this looks as if it will be the case for your market, you may prefer to move straight to developing your micro-segments and, in doing so, progressively compile a list of features which, by the way they have been identified, will be the KDFs.

---

In the majority of in-company workshops, moving straight to developing micro-segments is the preferred approach of the participants. However, you must adopt the approach you feel most comfortable in following.

**Marketing insight**

---

Whatever approach you choose to take, a useful structure for organizing this information is to consider 'what', 'where', 'when' and 'how' as four separate 'categories'. Within each of these categories it should then be possible to organize all the various specifications that are available into groups of alternatives. For example, within the 'what' category, 'colour' would be a feature group, while each of the colours available would be the alternative specifications in this group, in other words, the alternative features in that group. Information about the features would therefore be organized along the following lines:

*Category:* such as 'what', 'where' and so on.

> *Group:* such as 'package type', 'colour', 'brand' and so on.

>> *Specification:* such as 'multi-pack', 'red', 'high tech' and so on.

An example of this structure appears in Table 6.4.

**Table 6.4** Recording information on what, where, when and how

| Category | Group | Specification |
| --- | --- | --- |
| What | Speed | High; Medium; Low |
| | Loading | Top; Front |
| | Colour | Subtle; Loud; Neutral |
| | Service | Under 4 hours; 4–8 hours; Next day; Within 2 days |
| Where | Outlet | Superstore; Department store; Specialist shop; Catalogue company |
| | Channel | Face-to-face; Direct (mail); Direct (phone); Direct (Web) |
| | Buying Club | Trade body; Affinity group; Local club |
| When | Frequency | Daily; Weekly; Monthly; Yearly |
| | Season | Spring; Summer; Winter; Autumn; All year |
| How | Credit | 24 months; 12 months; 6 months; None |

## KDF guidelines

Before developing the micro-segments for your project there are some important guidelines to consider which will help ensure that the features you select for the micro-segments provide the required link to the next step in the process. These guidelines, each of which is discussed after this summary, are as follows. The numbers can be used to locate whichever guidelines are of particular interest to you.

1 Refer to the features, rather than their advantages or benefits.
2 Ensure the level of detail is appropriate for the defined market.
3 Exclude features that are basic market entry requirements.
4 Ensure the features reflect how customers categorize them and buy them.
5 Avoid hiding essential details behind meaningless feature descriptions.
6 Unbundle the components of a product or service.
7 Merge correlated features.
8 Focus on the influential features that drive the decision.

**Market research note**

In any market research subsequently commissioned to assist the segmentation project, an understanding of which features are the basic entry requirements, how customers refer to features, what lies behind generic descriptions, the importance of different features, the correlations that exist between features and how customers simplify complex offers are all important inputs to the project.

It is also important to collect the KDFs for each completed interview as it is useful to understand their relationship to the needs customers are looking to satisfy.

1 Features, advantages and benefits.

It is important when considering 'features' that you avoid covering a number of different products or services with what is really a description of either the advantage or the benefit being provided. For example, 'next day delivery' is a description of what is obtained by buying first-class postage or certain types of courier services. The features recorded in this example should be 'first-class postage' and 'next day courier service'.

**Marketing insight**

To assist in the distinction between a 'feature', an 'advantage' and a 'benefit' the following summary may help you:

- feature: what it is, consists of, or is made from;
- advantage: what it does;
- benefit: what the customer gets that they explicitly need.

For example, 'Teflon' is a surface coating for kitchen utensils (feature) which is non-stick (advantage), which means that less time is required for washing up (benefit).

The relationship between features, advantages and benefits is covered in Chapter 7. A detailed discussion about benefits can also be found in this chapter.

Features tend to crop up in conversation more often than the benefits as they are usually easier to talk about. It is possible, however, that in your discussions about features you may also highlight the benefit. If this happens, make a note of the benefit, as it is required for the next step in the process.

2 Ensure the level of detail equates to the degree of refinement in the market definition.

A finely defined market would refer to the specific features of individual products, while a more broadly defined market would refer to products or even product groups, possibly using generic descriptions. The following example helps explain this point.

When looking at which mode of transport is used for travelling between major cities it would be unnecessary, for example, to refer to the types and makes of car available as this level of detail adds nothing to understanding customer requirements. Referring to the alternative modes of transport available and their general characteristics would be more appropriate for this level of aggregation, as would frequency, journey time and en-route facilities.

However, if looking at family cars, referring to the types and makes of car available would be essential.

3 Exclude features that are basic market entry requirements.
In many markets there are certain features that all products or services must have in order to be considered by *any* customer. They are sometimes referred to as 'market qualifiers' or 'hygiene factors'. These features are those which the users expect to have as a matter of course, so much so that even if improvements are made to these features they are unlikely to generate any major gains in market share because they do not generate any major gains in customer satisfaction. However, once one company introduces improvements to these features, the entry level requirement moves up to this higher level. A good example can be found in the market for PCs, where the constant improvement in processor speeds simply moves the market up a further notch in terms of the customer's standard level of expectation.

Over time, features that were once used by customers to decide between alternative offers become the norm and begin to be regarded as basic entry requirements. It is important, therefore, that you periodically review your list of 'determining' features (the KDFs) with a cross-section of customers in your market.

---

Examples of features that have become basic entry requirements: radio and cassette players pre-installed in cars; advance programming for domestic video recorders (though understanding them is something else); built-in CD-ROM drives in PCs; colour televisions (with digital televisions eventually becoming the norm); 'family size' packs and multi-packs of various product lines such as savoury snacks and confectionary items; pre-shrunk clothes (apart from certain brands of jeans); loyalty programmes with airlines, hotel chains and credit cards; help desks and so on.

---

Two important considerations should be borne in mind, however, before concluding that a particular feature is a basic market entry requirement:

(a) Although all the products in a particular market may be required to contain a specific feature, possibly through legislation, it is only if *all* the customers in that market *require* the product to have this feature that it can be classified as a basic entry requirement. For example, all aerosol propellants are required to be ozone-friendly and while some customers are quite passionate about this, others are quite indifferent. From the customers' point of view, therefore, ozone-friendly propellants are not a basic market entry requirement.

(b) If you are in a market in which customers can select from a range of features and, in effect, 'design' their own product, be careful as to what you classify as 'basic entry items'. For example, in the market for car insurance in the UK the basic product consists of third party liability, fire and theft, which is a legal requirement. Every car insurance policy, therefore, contains this basic cover, which would seem to qualify it as a basic entry requirement. For some customers, however, this basic cover is all they buy, which means that it must remain as a KDF.

Marketing
insight

A feature that all products must have is only a basic market entry requirement if customers do not differentiate between alternative offers by reference to this feature.

4  Ensure the feature groups and the features reflect how customers categorize them and buy them.

In many markets the range and variety of features available are often far too numerous for the customers to cope with. To put order into the 'chaos', customers therefore simplify the options into more manageable sets, as in the following examples.

> There may be a range of supporting services available for a product which cover all sorts of options, but customers simply refer to them as 'basic' and 'premium' services.
>
> In a general drinks market, customers may want to retain the distinction between carbonated and still drinks but simplify the range of flavours available into more manageable groups.
>
> Rather than considering all the different 'bells and whistles' available with a particular product, customers who are interested in these additional features may simply refer to them as 'add-ons', or group them into various types of add-ons.
>
> The breakdown of retail outlets into specialist stores, department stores and so on may be irrelevant if customers simply see them as 'local' stores and make no other distinction between them.

This type of information can be established by listening to the way customers talk about the different features available. Capturing the features in this way is, therefore, perfectly valid (even if the 'bells and whistles' cross over different feature groups).

Companies know what they, and often what their competitors offer in great detail. In many markets, however, customers tend to discriminate between offers in much simpler terms. It is essential, therefore, that you ensure that the features used in the micro-segments reflect the views held by the market. Otherwise you will unnecessarily complicate this and subsequent steps.

Marketing
insight

5  Avoid hiding essential detail behind meaningless feature descriptions.

The three most frequent examples of this are 'brand', 'quality' and 'service' which are all meaningless on their own and could be hiding a range of specifications. Buying a 'good' brand for some customers could be associated with buying well-researched products, while for others it could be associated with a company's technical support staff. 'Quality' for some customers could refer to a material that is extremely durable, while for others it could mean the colour does not fade over time.

'Service' could refer to a returns policy or promptness in answering the telephone. It is important that your features consist of these more specific descriptions.

| **Marketing insight** | As a guideline: a description of a feature is meaningless if it does not describe what a company would need to do in order to offer it. Think of a feature in terms of how you would describe it on a product specification brief. |
|---|---|

6 Unbundle the components of a product or service.

In addition to covering the features that customers can choose to have included in the product or service such as, for example, the various features of a video recorder or washing machine or the different features associated with a life insurance policy, it is important to ensure that features *already* included as part of the offer are not overlooked. For example, buying a new personal computer often includes a technical support service as part of the 'package'. Buying a car in the UK often includes an extended warranty, whereas in some other countries it only covers the owner for the first year.

7 Merge correlated features.

It may be the case that features in one group may be highly correlated with features in another group and therefore having them appear as separate features adds nothing to this stage of the project. For example, 'home delivery' may appear as a feature in a group called 'type of delivery', and 'direct mail' appear as a feature in the 'channel' group. Now, if it was the case that for the market being segmented the only goods ever delivered to the home were those ordered by direct mail, rather than having them listed separately they could be combined, such as 'direct mail and home delivery', and placed in one or other of their original groups. In this example, the way the features are now being described suggests that it would appear sensible to place them in the 'channel' group.

It should be pointed out that it is important to ensure that the correlation is a two-way exclusive correlation before removing one or the other feature from their original group. For example, even if it was the case that *all* goods ordered by direct mail had home delivery, if customers visiting traditional retailers could also have home delivery, then the features would have to include all the options. The 'channel' group would therefore include 'direct mail and home delivery' along with 'direct mail' on its own, and 'home delivery' would still appear in the 'type of delivery' group.

8 Focus on the influential features.

Although the principle behind the KDFs is that they are all influential, there are occasions when the number of features appearing as KDFs are a little too numerous to handle. In these situations it is essential that you review the KDFs and home in on those that have the greatest influence on the decision. Applying the '80/20 rule' to the list of features can help you here, with only the features that account for, say, 80 per cent of the decision being those that are taken into the next stage of the project.

Use the '80/20 rule' to help identify the most influential features.

Sorting through the features in this way can be conducted at the 'feature category', 'feature group' or at the individual 'feature' level, and either across the market as a whole, by preliminary segment or by individual micro-segment. Adopt whatever appears to be the most appropriate. Clearly it is helpful if there is some information to hand which enables you to do this from the market's perspective.

Table 6.5 illustrates how to apply the '80/20 rule' and uses a set of feature groups as the example. This table has been arrived at by first arranging the feature groups in a descending order of importance and then allocating 100 points between them in a way which represents their relative importance to each other from the market's perspective (or from the perspective of the preliminary segment or micro-segment as appropriate). It is as if a value of £100 is placed on the feature groups as a whole and then distributed between each of them to indicate their individual value. The cumulative score has then been calculated by progressively adding up the individual scores.

**Table 6.5** Identifying influential features

| Feature group | Individual score | Cumulative score |
|---|---|---|
| 'What' – colour | 35 | 35 |
| 'What' – country of origin | 25 | 60 |
| 'What' – product type | 15 | 75 |
| 'Where' – retailer | 10 | 85 |
| 'What' – brand | 5 | 90 |
| 'What' – type of delivery | 4 | 94 |
| 'How' – payment | 3 | 97 |
| 'When' – frequency | 3 | 100 |

*Note:* Pinpoint accuracy in the distribution of the total sum between the feature groups is not essential. What is required is a clear distinction between those feature groups that really count in the decision and those which are less important.

**Marketing insight**

When compiling a table similar to Table 6.5 it is often easier to first score the most influential feature group out of 100 and then score the other groups relative to this score. Once completed, you add up all the individual scores, divide each individual score by this total and multiply the answer by 100. So, if the total comes to 230, divide each individual score by this figure and multiply by 100. A worked example for the Agrofertilizer Supplies case study can be found in Table 6.11.

Trying to ensure the figures add up to 100 at the outset often requires the figures to be reworked a number of times.

Although it is referred to as the '80/20 rule', the scores rarely provide you with a clear 80 per cent cut-off point. In Table 6.5 there are cumulative scores of 75 per cent and 85 per cent, but not 80 per cent, so in this example we would first use the 85 per cent cut-off point and include 'retailers' in the list of KDFs. If the concluding list of KDFs was still too onerous, we could then decide to use the 75 per cent cut-off point and exclude 'retailers' from this list.

## What, where, when and how

This is a useful point at which briefly to review the four categories that make up the KDFs.

### What is bought

Here we are primarily referring to the specific features of all the products and services covered by the market definition. In addition, it is important

**Definition reminder:**
A market is the aggregation of all the products or services which customers regard as being capable of satisfying the same need.

not to overlook any product or service 'add-ons' provided by any intermediaries on your market map, such as maintenance contracts, delivery services, installation and so on. These may be out of your control, but that doesn't mean they can be excluded from considering how a market splits into segments. It is also appropriate to include in 'what is bought' the role of 'influencers' as defined in Step 2 (Chapter 5), along with technical advisers and consultants.

**Definition:**
A product (or service) is the total experience of the customer when dealing with an organization.

When referring to a product or service we are including the total experience of the customer when dealing with the organization, which means that both the tangible and intangible aspects have to be covered. This is captured in Figure 6.2.

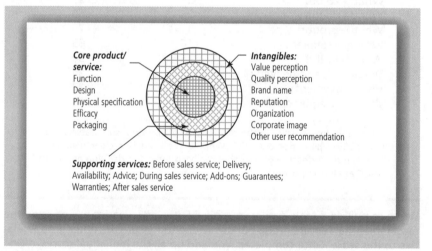

**Figure 6.2   What is a product?**
(*Note:* A number of items in the figure, such as 'quality', 'service', 'image' and so on require to be explained in your list of features. For further details, please refer to 'KDF guideline' number 5, 'Avoid hiding essential detail behind meaningless feature descriptions'.)

## Marketing insight

The two outer circles in Figure 6.2 are sometimes referred to as 'product surround' and can account for as much as 80 per cent of the impact of a product. Often, these only account for 20 per cent of costs, whereas the reverse is often true of the 'core' product.

It is clearly important to be pragmatic when listing the features for a micro-segment. So, for example, if it is known that customers rely on what their supplier stocks, exclude those feature groups which customers are clearly indicating they have no interest in, such as manufacturer's brand.

Some of the feature groups you could take into account when drawing up your list of what is bought, along with examples of features selected from a range of markets, appear later in this chapter when we look at further examples.

Finally, in those markets where competing products or services are used for different end-uses and these different applications have not been considered in the definition of the market or for identifying different preliminary segments, they should now be listed here as if they were an extension to your feature list. It is highly likely that these different applications will have an important input into your segmentation project.

---

If you are progressing a project for a market in which there are quite different applications but, as yet, have chosen not to run the project with these applications represented by different preliminary segments, it is recommended that you now regard these different applications as distinct preliminary segments. Attempt to size each of them as this will help you later in the process.

Marketing insight

---

## Where it is bought

In addition to covering all the different types of outlet from which the competing products are purchased, 'where' also includes all the different channels used to place orders along with all the different channels used to deliver the orders. Please note that this only refers to the sourcing of the products and services covered by the market definition and does not include the details of how independent influencers, advisers and consultants are sourced.

Depending on the detail contained in your market map in Step 2, this information may already be available on the market map.

Although the outlets and channels used by customers are often owned and run by companies other than your own, they are an integral part of the purchase as far as the customer is concerned. Being able to obtain the product from particular outlets or through particular channels could be crucially important for some customers and may, therefore, be the key to differentiating them from other customers in your concluding segments.

---

For example, publishers of books can only reach some segments by having their books available at supermarkets and other outlets that are similarly 'distant' from traditional bookshops. This is because some customers have an aversion to going into a traditional bookshop as they feel uncomfortable in that type of environment.

If you want to reach the serious sports enthusiasts you will find that some of them will only buy their equipment from professional sports outlets.

> Today, of course, there are segments that are dedicated to shopping over the Web, especially for items that they do not feel the need to preview beforehand. Whereas in the past they may have used mail order or placed an order by telephone, they now have a new route to market which, with its real time capabilities and sense of putting the customer in control, has attracted new users to direct marketing.

The list of where it is bought could include: direct telephone, mail order, internet, distributor, department store, national chain, regional chain, local independent retailer, tied retailer, supermarket, wholesaler, specialist supplier, street stall, through a buying group, through a buying club, door-to-door, local/high street/out-of-town shop and so on.

Even if the outlets and channels do not qualify as KDFs, it is important to record which of them are used by the customers in each micro-segment. This information will be included as part of the profile for each micro-segment (discussed later in this chapter) as it may provide the vital link between a specific proposition and its target segment. It is also used in the second part of market mapping (which follows the completion of the segmentation process).

## When it is bought

The frequencies at which customers prefer to make their purchases should not be overlooked, as they may once again be crucial for some segments.

> For example, some grocery shoppers prefer to make fortnightly shopping trips at weekends, others weekly shopping trips at weekends and some prefer daily shopping trips especially for fresh fruit, vegetables and meat.

The purchase frequencies found in markets could include: daily, weekly, monthly, seasonally, biannually, every two years, at 50 000 miles, occasionally, as needed, on impulse, only in emergencies, degrees of urgency, infrequently, rarely, special events, only during sales, at the bottom of the market and so on.

## How it is bought

Finally it may be necessary to consider the different methods of purchase customers prefer to use.

Examples which may help in drawing up your list include: credit card, charge card, debit card, cash, direct debit, standing order, credit terms, outright purchase, lease-hire, lease-purchase, negotiated price, sealed bid and so on.

Although many of these methods of purchase will be available across the market and therefore unlikely to act as differentiators, the ability, or otherwise, to include financing as part of the offer in some markets can still win, or lose, a sale.

> In segmentation projects for some capital goods, the provision of financing packages has been a crucially important factor in deciding between alternative suppliers for segments consisting of chief executive officers or chief financial officers. In such situations, having your own in-company financing facility or close liaison with a financing institution has been a critical factor for a successful bid.

## Price

It is *not* appropriate at this stage of the process to associate customers with the degree of focus they may have on 'price', even though a number of customers in your market may simply buy the cheapest. Price is better covered in the next step of the process when it can be allocated an importance rating relative to the benefits being delivered by the features being bought. This topic, therefore, is discussed in more detail in the next chapter.

---

In most markets, rarely more than around 10 per cent of customers have 'price' as their overriding requirement and can be regarded as true price chasers. Customers who act this way willingly give up KDFs in order to obtain the cheapest price. This should not be confused with customers who look for the best price for their KDFs as these customers are 'value' chasers.

Marketing insight

---

It is, however, an appropriate opportunity to point out that if your market is one in which customers hold different views as to what the 'price' consists of, the features appearing in the micro-segments need to reflect this. Here we are specifically referring to a market in which some customers evaluate alternative products according to their lifetime cost and other customers evaluate alternative products based on the initial purchase price. The KDFs for customers who evaluate competing offers in terms of their lifetime costs would clearly need to include features that they consider are important elements of the lifetime cost equation.

> Some operators of heavy goods vehicles consider only the initial purchase price when assessing the relative value of different vehicles. Other operators consider maintenance costs and residual value (second-hand value) along with the initial purchase price when making their comparisons.

# Profiling and ensuring it is practical

The second component of a micro-segment is the description of who is found within it in terms of their personal and, if appropriate, their company's characteristics. This detail is required because, once you have combined likeminded micro-segments to form market segments based on their needs, you will be looking for the personal attributes that can be used to identify clearly which customers are to be found in each of the concluding segments. This is important for the successful targeting of your segment-specific offers.

## Marketing insight

It is not always possible to find a single profile, or manageable number of profiles that can be used to identify *all* the customers found in a particular segment. What we are looking for is a profile, or small number of profiles that fit a meaningful majority of the customers found in each segment. It is worth pointing out, however, that with the increasing sophistication of multidimensional profiling packages, many of which are capable of being run on desktop PCs, this is becoming less of a problem.

At this point, you may find it useful to refer to Table 6.9 that appears later in this chapter so that you can see the format for recording the profiling attributes of micro-segments.

Finding the means by which you can reach the customers found in each needs-based segment is not always an easy task, and at this stage of the project, particularly if it is the first time you have approached segmentation along the lines presented in this book, you are unlikely to know what characteristic(s) can be used to distinguish one segment from another. Tackling this issue at an early stage in the project, and using a number of different profiling attributes is, therefore, of critical importance to the success of the project. What you have to bear in mind, of course, is that it is of no concern to the customers whether or not you are able to identify which segment they belong to by reference to their personal characteristics. You can be sure that they will not change their buying criteria simply to make this aspect of segmentation easy for you and it will make no difference to the way the *market* splits into segments. Simply ask yourself, have you ever changed your buying criteria to help a supplier segment their market?

> Customers do not change their buying criteria in order to slot themselves into segments for your administrative convenience.

## Marketing insight

Although we are at an early stage of considering how to reach segments, it is appropriate to point out that even if the association between a segment and the profile of its members proves to be difficult, it does not spell the end of your needs-based segmentation project. One or more of the following may apply to your market and/or your company:

- The strength of the individual segment propositions will self-select their target customers.
- The outlets and/or channels used by the segments are different, thereby forming the link between propositions and their customers.

- A short series of questions (often referred to as the 'golden questions') can be used when in direct contact with customers, and how they answer these questions will identify the segment they are from.
- Your sales staff are able to allocate customers into their segments based on prior knowledge or after a sales call.

If at all necessary, you may simply have to be pragmatic with your conclusions and modify the ideal segment model into one that can be effectively implemented.

---

A major computer manufacturer discovered that the market really segmented according to the application for which the computer was used, such as accounting, stock control, marketing and so on. Unfortunately, the company had no data on this and all its records were by company name and hence industry segment. Remedying this involved changing its order taking procedure to track at the time of purchase what use was envisaged by the customer. This extra data had to be gathered through whatever channel was used to place the order, be that through distributors, direct sales force, telesales or the internet.

---

The characteristics used to profile customers represented by each micro-segment can be based on a single type of descriptor, such as age or company size, or from a range of descriptors. We would strongly recommend, however, that you use a range of profiling descriptors for your micro-segments. How many will depend on the number you can handle and what is accessible to you, either from your own records or from third parties who specialize in holding information on their own databases about customers in your market. This is unless, of course, you already know which profiling characteristics can be used to identify the segment individual customers belong to. For most projects, however, it is not known in advance which profiling characteristics distinguish between segments as this only becomes apparent once the segments have been formed. What you have to bear in mind is a situation where, say, by simply adding the type of car owned by customers to their age and income profiles you would be able to distinguish between segments, but all you collected were age and income profiles which, unfortunately, overlapped various segments.

Whatever number of profiling descriptors you select for your project, each should be governed by its practical use in enabling you to identify the members of each concluding segment. They should be thought through carefully, related to observations in the market place and tested for their validity whenever possible.

*Add a number of profiling characteristics to each micro-segment as this improves the success of identifying customers by their segment and, therefore, targeting them with their specific offer.*

---

In any market research carried out as a requirement for segmentation, questions should be included which collect profiling information about each respondent. This will be used later in the segmentation process. Until you are at the stage where you know which characteristics can be used to distinguish between segments, the choice of profiling information you collect will have to be a matter of judgement.

**Market research note**

Definition: ●
Demographics are
measurable descriptions
of customers.

Definition: ●
Geographics are
identifiable locations
of customers.

Definition: ●
Psychographics are a
customer's inner feelings
and predisposition to
behave in certain ways.

# Profiling – standard categories

The standard categories of profiling information collected about customers tend to be **demographic** (sometimes referred to as 'firmographic' in business-to-business markets), **geographic**, geodemographic (which, as the name implies, is a combination of the previous two categories) and **psychographic**. Each of these can be broken down into a series of different profiling groups within which are found the individual profiling specifications. This gives us a data structure along the following lines, which is exactly the same structure suggested for the KDFs.

*Category:* such as 'demographic', 'geographic' and so on.

*Group:* such as 'age', 'industry', 'region', 'country' and so on.

*Specification:* such as 'under 18', 'services', 'Canada' and so on.

The 'specifications' provide the profiling detail used for the micro-segments.

The use of profiling appeared in the example presented earlier in this chapter of a completed segmentation project for the users of toothpaste. Here, the typical profile of customers to be found in each of the concluding segments was clearly identified. The profiling section of this example is repeated in Table 6.6.

**Table 6.6** Customer profiles for segments in the market for toothpaste

|  |  | Segment name | | | |
|  |  | Worrier | Sociable | Sensory | Independent |
| --- | --- | --- | --- | --- | --- |
| *Profile* | Demographic | C1 C2<br>25–40<br>Large families | B C1 C2<br>Teens<br>Young smokers | C1 C2 D<br>Children | A B<br>35–40<br>Male |
|  | Psychographic | conservative:<br>hypochondriacs | high<br>sociability:<br>active | high self-<br>involvement:<br>hedonists | high<br>autonomy:<br>value<br>orientated |

*Note:* 'C1', 'C2' and so on appearing in the demographic profiles of each segment represent socio-economic groups which were in use in the UK until 2001, now replaced by eight analytic classes numbered from 1 through to 8. A summary of the 2001 classification system appears in the Examples section of this chapter. Although not listed in the example here, geographic and geodemographic details could be added if they further helped identify customers by their segments.

Definition: ●
Socio-economic
classifications group
individuals according to
their level of income
and/or occupation (or
that of the head of
household).

What Table 6.6 also illustrates is that for this market, as in many markets, it is characteristics from a range of profiling groups that help identify the segments rather than the characteristics of a single profiling group.

The growing variety and sophistication of profiling possibilities available in many of the developed economies is making a major contribution to the success of targeted propositions, with some suppliers of profiling services stating that they can now tell the difference between two people in the same household. A selection of standard approaches to profiling in both business and consumer market segmentation appears in the Examples section of this chapter. It is, however, their practical application in isolating specific segments and enabling you to reach them that determines whether or not they have any value to you. A simple example illustrates this point.

---

In the UK, if you have a segment which consists of individuals from the professions and senior management, it is known that they tend to be light television viewers; consequently, if this is a target segment, it does not make sense to advertise your product or service heavily on television. However, they can be effectively reached by means of certain newspapers and magazines, where they comprise the principal readership.

Here we are seeing a useful correlation between readership and viewing patterns and the socio-economic groups which consist of the professions and senior management, and this can be most useful in helping us to communicate cost-effectively with our target market by means of advertising.

---

Using consumer demographics, banks and insurance companies have realized that at different stages in the family life cycle their customers have different needs, so this has become another most useful way of describing some of their segments. As a result, these financial institutions have been particularly adept at developing products especially for certain age categories. In this respect, because of the gradually reducing relevance of socio-economic classifications as a predictor of behaviour, there is an emerging concept of 'contexts', such as 'wellness', 'awareness', 'Euroness', 'traditionalism', 'expectism' and 'home-centredness', each one related to life stages such as 'singles', 'nesters', 'developers' and 'elders'. Thus, Laura Ashley would clearly be in the 'traditionalism' context, while Body Shop would probably be in the 'wellness' context.

For the geodemographic category, ACORN (A Classification of Residential Neighbourhoods from CACI Ltd[1]), for example, which classifies all households in Great Britain at postcode level into 56 different types based on key demographic variables, Census information and lifestyle data, is particularly useful for the retailing business because, when used in conjunction with market research, it can accurately predict consumption patterns in specific geographic locations.

Psychographic profiling differences are particularly useful in the creative execution of advertising and other promotional campaigns, especially in mass markets, thereby homing the offer into their target segment. In the market for toothpaste, for example, advertisements that play on people's concerns about the health of their teeth, especially the health of their children's teeth, have supported a number of brands targeted at the 'Worrier' segment in Table 6.6. However, brands targeted at the 'Sociable'

---

[1]ACORN and CACI are trade marks of CACI Ltd.

segment often feature young people socializing and instantly being attracted to each other simply because they use a specific toothpaste that gives them the smile that gets them noticed!

Briefly turning to business-to-business markets, Standard Industrial Classification (SIC) systems, number of employees, job titles, turnover and production processes have been found to be useful demographic descriptors. Unfortunately in business-to-business marketing the development of tools for sophisticated targeting of business customers has lagged behind the developments that have taken place in the consumer markets. This opportunity gap, however, has not been overlooked and geodemographic profiling packages have become available along with some psychographic lists and classifications systems combining demographics with behavioural characteristics, such as Commercial MOSAIC from Experían Ltd[2] in the UK. Summaries of both the UK/European and North American SIC systems appear in the Examples section of this chapter, with a more detailed listing found at www.marketsegmentation.co.uk.

**Definition:** Standard Industrial Classification (SIC) systems are lists of business categories for which most governments keep production statistics.

---

**Marketing insight**

On occasions, sophisticated profiling packages are seen as a method of defining segments. Segments, as has already been discussed, are defined by their particular needs, while profiling is the means by which you identify the membership of each segment.

---

## Profiling – additional categories

Two possibilities are discussed here:

1 Acquisition routes – outlets and channels.
2 Other interests and product usage.

Earlier in this chapter we touched on the possibility of using outlets and channels to reach individual segments and suggested that recording the acquisition routes used by the micro-segments, even when they are not KDFs, may provide the vital link between a specific proposition and its target segment. Whether this proves to be the case or not, it is essential that you record this information anyway because knowing which outlets and channels are used by each of the concluding segments will enable you to complete your market map and develop your distribution plan. We revisit market mapping at the end of the segmentation process.

With respect to a customer's other interests and product usage, the most obvious inclusions in this category would be leisure interests, such as sports, music, theatre and gardening, readership preferences covering newspapers, magazines and so on, and a customer's viewing and listening preferences on the television and radio, such as news, soaps and natural history. All of these, however, are often included in the demographic category.

It is the possibility of extending a customer's other interests and product usage beyond the obvious that is being considered here. The value of

---

[2]MOSAIC and Experían are trade marks of Experían Ltd.

using these additional profiling possibilities is illustrated by the following example:

> A publishing company that specializes in a particular format for its printed material has found that customers in their most important segment are strongly correlated to a particular approach to credit and their ownership of pets. This company, it should be noted, does not publish material on either financial matters or pets.
>
> When requesting lists of prospects from database companies for campaigns targeted at this segment, the company now only requests individuals who match this profile. As a result, the company has reduced its expenditure on lists, reduced its expenditure on prospecting for new business, and improved the success rate of its new business campaigns.

The broad nature of this profiling category, however, opens up an overwhelming number of possibilities at this stage of a segmentation project, so the following guidelines are suggested:

1 Limit the possibilities to those which are known, or suspected to correlate with different needs.
2 Keep the number down to what you can handle in an internal workshop and, if it is commissioned, to what an interviewee can be expected to handle in a market research questionnaire, and do not forget that the total number includes characteristics you select from other profiling categories.
3 If the number is too large to work through manually, ensure there is access to a software package that can sort through the profiling data and determine which attributes can be associated with particular groups of customers

Looking at other interests and product usage to help link customers to segments is often left until a project has been completed and it is proving difficult to find standard profiles that fit the various segments. It is, of course, a facility limited to countries where externally held databases are available which hold this type of information about individual customers.

What it requires is for a statistically valid sample of named customers to be identified for each segment, along with their addresses. An external agency takes these lists and enhances the profiling data associated with each customer using their own profiling records, which may include the addition of any demographic data that is missing. The customer records in each segment are then analysed by appropriate software to find which attributes when taken together are good identifiers of customers in each segment.

(Alternative approaches to getting round any difficulties with associating segments to particular profiles were discussed earlier in this chapter.)

## Profiling – keeping it practical

The profiling attributes you propose to record should focus on those you can use in your sales and marketing activity to identify customers. For example, although the size of garden may be appropriate in distinguishing between segments for garden equipment, unless there is a database somewhere which records this information for each address, it has no practical use for your sales and marketing activity. Certain postcodes may, however, correlate to particular garden sizes. Exploring the existence of such a relationship in any research you undertake would therefore prove useful. If a relationship between garden sizes and postcodes is then found to exist, the 'practicality' problem will have been overcome. Likewise, be careful about using psychographic profiles of customers as the method of distinguishing between segments, as this is often only suited to certain types of markets. Psychographic differences can be used in the creative execution of advertising and promotional campaigns in mass markets, thereby homing the offer into the target segment. Its use in other types of markets is not so easy.

Fortunately, in many countries the range of data held about individual customers by companies that specialize in this area, along with sophisticated software packages capable of uncovering predictive profiling patterns, is proving to be of great value to the practical side of profiling. The ability to target specific customers with the proposition that suits their needs has improved substantially and continues to improve.

However, as mentioned earlier, some of these sophisticated profiling packages are portrayed as methods of defining segments when, in reality, their use is to identify the membership of each segment.

# Developing micro-segments

A reminder: For projects which include current decision-makers and potential decision-makers, this book now uses the term 'decision-maker' to refer to both.

Definition reminder: A micro-segment is a group of decision-makers who share a similar level of interest in a specific set of features.

In this section we look at how to develop a representative sample of all the different decision-makers you have included in your segmentation project by utilizing data already available from within, or easily accessible to your company. This sample will consist of a number of micro-segments, each of which will be based on a distinct group of decision-makers in your market. In arriving at this model of the market, you may need to involve a cross-section of representatives from sales, marketing, customer services, customer enquiries, ordering and distribution. Revisiting appropriate past market surveys may also provide valuable input, so involving someone familiar with what these surveys contain can be especially useful. In addition, including representatives from selected intermediaries because of the contact they have with customers has proved useful to a number of projects.

To recap briefly, each micro-segment consists of:

1 a specific set of key discriminating features (KDFs) in which there is a similar level of interest shared by the decision-makers the micro-segment represents;
2 one or more profiling characteristics that identify who these decision-makers are;
3 a volume or value figure to indicate its size (discussed later in this section).

In developing micro-segments for your market, you will almost certainly end up with too many in number to consider each of them as a possible segment in their own right. You could well end up with around twenty or possibly around thirty micro-segments at the end of this step, though on extremely rare occasions the number has been higher. It is worth noting, however, that for most of the in-company segmentation projects the authors have been involved in, the number of micro-segments seen as necessary to represent the different decision-makers in a market has usually been less than twenty.

As regards the number of micro-segments a market should have for this stage of the project, there is no simple answer. It is whatever number is required to represent the different decision-makers in the defined market.

> There is no simple answer to the question about the number of micro-segments a market should have for this stage of the project. It is whatever number is required to represent the different decision-makers in the defined market.

---

This is an appropriate point at which to remind ourselves that the individual size of the micro-segments often means that they are too small to qualify as distinct segments and, therefore, justify the cost of developing specific offers for them. In addition, micro-segments are based on features, while segments are based on needs. Reviewing the micro-segments after their features have been replaced by the needs they satisfy, which we look at later in the process, allows like-minded micro-segments to be brought together to form segments which, by its very nature, means that the number of concluding segments is more manageable.

**Marketing insight**

---

Just in case your project looks as if it is developing an unmanageable number of micro-segments and you therefore need to scale it back, there is a section later in this chapter called 'Managing micro-segments – keeping control' which you can refer to.

---

Each completed interview for a segmentation project can be equated with the general concept of a micro-segment in that they represent the different decision-makers in the market as a whole.

**Market research note**

---

## Getting micro-segments up and running

It is crucial to remind yourself and the segmentation team that:

- micro-segments are based on actual decision-makers, not fictional individuals;
- they represent the defined market as a whole, not just your own customers;
- their KDFs are from the market as a whole, not simply limited to the features you and your particular intermediaries offer; and,
- their KDFs are what they see as important, not what you would prefer them to see as important.

Therefore, the approach to take when developing micro-segments is to put yourself in the shoes of a customer and evaluate the features from their perspective.

**Marketing insight**

Please note that in order to put on another person's shoes, you first have to remove your own!

The procedure to follow when developing micro-segments can be summarized as follows:

1 Divide the market into identifiable groups of customers you can visualize and talk about (preliminary segments are a good starting point here) as this equips you with useful points of reference for developing micro-segments, and size each of these 'reference groups'.

2 Take one of these reference groups, familiarize yourself with the individuals it represents and develop it into a micro-segment by carefully listing what the customers in this group regard as their KDFs, with any differences within the group captured as separate micro-segments.

3 Now attempt to indicate the relative importance of each KDF to the micro-segment(s) using a simple grading structure initially based on, for example, one to three stars.

4 Consider a cross-section of customers included in a micro-segment to confirm if they would all generally agree with the list of KDFs and their grading, and if they would not, develop additional micro-segments to cover any meaningful differences.

5 Verify each micro-segment by checking that it is based on actual decision-makers, its reality check, further verified by checking that its KDFs either represent a known transaction, or actually make sense.

6 Attach profiling characteristics to each micro-segment and use a simple grading structure to indicate what proportion of its customers each characteristic applies to with, for example, three or four tick marks identifying characteristics applicable to all of them.

7 Size each micro-segment, by referring back to the reference group it originated from and utilizing any market figures that may be available.

Repeat steps two to seven of this procedure for each group of customers until they have all been converted into micro-segments and then review each micro-segment against the complete list of KDFs and make any appropriate additions to the KDFs that have been listed for them.

Finally, review and compare the finished micro-segments with each other and increase or decrease the importance of appropriate KDFs if this better reflects the differences between individual micro-segments. If you come across duplicate micro-segments, the duplicates can be merged only if their intended end-use is the same and you believe the benefits they are looking for are the same (which may require you to wait until the next step).

**Marketing insight**

An often incorrectly held belief is that one company's customers form a microcosm of the market as a whole and can therefore be regarded as forming a representative sample of the complete market. Slipping into this belief without some independent validation could well result in the company failing to identify new opportunities in their market.

However, even if you know that the micro-segments you develop will not truly represent the market as a whole, it is still worth progressing the project through this and the following two process steps (Steps 4 and 5). This will enable you to gain an appreciation of what is involved in the segmentation process as a whole and provide a better informed and much more productive brief for the more statistically sound study which should follow.

Taking each step of the above procedure in turn:

1  Divide the market into identifiable groups of customers.

It usually helps when developing micro-segments to first divide the customers being segmented into recognizable groups of individuals that you and your team can visualize and talk about. Grouping customers in this way equips you with useful points of reference for developing micro-segments, and working with such 'reference groups' is far better than starting from an entity called 'the market'. If you have already divided the market being segmented into preliminary segments, these clearly form, or at least provide the basis for, such reference groups and you should develop micro-segments for each of them. You may want to break down the preliminary segments further if this helps associate them with particular groups of customers.

The complete hierarchy we are suggesting is presented in Figure 6.3.

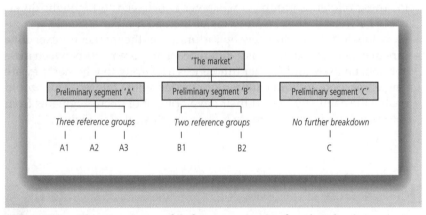

**Figure 6.3**   The structure of reference groups for developing micro-segments
(*Note:* If you have not introduced preliminary segments into your project, each reference group would originate from 'The market'. For projects with preliminary segments, referring to them is made easier if they are each now given a letter in addition to any name given to them in the previous chapter. If preliminary segments are then broken down into smaller groups of customers, each individual group can then be labelled in a way that links it to the preliminary segment it originated from, as is shown by the use of A1, A2 and so on. This provides a quick and easy way of identifying for each concluding segment the source of its customers. The addition of a name to each reference group which currently only has a label may help you identify with, and relate to the customers it represents. As for naming preliminary segments, it helps if this name reflects who is being represented by the reference group.)

**Marketing insight**

When breaking down a market, or preliminary segment, into reference groups you can either:

1 start by identifying all the reference groups, and then develop micro-segments for each one in turn; or,
2 identify one group and develop micro-segments for it, then identify another group and develop its micro-segments, and repeat this until you believe all the customers have been covered.

Adopt the approach you feel most comfortable in following.

The guideline for selecting the criteria on which to base these reference groups is to use whatever enables you to visualize particular customers and see the KDFs from their perspective. We would suggest, however, that in order to re-enforce the point that you are referring to individuals, the criteria should be based on either some standard profiling attribute such as size of company, size of family, age, type of company, type of family, geographic location and so on, or on some other criteria that equally links it to a particular group of customers, such as differences in the volume used, which could simply be broken down into large, medium and small users. What often determines the choice of criteria for these reference groups is whatever is believed to highlight differences between customers in terms of their KDFs. For example, a company looking to develop new opportunities in the market for executive cars may believe that there is a difference in requirements between male and female users and further differences according to whether they are single, married without children or married with children. This would enable the company to start their development of micro-segments from six easily identifiable reference groups, as illustrated in Figure 6.4.

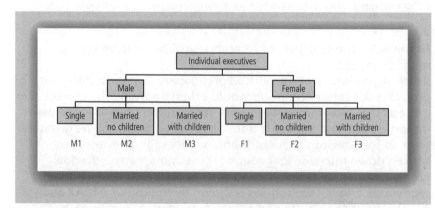

**Figure 6.4** Reference groups for developing micro-segments (*Note:* M1, M2 and so on are the identification labels for each reference group. In this example, using 'M' and 'F' in the labels clearly associates each reference group with where it originated from.)

An alternative to using profiling attributes as a basis for the reference groups could be to use specific features, especially features that tend to dominate the choice of competing products. Choose whichever you feel most comfortable in using.

Because the resulting reference groups originate from preliminary segments or the market as a whole, and they will already have been given a value or volume figure, it is an appropriate point at which to distribute this figure between the reference groups as best as you can. This will help in sizing the final micro-segments later.

---

If you are segmenting a market in which there are a limited number of customers (how you define 'limited' may depend on time and resource available to the project), you may wish to create a micro-segment for each individual customer and proceed through the next steps at this individual customer level.

**Marketing insight**

---

2  Develop each group into a micro-segment by listing its KDFs.

Select one of these groups and begin by putting yourself into their shoes and familiarizing yourself with the customers it represents. Discussing such topics as the type of life they lead (family, social, work), their personal situation and responsibilities, the issues that concern them, their background and their aspirations for the future can all help bring a reference group to life. This discussion may also highlight characteristics that can be used later as part of their profile.

Now, develop this group into a micro-segment by carefully listing the features that the customers in this group particularly look for and use to discriminate between competing propositions in your market (the KDFs), with any differences within the group captured as separate micro-segments. In addition to knowing what they look for, also knowing what they reject and what causes disappointment can help in compiling the relevant list of features. If you elected to draw up a full list of features in preparation for this stage, simply select these KDFs by reference to that list. If, on the other hand, you are using the development of micro-segments progressively to compile the list of KDFs, organizing this list along the lines suggested earlier in this chapter can be helpful. A worksheet for this part of the process appears in the Exercises section of this chapter. Table 6.7 illustrates a suggested layout for recording micro-segments and their KDFs.

> In addition to knowing what individuals particularly look for, also knowing what they reject and what causes disappointment can help identify the KDFs.

Whenever more than one micro-segment emerges from a single reference group, remember to attach an identifier to each of them along the lines you have adopted for your project. If this includes a name, ensure that the names continue to reflect who each micro-segment represents.

For this step, and those that follow, consider splitting the participants into a number of teams, with each team adopting the standpoint of a particular reference group.

**Table 6.7** Recording micro-segments and their KDFs

| Feature category | Group | Specification | Micro-segments | | | | |
|---|---|---|---|---|---|---|---|
| | | | A1 | A2 | B | C1 | C2 |
| 'What' | Finish | Dark hardwoods | ✓ | | | | |
| | | Light hardwoods | | ✓ | | | |
| | | Pine | | | ✓ | ✓ | |
| | | To paint/stain | | | | | ✓ |
| | Country of origin | Scandinavia | ✓ | | ✓ | | |
| | | UK | | | | | ✓ |
| | Format | DIY kits | | | | ✓ | |
| | | Made up | ✓ | ✓ | ✓ | | |
| 'Where' | Retailer | Department store | ✓ | ✓ | | | |
| | | Direct mail | | | | ✓ | |
| | | Sheds | | | | | ✓ |

*Note:* Rather than using a tick mark (✓) to indicate which features are the KDFs for each micro-segment you could use a star (*). As you will see in the above, A2 and C1 have no KDF related to the country of origin, B has no KDF related to retailers and C2 has no KDF related to the format. 'Sheds' is the name sometimes used to refer to hardware superstores.

**Marketing insight**

Using a spreadsheet or database package on a PC is particularly helpful for this part of the process. The PC-based segmentation package developed in association with the authors can be used here.[3]

3 Indicate the relative importance of the KDFs for each micro-segment.
Once you have agreed the KDFs for a particular micro-segment, indicate their relative importance to each other for that micro-segment, thereby indicating their level of interest in this specific set of features (as per the definition). The simplest way of indicating the relative importance of the KDFs is to increase the number of tick marks or stars given to each of them. This is illustrated in Table 6.8. At this stage it helps if you use no more than three tick marks or stars to identify the most important KDFs. This is because when you later review and compare the finished micro-segments with each other, you may feel that you have not adequately indicated the differences between them and need to increase, or decrease, the importance of certain KDFs for individual micro-segments to redress this. It helps if you can add further tick marks or stars without turning the 'picture' into a visual nightmare. You really need to avoid having too many stars in front of your eyes!
If you do not feel able to indicate the relative importance of KDFs for micro-segments, simply leave them as they were, each with a single tick mark or star (as in Table 6.7), thereby implying that they have the same

[3] Details of this package, called Market Segment Master®, can be obtained from Ian Dunbar using info@marketsegmentation.co.uk. Full contact details can be found in the Preface of this book.

**Table 6.8** Indicating the relative importance of KDFs to micro-segments

| Feature category | Group | Specification | Micro-segments | | | | |
|---|---|---|---|---|---|---|---|
| | | | A1 | A2 | B | C1 | C2 |
| 'What' | Finish | Dark hardwoods | *** | | | | |
| | | Light hardwoods | | ** | | | |
| | | Pine | | | ** | * | |
| | | To paint/stain | | | | | *** |
| | Country of origin | Scandinavia | ** | | * | | |
| | | UK | | | | | * |
| | Format | DIY kits | | | | * | |
| | | Made up | *** | *** | *** | | |
| 'Where' | Retailer | Department store | * | * | | | |
| | | Direct mail | | | | *** | |
| | | Sheds | | | | | ** |

*Note:* The most important KDFs are identified by three stars (***) in this table.

level of interest in their specific set of features. This does not prevent you from progressing to the next stage of the segmentation process, though these indications of importance are useful to this stage.

---

Once a micro-segment is associated with a specific set of features along with their level of interest in these features, it meets the definition of a 'micro-segment'.

Marketing
insight

---

4 Confirm that the customers in the micro-segment all generally agree. Although you have developed a micro-segment based on a recognizable group of individuals interested in a particular set of features, it is suggested that you now consider a cross-section of the customers this micro-segment represents to confirm that they would all *generally* agree with what is currently being said about them. By 'generally agree' we mean that they would positively respond to an offer based on the KDFs listed for them. This clearly has to be a matter of judgement at this point.

In those situations where you believe they would not all generally agree, develop new micro-segments to accommodate any meaningful differences. Attach identification labels to each new micro-segment which continue the practice you have adopted for your project, ensuring, once again, that any names retain their association with the individuals each micro-segment represents. This may require you to revise the name of the originating micro-segment if this would better describe who it now represents.

---

If in doubt, split them out! They will be reviewed again later.

Marketing
insight

5  Verify each micro-segment.

Although the first guideline for developing micro-segments is to ensure that they are based on actual decision-makers, as opposed to fictional individuals, it has been known for some projects occasionally to lose sight of the real world during this stage of the process. A useful reality check is to challenge the team to put forward their understanding of who the micro-segment is representing (which will provide details for its profiling). This can be further verified by simply looking through a micro-segment's KDFs to check that such a combination is either known to occur, and therefore represents an existing transaction, or actually makes sense. For example, if in the market represented by Table 6.8 it was known that when individuals wanted to paint or stain an item themselves they only ever bought UK products, any micro-segment showing that they bought Scandinavian products would be rejected.

> A segmentation project conducted by a components manufacturer initially generated just under 150 micro-segments, but when challenged to match these micro-segments to transactions known to take place in their market, the number of micro-segments dropped substantially (by just over 80 per cent) to a much more manageable number.
>
> What had happened was that micro-segments were being generated to cover *possible* combinations of KDFs rather than being based on customers and the *actual* KDF combinations that occurred.

6  Attach profiling characteristics to each micro-segment.

For each completed micro-segment, add some details about who it represents using applicable profiling characteristics, along with their outlet and channel preferences. Because specific profiling characteristics and distribution alternatives may not be applicable to every customer in a micro-segment, for example they may not all be in the same age range or use the same retail outlet, use a scale to indicate the proportion of customers associated with each of the alternatives. Once again, use your best judgement. If you are not sure about the proportions, just indicate each profiling characteristic, outlet and channel that is applicable. You can once again use tick marks or stars for this, but it makes it clearer if it is the opposite symbol to that used to indicate the KDFs, as illustrated in Table 6.9. The worksheet for developing micro-segments in the Exercises section of this chapter also covers profiling.

## Marketing insight

Try to ensure that each micro-segment has profiling characteristics selected from all the profiling groups you are using. This will be appreciated later during the analysis of segments when you are looking for the personal attributes that can be used to identify the customers in each of them.

**Table 6.9**  Adding profiling characteristics to micro-segments

| Feature category | Group | Specification | Micro-segments | | | | |
|---|---|---|---|---|---|---|---|
| | | | A1 | A2 | B | C1 | C2 |
| 'What' | Finish | Dark hardwoods | *** | | | | |
| | | Light hardwoods | | ** | | | |
| | | Pine | | | ** | * | |
| | | To paint/stain | | | | | *** |
| *... and so on* | | *... and so on* | | | | | |

| Profiling category | Group | Specification | | | | | |
|---|---|---|---|---|---|---|---|
| Demographic | Age | Up to 30 | | ✓ | ✓ | ✓✓ | ✓✓ |
| | | 31 to 50 | ✓ | ✓ | ✓✓ | ✓ | ✓ |
| | | 51 and over | ✓✓ | ✓ | | | |
| | Socio-economic group | 1a and 1b | ✓ | | | | |
| | | 2 and 3 | ✓✓ | ✓✓ | ✓ | ✓ | |
| | | 4 and 5 | | ✓ | ✓✓ | ✓ | ✓ |
| | | 6 to 8 | | | | ✓ | ✓✓ |
| | Family stage | Single | | ✓ | ✓ | ✓ | ✓ |
| | | Married no kids | ✓✓✓ | ✓✓ | ✓ | | |
| | | Married and kids | | | ✓ | ✓✓ | ✓✓ |
| Acquisition routes | Outlet | Department store | ✓✓✓ | ✓✓✓ | ✓ | | |
| | | Specialist | | | ✓✓ | ✓ | |
| | | Shed | | | | | ✓✓✓ |
| | | Catalogue co. | | | | ✓✓ | |
| | Channel | Face-to-face | ✓✓✓ | ✓✓ | ✓ | | ✓✓✓ |
| | | Direct – tel. & mail | | ✓ | ✓✓ | ✓✓ | |
| | | Direct – internet | | | | ✓ | |

*Note:* The distribution of a micro-segment between the alternative characteristics in each profiling group has to be looked at separately. Three tick marks (✓✓✓) are used in this table to indicate characteristics applicable to all the customers represented by a micro-segment.

It sometimes helps when profiling a micro-segment to consider the characteristics you would associate with the preliminary segment it came from (assuming this is how it originated), as some if not all of these characteristics could have been inherited by the micro-segment. It also helps to consider if any of the KDFs could be associated with any particular profiling characteristics. For example, customers who use certain retailers may be associated with particular socio-economic groups, a certain type of IT support package may be associated with customers from smaller companies, and individuals who select marketing books designed to help practitioners put marketing into practice may be associated with particular types of jobs.

Do not be concerned if you are associating a micro-segment with a number of specific characteristics from a single profiling group, such as two or three age bands as seen in Table 6.9. What we are looking for here is a full profile of each micro-segment so that your project has the best opportunity of finding the specific characteristics that can be associated with each concluding segment.

It is also possible to use 'other interests and product usage' as part of the profiling if they are known, or suspected to correlate with different needs. However, care needs to be taken when including these in the customer attributes and it is suggested that readers refer back to 'Profiling – additional categories' for guidelines.

7 Size the micro-segment.

It is important for later stages of the process to have a volume or value figure attached to each micro-segment, especially as these figures will be used to determine the size of each concluding segment. You may, of course, already be in a position where you can attach a volume or value figure to each micro-segment, but if this is not the case, the following may assist you.

The most obvious starting point for sizing micro-segments is the reference group they originated from and to apportion to each micro-segment the amount they would account for in their group.

> When there are no sources of information available to help you, assume that the micro-segments developed for a particular reference group are equal in size.

At the simplest level, this apportioning could be achieved by dividing the total given to the reference group equally between its micro-segments. You may, however, believe you can be a little more sophisticated than this, either because you feel sure that certain micro-segments are larger than others, with the apportionment based on your best guess, or there is information to hand that may help determine these figures.

There may be, for example, some profiling differences between the micro-segments, such as age or size of company, that enable you to determine the ratio of one micro-segment to another based on published national statistics. You may even be fortunate enough to be segmenting a market for which there are annual figures about the different products sold into that market or about the sales made through different outlets or through channels. If this is the case, you could check your micro-segment totals for these products, assuming they have appeared as KDFs, or their totals for the different outlets and channels. Depending on how close the figures match up, you may feel that some adjustments are or are not required.

Referring to Table 6.9 and using this as an example: if this market was valued at 2000 units and there was published information available that illustrated how this was divided between the four types of distribution outlet, you could work out from the micro-segment profiles, along with their proposed size, the total amounts you were suggesting came through these outlets. Micro-segment B, for example, is showing one-third of its purchases coming through department stores and two-thirds coming through specialists, so if your suggested size of this segment was 300 units you could allocate this total between these two outlets using the ratio 1 : 2. By applying this reasoning to all the micro-segments you would be able to work out what your totals were for the four outlets. You could then compare your totals to the published totals, and if you needed to make any changes, you would now at least have a feel for the scale of the adjustments to be made. Pinpoint accuracy, however, is not required and an informed approximation will be sufficient.

In carrying out the above, you may find that the original figures you gave to your reference groups, and, if applicable, the preliminary segments before them, should be changed. Clearly this would only be a problem if these figures had been developed from reliable data to start with as opposed to your best estimate at the time.

It is crucial that research conducted for the quantitative stage of segmentation is structured so that the concluding segments can be sized.

**Market research note**

Now repeat steps two to seven for each group of customers.

It helps if you occasionally remind the team as they work through the micro-segments that:

**Marketing insight**

- micro-segments are based on actual decision-makers, not fictional individuals;
- they represent the defined market as a whole, not just your own customers;
- their KDFs are from the market as a whole, not simply limited to the features you and your particular intermediaries offer; and,
- their KDFs are what they see as important, not what you would prefer them to see as important.

Once all the reference groups have been converted into micro-segments, you can review each micro-segment against the complete list of KDFs and make any necessary changes to the KDFs that have been listed for them. It is possible that, as you have progressively been developing micro-segments, new KDFs have been identified that may be applicable to micro-segments developed earlier.

Finally, review and compare the finished micro-segments with each other to ensure that you have adequately indicated the differences between them in terms of the importance of their various KDFs. Where required, increase or decrease the importance of appropriate KDFs for individual micro-segments to redress any 'imbalances' and better reflect the differences between them. It is suggested, however, that no more than five stars (or tick marks) are used to highlight the most important KDFs, as this will ensure that the final picture remains visually comprehensible.

If you come across duplicate micro-segments, the duplicates can be merged only if you feel confident that:

- the micro-segments have the same intended end-use for their purchase; and,
- they are looking for the same benefits from their KDFs.

Checking the second requirement, however, may need to wait until the next step in the process. It is not unknown for different customers to have varying views about the benefits delivered by a particular feature, and a possible indicator of this is if the individuals in the duplicate micro-segments are quite different from each other in terms of who they are. Therefore, whenever the individuals they represent are quite different from each other, it is safer to retain the duplicate micro-segments at this stage.

When duplicate micro-segments are merged, this clearly requires their profiling characteristics and sizes to be combined; in addition, it is useful to give the 'new' micro-segment an identification label that reflects what has occurred. The simplest way of doing this is to give it the labels of its predecessors. These labels, as pointed out earlier, provide a quick and easy way of identifying for each concluding segment the source of its customers.

## Managing micro-segments – keeping control

The principal controlling mechanism for companies segmenting their market using data available from within, or easily accessible to the company and to the segmentation project team, is to check that their micro-segments match with reality.

A further series of checks can be based on the features that are listed for the micro-segments:

- Do any micro-segments contain features which are basic entry requirements?
  This was discussed in the 'KDF guidelines' section earlier in this chapter under point 3. Remove these features and then check if this now means there are micro-segments that duplicate one another. Duplicate micro-segments can be removed as per the guidelines at the end of the previous section.
- Are you sure the features reflect how customers categorize them and buy them?
  This was point 4 of the 'KDF guidelines'. By revising micro-segments better to reflect the way customers consider the features and talk about them you may find that duplicate micro-segments appear which can be removed.
- Have you merged correlated features?
  Micro-segments that differ by features that are in fact correlated, point 7 of the 'KDF guidelines', should be revised and the duplication check carried out.

● Do any micro-segments contain features that are only marginal in their importance?

Although only a simple grading structure has been suggested for indicating the relative importance of features to a micro-segment, it may be that by applying a little more sophistication to this grading you can identify features that are really only playing a very small role in the purchase decision and can be removed. You could also consider applying the 80/20 rule as suggested in point 8 of the 'KDF guidelines' to all your micro-segments. Once again, if this now produces duplicate micro-segments, the duplicates can be removed as per the guidelines at the end of the previous section.

If, after following the above, you still find the number of micro-segments rather daunting, the following may finally bring them under control.

● Combine micro-segments that are known to be unattractive to your company.

This removes such micro-segments from the detailed analysis which follows this chapter but does not remove them completely from the process, because to do so would distort the picture of the market being looked at. How you define 'unattractive' is a topic we indirectly address later in this book when we consider how to prioritize and select segments for Steps 6 and 7 of the segmentation process. Great care should be taken when removing micro-segments from the detailed analysis in this way. *Micro-segments may be unattractive today, but could well form the attractive segments of tomorrow*. For example:

– some micro-segments may be currently unattractive because no company has put together the right offer to stimulate demand from this particular group and/or generate the required margins from it;

– some micro-segments may be unattractive today because they account for only a very small volume or value of business, but this may be because they are at an early stage of their development.

Individually, micro-segments may represent only a small quantity in the market, but their requirements may be the same as those of other micro-segments. Later stages of the process would see these micro-segments combined and, as a segment, they may then represent a significant quantity of the market. This possibility, therefore, should be borne in mind before removing micro-segments from the detailed analysis based on their size.

If it is necessary to reduce the number of micro-segments as described here in order to progress to the next step in the process, the resulting group of micro-segments can always be revisited later, an option you may have to consider when looking for opportunities to achieve the company's revenue targets.

You should now have around twenty, or possibly around thirty micro-segments, each of which represents a distinct group of decision-makers in your market and which forms the sample for the next stage of your project. If, however, this is not the case and the number is substantially higher, it could be worth reviewing your market definition, as it may, in fact, be too broad.

Finally, if despite all of these checks you are still having to consider a large number of micro-segments, it may help in progressing the project if, when entering the final stage of the next step which indicates the importance of the needs-based buying criteria for each micro-segment, you initially take around thirty of them through this particular sequence and then through the subsequent step (Step 5), 'Forming Segments'. Once this initial batch has been through Step 5, repeat this sequence for further batches of micro-segments, not forgetting to consider each new batch taken into Step 5 alongside the market segments already established in that step.

# Process check

The primary purpose of this, the third step in the segmentation process, is to provide guidelines on how an in-company segmentation team can develop a representative sample of decision-makers for their market using internal resources. In doing so, it identifies the features which customers look for when deciding between competing offers and captures information about the decision-makers themselves which describes who they are and their acquisition routes. This detail provides critical links to other steps in the process:

- The features are used to develop an understanding of why decision-makers select the products and services they specify, thus converting behaviour into motivation, which, in turn, becomes the basis on which segments are formed.
- The information about the decision-makers is used to determine how you reach the customers found in each of the concluding segments, as this is important for the successful targeting of segment-specific offers and is, therefore, a key question in the segmentation checklist used to validate the final segments.

This step, therefore, is a major stage in the segmentation process and requires a great deal of careful thought.

We began by briefly discussing how distinct groups of decision-makers in your market can be represented by 'micro-segments' and summarized the three components that make up a micro-segment, namely features, profiling attributes and a volume or value figure. We also highlighted that the uniqueness of a micro-segment is that when determining which of the alternative offers is to be bought, the decision-makers it represents demonstrate a similar level of interest in a specific set of features. It was pointed out that issues to do with size and the fact that it was based on features, as opposed to needs, were the reasons for using the term 'micro-segment'.

A detailed section then looked at the features that are of interest to a segmentation project, the 'Key Discriminating Features' (KDFs), sometimes referred to as 'determiners' or 'differentiators', and began by emphasizing that it is essential that these features are looked at from the customer's perspective, not your own. It was pointed out that you could either develop KDFs initially by drawing up a list of *all* the features available across the market, with those selected from this list for the micro-segments becoming the KDFs, or progressively compile the list of KDFs while developing the micro-segments. We then suggested a structure for organizing the features and presented eight important guidelines to follow, their purpose being to ensure that the features you select for the micro-segments provide the required link to the next step in the process. This was followed by a brief review of the four categories that make up the KDFs, namely 'what' is bought, 'where' it is bought, 'when' and 'how' it is bought.

To conclude the section on features, we pointed out that at this stage of the process it was *not* appropriate to associate customers with the degree of focus they may have on 'price' and that this topic was best left to the next step. However, we did use this as an opportunity to emphasise that if your market was one in which some customers considered lifetime costs and others considered only the initial purchase price, features should be included which reflect these differences.

We then looked at the issue of customer profiling and highlighted its importance in later stages of the project. We also took this opportunity to point out that, even if the association between a segment and the profile of its members proves to be difficult, it does not spell the end of your needs-based segmentation project. Four ways round this difficulty were presented, one of which we suggested you include as part of a micro-segment's profiling, namely the outlets and channels they use.

The discussion on profiling then moved on to suggesting that it was better to attach a number of profiling descriptors to each micro-segment, as opposed to a single type of descriptor, such as age or company size, as this improves the success of identifying customers by their segment. We then summarized the four main profiling categories, namely 'demographic', 'geographic', geodemographic' and 'psychographic', and suggested a structure for organizing the profiling data. Two additional profiling categories were introduced, one of which has already been mentioned, namely the outlets and channels used by customers, with the other looking at the possibility of including other interests and product usage, though care needs to be exercised if this is a profiling category you elect to use. We closed the section on profiling by emphasizing that the profiling attributes selected need to be practical and therefore ones which you can use in your sales and marketing activity to identify customers

With the scene setting now complete, we then presented the seven steps to follow when developing micro-segments. This started with dividing the market into identifiable groups of customers you can visualize and talk about (reference groups), then identifying their KDFs and grading them, checking that everyone in the micro-segment would agree with what is being said about them, conducting a reality check, profiling the micro-segment and finally sizing the micro-segment. We also suggested that the approach to take when developing micro-segments is to put yourself in the shoes of a customer and evaluate the features from their perspective, with a note to emphasize that in order to put on another person's shoes, you first have to remove your own!

Finally, we put forward suggestions on how to keep micro-segments under control to help ensure that you complete this step with a manageable number of them.

Careful and thoughtful consideration of the segmentation steps presented so far, assisted by a healthy dose of realism, will ensure your company is ready to take its project into the next step.

## Case study

As you may recall, the segmentation team at Agrofertilizer Supplies have decided to include in their segmentation project both those farmers who do and those who do not currently decide on which product to buy. They have also divided the farmers into three preliminary segments based on the primary focus of the farmer's business, namely 'Arable', 'Grassland' and 'Mixed'.

Given that the project is now at a stage where understanding the customers in the market is becoming increasingly important, it is worth noting that throughout the project the team spoke to members of the sales force on a number of occasions. In addition, for all but one of the team, the very nature of their positions, both at the time of the project and in the past, along with the length of time in the company, meant that they had met and talked to a wide variety of farmers.

The team decided that they would start by drawing up a list of all the features in their market which they would then refer to, and possibly add to, as they developed micro-segments for each of the three preliminary segments.

The potential list of features to be considered by the team was quite large. The company itself had over forty products on its list. However, when these lists were looked at from the customers' point of view, they could be simplified quite substantially and with confidence. For example, although most bags of fertilizer contain three different fertilizer components which can be mixed (blended) in a wide variety of ratios, farmers tended to distinguish between the blends according to whether they were part of a range, therefore made up and bagged by the manufacturers (manufactured blends), or whether the farmer had specified the ratio they wanted and had the blend made up specifically for them (bespoke blends). It is rather like paint: paint can be bought in a particular colour and used as it is, or a customer can request a specific colour to be made up for them.

In addition to the blends, farmers also bought one of the fertilizer components (nitrogen) on its own, nitrogen being the nutrient in most demand by the crops. Nitrogen could be bought in one of two forms, ammonium nitrate (AN) or Urea.

Farmers were therefore seen to buy one of four product combinations:

1  AN and manufactured blends
2  AN and bespoke blends
3  Urea and manufactured blends
4  Urea and bespoke blends

Thus, by putting themselves into their customer's shoes a large range of product types could be captured quite simply.

Other features were also looked at from the farmers' point of view and adjusted accordingly. For example, fertilizers could be purchased from three different types of distributor (national, independent or the co-operative), as well as from an importer or direct from the manufacturer. However, the three different types of distributor tended to be subsumed under the general description of 'local' distributor, regardless of ownership. The resulting feature list appears in Table 6.10.

**Table 6.10** Feature list for the case study

| Category | Group | Specification |
|---|---|---|
| What | Product | AN and manufactured blends; AN and bespoke blends; Urea and manufactured blends; Urea and bespoke blends |
| | Package | 50 kg; 500 kg |
| | Brand | Well-established; Any brand |
| | Quality | High consistency; Any quality |
| | Concentration | High nitrogen level; Low nitrogen level |
| | Consultants/services | Manufacturer's; Distributor's; Independent |
| | Publication | Specialist technical; General |
| Where | Channel | Local distributor; Importer; Direct from the manufacturer |
| When | Frequency | As required; Bulk in advance |
| How | Payment method | Standard terms; Long-term finance from the manufacturer; Long-term finance from the bank |

*Note:* 'Quality' referred to the consistency of fertilizer granule size with no lumps or very fine (dusty) particles and the consistency of nutrients throughout the granules (nitrogen, N, phosphate, P, and potash, K; NPK). It is also worth noting that consultancy, along with some agronomic services, was often available from the manufacturers and distributors at no charge. Even so, many farmers preferred to pay for independent advice while others chose not to use these facilities from any supplier.

The next stage was to develop micro-segments for the market using each of the three preliminary segments as reference groups. The team selected a preliminary segment and began by having a general discussion about the farmers it represented, covering such topics as the way they ran their farms, the issues they faced, the different characters they had come across, what had happened to this type of farming over the past decade and what the future appeared to hold for it. Once they had immersed themselves into a preliminary segment it became clear that the general feature list they had compiled contained items that contributed very little to a farmer's decision on which competing offer to buy. They therefore decided to tidy up the list by applying the 80/20 rule to the feature groups, though this clearly does not prevent them from selecting one of the 'discarded' features if a micro-segment requires it. The result of this exercise for the grassland preliminary segment appears in Table 6.11.

To arrive at the figures in Table 6.11, the team first identified what they believed was the most important feature group for the preliminary segment – there were in fact two of them,

**Table 6.11** Prioritizing feature groups for a preliminary segment in the case study

| Feature group | Initial individual score | Total | Reworked individual score | Cumulative score |
|---|---|---|---|---|
| 'What' – product | 80 | | 20 | 20 |
| 'What' – brand | 80 | | 20 | 40 |
| 'What' – quality | 60 | | 15 | 55 |
| 'Where' – channel | 60 | | 15 | 70 |
| 'What' – concentration | 40 | | 10 | 80 |
| 'What' – consultant/svc | 30 | | 8 | 88 |
| 'When' – frequency | 20 | | 5 | 93 |
| 'How' – payment | 10 | | 3 | 96 |
| 'What' – publication | 8 | | 2 | 98 |
| 'What' – package | 8 | 396 | 2 | 100 |

*Note:* The dotted line indicates the suggested cut-off point. Given the closeness of the scores for 'concentration' and 'consultant/svc' (consultants/services – see Table 6.10) it would be perfectly in order to drop the cut-off point to 88.

**Table 6.12** A selection of micro-segments and their KDFs for a preliminary segment in the case study

| Feature group | Specification | Micro-segments | | | | |
|---|---|---|---|---|---|---|
| | | G1 | G4 | G8 | G9 | G12 |
| 'What' | AN & manufactured blends | *** | ** | * | | |
| – product | AN & bespoke blends | | | | ** | |
| | Urea & bespoke blends | | | | | *** |
| – brand | Well-established | * | ** | | * | |
| – quality | High consistency | *** | * | | | |
| – concentration | High nitrogen | ** | | ** | ** | ** |
| | Low nitrogen | | *** | | | |
| – consultants/ | Manufacturer's | * | | | * | |
| services | Distributor's | | * | | | |
| | Independent details | | | | | |
| 'Where' | Local distributor | * | *** | | * | * |
| – channel | Importer | | | *** | | |

*Note:* The most important KDFs are identified by three stars (***) in this table. G1, G4 and so on are the identification labels for each micro-segment, with 'G' indicating that they originated from the Grassland preliminary segment (the letters 'A' and 'M' were used for the Arable and Mixed preliminary segments respectively). This table only shows the KDFs for the micro-segments in the grassland preliminary segment which, as you will have noticed, includes 'consultants/services' (please refer to Table 6.11). Although 'Independent consultants/services' appears redundant in this table it was in fact a KDF for one of the other grassland micro-segments. The full list of KDFs for the market included 'Urea and manufactured blends' along with the 'Direct' channel.

'product' and 'brand' – and gave each of these feature groups a score out of 100 to represent their importance to the farmers. The next most important feature group was then selected and given a score that reflected its relative importance to those already on the list. This was repeated until all the feature groups had been given a score, as illustrated in the table. These scores were then added up and the total came to 396, but in order to apply the 80/20 rule it is easier if they total 100. In order to reset these scores so that when added together they came to 100, each individual score was divided by the total of 396 and the answer multiplied by 100.

The initial discussion about each preliminary segment also highlighted to the team that the farmers in these reference groups were not all the same. They therefore developed their micro-segments from more precisely defined reference groups, adding to these groups as they progressed with their analysis until they were satisfied that they had covered all the farmers. A selection of the micro-segments developed for the grassland preliminary segment and their KDFs appear in Table 6.12.

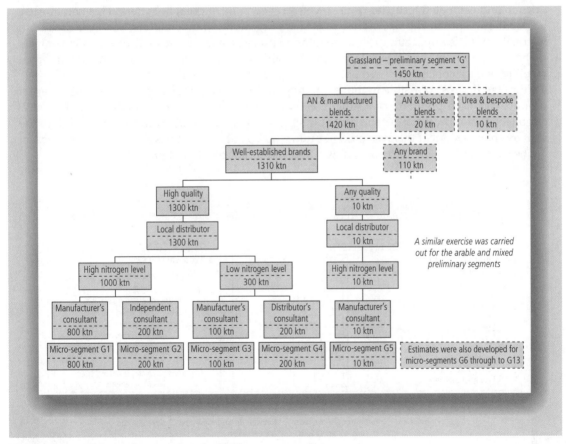

**Figure 6.5**  Sizing micro-segments in the case study
(*Note:* To construct a cascade along the lines in this figure it helps if you include 'features' such as 'Any quality', 'Any brand', 'Any colour' and so on to cover the customers who do not have an interest in particular features. Both 'Any quality' and 'Any brand' have been used in the above cascade.)

A total of 13 micro-segments were identified for the grassland preliminary segment, a further 17 for the arable preliminary segment and a final four to represent farmers in the mixed preliminary segment, a total of 34. Although this number was at the high end, the team were confident that all 34 represented actual farmers in the market. In hindsight, however, the number could have been lower as they had differentiated between some farmers on the basis of features that played only a minor role in their decision and, therefore, were not KDFs, a fact picked up when the team looked at the real needs of the farmers (the next step in the process). Even so, this still meant that the team had covered the full range of farmers in their market (later verified by market research).

Attached to each micro-segment were a number of profiling characteristics such as size of farm, the farmer's formal level of agricultural training, level of investment, production focus (a more detailed breakdown of 'arable', 'grassland' and 'mixed'), farming style and some personality descriptions. Of these, there was a particular interest in seeing whether farm size and training could be used to distinguish between segments but, in the end, neither of these characteristics could be reliably used for this purpose.

Finally the team looked at sizing each micro-segment and, although some guesswork inevitably went into these calculations, the availability of sales figures from the industry trade body, access to government statistics on the amount of farmland used for various types of production and estimated fertilizer usage levels proved to be of great help here. This had already helped them estimate the size of the preliminary segments. Many markets, however, are not so fortunate, but it is important to all segmentation projects that at least some reasonable approximations are arrived at as this information becomes essential when assessing the commercial viability of each concluding segment.

From the figures accessible to the team, they could estimate the splits between the different products for each preliminary segment, estimate the proportion accounted for by the 'well-established' brands, work out the probable split between high and low nitrogen levels and the split by channels. All of this was used to build a picture along the lines appearing in Figure 6.5.

The status of the case study as it now stands is summarized in Figure 6.6.

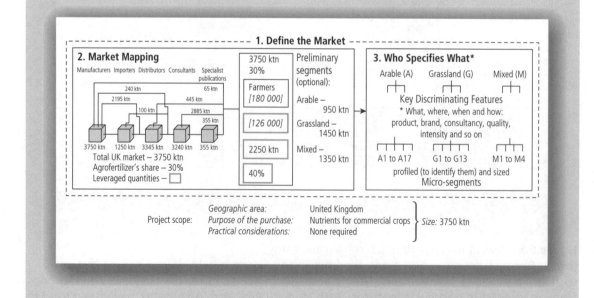

**Figure 6.6** The segmentation process – Steps 1 to 3

# Further examples

In general, it is by listening to customers, in addition to observing their buying behaviour, that companies arrive at the lists of key features for their market.

The first example presents some of the feature groups you could take into account when drawing up your list of what is bought, along with a selection of features from a range of markets:

| | |
|---|---|
| *Type of product* | Cleaners, galvanizers, installed, flat pack, ready made, on-call engineers, resident engineers, included with a service package and so on. |
| *Specification* | 100% purity, 98% purity, tolerance levels, percentage failure rate and so on. |
| *Colour* | Red, white, blue, pastel, garish and so on. |
| *Size of package* | Single, multiple, family pack, 5 litre, 10 litre, 20 kg, bulk and so on. |
| *Area occupied by equipment (footprint)* | Small, medium, large, very large, or by specific areas. |
| *Volume used* | Small, medium, large, very large, or by specific quantities. |
| *Type of service* | Testing service, design service, technical advice (which is sometimes, unintentionally, provided by the sales force), evaluation, evaluation analysis and so on. |
| *Brand* | Innovative, youthful, sober, luxury, local, international, own label, high profile and so on. |
| *Country of origin* | UK, German, French, European Union (EU), Scandinavian, North American, Arabian, Asian, African, Japanese and so on. |
| *Independent influencers* | Advisers, consultants (complementing or competing with the technical/advisory services provided by the manufacturers/suppliers), specialist publications, consumer publications, accountants, financial advisers, financial consultants and so on. |
| *Type of delivery* | Courier, first class, within four hours, collected, automatically triggered (via links with inventory control systems) and so on. |
| *Volume of purchase* | Large, medium, small, or in particular quantities. |
| *Value of purchase* | High, medium, low, or in specific expenditure bands. |
| *Range bought* | All, single, across the range, those at the top, middle, bottom and so on. |

This next example contains extracts from the final, summary feature lists pulled together for three different projects:

| | |
|---|---|
| *Lawnmowers* | Hover, cylinder, rotary, petrol driven, manual, electrically driven, 12″ cut, 16″ cut, engine |

Paints
from specialist manufacturer, extended warranty, metal structure, with after sales service and so on.

Paints
Emulsion, gloss, oil-based, water-based, non-drip, one coat, 5 litre cans, 2 litre cans, environmentally friendly, 'homely' brand, own label and so on.

Petrol Stations
Self-service, forecourt service, with convenience store, with 'newsagent's' products, cash-based loyalty programme, travel-based loyalty programme and so on.

Rationalizing complex feature lists often proves difficult for companies, but customers are very skilled at doing this, as the following three examples illustrate:

1 For one particular company, listening to their customers enabled them to simplify an extensive catalogue of components into those which were:
   – off-the-shelf; or
   – bespoke.
   Further divided into those which were of:
   – materials able to survive 'harsh' operating environments (varying temperatures and pressures); or
   – materials required to function in 'benign' operating environments.
2 In yet another market, it quickly became apparent that the features customers focused on in their market were split between:
   – features linked to the latest technology;
   – features which were of the most exacting specifications;
   – features related to the productive capacity of the equipment;
   – the product being available on demand and stocked at their local supplier.
3 For a company providing information on how to carry out particular tasks, the extensive range of products that they and their competitors supplied to the market were categorized by customers along the following lines:
   – illustrative, guiding them through what to do with sequential diagrams illustrating how to do it;
   – factual, leaving them to decide how to do it;
   – minimalist, containing just basic information expressed in as few words and in as few diagrams as possible.

The following example is a simplified illustration of avoiding the mythical customer. You may recall that the reality check for a micro-segment is whether or not it truly represents a group of customers in the market.

Assume that for a particular reference group in a market served by florists just two feature groups exist, 'colour scheme' and 'type of bouquet'. Within the colour scheme the KDFs are 'red-based', 'blue-based' and 'pastel-based', and the types of bouquet are either 'bespoke' or 'ready made'. A feature combination known to occur is that of 'red-based, bespoke bouquets', so this would form one micro-segment. For some reason, no customer in this reference group ever requests a 'pastel-based, bespoke bouquet', therefore, no micro-segment should be developed for this particular reference group based on the combination of 'pastel-based' and 'bespoke' KDFs.

An extremely simple example, but it is not unknown for companies to develop micro-segments from a mathematical standpoint based on all the KDF combinations that are possible. Even in the above example, only six micro-segments are technically possible, but if one of these possibilities does not occur, creating a mythical micro-segment to accommodate it is of no help to the segmentation process.

The final example is of a company which used market research to understand which features were basic market entry requirements, and which features were the differentiators, from the customer's perspective. The particular products they were interested in were printers and photocopiers and what follows is a selection from the resulting lists drawn up some years ago.

- Basic market entry requirements:
  - Clarity of the image (based on the fact that above a certain number of dots per inch the improvement in clarity is hardly detectable);
  - Number of copies per minute (the entry level requirement going higher with each increase in speed);
  - Helpline (available during normal office hours).
- Differentiators:
  - Short warm-up times;
  - Understandable error messages;
  - Multiple paper trays (accommodating different types of paper);
  - Built-in finishing technology (stapling, folding, hole punching);
  - High capacity paper trays.

As pointed out earlier in this chapter, it is important to review these lists periodically as what were once used by customers to decide between alternative offers can, over time, become the norm and be regarded as basic entry requirements.

# A selection of standard approaches to profiling businesses

## Demographic characteristics

- Standard Industrial Classification (SIC)
  The latest details are available from the appropriate statistical office. Summaries of both the UK/European and North American SIC systems appear below, with a more detailed listing found at www.marketsegmentation. co.uk.

*United Kingdom and Europe*
Agriculture, Hunting and Forestry (01–02)
Fishing (05)

Mining and Quarrying (10–14)
Manufacturing (15–37)
Electricity, Gas and Water Supply (40–41)
Construction (45)
Wholesale and Retail Trade; Certain Repairs (50–52)
Hotels and Restaurants (55)
Transport, Storage and Communication (60–64)
Financial Intermediation (65–67)
Real Estate, Renting and Other Business Activities (70–74)
Public Administration and Defence; Compulsory Social Security (75)
Education (80)
Health and Social Work (85)
Other Community, Social and Personal Service Activities (90–93)
Private Households with Employed Persons and Miscellaneous (95–97)
Extra-territorial Organizations and Bodies (99)

*North America (USA, Canada and Mexico)*
Agriculture, Forestry, Fishing and Hunting (11)
Mining (21)
Utilities (22)
Construction (23)
Manufacturing (31–33)
Wholesale Trade (42)
Retail Trade (44–45)
Transportation and Warehousing (48–49)
Information (51)
Finance and Insurance (52)
Real Estate and Retail and Leasing (53)
Professional, Scientific and Technical Services (54)
Management of Companies and Enterprises (55)
Administrative and Support and Waste Management and Remediation
   Services (56)
Education Services (61)
Health Care and Social Assistance (62)
Arts, Entertainment and Recreation (71)
Accommodation and Food Services (72)
Other Services (except Public Administration) (81)
Public Administration (92)

- Size of company
  Size is usually based on the number of employees or on turnover,
  though the figures used for different categories vary a great deal, as
  does the number of categories that are used.

| | | | |
|---|---|---|---|
| Very small | Small | Small-Medium | Medium |
| Medium-Large | Large | Very large | Very large+ |

Other descriptions include: SoHo (small office/home office), SME
(small-medium enterprise), mid-cap or mid-market (medium size), corporate (large and very large), global (very large+).

- Ownership
  Private, public; quoted, private; independent, wholly owned, subsidiary
- Department/section
  Although a number of functions can be found in most organizations, variations will occur in different sectors, such as health care.

| | | |
|---|---|---|
| Manufacturing | Distribution | Customer services |
| Sales | Marketing | Commercial |
| Engineering | Office services | Estates |
| Planning | Finance | Personnel/Human resources |
| Health and safety | Legal | Information Technology (IT) |
| Purchasing | Secretariat | Board |

  Where appropriate, use more specific descriptions, such as telesales, internet sales and face-to-face sales, specialist purchasing units and general purchasing units.

- Job title
  Variations in job titles clearly occur by sector. This list is of the more general titles that are found.

| | | |
|---|---|---|
| Director | General manager | Departmental head |
| Manager | Inspector | Officer |
| Supervisor | Foreman | Technician |
| Operative | Fitter | Senior executive |
| Junior executive | Assistant | Clerk |

- Multi-demographic
  Combining a selection of demographic criteria, such as size of company with job title along with whether the company is public or private.

## Geographic

Postcode/zip code (many schemes take location down to a very low level of geography)
Metropolitan, urban, rural; city, town, village; out-of-town, suburban, central; county, province, state
Region (frequently defined in the UK by TV areas, listed in the following section which summarizes the approaches to profiling individuals)
Country
Economic/political union or association (for example, ASEAN)
Continent

## Geodemographic

Associating geographic areas with, for example, the type (SIC) and size of businesses found there. Areas down to postcode level are then described as being retail, financial, light industrial, large manufacturing, dairy farming, cereal farming and so on.

## Psychographic characteristics

- Personality
  Stage in its business life cycle (start-up, growth, maturity, decline, turn-round)

Style/age of staff (formal, authoritarian, bureaucratic, disorganized, positive, indifferent, negative, cautious, conservative, old-fashioned, modern, ageing, youthful)

Style of decision-making (centralized, decentralized, consensual, individual, committee)

- Attitude
  Risk takers, risk avoiders
  Customer relationship orientation (high, medium, low)
  Approach to technology, new products and/or new services (innovator, early adopter, early majority, late majority, laggard)
  Approach to sharing information (open, secretive)

Many of the adjectives used to describe different types of personality can also express a company's attitude towards your product line (as opposed to their distinctive personal character).

- Lifestyle
  Environmentally concerned; involved with the community; sponsor of sports and/or the arts.

## Multidimensional

This is the most recent addition to business profiling and combines a range of profiling attributes into a number of distinct business types. For example, Experían's Commercial MOSAIC[4] classifies over 3 million businesses in the UK into 13 broad groups and 50 distinct types based on a selection of demographic data and behavioural characteristics. These 13 broad groups are as follows:

| | | |
|---|---|---|
| A Major Retail | F Specialist Suppliers | K Independent Entrepreneurs |
| B Industrial Blue Chips | G Local Solid Rocks | L Energetic Enterprises |
| C National Service | H Hotels and Catering | M Cottage Industry |
| D Fleet and Finance | I Health and Social Work | |
| E Monumental Monoliths | J Property Portfolio | |

The types include such descriptions as: New Born Subsidiaries (B3); Large Subsidiary Specialists (C6); Major Money Movers (D9); Vehicles and Veg (D13); Farsighted High Fliers (E17); Expert Engineers (F22); Small Town Stalwarts (G29); Inns and Eats (H32); Nurses and Nannies (I34); Landlords and Ladders (J39); Developing Dynamos (K42); Supply Chain Sophisticates (L46).

---

[4] 'Experían' and 'MOSAIC' are trade marks of Experían Ltd. Further details can be found at www.commercialmosaic.com.

# A selection of standard approaches to profiling individuals

## Demographic characteristics

- Age
  The most appropriate breakdown will vary according to the market being segmented.

  | | | | | |
  |---|---|---|---|---|
  | <5 | 5–10 | 11–15 | 16–19 | 20–24 |
  | 25–34 | 35–44 | 45–54 | 55–64 | ≥65 |

- Gender
  Male, female

- Family life cycle
  Bachelor (young, single), split into dependants (living at home or full-time student) and those with their own household; newly married (no kids); full nest (graded according to the number and age of children); single parent; empty nesters (children left home or childless couple); elderly single.

- Number of children

  | | | | |
  |---|---|---|---|
  | 0 | 1–2 | 3–4 | ≥5 |

- Type of residence
  Flat/maisonette, bungalow, house
  Terraced, semi-detached, detached
  Owned, rented (private, housing association, council)
  Number of rooms, bedrooms
  No garage, single garage, double garage

- Income
  Usually recorded as household or family income.

  | | | | | | |
  |---|---|---|---|---|---|
  | <£10k | £10k–£19k | £20k–£29k | £30k–£39k | £40k–£49k | ≥£50k |

- Occupation
  These are usually grouped into a manageable number of categories due to the range of occupations that exist.

  Manager, administrator, proprietor; scientist, lawyer, engineer, accountant, clergy, teacher; nurse, entertainer, surveyor, journalist; supervisor, foreman; secretary, telephonist, flight attendant; fitter, mechanic, rail guard, operative; security guard, cook, carpenter, bus driver; machinist, labourer, courier, cleaner; housewife/husband; student; retired; unemployed; white collar (professional, managerial, supervisory, clerical); blue collar (manual).

  The socio-economic classification scheme in the UK introduced in 2001 is occupationally based and provides groups that are linked to official statistics and surveys (see later).

- Qualifications
  The highest level is usually recorded.

  None; secondary education (GCSE, AS level, A level); vocational education (NVQ); first degree, higher degree, professional

- Readership
  Listed by title, type, topic and/or target group

  Newspapers (tabloids, broadsheets; daily, Sunday), journals, magazines

- Viewing and listening
  Sports, news, current affairs, drama, soaps, contests, 'reality' TV, natural history

- Leisure interests
  Football, rugby, cricket, baseball, golf, hiking, keep-fit; art, theatre, cinema, opera, classical music, pop, jazz; gardening, cooking, needlecraft, DIY, reading; wildlife, countryside, history; travel (with holidays split by type of accommodation, by type of destination and by selected geographical areas)

- Religion
  Christian, Muslim, Jewish, Sikh, Hindu, Buddhist, other, none

- Ethnic origin
  African, Asian, Caribbean, Chinese, Caucasian, Polynesian, other

- Socio-economic
  Table 6.13 contains the eight-class version of the socio-economic classification (SEC) scheme introduced by the Office for National Statistics (UK) in 2001. The new SEC is an occupationally-based scheme with rules to provide coverage for the whole adult population and has replaced 'Social Class based on Occupation' (formerly the Registrar General's 'Social Class') and 'Socio-economic Groups' in all official statistics and surveys.

  Also illustrated in Table 6.13 is the approximate relationship between the eight-class version of the new SEC with the former Registrar General's 'Social Class' and the socio-economic class indicators used by advertisers, market researchers and pollsters.

  A more detailed listing of the new SEC, including examples of occupations in each of the classes, can be found at www.marketsegmentation.co.uk. Full details can be found on the National Statistics website, www.statistics.gov.uk.

- Multi-demographic
  Combining a selection of demographic criteria, such as life-cycle stages and occupation groupings, on the basis that these are indicative of different aspirations and behaviour patterns.

## Geographic

Postcode/zip code (many schemes take location down to a very low level of geography)

Metropolitan, urban, rural; city, town, village

County, province, state

**Table 6.13** Eight-class analytic version of the 2001 Socio-economic Classification (UK) and its approximate relationship with other schemes

| *New eight-class SEC* | *Former Registrar General's Social Class* | *Former socio-economic class indicators* |
|---|---|---|
| 1  Higher managerial and professional occupations | | |
|   1.1  Large employers and higher managerial occupations | I  Professional, administrative | A  Upper middle class |
|   1.2  Higher professional occupations | II  Managerial and technical | B  Middle class |
| 2  Lower managerial and professional occupations | III Skilled workers N (non-manual) | C1 Lower middle class |
| 3  Intermediate occupations | | |
| 4  Small employers and own account workers | III Skilled workers M (manual) | C2 Skilled working class |
| 5  Lower supervisory and technical occupations | | |
| 6  Semi-routine occupations | IV Partly-skilled | D  Working class |
| 7  Routine occupations | V  Unskilled labour | E  Subsistence level |
| 8  Never worked and long-term unemployed |    Other |    Other |

*Source:* Based on the National Statistics website: www.statistics.gov.uk. Crown copyright material is reproduced with the permission of the Controller of HMSO and the Queen's Printer for Scotland.
*Note:* The alignment is only approximate due to the differences in criteria used to allocate individuals to their respective classes in the above schemes. 'Large employers' refers to individuals who employ others in enterprises employing 25 or more persons.

Region (frequently defined in the UK by TV areas – Anglia, Border, Carlton London, Carlton Central, Carlton West Country, Channel, Grampian, Granada, HTV, LWT, Meridian, Scottish, Tyne Tees, UTV, Yorkshire)
Country
Economic/political union or association (for example, ASEAN)
Continent
Population density
Climate

## Geodemographic

A Classification of Residential Neighbourhoods (ACORN) produced by CACI Ltd[5] is one of the longer established geodemographic classifications in the UK, updated with Census information and lifestyle data. ACORN covers every street in Great Britain and classifies the whole population into 56 types, summarized into 17 groups, which in turn are condensed into five broad categories. These five broad categories act as a simplified reference to the overall household classification structure. The categories and their respective groups are as follows:

| | | |
|---|---|---|
| 1 'Affluent Achievers' | A | Wealthy Executives |
| | B | Affluent Greys |
| | C | Flourishing Families |
| 2 'Urban Prosperity' | D | Prosperous Professionals |
| | E | Educated Urbanites |
| | F | Aspiring Singles |
| 3 'Comfortably Off' | G | Starting Out |
| | H | Secure Families |
| | I | Settled Suburbia |
| | J | Prudent Pensioners |
| 4 'Modest Means' | K | Asian Communities |
| | L | Post Industrial Families |
| | M | Blue-collar Roots |
| 5 'Hard Pressed' | N | Struggling Families |
| | O | Burdened Singles |
| | P | High Rise Hardship |
| | Q | Inner City Adversity |
| | Z | Unclassified |

The types include such descriptions as: Villages with wealthy commuters (A3); Mature couples, smaller detached homes (B8); Well-off working families with mortgages (C10); Older professionals in detached houses and apartments (D14); Young educated workers, flats (E17); Singles and sharers, multi-ethnic areas (F21); White collar singles/sharers, terraces (G25); Mature families in suburban semis (H29); Middle income, older couples (I33); Elderly singles, purpose built flats (J35); Low income Asian families (K38); Young family workers (L40); Home owning, terraces (M42); Low income, routine jobs, unemployment (N46); Council terraces, unemployment, many singles (O51); Singles and single parents, high rise estates (P54); Multi-ethnic, crowded flats (Q56).

Geodemographic data is also combined with financial data to provide detailed information on financial product ownership. For example, Financial ACORN combines Census and financial research data into 51 types, 12 groups and four categories.

---

[5] 'ACORN' and 'CACI' are trade marks of CACI Ltd. Further details can be found at www.caci.co.uk.

## Psychographic characteristics

- Personality
  Compulsive, extrovert, gregarious, adventurous, formal, authoritarian, ambitious, enthusiastic, positive, indifferent, negative, hostile.

  Specific personality profiles by gender have also been developed.

- Attitude
  Degree of loyalty (none, total, moderate)
  Risk takers, risk avoiders
  Approach to technology, new products and/or new services (innovator, early adopter, early majority, late majority, laggard)

  Many of the adjectives used to describe different types of personality can also express an individual's attitude towards your product line (as opposed to their distinctive personal character)

- Customer status
  Purchase stage (aware, interested, desirous, ready for sale); user classification (non-user, lapsed, first time, potential).

- Lifestyle
  Lifestyle data is obtained from consumer questionnaires which are then combined with publicly available information such as share registrations, Census data and the Electoral Roll to provide extensive coverage of the population. The number of different attributes which can be used to select individuals is quite extensive and can cover:
  Product and service usage
  Activities, including work, social, sports and holidays
  Interests, including family, home, community, recreation, fashion, food and media
  Opinions, covering themselves, social issues, politics, economics, education, the future and culture

  Because the data is based on individuals, variations in the attributes to be used can result in different people in the same household being selected.

## Multidimensional

Combining psychographic profiles with selected demographic data and identifying geographic areas where the resulting 'behavioural' types are found. For example, Experían's MOSAIC[6] classifies all the households and neighbourhoods (postcodes) in Great Britain into 52 distinct types which describe their socio-economic and socio-cultural behaviour. These 52 types are aggregated into 12 broad groups:

| | | |
|---|---|---|
| A High Income Families | B Suburban Semis | D Low Rise Council |
| | C Blue Collar Owners | E Council Flats |

[6]'Experían' and 'MOSAIC' are trade marks of Experían Ltd. Further details can be found at www.micromarketing-online.com and www.experian.co.uk.

| | | |
|---|---|---|
| F  Victorian Low Status | I  Independent Elders | L  Institutional Areas |
| G  Town House and Flats | J  Mortgaged Families | |
| H  Stylish Singles | K  Country Dwellers | |

The types include such descriptions as: Clever Capitalists (A1); Ageing Professionals (A4); Pebble Dash Subtopia (B8); Smokestack Shiftwork (C12); Low Rise Subsistence (D16); Victims of Clearance (E19); Inner City Towers (E23); Rejuvenated Terraces (F29); Town Centre Singles (G32); Chattering Classes (H36); Aged Owner Occupiers (I39); Nestmaking Families (J43); Rural Retirement Mix (K46); Tied/Tenant Farmers (K49); Military Bases (L51).

In addition to MOSAIC for Great Britain as a whole, there are separate MOSAICs for Scotland, Northern Ireland and London which identify differences only found in those areas. Experían has also extended MOSAIC to areas outside Great Britain.

For supermarket retailers in Great Britain, Experían has developed Grocery MOSAIC which is a classification system based on shopping behaviour, attitudes to shopping and demographics. This classifies households and neighbourhoods (postcodes) into ten types. As well as differences in product category and brand preferences, the ten types also differ in terms of how they trade off price against service, convenience against variety, promotional orientation, pack size preference and attitude towards own brand.

# Exercises

**Exercise 6.1**

Among the list of KDFs drawn up by one company were 'brand', 'quality', 'service' and 'performance', all of which are meaningless as they tell you nothing about what is being bought. For this exercise, consider a market in which you are a decision-maker and in which these four 'features' are issues for you when choosing between alternative offers. You may need to consider more than one market to cover all four 'features'. Identify for each of these 'features' the particular specification you are actually looking for. A copy of the worksheet appearing in Table 6.14 can be used for this exercise.

Now identify for your market the particular specification(s) customers are looking for with respect to each of these four 'features', assuming, of course, that they apply to your market. The guideline is to think of these 'features' in terms of how you would have to describe them on a product or service specification brief. Further copies of Table 6.14 can be used for this part of the exercise.

**Table 6.14**  Worksheet – making sense of meaningless features

| 'Feature' | More meaningful specification |
|---|---|
| Brand<br>Quality<br>Service<br>Performance | |

For this exercise, take a product or service you use at home or at work and list the features you particularly focus on when deciding between the alternative offers available in the market you have selected, in other words, your KDFs. As discussed in this chapter, 'price' is better left until the next step in the process. You can capture your KDFs on the first part of the worksheet appearing in Table 6.15. Make as many copies of this worksheet as you need.

**Exercise 6.2**

**Table 6.15** Worksheet – recording micro-segments, their KDFs, profiling characteristics and size

| Feature | | | Micro-segments | | | | | |
|---|---|---|---|---|---|---|---|---|
| Category | Group | Specification | | | | | | |
| | | | | | | | | |
| | | | | | | | | |
| Profiling | | | | | | | | |
| Category | Group | Specification | | | | | | |
| | | | | | | | | |
| Acquisition routes | | | | | | | | |
| | | Size | | | | | | |

Using one of the micro-segment columns, indicate the relative importance to you of each feature using one to three stars or tick marks.

In order to extend this exercise to some of the other micro-segment columns, consider someone else known to you who is also a customer in this market, but who is different to you in the features they look for, and complete the entries in Table 6.15 for them. You can repeat this as many times as you wish.

Now attempt to complete the profiling and acquisition details for each micro-segment. You may also be able to make some estimate of the quantities each of these micro-segments accounts for, even if, at this stage, it is simply along the lines of the ratios they account for (such as, micro-segment 2 buys three times more than micro-segment 3).

## Exercise 6.3

Now apply the last exercise to the market your company is in. After drawing up an initial list of micro-segments, discuss them with others in the organization to obtain their views on the KDFs, how they see customers differing with respect to these KDFs along with the profiles and acquisition routes they associate with these micro-segments.

Chapter 7

# Accounting for the behaviour of decision-makers

# Summary

To really understand what lies behind the choices made by customers requires their behaviour to be understood in terms of the needs they are seeking to satisfy. This is the most useful and practical way of explaining customer behaviour as it provides the insights required for putting together the most appropriate offer for each of the concluding segments, thereby realizing the most valuable benefits of segmentation. It is the needs of decision-makers that are identified by this, the fourth step in the segmentation process, as illustrated in Figure 7.1.

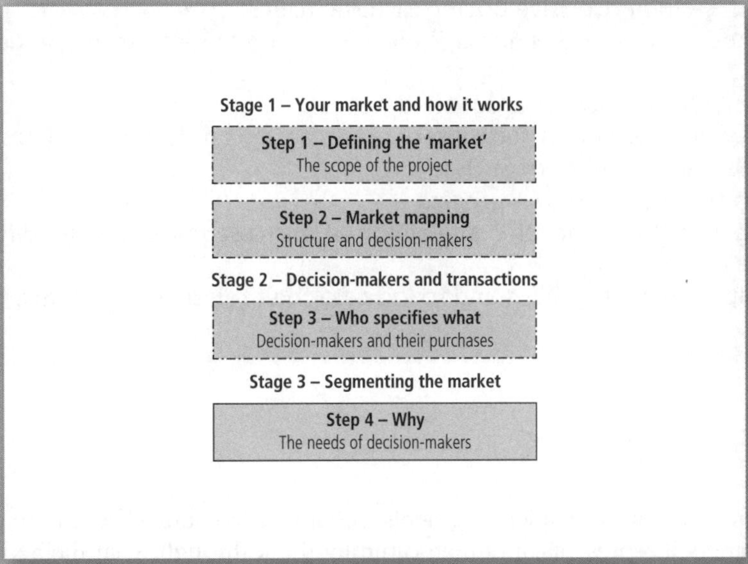

Stage 1 – Your market and how it works

**Step 1 – Defining the 'market'**
The scope of the project

**Step 2 – Market mapping**
Structure and decision-makers

Stage 2 – Decision-makers and transactions

**Step 3 – Who specifies what**
Decision-makers and their purchases

Stage 3 – Segmenting the market

**Step 4 – Why**
The needs of decision-makers

**Figure 7.1**
The segmentation process – Step 4

This chapter uses the details put together in the previous step to determine the needs-based buying requirements of the decision-makers who now form the sample for your project, and takes account of the role of 'price' in their decision-making. As these are the criteria on which the concluding segments for your market will be based, this step, when completed, provides the framework for comparing the different decision-makers with one another.

When conducting a segmentation project using internal resources, information for this step potentially can be found among the same individuals involved in the previous step, supplemented, where possible, by lost sales reports and appropriate past market surveys. It is important to remember, however, that the project is looking at the needs of the market as a whole, not just the needs that your company can satisfy.

While we would still recommend that your internal segmentation project completes the phase of developing segments before commissioning an external market research company to fill in any information gaps, a substantial part of the brief can usefully be pulled together once you have taken the project through this step of the process.

This chapter is organized as follows:

■ A 'fast track' for those looking for a quick route through the key points
■ A brief discussion about the two principal theories of customer behaviour and why explaining this behaviour in terms of 'benefits' is preferred
■ How to progress from a feature, through its advantage, to the benefit a customer is looking for
■ The distinction between 'standard', 'company' and 'differential' benefits
■ How to avoid providing answers to the question 'why?' that simply represent the status quo, and keeping alert to the possibility of there being unsatisfied needs
■ A discussion about the role of price in segmentation and its inclusion in this step
■ The procedures to follow when identifying the benefits that lie behind the choices made by micro-segments – their 'Decisive Buying Criteria' (DBCs)
■ How to indicate the importance of DBCs numerically as opposed to using stars and tick marks
■ Techniques that can be used to uncover unsatisfied needs
■ A brief note for those whose project is focusing on one strategic business unit (SBU), but whose market straddles a number of SBUs
■ A review of this step in the segmentation process
■ DBCs for the case study and their scores for a selection of micro-segments, along with some further examples of benefits
■ Exercises further to help you identify DBCs and to indicate their relative importance to micro-segments

# Fast track

● Take one of your micro-segments, re-familiarize yourself with the customers it represents, and then carefully think through what their KDFs, both individually and as a package, really mean to these customers in terms of the underlying needs they are satisfying. These are referred to as their 'Decisive Buying Criteria' (DBCs). To progress from a feature to a benefit, first describe the feature in terms of what it is, consists of, or is made from, then its advantage, what it does, and then describe what this gives the customer that they explicitly need, in other words, the benefit. For example, 'Teflon' is a surface coating for kitchen utensils (feature) which is non-stick (advantage), which means that less time is required for washing up (benefit). To check that you have arrived at the benefit, ask, 'so what?', and if this prompts you to go further in explaining what this means to the customer and why it is of interest to them, it is likely that you have yet to identify the benefit.

Ensure you get to their true motivations by understanding what it is they are really trying to achieve and what it is they would like to achieve, keeping alert to any possible unsatisfied needs, so as to avoid providing answers that simply represent the status quo. Refer to 'Looking beyond the status quo' and 'Techniques for uncovering unsatisfied needs' later in this chapter.

**Table 7.1** Fast track – recording DBCs and indicating their relative importance to micro-segments

| Features | DBCs: benefits + price | Micro-segments | | | | |
|---|---|---|---|---|---|---|
| | | B1 | B2 | C | D | E |
| Modern design | Eye-catching | | | *** | | |
| Latest technology 'Blue-chip' brand | Holds value better | | | | | ** |
| Latest technology | Innovative functionality | | | ** | | *** |
| Upgradeable | Future-proofed | | | | | *** |
| Proven technology | Unlikely to go wrong | *** | *** | | ** | |
| 'Blue-chip' brand | Trusted performance | *** | *** | | | |
| Local retailer | Able to touch and see | ** | | | | ** |
| Reputable retailer | Confidence in choice | ** | ** | | * | |
| On-line retailer Telephone ordering | Armchair shopping | | | ** | | |
| On-line retailer Mail order | Avoids sales patter | | * | | | |
| | Price | * | * | * | ** | * |

*Note:* While it is useful to show the link between DBCs and their KDFs, it is optional. The most important DBCs are identified by three stars (***) in this table. As you will see in the above, a single feature can have more than one benefit and different features can deliver the same benefit.

A suggested layout for recording micro-segments and their DBCs appears in Table 7.1 (used to illustrate a grading structure for DBCs).

- Complete the list of DBCs by adding 'price' and attempt to indicate the relative importance of the DBCs to each other for that micro-segment. Ensure that the relative importance of 'price' only reflects how readily customers will give up their KDFs and associated benefits to get a cheaper price. Up to three tick marks or stars can, once again, be usefully employed for the grading structure here, as illustrated in Table 7.1. If required, extend the range at this stage by using 'half' tick marks ($^1/_2$) or an equivalent 'half' star, such as an outline star '☆'.

  Numbers can be used to indicate the relative importance of the DBCs to each other if preferred (please refer to 'Expressing the relative importance of DBCs numerically' later in this chapter for guidelines). Use a single tick mark or star if you are unable to indicate the relative importance of DBCs (this does not prevent you from completing the project, though it could have implications for the next step).

  Add this information to any spreadsheet or database file set up on your PC for the previous step.

- Consider a cross-section of customers included in the micro-segment to confirm if they would all *generally* agree with the list of DBCs and their grading, and if they would not, develop additional micro-segments to cover any meaningful differences. Redistribute the size of the original micro-segment between them as best as you can and check their profiling characteristics.

- Once all the micro-segments have had their DBCs identified for them, review each micro-segment against the complete list of DBCs and make any appropriate additions to the DBCs that have been listed for them.
- Finally, review and compare the micro-segments with each other and increase or decrease the importance of appropriate DBCs if this better reflects the differences between individual micro-segments, but avoid imposing differences if such differences do not really exist. Use no more than five tick marks or stars to highlight the most important DBCs, as this will ensure that the final picture remains visually comprehensible. Use half-values if this better helps to reflect the differences between micro-segments.
- While identifying benefits it is crucial to remind yourself and the team that:
  - the benefits are for the market as a whole, not simply limited to those that you deliver to your customers; and,
  - these benefits are what the decision-makers regard as their decisive buying criteria, not what you would prefer them to see as their decisive buying criteria.
- A worksheet for developing KDFs into benefits and a worksheet for recording DBCs and their relative importance by micro-segment appear in the Exercises section of this chapter.

Readers who are reasonably confident that they have captured the needs-based buying requirements of micro-segments may go straight to Chapter 8.

This concludes the fast track for Step 4 of the segmentation process.

# Explaining customer behaviour

Basically, there are two principal theories of customer behaviour. One theory refers to the rational customer, who seeks to maximize satisfaction or utility. This customer's behaviour is determined by the utility derived from a purchase at the margin compared with the financial outlay and other opportunities foregone. While such a view of customers provides some important insights into behaviour, it must be remembered that many markets do not work this way at all, there being many examples of growth in demand for every rise in price.

Another view of customer behaviour which helps to explain this phenomenon is that which describes the psycho-socio customer, whose attitudes and behaviours are affected by family, work, prevailing cultural patterns, groups they relate to, perceptions, aspirations, and lifestyle.

While such theories provide useful insights, they rarely explain the totality of customer behaviour.

The most useful and practical way of explaining customer behaviour has been found to be **benefit** segmentation, in other words, the benefits sought by customers when they acquire a product or service in order to satisfy

Definition: A benefit is a perceived or stated relationship between a feature and what a customer gets that they explicitly need.

their explicit needs. For example, some customers choose products for their functional characteristics (product), for economy (price), for convenience and availability (place), for emotional reasons (promotion), or, as is often the case, for a combination of these reasons (a trade-off). Otherwise, how else can the success of car firms like Bentley, retailers like Harrods, and many others be explained? Understanding the benefits sought by customers helps us to organize our marketing mix in the way most likely to appeal to our target groups.

● Definition:
A company's marketing mix consists of the 'tools' or means available to the organization to improve the match between benefits sought and those offered by the organization so as to obtain a differential advantage. Among these tools are product, price, promotion and place (services and distribution) – the four Ps

The most useful and practical way of explaining customer behaviour has been found to be benefit segmentation.

Marketing
insight

'*Customers don't buy products; they seek to acquire benefits*'. This is the guiding principle of the marketing director of one of America's more innovative companies in the hair-care business. Behind that statement lies a basic principle of successful marketing. When a customer selects a particular product or service, they are not motivated in the first instance by physical features, or objective characteristics of the product, but by the benefits that those attributes bring with them. In a sense, therefore, all products and services are problem-solvers.

> For example, a purchaser of industrial cutting oil is not buying the particular blend of chemicals sold by leading manufacturers of industrial lubricants; rather, they are buying a bundle of benefits which include the solving of a specific lubrication problem.
>
> The motivation behind employing a surveyor when contemplating moving into a new home is not to preserve the sub-species *Homo sapiens 'surveyorcus'*; rather, they are employing the surveyor because they want to be assured the proposed new property is structurally sound.
>
> Analgesics are not bought to keep the pharmaceutical companies in business; they are bought to relieve pain.
>
> The do-it-yourself 'handyman' does not buy drill bits out of an interest in preserving the precision engineering industry of a particular country's industrial heartland; rather, as a drill manufacturer is quoted as saying, 'Last year we sold 1 million quarter-inch drills [approximately 0.65 centimetres], not because people wanted quarter-inch drills, but because they needed quarter-inch holes' (although this could be seen as a blinkered understanding of the real need, which is usually to attach two items together and could therefore be achieved by using an appropriate glue!).

The difference between benefits and products is not just a question of semantics. It is crucial to any company seeking success on two important counts:

1 Unless the benefits are clearly identified, the strength of a company's product may simply go unnoticed, even if the features outperform those of competing products in terms of satisfying the needs of its target group. Many companies, however, still fall into the trap of talking to customers about features, rather than about what those features mean to the customer.

2 A company's output is only saleable for as long as it provides the benefits the customer requires, and for as long as it is seen by the customer to be good value when compared with other possible methods of solving their problems. Once there is a better, cheaper, quicker, tidier, more enjoyable way of putting holes in walls, the drill manufacturer will go the way of the buggy-whip maker.

Therefore it is vitally important to know just as much about the benefits you supply as it is to know about the products or services themselves.

## From 'features' to 'benefits'

When looking at the benefits for your market, it is useful if you first consider what issues are of particular concern to the customer. This, as you may recall from the last chapter, was a topic we suggested you discussed when visualizing the different customer groups in your market, as it helps set the scene for developing their key discriminating features. Then to get from a feature to a benefit, describe what the feature does, its 'advantage', and, finally, identify the particular appeal this has to the customer, the 'benefit', this being the reason why the feature is of interest to them: in other words, the particular need that it satisfies.

A summary of the distinction between a 'feature', an 'advantage' and a 'benefit' appeared in the last chapter and is repeated here for convenience:

| Marketing insight | The distinction between a 'feature', an 'advantage' and a 'benefit' can be summarized as follows: |
|---|---|

- feature: what it is, consists of, or is made from;
- advantage: what it does;
- benefit: what the customer gets that they explicitly need.

The advantage of applying the above sequence to your market's KDFs is that it ensures the benefits you identify are deliverable by the features, which means that the needs you are highlighting can be used to form segments. This systematic approach to developing benefits appears in Table 7.2, along with three examples. A worksheet based on this table appears in the Exercises section of this chapter.

A simple formula to ensure that a benefit-orientated approach is adopted is to use the phrase 'which means that' to link a feature to its advantage,

**Table 7.2** Benefit analysis

| Customer appeal | Features | Advantages | Benefits |
|---|---|---|---|
| What issues are of concern for this customer? For example, availability, safety, reliability, simplicity, fashionable, leading-edge and so on. | What features of the product or service, channel and so on in the customer's view best represent these issues? What are they? How do they work? | What advantages do these features provide? In other words, what do they do for the customer? | How can tangible benefits be expressed to give maximum customer appeal? In other words, what does the customer get that they explicitly need? |
| *Example – credit cards* Ease of use. Safer than carrying money. Less bulky than cash or cheque book. Speedy transaction. Provide credit. International. | MasterCard credit card. | Enables purchases to be made world-wide. | Eliminates the need to carry large amounts of cash. Eases cash flow problems and so on. |
| *Example – saucepans* Ease of use. Ease of washing up. Attractive end product. | Teflon coated. | Non-stick. | Trouble-free cooking. Quicker washing up. Better presentation of food and so on. |
| *Example – office service bureaux* Accuracy. Speedy turnaround of work. | Latest equipment. Very skilled staff. | Extremely versatile. | Minimum of errors. Able to meet tight deadlines. |

and then to the benefit it brings. For example, 'This product is coated in new formula paint (*feature*) which means that the colour will never fade (*advantage*) which means that it will require repainting less often (*benefit*)'. Once you *know* this is what the customer *needs*, then you have arrived at a *benefit*.

Sometimes the expression 'which means that' can sound rather clumsy. When this happens, an alternative linking word is 'because': for example, 'You can be sure of personal attention from us because we are a small family business'.

To check if you have arrived at a benefit and not just an advantage, apply the 'so what?' test. Ask this question after the benefit. If the 'so what?' prompts you to go further, it is likely you have not yet reached the real benefit. For example, 'The products are hand-made (*feature*), which means they are of better quality than machine-made ones (*benefit?*) – 'so what?' – which means they last longer (*the real benefit*).

| **Marketing insight** | It is important to note that a particular feature may be seen by different customers as providing them with different benefits. For example, an airline's non-stop service between two cities could mean: |

- a better use of time (less of it spent at 35 000 feet);
- less opportunity to go missing at transit airports (a concern of parents when their children are travelling alone to and from overseas boarding schools for example);
- a better chance of arriving on time (a transit stop being an opportunity for a delaying incident to occur).

| **Marketing insight** | It is also important to note that a single feature may also provide more than one benefit to the same customer. For example: |

- a business traveller may be attracted to an airline's non-stop service both because it is a better use of time and because it means that they are more likely to arrive in time for their appointments;
- canned food may appeal to some customers because it both provides easy storage (no special storage conditions) and reduces the frequency of shopping trips (long shelf-life).

| **Marketing insight** | And finally, the possibility that different features may provide the same benefit should not be overlooked. For example: |

- the provision by airlines of on-board power connections for portable PCs, along with facsimile and telephone services enable business travellers to make better use of their time while at 35 000 feet;
- frozen food reduces the frequency of shopping trips because it too has a long shelf-life.

## Standard, company and differential benefits

Benefits generally fall into one of three categories, namely 'standard' benefits, 'company' benefits and 'differential' benefits:

1 Standard benefits

These are basic benefits provided by product features but are not in any way unique to any particular manufacturer/supplier: for example, 'the aerosol propellant is one that does not damage the ozone layer'. Although in this respect your product might be like all others, it is still worth noting if it is an important consideration in the purchasing decision for your market. Its importance may also differ between customers. Not to make customers aware of this standard benefit could imply that you still use environmentally-unfriendly materials. Clearly this would be to your disadvantage.

2 Company benefits

Whenever a purchase is made, the transaction links the customer to the company supplying the item. Links will be forged between the two at many levels. For example, in business-to-business transactions, their accounts departments will be in contact to deal with payment or financial matters; people on installation work or after-sales servicing will interact with the personnel at the buyer's company; delivery personnel with storekeepers; designers with technicians and so on. When a buyer selects one of a number of competing suppliers, there ought to be some benefits to that buyer for making that choice.

Customers will prefer to deal with companies that, for example, provide better customer service, inspire confidence, have a reputation for fair trading policies, are known to be flexible, have a particular image associated with them, and so on. Company benefits are a means of differentiating your products or services from competing ones if, to all intents and purposes, they are similar. For example, some UK banks are trying to establish specific identities for the benefits they supply. Hence there is 'the world's local bank', the bank that is 'always giving you extra' and one that promises 'banking worth talking about'. There has also been the 'listening bank', 'the action bank' and the bank that liked to say 'yes'. There are now even banks which are 'open when their customers want them to be'!

3 Differential benefits

In a competitive market place, most suppliers vying for the available customers will not be able to claim that their standard, or company, benefits are, in truth regarded as being a great deal different from those of the competition. The benefits that only your products or services provide, which are also benefits in the eye of the customer, give your company its competitive advantage and are known as 'differential benefits'. To understand your market dynamics fully, however, particularly in the context of developing a segmentation structure for it, you not only need to be aware of your own company's differential benefits, you also need to note those differential benefits of your competitors which attract some of the market to them, as opposed to you. Differential benefits could include, for example:

- the only breakdown service genuinely open 24 hours a day and therefore available at any time to get the customer back on the move again;
- the only product with self-cleaning heads, so once installed there are no maintenance worries.

These are, of course, only benefits if they meet an explicit customer need.

## Looking beyond the status quo

It is important when considering the reasons why a customer shows interest in certain features that you are not simply providing answers that represent the status quo. To help uncover their real needs and their true motivations, we must be able to answer the question, 'What are they really trying to achieve?' Examples of this can be found in the case study being used to illustrate each step of the segmentation process:

In the agricultural market covered by the case study, the focus of some farmers was to buy products which produced lush, green grass for their livestock to graze on. For another group of farmers, their concern was how well their livestock looked (the appearance of the grass being a minor concern). In the arable sector, one group of farmers concentrated solely on producing crops which met the needs of the market they were selling into, again regardless of how the crop looked whilst in the field. This particular group also demonstrated another important point when looking at the reasons 'why' particular products are bought.

This point concerns the 'market-orientated' arable farmers, who bought a great deal of this product in its constituent parts, rather than already mixed (which was how the majority of it was sold in various standard combinations), and they always looked for the cheapest buys. The initial conclusion was that this group bought on price, a conclusion which, it was later discovered, combined them with another group of farmers who *were* driven by price. However, on probing what they were really trying to achieve, it became apparent that they were combining the constituent parts in a variety of ways to make up a number of different mixes. This was being done because the standard, off-the-shelf combinations produced by the manufacturers were not sophisticated enough for the needs of this particular group of farmers. These bespoke combinations improved their farm's output and had nothing to do with price. In addition, a further driving force for this group of farmers was innovation, and their own bespoke mixing operation was also seen to be innovative.

Also understanding why customers show little interest in a product and asking, 'What would they really like to achieve?', can help take the analysis of benefits beyond the status quo, as in the following example:

In quite a different market from that covered by the case study, one segment was found to consist of unenthusiastic buyers who stated they were not really interested in the product class at all and only made purchases in this product class for the functional needs it satisfied. For example, they bought cars simply to travel between 'A' and 'B'. However, a research project discovered that this segment did have aspirations, in addition to the functional requirements, which could be met by the product if only it was designed and specifically targeted at this distinct group (which, usefully, had a distinct demographic profile). An example of this would be a car specifically designed to meet the requirements of the female executive and specifically positioned to appeal to this group of customers. A car manufacturer who pursued a strategy similar to this was Jaguar, who in the USA positioned their XJS model as one targeted at (wealthy) women.

Be alert to any possible unsatisfied needs manifesting themselves in the guise of something else.

Thus, it is crucial at this stage to be alert to any possible unsatisfied needs manifesting themselves in the guise of something else, rather than accepting the status quo. For example, 'price' may be given as the sole or major criterion for choice, but it *could* be hiding the fact that customers are currently dissatisfied with the present alternative offers available, as their real needs are not being met. What they are currently limited to buying in order to meet a functional need is, therefore, second rate, for which they certainly would not pay a premium, as in the following example:

> There is a functional need of (most) garden owners to mow the grass. To meet this need, there used to be only cylinder mowers available. Despite a close cut, a collecting box and roller providing an attractive finish, the cylinder mower was regarded as cumbersome by some gardeners and, because of this, they would buy cheap versions.
>
> Then the hover mower arrived, which was light and quick, thus enabling a substantial amount of the time previously allocated to a chore to be better spent. Many individuals in the group dissatisfied with the cylinder mower switched to the hover mower as this met their need for a fast method of keeping their grass in check. In contrast, the need of the group choosing to use a cylinder mower was, in many instances, to present the lawn as a 'show piece'.

To assist in identifying whether there are any unsatisfied needs in a market, current products can be looked at in terms of the functional requirements they meet and by the views and attitudes customer have of them. By positioning today's products along these dimensions, unfilled *potential* opportunities may then become apparent. They could be unfilled, of course, because there is no demand. Details of this approach appear later in this chapter.

It is often by considering the possibility of unmet needs that the reasons why there are lapsed users and prospects become clear. We last mentioned these two groups when considering the options for preliminary segments in Chapter 5 and this is an appropriate point at which to reintroduce them into your project as suitably identified micro-segments with an estimate of what these potential new marketing opportunities could represent in terms of the quantities they might buy.

---

When commissioning research to uncover the real needs of customers, it is essential that the agencies you consider for this work clearly demonstrate their skills in carrying out and, in particular, interpreting qualitative discussions. The emphasis is deliberately placed on 'interpreting' as this tends to be the area where weaknesses, if there are any, are to be found.

**Market research note**

---

## Price

Clearly, 'price' has an important part to play in explaining customer behaviour and is obviously a component of customers' 'buying criteria'. Everything has its price!

However, a detailed discussion of 'price' has deliberately been kept out of the process up until this point because it can too easily be used as a 'catch all' or 'get out' in answer to some of the more difficult questions you need to address in a *market*-based segmentation project. All too often, 'price' is given as the reason for particular buying activity. Not everyone buys the cheapest, and for those who do, it could be because there is nothing available in the market that really meets their requirements, as was pointed out in the previous section. Produce the product or service they are looking for, and price becomes less of an issue.

'Price' is simply a measure of value placed by the customer on both the tangible and intangible components of a purchase. Three simple examples should suffice to illustrate this point.

> 'Price' is a measure of value placed by the customer on both the tangible and intangible components of a purchase.

---

A company launched a new pure juice product on the market after tests had indicated an overwhelming acceptance by the target group. When sales fell far short of expectations, research indicated that the target group simply did not believe that the claims on the container about the product could be true at such a low price. So the company doubled the price and relaunched it, and the product was a resounding success.

Jaguar launched a luxury car in the 1960s and priced it on their cost-plus basis. Demand far outstripped supply and a lengthy waiting list developed. This resulted in some customers buying the car and reselling it immediately after delivery at a much inflated price. In other words, the *value* of the car to the customer was much greater than the actual price charged.

Likewise, some tertiary educational establishments claim that their courses are the best in the world, then charge lower prices than their competitors. Research indicates that for directors and very senior managers in industry, a low price is more likely to be counter-productive, because in this particular product field, it is considered to be an indicator of educational standard.

---

For the purposes of segmentation, we are concerned with the relative importance of price to the other components of the purchase: in other words, to what extent will the customer sacrifice their requirements for a lower price? Alternatively, when will they start trading in their requirements in order to keep the price at an acceptable level? The ability of one supplier to supply the market at lower prices than everyone else for a directly comparable offer is not the issue we are addressing here, or need to address, when segmenting markets and the failure to recognize this often leads to the wrong conclusions. This is illustrated in the following example:

---

The UK market for car insurance is characterized by customers phoning round different suppliers for a price quotation. It would be wrong, however, instantly to conclude that this market was dominated by price chasers.

Many will be phoning round a selected list of preferred suppliers, having rejected other possible suppliers, indicating that they attribute some value to particular brands. In addition, many will be phoning round their preferred suppliers with a particular list of requirements they want to include in their car insurance and regard as being important.

In this market, therefore, the segmentation project would need to focus on the lists of alternative suppliers and the lists of require-ments, the phoning round basically indicating that the customers regard the suppliers on their list as all being very similar to each other. They are, therefore, comparing one with another in order to obtain the best value. Inevitably, of course, some of those phoning round will be looking for the cheapest, willing to take out a car insurance policy with any supplier and ready to sacrifice any of their requirements in order to get a lower price (assuming they have any requirements other than the basic legal minimum).

In the above situation there is, of course, a serious competitive issue to be addressed, namely how to differentiate your offer in the market. This brings into sharp focus the whole question of market segmentation and what ingredients of the marketing mix a company should put together so that their 'offer' to the customer cannot be compared directly with anyone else's 'offer'. For if two offers *can* be directly compared, it is obvious that the one with the lowest price will win most of the time.

> If two products are the same, it is obvious that the one with the lowest price will win most of the time.

## Market research note

In any market research project commissioned to assist you with your segmen-tation project, it is crucial that the questionnaire and/or interviewer makes it very clear to the respondent what is meant by 'price', so that when the respondent is asked to give it an importance score, they understand how it is to be related to the other benefits they are being asked about. If this is not correctly understood, the conclusions drawn for the project will be mislead-ing. This, in turn, will result in marketing objectives and strategies failing to deliver the best financial returns available to the company.

For respondents who give 'price', or, as it is sometimes phrased, 'buying the cheapest', a high level of importance, introducing a check question can be a useful way of confirming that this means they would be willing to lessen their demands for, or even give up, the other benefits they value in order to obtain a lower price.

To conclude these comments on price, it is worth noting that, in some instances, the role played by price can be distorted, as in the case, for example, of company car purchases by individual employees. This will certainly be true when none of the options available are really what the employee wants, yet they 'have' to spend their allowance! This should, however, have been picked up earlier in the process and these individuals established as a distinct group of customers.

# Micro-segments and their Decisive Buying Criteria (DBCs)

Definition: ●────
Decisive Buying Criteria are the perceived or stated attributes of a purchase that customers evaluate when choosing between alternative offers.

In this section we look at your micro-segments and, by reference to the picture you have built about the individuals they represent, along with their KDFs, determine what lies behind the choices they make so that we can understand their needs-based buying requirements. The benefits that are uncovered by this analysis are referred to in this book as 'Decisive Buying Criteria' (DBCs). They have been called this to emphasize the point that it is these attributes that determine which of the alternative offers the decision-makers will choose. 'Price' is therefore included as one of the DBCs.

## Marketing insight

This is a critical stage in the process as, once this analysis has been completed, the resulting list of DBCs are used to determine the segmentation structure of your market, as they provide the framework for comparing the micro-segments with each other. It is, therefore, important that you spend as much time as necessary in compiling these benefits.

To help identify the benefits for your market, you may need to involve some, or maybe all of the colleagues who helped you with the previous step. This included a cross-section of representatives from sales, marketing, customer services and so on, along with any individual familiar with appropriate past market surveys. If your company also follows the practice of putting together lost sales reports, or simply logs ad-hoc feedback of this nature, involving someone familiar with this information could also provide some useful input. Continuing the involvement of any intermediaries you included in the last step may also be appropriate.

Although the principle of approaching each step of the segmentation process from the customer's point of view is probably well-established by now, it is timely to highlight this requirement once again, as it is crucial that the benefits identified in this step are looked at from the customer's perspective, not your own. The two pertinent points to remind yourself and the segmentation team about while working through this step are that:

1 the benefits are for the market as a whole, not simply limited to those that you deliver to your customers; and,
2 these benefits are what the decision-makers regard as their decisive buying criteria, not what you would prefer them to see as their decisive buying criteria.

Although the segmentation process moves from KDFs to DBCs in this step, it is still useful to track the KDFs through to the concluding segments. The performance of your company with respect to these features, and those that may, in time, supersede them, is how customers assess your ability, and that of your competitors, to satisfy their needs. Your company's competitive position in each segment is looked at in Step 7 of the segmentation process.

In addition, this insight enables you to review the actual purchasing practice of the customers found in each segment. This is useful when determining the most appropriate strategies for the segments you elect to target. Setting marketing objectives and strategies for identified segments is looked at in Chapter 13.

**Marketing insight**

## Defining micro-segments by their needs

As a preparatory step, you may find it a useful exercise to draw up an initial list of benefits based on each KDF identified for the market as a whole and add these to any benefits you noted while developing the micro-segments. This can then be followed by the analysis of benefits for each micro-segment. Alternatively, you may prefer to leave any list of benefits you have developed this far as it is and move straight to the analysis of benefits for each micro-segment. Adopt the approach you feel most comfortable with. It is important to note, however, that only the benefits highlighted during the analysis of each micro-segment's needs, whether from a previously prepared list or additional to this list, become the DBCs.

The procedure to follow when identifying the benefits for each micro-segment can be summarized as follows:

1 Take one of your micro-segments, re-familiarize yourself with the customers it represents and carefully list the benefits being sought from their KDFs in order to identify their decisive buying criteria.
2 Now attempt to indicate the importance of each DBC to this micro-segment, including the importance of price, using a simple grading structure initially based on, for example, one to three stars.
3 Consider a cross-section of customers included in the micro-segment to confirm if they would all generally agree with the list of DBCs and their grading, and if they would not, develop additional micro-segments to cover any meaningful differences, redistribute the volume or value figure between them and, if required, adjust their profiling characteristics.

Repeat all three steps of this procedure for each micro-segment and, when completed, review each micro-segment against the complete list of DBCs and make any appropriate additions to the DBCs that have been identified for them.

Finally, review and compare the micro-segments with each other and increase or decrease the importance of appropriate DBCs if this better reflects the differences between individual micro-segments.

It is important not to force differences between micro-segments, as this will distort the final segmentation structure for your market.

**Marketing insight**

Taking each step of the above procedure in turn:

1 List the DBCs for each micro-segment.

Select one of your micro-segments and begin by re-familiarizing yourself with the customers it represents in order to put yourself back in their shoes once again (removing your own while doing so!). In the previous chapter we suggested that topics such as the type of life they lead (family, social, work), their personal situation and responsibilities, the issues that concern them, their background and their aspirations for the future can all help bring customers to life. We also suggested in the previous chapter that for the equivalent step in developing micro-segments, and for the steps that followed, you could consider splitting the participants into a number of teams with each team adopting the standpoint of particular customers. This approach could also be usefully applied here.

Now carefully think through what the micro-segment's KDFs really mean to these customers in terms of the underlying needs they are satisfying, taking the KDFs both individually and as a 'package'. It is sometimes only through specific combinations of features that customers obtain the benefits they are looking for. To help identify these needs, consider such questions as:

- Why do they look for these features?
- What do these features do for them?
- What are they really trying to achieve?
- Why are some features not of interest to them?
- What would they really like to achieve?
- What causes them disappointment?
- Why are they customers of ours and not of our competitors (and vice versa)?

Do not forget that a single feature can have more than one benefit and that different features can deliver the same benefit.

Apply the 'so what?' test suggested earlier in this chapter to ensure that you arrive at the real benefits, and consider using the benefit analysis worksheet in the Exercises section to take you through the sequence of features, advantages and benefits.

**Marketing insight**

You should find that around five benefits are sufficient to explain the motivations that drive the choices a micro-segment makes and, in turn, can truly be regarded as their *decisive* buying criteria. It certainly can be less than this, but rarely is it more than seven (which can occur for more complex products). If it is running at a high number, it may be because the benefit analysis is simply highlighting that the customers represented by the micro-segment are not as similar to each other after all (which is looked at in the third step of this procedure).

As you progressively pull together the full list of DBCs it is useful to show which particular KDF, or KDFs, each of them relate to. This is illustrated in Table 7.3 which appears as part of the next step. A further refinement you may be able to apply to the structure of this list is to arrange the benefits by the specific part of the marketing mix that delivers them, such as by product, promotion and place (price is covered in the next step), which is sometimes extended into a number of other 'Ps' such as people and processes. This assumes, however, that the 'Ps' do not share the same benefits. Alternatively, record the benefits as a straight-forward list if this is what you would prefer to do.

2 Indicate the importance of the DBCs for each micro-segment.
Once the benefits have been agreed for the micro-segment, complete the list of DBCs by adding 'price' and indicate the relative importance of all the DBCs to each other for that micro-segment. The importance given to their respective KDFs in the previous chapter is helpful here. Adopting the approach you took in the previous chapter to indicate importance can also be applied to the DBCs, the simplest approach being the use of tick marks or stars, as illustrated in Table 7.3.

---

A reminder: when considering the relative importance of 'price' to the other DBCs it is in terms of how readily the customers will give up other benefits to get a lower price. It is important that this is clearly understood by the team involved at this stage of the segmentation project, otherwise, as mentioned in the section on price, the conclusions will be misleading and the resulting marketing objectives and strategies will fail to deliver the best financial returns available to the company.

In most markets it is unusual to find more than around 10 per cent of customers who are true price chasers.

**Marketing insight**

---

**Table 7.3** Recording DBCs and indicating their relative importance to micro-segments

| Features | DBCs: benefits + price | Micro-segments | | | | |
|---|---|---|---|---|---|---|
| | | D | E1 | E2 | F | G |
| Light-weight Mounted on wheels | Easily moved around | | *** | *** | | * |
| Heavy-weight | OK in production areas | | | *** | | |
| Latest technology | Innovative functionality | *** | * | | | ** |
| Proven technology | Reduces training time | | | ** | *** | |
| 24/7 support staff | Fewer hold-ups for users | *** | | | ** | |
| Staff answer calls | Faster call handling | * | | | ** | *** |
| Small supplier | Personalized service | | | ** | | *** |
| Large supplier | Dependable back-up | ** | ** | | ** | |
| Large supplier | Easier approval of choice | | * | | | |
| | Price | * | * | * | ** | ** |

*Note:* While it is useful to show the link between DBCs and their KDFs, it is optional. The most important DBCs are identified by three stars (***) in this table.

A worksheet for recording DBCs and their relative importance by micro-segment appears in the Exercises section of this chapter. This worksheet also contains the option of showing the link between DBCs and their KDFs.

Although at this stage it helps if you use no more than three tick marks or stars to identify the most important DBCs, you may find that this does not adequately portray the relative importance of the DBCs to the micro-segment. Rather than increasing the number of tick marks or stars at this stage use 'half' tick marks ($^1\!/_2$) or an equivalent 'half' star, such as an outline star '☆', to extend the range.[1] Increasing the number of tick marks or stars above three is best left until you later review and compare the micro-segments with each other. This will ensure that the final picture remains visually comprehensible. Alternatively, you can use numbers to indicate the relative importance of the DBCs to each other. This is looked at in the next section.

| **Marketing insight** | Using a spreadsheet or database package on a PC is, once again, particularly helpful when putting together these lists. |
| --- | --- |

If you really do not feel able to indicate the relative importance of DBCs for micro-segments, simply indicate the applicable DBCs for each micro-segment with a single tick mark or star. This does not prevent you from completing your internal look at how your market splits into segments, though it could well have implications when you look at forming the segments in the next chapter. This will particularly be the case if the actual segments in the market share a number of DBCs but the importance they give to them is different and these differences need to be recognized in the offers designed to attract them.

3 Confirm that the customers in the micro-segment all generally agree.

Although the micro-segment consists of a recognizable group of decision-makers who have a similar level of interest in a specific set of features, and what is now being said about them is based on this, it is still appropriate to consider a cross-section of these customers to confirm that they would all *generally* agree both with the DBCs and their import-ance ratings. By 'generally agree' in this step we mean that they would positively respond to an offer presented to them on the basis of the bene-fits listed for them and have a similar level of sensitivity to price. This clearly has to be a matter of judgement at this point.

In those situations where you believe they would not all generally agree, develop new micro-segments to accommodate any meaningful differ-ences. Redistribute the size of the original micro-segment between them using, once again, your best guess and replicate the profiling character-istics, making any changes that are required. As on previous occasions, attach identification labels to each new micro-segment which continue the practice you have adopted for your project. Also ensure that any names retain their association with the individuals each micro-segment represents, which may require you to revise the name of the originating micro-segment if this would better describe who it now represents.

---

[1] This refinement is suggested for DBCs and not for KDFs because it is the DBCs that are used to compare one micro-segment with another when forming the concluding segments. Being more precise about the relative importance of the needs-based buying requirements and price can play a crucial role in these conclusions.

If in doubt, split them out! They will be reviewed again later.

Now repeat the above three steps for each micro-segment.

To keep the team on track, occasionally remind them that:

- the benefits are for the market as a whole, not simply limited to those benefits that you deliver to your customers; and,
- these benefits are what the decision-makers regard as their decisive buying criteria, not what you would prefer them to see as their decisive buying criteria.

Once all the micro-segments have been taken through these steps, you can review each micro-segment against the complete list of DBCs and make any necessary changes to the DBCs that have been identified for them. It is possible that as you have progressively been identifying the DBCs for each micro-segment, new DBCs have been uncovered that may be applicable to micro-segments looked at earlier.

Finally, review and compare the micro-segments with each other to ensure that you have adequately indicated the differences between them in terms of the importance of their various DBCs. Where required, increase or decrease the importance of appropriate DBCs for individual micro-segments to redress any 'imbalances' and better reflect the differences between them, but avoid imposing differences between micro-segments if such differences do not really exist. As was suggested for the final review of the micro-segments and their KDFs, it helps ensure that the final picture remains visually comprehensible if no more than five stars (or tick marks) are used to highlight the most important DBCs. Where necessary, however, use half tick marks ($^1/_2$) or 'half' stars (☆) if this better helps to reflect the differences between micro-segments.

The final list of DBCs is, of course, a list of the 'Market's DBCs'.

At this point you are in a position to pull together a substantial part of the brief for any external research you may be considering. It is suggested, however, that this is best deferred until your internal segmentation project has completed the phase of developing segments before finalizing the brief and commissioning the research.

## Expressing the relative importance of DBCs numerically

Numerically indicating the importance of DBCs was suggested as a possible option in the previous section and it is the approach most likely to be adopted for the quantitative stage of a segmentation research project as it is relatively quick and easy to administer, especially if this stage is conducted over the telephone. Two methods of numerically rating the importance of DBCs are reviewed here:

1 scoring each DBC out of ten;
2 apportioning a total score between the DBCs.

Taking each of these in turn:

1 Marks out of ten

Alternative importance scales can be used, such as a seven-point or a nine-point scale, and '0' is sometimes used instead of '1' for indicating 'no importance'. Whichever scheme is chosen, the principle behind the approach is the same.

With this approach, each DBC is rated on an importance scale of one to ten where '1' means the DBC is of no importance at all and '10' means it is extremely important. This approach to scoring is often suggested by research companies as the preferred method because it is the most time efficient and the simplest to administer, particularly if telephone interviews are being conducted. It also has to be said that this approach is, in the main, easily understood by respondents. However, its simplicity has a downside, as illustrated in the following example:

Assume there is a micro-segment that is not very price sensitive and values five DBCs, one of which is very dominant. The highest score that can be given to any DBC is '10', so the respondent gives the dominant DBC a score of '9'. As this micro-segment values four more DBCs, the inclination will be to give each of them a reasonable score in order to indicate their individual importance to the micro-segment. If we assume the scores for these four DBCs range from, say, '6' down to '4', averaging out at a score of '5', the total for these four DBCs comes to 20. Add a score for price of, say, '2' and the total for these less dominant criteria comes to 22. Although the dominance of one DBC when compared with everything else still remains, its true relative importance to the micro-segment is highly likely to be masked. A very dominant DBC could well account for 50 per cent or more of a decision. This could have crucial implications for the marketing strategy put together for a particular segment.

Table 7.4 summarizes the situation presented in the above example and illustrates how the 'rating' approach to scoring can hide the true relative importance of DBCs.

A further difficulty with using this approach in surveys is that some respondents are inclined to give low scores to everything and some inclined to give high scores, which means that comparing such respondents with each other and with the rest of the respondents distorts the results. It is usually anticipated, however, that the number of interviews conducted for the quantitative phase will minimize this problem.

2 Apportioning a total sum

While this is not the simplest of the two approaches being reviewed here and, therefore, the less easy to administer, it is better at indicating the true relative importance of the DBCs to each other and in itself generally

**Table 7.4** The 'rating' approach to scoring DBCs

| Decisive Buying Criteria | Individual rating: 1 to 10 | Re-scored to total 100 |
|---|---|---|
| Maintains 'pioneering' status | 9 | 29 |
| Enables precision work | 6 | 19 |
| Reduces labour requirement | 5 | 16 |
| Occupies little floor space | 5 | 16 |
| Easy to move | 4 | 13 |
| Price | 2 | 7 |
| Total | 31 | 100 |

*Note:* Re-scoring the individual ratings so that the total 100 is calculated by dividing each individual rating by the total of the ratings column (being 31 in this example) and multiplying the answer by 100 (as if you were expressing each individual rating as a percentage of the total). Although the dominance of 'maintains pioneering status' survives, its true relative importance, which in the example given could mean it accounted for over 50 per cent of the decision, is masked. Only the DBCs of importance appear in this table.

overcomes the problem of some respondents giving low scores and others high scores. We have, in fact, already touched on this method of scoring in the last chapter when discussing the 80/20 rule for identifying the features with the greatest influence.

In this approach, a total sum of, say, 100, is apportioned between the DBCs to indicate their relative importance to each other, with benefits that play no part in the decision being given no score at all. A useful starting point is to arrange the DBCs for the micro-segment in a descending order of importance, or simply number each of them accordingly. The total sum being apportioned is then distributed between the DBCs to represent their relative importance to each other. The simplest way of administering this method of scoring, you may recall, is to first score the most important out of 100 and then score each of the others relative to this score. This is then reset back to 100 by adding up all the individual scores, dividing each individual score by this total and multiplying the answer by 100. A fully worked example of this approach appeared for the case study in Table 6.11. Administering this approach along these lines is far better than trying to ensure that the total adds up to 100 at the outset. Table 7.5 shows what this looks like and uses the same example appearing in Table 7.4.

As will be apparent, when this approach to rating DBCs is adopted in research projects, it gets round the problem of some individuals always giving low scores and others always giving high scores.

Administering this approach during a research project is made easier if the respondents have the list of DBCs in front of them. This is easily done with face-to-face interviews or online questionnaires, and when conducting telephone interviews it can be achieved by either e-mailing or faxing this part of the questionnaire to the respondent. The alternative when conducting a telephone interview is to read through the list to the respondent and ask them to note down those that they care about (suggesting that this is kept to around five, but no more than seven).

**Table 7.5** The 'total sum' approach to scoring DBCs

| Decisive Buying Criteria | Initial individual score | Re-scored to total 100 |
|---|---|---|
| Maintains 'pioneering' status | 95 | 50 |
| Enables precision work | 50 | 26 |
| Reduces labour requirement | 15 | 8 |
| Occupies little floor space | 15 | 8 |
| Easy to move | 10 | 5 |
| Price | 5 | 3 |
| Total | 190 | 100 |

*Note:* Re-scoring the initial individual scores so that the total 100 is calculated by dividing each individual score by the total of the individual scores (being 190 in this example) and multiplying the answer by 100 (as if you were expressing each individual score as a percentage of the total). Only the DBCs of importance appear in this table.

The respondent then gives a score to their most important and using this as a reference point, they then score all the other relevant DBCs accordingly. During a telephone interview it is often necessary to run through the list a couple of times.

**Market research note**

For some respondents, scoring their most important DBC out of a lower figure is preferred. Clearly, the preference of the respondent should be respected, as it is important that they feel comfortable with what they are being asked to do. This flexibility is also more likely to produce a more accurate reflection of the respondent's priorities and, therefore, a more accurate segmentation result.

Because of what this approach involves, it is not as administratively easy or as fast as awarding each item a mark out of ten, but it is more accurate.

**Marketing insight**

The 'total sum preference' approach to scoring benefits is the least used of the two approaches summarized here, mainly because the extra time it requires increases the cost of the survey and reduces the time available for other questions, there being a finite time over which a respondent can be expected to participate. However, when it has been administered, the distinction between the concluding segments has usually been clearer.

# Techniques for uncovering unsatisfied needs

There are usually several main motivations in any market, just a few of which are of real importance to the decision-makers. These dimensions can be viewed as bipolar scales along which current offers in the market can be positioned. For example:

- Expensive/inexpensive
- Strong/mild
- Fast/slow
- Large/small
- Complex/simple
- Garish/subtle
- Masculine/feminine

The possibility of there being unsatisfied needs in a market can be determined by putting together a two-dimensional matrix with the axes selected from the list of main motivations and the current offers positioned accordingly. The resulting picture is often referred to as a 'bipolar map'. A simple example appears in Figure 7.2 which shows a bipolar map for detergents.

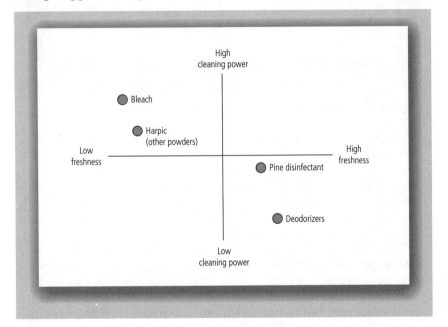

**Figure 7.2**
Bipolar map for detergents

Figure 7.2 would appear to suggest that there are a number of possible 'opportunity gaps' in the market for detergents where customers with unsatisfied needs could be found. But before investing resources in new products targeted at these gaps it is essential to ensure that the gaps do not exist simply because they represent products for which there is no demand.

Uncovering an opportunity gap populated by potential customers and then targeting these customers with an appropriately designed product enabled a struggling car company of the 1960s to become one of the world's top brands:

> Bayerische Motoren Werke, a motor company struggling to survive in the 1960s, desperately set out to uncover whether there were any unmet market opportunities in an already seemingly saturated market.

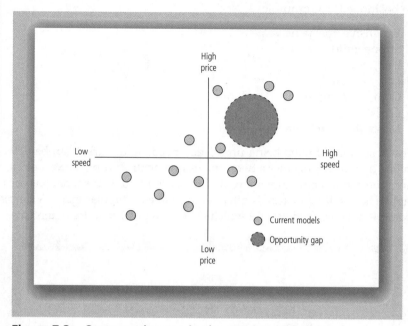

**Figure 7.3**   Opportunity gap in the 1960s' market for cars

After undertaking extensive market research to uncover both the needs of car buyers and how well the models available at that time met these needs, it became apparent that buyers of motor cars in the 1960s made their choice of model based primarily on two criteria, speed and price. The company then sat down and plotted out on a simple, two dimensional, matrix a 'picture' of the total market for cars as it was then, as shown in Figure 7.3.

The resulting picture revealed that there was a gap in the market, a gap with sufficient sales potential to justify the required capital investment, so the company set about building cars for it.

Today this motor company has only a small share of the total market for cars, but has a large share of the particular segment its namesake brand has become associated with. Rarely has the brand stepped outside its specialist segment. Today, many car manufacturers have fluctuating financial results, but BMW, as it is better known, continues to be one of the more profitable brands.

Not being alert to unsatisfied needs and having these opportunity gaps filled by competitors has sharply dented the performance of some companies:

In 1972, Rank Xerox, as it was then known, had an 80 per cent share of the UK market for replicating printed material in offices, schools and so on, and a margin of 40 per cent. This dominant position was principally down to the company's patented imaging technology, a patent that expired in 1972. Once the patent had

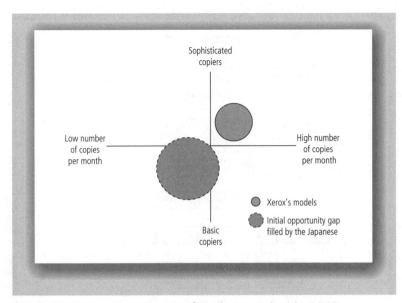

**Figure 7.4**  Opportunity gap for photocopiers in 1972

expired, Japanese companies came into the market with photo-copiers aimed at companies who did not need the sophisticated, high volume photocopiers produced by Xerox. By 1977, Xerox's share had dropped to 10 per cent and their margins had also dropped to 10 per cent. By 1983, however, helped by producing products better tuned to the needs of different segments in the market, Xerox had recovered some of its former position and had a 30 per cent share and 20 per cent margins. The bipolar map for 1972 appears in Figure 7.4.

A further technique which can be used to identify where there are needs not being fulfilled is to construct what could be termed a 'needs cascade'. This is simply a build-up of needs based on an analysis of functional requirements: in other words, requirements that do not take into account the less tangible aspects of buying such as attitudes and perceptions. In the pharmaceuticals market, for example, a needs cascade for the 'relief of pain and inflammation' could be constructed as illustrated in Figure 7.5.

The precise structure of this cascade may differ, of course, by sex, and further differ by age. Separate cascades would therefore need to be constructed for each of these different user groups, who could well have entered the segmentation process earlier as preliminary segments.

Clearly, however, it would be essential to qualify the size of the opportunity each distinct need represented. It may be necessary to 'backtrack' up the cascade and combine some of the needs before a distinct marketing strategy can be justified.

The examples presented so far have focused on the more functional needs of a market. Bipolar maps can also be based around the views and attitudes of customers and such maps are sometimes referred to as 'perceptual' maps. These maps have the advantage of being able to illustrate the changes which

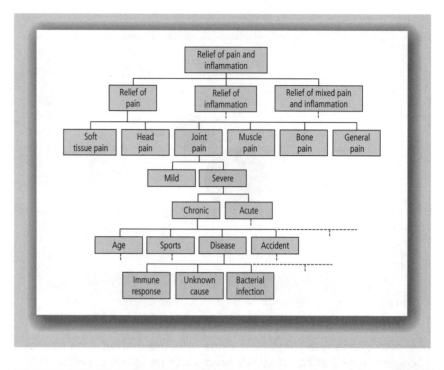

**Figure 7.5**
Extracts of a 'needs cascade' for the 'relief of pain and inflammation' (*Source:* Lidstone, J. (1989). 'Market segmentation for pharmaceuticals'. *Long Range Planning*, Vol. 22, No. 2, 54–62.)

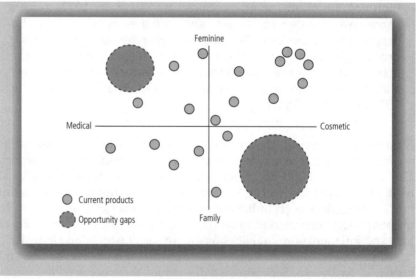

**Figure 7.6**
A perceptual map of the market for soap

can occur in a market's view of what a particular product line can represent. By plotting the position of currently available products on this map, opportunity gaps can be seen for positioning new products in the market, or even repositioning current brands, assuming, of course it is a gap waiting to be filled by currently under-served or potential new customers.

The example in Figure 7.6 looks at the market for soap in terms of soap being positioned between feminine brands and family brands, and between soaps with medical benefits and those with cosmetic benefits. Clearly, other dimensions are possible.

There appear to be two areas of opportunity in the market for soap as represented above. These new opportunities clearly would have to be evaluated before resources were committed to developing and launching suitable products in case they were actually representing areas where little or no demand existed. It is interesting to note that in the male toiletries market, there are an increasing number of new products positioned as having a cosmetic value. There has clearly been a major shift in this market which has opened up the 'cosmetic' area of the male's perceptual map.

As a final example, it is interesting to go back a few years and look at the perceptual map of the tabloid newspapers in the UK as they were in 1993, because it is a good example of a market in which brands (titles) have been steered towards new positions:

The dimensions used for the perceptual map in Figure 7.7 show the extremes of 'upmarket' and 'downmarket', which can, in some cases be associated with socio-economic group, and 'serious' and 'entertaining', the latter often being associated with 'exclusive' stories about individuals which the individuals concerned would prefer not to be highlighted!

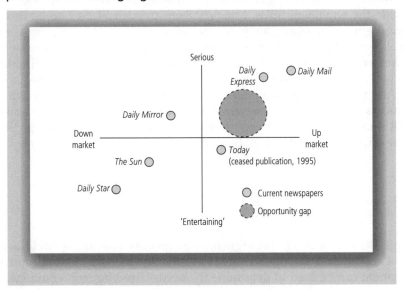

**Figure 7.7** Perceptual map of the market for tabloid newspapers (1993)

In this market, the *Daily Mail*, for example, was gradually steered towards its 'upmarket' position and the *Today* newspaper also changed position and became more 'serious', a move which possibly contributed to its demise. More recently, *The Sun* and the *Daily Mirror* have seen themselves as occupying about the same position, and in 2002 the *Daily Mirror* sought to distance itself from its arch rival by dropping its 'red top'[2] to look more 'serious'.

[2] A number of tabloids in the UK have their brand name appearing on a red banner at the top of the front page and are referred to as the 'red tops'. They tend to be from the less serious stable.

With respect to the moves that have occurred in the above example, it is important that we do not confuse deliberate repositioning with drifting. The danger of drifting is that it can often take a product into the weak, middle ground.

# Addendum for those intending to test the validity of a current SBU structure

This note is for those of you who are segmenting a market that straddles a number of strategic business units (SBUs) in the company, and have, so far, been looking at only one of them, though the intention is to take the other SBUs through the process. We covered this situation in Chapter 4 when discussing how to define the market.

You are now at a stage in the process where it is useful to take stock and tackle the remaining SBUs, bringing them through Steps 1 to 4. This is because Step 5 is where the process combines like-minded micro-segments. If all your SBUs are, therefore, included in Step 5, it will enable you to see whether your current SBU structure is the most appropriate for the market, or whether a more customer-focused structure for your business is required.

Alternatively, you may prefer to take the first SBU through the whole process in order to become familiar with it, after which, the remaining SBUs are taken through Steps 1 to 4, with the first SBU taken through Step 5 again, once the remaining SBUs are ready.

# Process check

This, the fourth step in the segmentation process, provides guidelines on how the information pulled together in the previous step for each micro-segment can be used to determine the needs-based buying requirements of the decision-makers they each represent. These findings will then provide the basis on which the final segments will be formed, which means that this step must be worked through both carefully and thoroughly.

We began by briefly discussing the two principal theories of customer behaviour, the rational customer and the psycho-socio customer, but pointed out that although they provided useful insights, they rarely explained the totality of customer behaviour. The clear conclusion was that explaining customer behaviour in terms of the 'benefits' they were looking for from the choices they made was by far the most useful and practical approach. In particular, this approach provides the insights that can be used to organize the most appropriate proposition for each concluding segment, which is a key deliverable from a segmentation project.

The section explaining customer behaviour then moved on to a more detailed discussion about features and benefits, starting with a useful sequence for advancing from a feature to a benefit. We pointed out that a single feature can deliver more than one benefit and that the same benefit can be delivered by more than one feature, and explained the distinction between 'standard' benefits, 'company' benefits and 'differential' benefits. We also pointed out that in order to uncover the real needs and true motivations of customers, it was essential that the explanation of their behaviour went beyond the status quo.

The final topic in our discussion about customer behaviour covered the role of 'price'. Here we emphasized that it was the relative importance of price to the other buying criteria that was of interest to a segmentation project, 'price' being a measure of value placed by the customer on the tangible and intangible components of their purchase. We highlighted that the ability of one supplier to price its products lower than everyone else was not an issue in segmentation, though it clearly would be of major concern to the other suppliers.

With the discussion of benefits complete, we then presented the three steps to follow when determining the needs-based buying requirements of the decision-makers in each micro-segment. We refer to these benefits, along with price, as their 'Decisive Buying Criteria' (DBCs). The steps began with an analysis of the benefits customers were seeking from their KDFs. These were then graded, along with price, to indicate their relative importance to each other, followed by a check to ensure that everyone in the micro-segment would agree with what was now being said about them. We emphasized the importance of approaching all of this from the customers' perspective and suggested that the approach to take when developing and grading the DBCs was to place yourself back in the shoes of the customers once again.

While tick marks and stars can be used to indicate the relative importance of the DBCs we also discussed the option of using numeric scales. Two approaches were presented, one which scored each DBC out of 10 and another which distributed a total sum of, say 100, between the DBCs.

We then moved on to discuss some techniques that could be used to help identify unsatisfied needs in the market, but at the same time pointed out that 'gaps' sometimes appear in markets because there are no customers with that particular need rather than there being an untapped opportunity.

Finally, we included a short addendum in which we suggested that for those who were segmenting a market that straddled across a number of strategic business units in their company but, so far, had only been looking at one of them, this was a suitable stage in the process to consider bringing all of them into the process.

## Case study

Spread across the 34 micro-segments the segmentation team at Agrofertilizer Supplies had developed in the previous step, were 14 KDFs (the two additional KDFs to those appearing in Table 6.12 in the previous chapter being 'Urea and manufactured blends' and 'direct' sales). The team now had to look at these KDFs in terms of the real needs their representative sample of different decision-making farmers were looking to obtain from them, not overlooking the possibility that the choices made by some farmers could be reflecting unsatisfied needs.

Identifying the needs-based buying requirements of their market and understanding what the farmers were really trying to achieve proved to be quite challenging for the segmentation team. This was primarily down to two key reasons:

1 the company had sold fertilizers from the very first day based on their technical specification and what this gave the crops in terms of the nutrients they required, not what the farmer was actually trying to achieve in totality;
2 with fertilizers 'officially' declared to be a commodity it was, for many in the industry, all down to price and moving the analysis of buying behaviour out of this death trap had been given very little thought.

The team also believed that any list of benefits they developed would be contested, even with the sales force involved.

Input for this stage of the project finally came from a qualitative piece of market research they commissioned conducted by an independent research company skilled in this particular area of market research. This resulted in a total of ten market DBCs with the inclusion of price, and these were graded for each of the micro-segments. A selection of micro-segments and their DBCs appears in Table 7.6 and, as you will see, the team used the total sum approach for illustrating the relative importance of the DBCs to each micro-segment.

**Table 7.6** DBCs and their scores for a selection of micro-segments in the case study

| Features | DBCs: benefits + price | Micro-segments | | | | |
| --- | --- | --- | --- | --- | --- | --- |
| | | A1 | A6 | G3 | G9 | M1 |
| AN & bespoke blends Urea & bespoke blends | Innovative/new | – | 38 | – | 22 | – |
| AN & bespoke blends Urea & bespoke blends | Sophisticated | – | 14 | – | 5 | – |
| AN & manufactured blends Well-established brand | Proven/traditional (reassurance) | 24 | – | 21 | – | 35 |
| High consistency (of nutrients – NPK) | Healthy-looking crop or grass | 6 | – | – | – | 5 |
| High consistency (of nutrients – NPK) Low nitrogen level | Healthy-looking animal stock | – | – | 26 | – | 5 |
| Well-established brand | Service (qualified help) | 23 | – | – | – | 15 |
| High consistency (no lumps or dust) | Ease of handling | 21 | – | 9 | – | 25 |
| High nitrogen level | Maximum output/ yield per acre | – | 32 | – | 9 | – |
| Local distributor | Convenience/easy access to supplies | 16 | – | 39 | – | 10 |
| | Price | 10 | 16 | 5 | 64 | 5 |
| *Total* | | 100 | 100 | 100 | 100 | 100 |

*Note:* 'A' identifies micro-segments originating from the Arable preliminary segment, 'G' for micro-segments from the Grassland preliminary segment and 'M' for micro-segments from the Mixed preliminary segment. Although the benefit of having 'healthy looking crop or grass' receives only small scores in the above table, there were other micro-segments who were seen to score it at around 25.

Once the potential implications of the results were realized, the initial conclusions were tested by commissioning a detailed quantitative market research project. The results from this illustrated that while the team had miscalculated the importance of benefits in some areas, their overall conclusions had provided a general indication of the reality. The research project, however, provided not just accuracy, but also the robustness the team would need when presenting the results and the strategic messages it carried.

The status of the case study at the end of Step 4 is summarized in Figure 7.8.

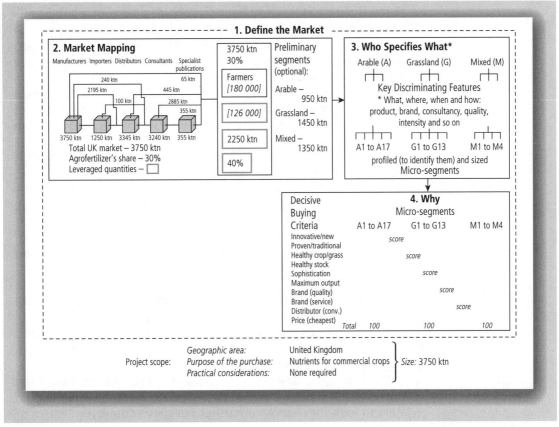

**Figure 7.8**
The segmentation process – Steps 1 to 4

# Further examples

Success in identifying the real benefits being sought by customers in a market can lead to remarkable increases in market share when the right offer is put in place. Unfortunately, getting it wrong can have exactly the reverse effect.

The first example is an extract from an article which appeared in the mid-1980s. Here we see that one overseas tour operator has correctly identified a growing preference in the UK market for self-catering holidays, while some of its competitors have not caught on so quickly. In fact, one of the competing tour operators makes an overall assumption that the holidaymakers buying this type of holiday have traded down and bought on price. This fails to acknowledge that there could well be other benefits associated with self-catering holidays which are more important to these holidaymakers than price, such as the freedom to eat *what* they want, at a place *where* they want and at a time *when* they want.

---

Shrewd anticipation of holiday trends has paid off for Intasun by nearly doubling its share of the Greek market.

By buying heavily into the Greek self-catering sector for 1985 the leading operator has captured a 17 per cent stake compared to the nine points held last year.

According to the latest figures produced by the British Market Research Bureau this means it is breathing down the necks of flagging front runner Thomson Holidays which has plunged from 28 points to 19.

Horizon's share has fallen five points to 11, while Olympic Holidays has dropped two points to four.

Apart from Intasun, the other star performers are Sunmed – whose share has doubled to ten points – and Grecian which is up to 11 from eight.

Commenting on overall trade, the managing director of Olympic Holidays said that holidaymakers had traded down and bought on price.

'Specialists at the bottom of the market such as Grecian and Sunmed and Intasun have done well, while those offering more expensive hotel holidays are down on last year.

'But only 35 per cent of the Greek market is self-catering, and Sunmed is probably around 70 per cent sold out, so the hotel holidays will have to start filling soon.'

The managing director of Olympic Holidays warned that if the British did not fill up the beds in Greece, then hoteliers would start to look for clients from other European countries.

*Source: Travel Trade Gazette, UK.*

---

The understanding of customer needs and the provision of holidays to match them has moved on a great deal since this article appeared.

The second example consists of a short series of mini-case histories:

*Pampers*   When 'Pampers'[3] were first test-marketed by Procter & Gamble (P&G), the results were extremely disappointing. The 'convenience' offered by the product, along with its high price, failed to impress its target customers. The real benefit that turned this product into a winner, supported by a price

---

[3] 'Pampers' is a registered trade mark of Procter & Gamble.

that presented the offer as a value proposition, was its ability to keep babies drier and that it could be used as a permanent replacement for nappies, rather than a convenient stand-by for when you were out.

*New Coke*  The failure to recognize a particular benefit was the undoing of 'New Coke', launched in 1985 by the Coca-Cola Company to replace 'Coke' with the claim that it was offering a better taste. We briefly mentioned this case in Chapter 3. What the new product could not inherit from its stable mate was the emotional association the original drink had, particularly in its home market, with all that was American.

*Plastic*  In a car showroom for a brand of cars made by General Motors a sales executive was challenged by a customer over the amount of plastic in the car. Without batting an eyelid, the sales assistant pointed out that this reduced the overall weight of the car, which clearly meant that the power to weight ratio was much better. The customer bought the car.

Not long afterwards, a second customer was being shown round the various cars on display by the same sales executive. This customer also made exactly the same comment about the amount of plastic in the car. Once again, the sales executive explained that this reduced the overall weight of the car. However, on this occasion, the reduction in weight, so the sales executive enthusiastically pointed out, meant that it improved the fuel consumption of the car. This customer also bought the car.

*Post-it Notes*  Sometimes a potential winner is developed, but the company struggles to recognize what it is about the product that makes it a valued proposition. This was the case when a section of 3M developed a glue that didn't bind items together, but merely attached them to each other. This, as far as the company was concerned, at least for a short time, was not what glue was about! But along with this new type of glue was the idea of adding it to square pieces of paper, sold in blocks, which could be used to write notes on, detached from the block and then conveniently attached to a desk, chair, wall, door, well, anything really, for the intended, but absent, recipient, knowing that it would still be there when the recipient returned. Conveniently, just as easily as it was attached, the recipient could then detach it and, if they wanted to keep it, reattach it to where they would not miss it, again knowing that it would still be there when they needed to refer to it. Obvious, isn't it!

The outcome was the launch of 'Post-it Notes'.[4]

---

[4] 'Post-it' is a registered trade mark of 3M.

*A handle*  A supermarket that sold drinks in large plastic bottles, as well as in other containers, was receiving feedback from some of its customers about the difficulties they were having in handling these large bottles. The customers, however, liked the large bottles as it meant that they could store larger quantities of these drinks in the storage space they had available, which, in turn, meant that they didn't have to shop as often. In addition, the price for these larger bottles of drink meant that the customer received better value for money. The supermarket took their customer's problem to the manufacturer of the plastic bottles and asked them to design a bottle that was easier to handle.

The manufacturer missed the point, and asked its engineers to design a more rigid bottle so that the customer would feel more confident in holding it. The engineers, responding to the brief, came up with a design consisting of a skeletal structure built inside the bottle which met the brief exactly. The manufacturer turned the design into a product, shipped them to the supplier of drinks, and these much improved plastic bottles were soon on the shelves of the supermarket.

It was still difficult to handle.

It's not often that the benefit being sought actually describes the feature that best delivers it!

Eventually, large plastic bottles with handles began to appear.

# Reference

Lidstone, J. (1989). 'Market segmentation for pharmaceuticals'. *Long Range Planning*, Vol. 22, No. 2, 54–62.

# Exercises

**Exercise 7.1**  The following is a list of various benefits:

Availability – when required
Convenience – where required
Reduces required stocks (of supplies) – prompt delivery
Proven/trusted performance
Innovative/leading edge
Efficient performance
Personalized service
Respects my personal 'space'
Eye-catching/grabs attention
Saves time

After-sales support (resolves issues, rather than logs them)
Long-lasting/robust
Looks good – streamlined/sleek
Looks good – chunky/solid
Looks extravagant – feels good
Child-proof (safety)
Sporty image
High-tech image
Space-saving design
Portable

Referring now to Exercise 6.2 in the last chapter which looked at your KDFs for a product or service you use at home or at work, select from the above list any benefits that apply to you when buying this particular product or service, and note the particular feature that delivers it. If there are other benefits you are looking for, also note these down, along with their associated KDF. When you have linked a benefit with a feature, capture this link on the worksheet in Table 7.7 and take it through the feature, advantage and benefit sequence. As for previous worksheets, make as many copies as you need of this, and the following worksheet.

Now transfer the list of benefits to the worksheet in Table 7.8, add price to the list, assuming it is not already there, and, using one of the micro-segment columns, score this list of DBCs so that it reflects their relative importance to you. Either score each of them out of 10, with '10' meaning it is extremely important (and '1' meaning it is of no importance, but that shouldn't apply at this stage), or apportion a total of 100 between the benefits to indicate their relative importance to each other (made easier if you score the most important out of 100 and score the other benefits relative to this score, and reset them so that they total 100, as described earlier in this chapter). The worksheet in Table 7.8 also enables you to record the relationship between the DBCs and their respective KDFs.

The exercise being referred to in the previous chapter also suggested that you created a micro-segment for someone else you knew who was also in this market. If this is the case, record the benefits and their relative importance to each other for this micro-segment using both worksheets.

**Table 7.7** Worksheet – developing KDFs into benefits

| Customer appeal | Feature | Advantage | Benefit |
|---|---|---|---|
| *What issues are of concern this customer?* *For example, availability, safety, reliability, simplicity, fashionable, leading-edge and so on.* | *What features of the product or service, channel and so on in the customer's view best represent these issues?* *What are they?* *How do they work?* *(The list of KDFs)* | *What advantages do these features provide?* *In other words, what do they do for the customer?* | *How can tangible benefits for be expressed to give maximum customer appeal? In other words, what does the customer get that they explicitly need?* |

Micro-segment:

| Customer appeal | KDF | *which means that:* | Advantage | *which means that:* | Benefit |
|---|---|---|---|---|---|
| | | | | | |

**Table 7.8** Worksheet – recording DBCs and their relative importance by micro-segment, along with their link to features (optional)

| Features | DBCs: benefits + price | Micro-segments and their DBC scores | | | | |
|---|---|---|---|---|---|---|
| | | | | | | |
| | Price | | | | | |
| | *(if apportioning a total sum)* Total | | | | | |

*Note:* While it is useful to show the link between DBCs and their KDFs, it is an optional entry on this worksheet.

**Exercise 7.2**     Now apply the last exercise to the micro-segments you have developed for the market your company is in. After drawing up the list of benefits and scoring them for a selection, or all, of the micro-segments, discuss your conclusions with others in the organization to obtain their views on the benefits and how the micro-segments would score them.

# Chapter 8

# Forming market segments out of like-minded decision-makers

The segmentation process has now reached the point where all the details required for segmenting the market are in place. This, the fifth and final step in the development of segments, as illustrated in Figure 8.1, constructs these segments based on the decisive buying criteria identified in the last chapter.

**Stage 1 – Your market and how it works**

**Step 1 – Defining the 'market'**
The scope of the project

**Step 2 – Market mapping**
Structure and decision-makers

**Stage 2 – Decision-makers and transactions**

**Step 3 – Who specifies what**
Decision-makers and their purchases

**Stage 3 – Segmenting the market**

**Step 4 – Why**
The needs of decision-makers

**Step 5 – Forming segments**
Combining like-minded decision-makers

**Figure 8.1**
The segmentation
process – Step 5

Once the segments have been formed, the picture is completed by consolidating for each segment the profiling attributes and estimates of size put together in Step 3 for the customers they now represent.

With a manageable number of micro-segments, internally resourced segmentation projects can conduct this step manually, and this chapter provides the guidelines you require to form your segments this way. Most internally resourced projects should, therefore, be able to construct their own segments along these lines. The alternative is to use a computer package specifically designed for the purpose, such as the PC-based software package developed in association with the authors,[1] the assistance of which will certainly be required for the quantitative stage of any market research you commission.

This chapter is organized as follows:

- A 'fast track' for those looking for a quick route through the key points
- An introduction to 'market segments' and an overview of their key components
- A discussion about the size of segments and economic viability
- Balancing market segments with the number of different marketing strategies a company can handle

---

[1] Details of this package, called Market Segment Master®, can be obtained from Ian Dunbar using info@marketsegmentation.co.uk. Full contact details can be found in the Preface of this book.

- The order of events for developing market segments (clustering) and the clustering routines to consider
- How to carry out visual clustering (pattern matching)
- How to progress through mathematical clustering
- The mechanics for isolating the most important buying criteria
- A brief discussion about 'acceptable differences' between customers
- Working through clustering outcomes that may not have been expected
- Some brief comments about computer-assisted clustering techniques and working with external agencies conducting this analysis
- The rites of passage for a cluster to become a segment, along with some further comments on customer profiling
- A review of this step in the segmentation process
- The concluding segments for the case study and some further examples
- Exercises further to help you with this step

# Fast track

- Ensure that all the DBCs appear for each micro-segment and in the same order, and remove any DBCs that appear in all the micro-segments with the same, or very similar importance ratings. Consider clustering the micro-segments using only their most important DBCs, such as those accounting for, say, 80 per cent of the decision.
- Arrange the micro-segments so that all of them with the same top-rated DBC are placed next to each other and merge those micro-segments that are exact or very close matches to each other to form some initial clusters.
- Transfer each micro-segment and, if appropriate, each initial cluster onto a separate sheet of paper with the importance of each DBC represented by one of the three formats in Figure 8.2.

  If you would prefer to follow a mathematical clustering routine, please refer to the relevant section that appears later in this chapter.
- Lay the micro-segments out on a table, select one of them and find its closest match and place them together. Take another micro-segment and repeat the same routine and build clusters of micro-segments by progressively decreasing the level of similarity customers or clusters must have with each other before they can be merged together. Periodically produce consolidated pictures for each cluster if this makes them easier to work with, and express the importance ratings of each DBC as an average (or weighted average) of the micro-segments it represents. Label each cluster CL1, CL2 and so on and make a note of the micro-segments each represents. Do not overlook the fact that a segment can consist of a single micro-segment, particularly if that micro-segment is of sufficient size to qualify as a segment (see later).
- Continue until you have produced a series of clusters, each populated by customers who share a similar level of interest in the same, or comparable, set of needs (the definition of a 'market segment'). If the number of clusters either corresponds to the number of segment-specific

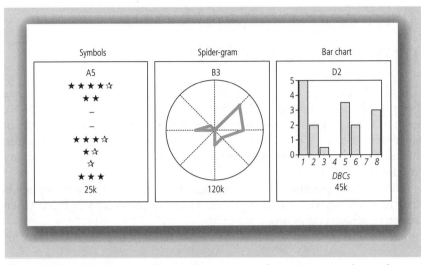

**Figure 8.2**  Fast track – alternative approaches to comparing micro-segments with each other visually
(*Note:* Consider transferring the details of each micro-segment onto acetates with white backing paper so that you have the option of overlaying them when checking how similar they are to each other. The 'Y' axis on the bar chart is the importance rating of the DBCs.)

marketing strategies your company could work with, or is up to 50 per cent more than this number, you have arrived at an ideal conclusion (you are unlikely to find all of the segments attractive to your company). Most markets tend to divide into between five and ten segments.

- Once completed, take each cluster and from the information associated with its constituent micro-segments, work out the importance rating for its DBCs (as an average or weighted average), produce its profiling characteristics and calculate its overall size. As a minimum, this size should at least equal the minimum size you require a segment to have to justify the expense of putting together a separate marketing strategy for it. If required, include future growth forecasts in this figure. Consolidating the KDFs for each cluster is optional at this stage of the process.
- For a cluster to qualify as a segment, it is essential that it is of sufficient size to make it worth being considered a business opportunity; it can be served by a distinct marketing strategy; it can be reached by sales and distribution channels currently used, or which could be used; the customers in it can be identified and reached by means of a distinctive and cost effective communications strategy; and a structure, information and decision-making system can be adopted which will enable it to be served effectively.
- A worksheet for recording market segments, their DBCs and profiling characteristics appears in the Exercises section of this chapter.

Readers who are reasonably confident that they have developed the segments found in their defined market may go straight to Chapter 9.

This concludes the fast track for Step 5 of the segmentation process.

# The components of a market segment

The whole purpose of this first phase of the segmentation process has been to develop segments within the defined market (market segments), each of them populated by decision-makers who share a similar level of interest in the same, or comparable, set of needs. This can then be used to develop the most appropriate offer for each of the segments the company chooses to target.

The first component of a market segment is, therefore, the list of needs that the individuals in that segment regard as important to them when selecting which competing offer to buy.

## Marketing insight

An important distinction to note here, and one first mentioned in Chapter 4, is that between a 'market' and a 'segment':

While a 'market' describes a customer need in a way which covers the aggregation of all the alternative products or services customers regard as capable of satisfying that need, 'segments' focus on specific products or services, their characteristics and properties, along with other components of the total marketing proposition, that different groups of customers are looking for in order to satisfy their particular needs within a market.

A key difference, therefore, between a 'market' and a 'segment' is that a specific marketing strategy can be defined for a segment, whereas for a market, we can only list the alternative products or services. It is simply a different level of aggregation of customer needs.

Successful targeting of segment-specific offers, however, requires an understanding of who is to be found in each of these segments so that there is some way of communicating with, and reaching them. Unless they can be isolated in this way, difficulties will be encountered when implementing strategies targeted at specific segments.

The second component of a market segment is, therefore, the profiling attributes of its decision-makers.

But before any resources are committed to developing segment-specific offers and in putting together the appropriate communication and distribution plans, it is essential that the level of business each segment represents is assessed. While this may need to be an informed best guess at this stage of an internal segmentation project, subsequent research can be used to provide a more thorough assessment.

The third and final component of a market segment is, therefore, its size.

In summary, each segment consists of:

1 The needs regarded as important by the decision-makers it represents.
2 Characteristics that tell us who these decision-makers are.
3 A volume or value figure.

If you have rigorously been following the steps in the segmentation process to this point, all the above information will now be embedded in your micro-segments; their profiling attributes and an estimate of their size developed for them in Step 3, and their needs identified in Step 4.

---

As pointed out in the previous chapter, it is also useful to track the KDFs through to the concluding segments. Your company's performance with respect to these features, and those that may, in time, supersede them, is how customers assess your ability, and that of your competitors, to satisfy their needs. Company competitiveness by segment is looked at in Chapter 10.

In addition, as we also pointed out, this insight enables you to review the actual purchasing practice of the customers found in each segment. This is useful when determining the most appropriate strategies for the segments you elect to target and is looked at in Chapter 13.

Consolidating the KDFs for each segment is not, however, essential for this step in the segmentation process.

**Marketing insight**

---

Before reviewing the micro-segments to determine which of them can be merged on the basis of the needs they share, there are two questions to consider:

1 What is the minimum volume or value you require each segment to have (or, perhaps, the minimum number of customers) for it to become an economically attractive group of customers?[2]
2 How many segments could the company actually work with?

For many companies, the more difficult of these two questions concerns the number of segments they will be able to support with different marketing strategies, especially if the performance of the company is judged by its *market* share.

## Size of market segments

The question about the economic size of a segment is one that has to be considered by those businesses where tailoring their propositions around the different needs of *individual* customers is unlikely to produce the returns required by the company. This is very likely to be the case for companies with limited resource flexibility, such as those producing products or services that require investment in large fixed/capital assets, and where tailoring is severely limited by technical considerations, as would be the case in pharmaceuticals.[3] Such companies would clearly need to establish minimum thresholds of segment viability that were fairly high. At the other end of the spectrum are those companies with a high degree of resource flexibility, such as those dependent on human resources, and with

---

[2] This figure should bear in mind, of course, that in most if not all segments you will have a share of their custom rather than all of it.

[3] 'Resource flexibility' and 'tailoring' were raised in Chapter 3 as considerations in effective market segmentation, along with the degree to which customer needs differ, which is mentioned in the next paragraph.

almost no technical limitations on their proposition flexibility, as would be the case for consulting services. However, even for these latter companies, unless they are offering full individual tailoring of every proposition, they will still need to establish some minimum threshold, but it would be substantially lower than that set by the capital intensive organizations. Figure 8.3 summarizes this relationship.

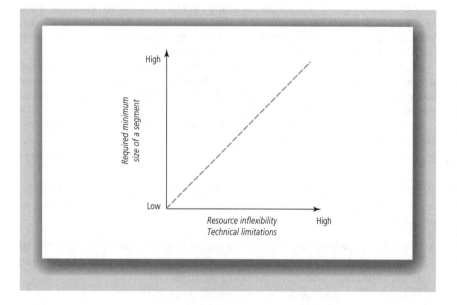

**Figure 8.3**
The relationship between resource inflexibility/ technical limitations and viable segment size

The impact this decision has on how far the concluding segments represent a compromise of the ideal from the customer's point of view will depend on the degree to which customer needs differ within the defined market. If they differ on only a limited number of specific needs and the minimum segment size is high, there will probably be very little, if any compromise. On the other hand, if they differ on quite a number of specific needs and the minimum segment size is high, then the degree of compromise could be quite high. It only 'could' be quite high because the aim of the clustering routines is to minimize the level of compromise between the customers that are merged to form a particular segment.

The degree to which customer needs differ in your market will, of course, be reflected to some extent in the number of micro-segments you finished with at the end of Step 4 in the last chapter. This number cannot, however, be taken as an absolute indication because it is possible that some of the micro-segments, when redefined in terms of their needs, are now very similar to each other.

**Marketing insight**

When customers are being merged to achieve an economic size but, as independent groups, they could support distinct propositions, consider the future size of business they could represent. If it looks as if this will go above the minimum threshold in an acceptable period of time (normally the time horizon for your marketing plan) then it would clearly be better to keep them separate.

This consideration would be particularly important for those customer groups you may have introduced into your project whose needs are not being currently met in the market.

The future size of segments is a topic covered in Chapter 9.

## Number of market segments

Turning now to the question about the number of segments the company could actually work with, it will be clear from what has already been said, that unless you are a company with a high degree of resource flexibility with almost no technical limitations on your proposition flexibility, you will need to consider how many different segment-specific marketing strategies your company could handle.

Most markets tend to divide into between five and ten segments, so if you were planning to serve every segment in the market, you could be looking at between five and ten different propositions.

Marketing insight

With respect to the number of segments you could work with, whatever this number is, increase it by, say, around one-half as it is unlikely you will find that all the concluding segments are actually attractive to your company, or that you can effectively compete in all of them. Segment attractiveness and your competitiveness are looked at in Chapters 9 and 10 respectively. If the number you arrive at is close to the resulting number of segments, you will have arrived at an ideal conclusion.

If the ideal conclusion evades you and the most appropriate number of segments from the customer's point of view is outside this range, it is interesting to continue merging customers until your ideal has been reached, but only after the customer's ideal conclusion has been recorded. The two results can then be compared with each other, with particular attention paid to the level of compromise that has had to occur with respect to the needs recorded for each segment. It will then be a matter of judgement on the strategy you adopt, the options being:

1 adopt the customer's ideal segmentation conclusion and run with the number of different propositions you are comfortable with handling effectively, thereby targeting a lower proportion of the market, but with competitive offers; or,

2 adopt the customer's ideal segmentation conclusion and work out how to run with a higher number of different propositions effectively, thereby targeting a higher proportion of the market with competitive offers; or,

3 adopt your ideal segmentation conclusion and run with the number of different propositions you are comfortable with handling effectively, thereby targeting a higher proportion of the market but with competitively weakened offers (especially if other companies have offers that are more precisely targeted).

# Building micro-segments into market segments – clustering

For internally resourced segmentation projects that have a manageable number of micro-segments, which tends to be most of them, it is possible to build the market segments manually. The alternative is to build the segments with the assistance of a suitable computer-based clustering package. The use of such packages will certainly be required for the quantitative stage of any market research. A short discussion about computer-assisted clustering techniques and working with external agencies conducting this analysis occurs later in this chapter.

The general order of events in clustering can be summarized as follows:

1 Begin by looking for customers who are an exact match with each other in respect of the benefits they are looking for and the importance they give these benefits and merge identical customers together to form some initial clusters.

2 Next, look for any customers and clusters that are a very close match with each other and merge them together to create a revised set of clusters.

3 Continue by progressively decreasing the level of similarity customers and clusters must have with each other before they can be merged together, revising the clusters until the best or desired result has been achieved.

| Marketing insight | Forcing customers together who are really quite different from each other in terms of their needs simply to achieve segment size targets and/or the preferred number of segments, should be avoided. By definition, they do not qualify as a segment, as they will not be sharing a similar level of interest in the same, or comparable, set of needs. In such situations, the guidelines you have set for the project should be reconsidered. If it is to do with segment size, don't overlook the future size of business the customer groups could represent.

Any competitor who is able to target a specific group of customers with an offer aligned to their needs is more likely to win their business. |
|---|---|

Whether you tackle clustering manually or with a computer, there are two clustering routines you can consider when forming segments and a third routine which is interesting to look at if your company currently segments customers on the basis of their profiling attributes.

*Routine 1*    This routine is the most obvious routine to follow as it merges micro-segments together according to how similar they are to one another with respect to the relative importance they have given to each Decisive Buying Criterion (DBC) identified for the market.

Once completed, the profiling attributes and estimates of size that accompanied each micro-segment should be consolidated for each concluding segment.

Although we refer to the 'similarity' between micro-segments, it is often described as determining the 'difference' between micro-segments, especially when clustering is conducted mathematically. To be more accurate, therefore, each segment should be described as consisting of customers who have an 'acceptable' level of difference between them.

A brief discussion on 'acceptable' differences occurs later in this chapter. It is based around the effect a merger of customers has on the most appropriate marketing strategy.

**Marketing insight**

Depending on how satisfied you are with the degree of 'fit' obtained by this first clustering, in other words, how well the micro-segments come together to form distinct segments, you may wish to explore the alternative routine to see whether or not this 'fit' can be improved upon:

*Routine 2*   A selective DBC clustering routine which follows the principles of the first routine, except that you select which particular market DBCs to include, which could possibly see 'price' taken out of the equation. This may be a useful routine if the score for one, or more, of the clustering criteria is/are similar across the micro-segments. It can also be useful if one, or more, of the benefits is, in fact, becoming an expected part of the offer and less of a differentiator. Seeing what would happen when this DBC becomes a market 'qualifier' (and therefore removed from the segmentation equation) can provide you with an interesting future vision of the market – a vision which could provide you with a valuable strategic advantage.

As for the first routine, once completed, the profiling attributes and estimates of size that accompanied each micro-segment should be consolidated for each concluding segment.

As already mentioned, a final routine which is sometimes interesting to look at concentrates on the profiling attributes of each micro-segment;

*Routine 3*   This routine merges micro-segments together to form segments based on the similarity of their profiling attributes.

When this routine is completed, the similarity (or otherwise) of the scores for their market DBCs are shown for each of the concluding 'segments'.

If segments are, however, about groups of customers with the same or comparable set of needs, the value of this third routine is limited to simply satisfying curiosity. However, if your company is currently following a segmentation structure built around customer profiles, such as industry types, and your needs-based segmentation project has identified that this is not in fact the case, being able to produce the results based on a current view held by the business can help the segmentation team persuade the company to change.

Two approaches to manual clustering are looked at in this chapter:

1 visual clustering; and,
2 mathematical clustering.

The second of these approaches will require the relative importance of the DBCs to be expressed numerically, which is also how they will have to appear if you are proposing to use a computer package for clustering.

At this stage, you need only to consider the micro-segments and their DBCs, along with their size. Bringing together their profiling details and their KDFs can occur once the segments have been formed.

**Marketing insight**

If at any stage of building your clusters:

1 a cluster is developed that matches or exceeds the size requirement of a segment, *and*
2 further additions to this cluster will weaken what is currently a very clear focus around one, or more key DBCs in this cluster,

put this particular cluster to one side in order to protect its position. However, for thoroughness, frequently review its position as you continue to build other clusters to reconfirm that keeping it 'protected' remains the best strategy.

## Visual clustering (pattern analysis)

There are three preparatory measures to follow before proceeding to merge like-minded decision-makers into clusters, the third of which you may prefer to implement only if an initial attempt at clustering proves to be too difficult and a reduction in the number of DBCs having to be considered would resolve the problem.

1 So that the micro-segments are directly comparable with each other, ensure that all the market's DBCs appear for each micro-segment, even those they have no interest in, and that the DBCs are in the same order.
2 Remove any DBCs that appear in all the micro-segments with the same, or very similar importance ratings, as they clearly have no role in differentiating between groups of customers, though it is helpful if they still appear in the list of DBCs for the concluding segments as they will need to be taken account of when putting together the segment-specific offers.
3 Consider clustering the micro-segments using only their most important DBCs by focusing on those that account for, say, 80 per cent of their decision (the mechanics for this are discussed after the section on mathematical clustering).

As a first step in visual clustering, look across the micro-segments to see if any obvious similarities appear, as these can be used to form some initial clusters. This will reveal if there are any exact matches and should enable you to identify the very close matches. If your micro-segments looked anything like those in Table 8.1 you would be able to form your clusters in a single move.

**Table 8.1** Looking for distinct patterns across micro-segments

| Market DBCs | Micro-segments and the importance of their DBCs | | | | | | | | | |
|---|---|---|---|---|---|---|---|---|---|---|
| | A1 | A2 | A3 | B1 | B2 | C1 | C2 | C3 | C4 | D |
| DBC 1 | – | 32 | – | – | 31 | 22 | – | – | 18 | – |
| DBC 2 | 16 | – | 15 | 42 | – | 8 | 40 | 21 | 11 | 18 |
| DBC 3 | 21 | – | 20 | 8 | – | 15 | 10 | – | 16 | – |
| DBC 4 | 5 | 40 | 5 | – | 38 | 11 | – | – | 9 | – |
| DBC 5 | – | 14 | – | – | 16 | – | – | – | – | – |
| DBC 6 | 19 | – | 20 | 20 | – | 4 | 20 | 29 | 5 | 32 |
| DBC 7 | 6 | – | 5 | – | – | 24 | – | – | 27 | – |
| DBC 8 | – | – | – | 25 | – | – | 25 | – | – | – |
| DBC 9 | 23 | – | 25 | – | – | 9 | – | 6 | 11 | 4 |
| DBC 10 | 10 | 14 | 10 | 5 | 15 | 7 | 5 | 44 | 3 | 46 |

*Note:* It is not necessary to list the actual DBCs themselves. There are five clusters in this table consisting of, A1 and A3, A2 and B2, B1 and C2, C1 and C4, C3 and D.

This first look across the micro-segments can sometimes be made easier if the micro-segments are arranged so that all of those with the same top-rated DBC are placed next to each other. If the micro-segments in Table 8.1 had been arranged along these lines then the final clusters would have been even more apparent.

**Marketing insight**

Assuming it was not quite as easy as the example in Table 8.1, once any initial clusters have been formed from this first look, it is now a case of building your clusters by progressively decreasing the level of similarity customers and clusters must have with each other before they can be merged together. This is continued until the best or desired result has been achieved (as described earlier).

Don't overlook the possibility that a segment could consist of one micro-segment, particularly if that micro-segment is of sufficient size to qualify as a segment.

Visual clustering can be made easier if you follow one or other of the following suggestions;

1 Transfer each micro-segment onto a separate sheet of paper with its list of DBC importance ratings and its size as illustrated in Figure 8.4.

Lay the micro-segments out on a table, select one of them and find if it has a close match and put it with the matching micro-segment (which would see A5 and D2 in Figure 8.4 being brought together). Take another micro-segment and follow the same routine. Build the clusters by progressively decreasing the level of similarity customers and clusters must have with each other. Focusing on the DBCs that account for the major part of a customer's decision and putting aside the DBCs with very low scores can help here.

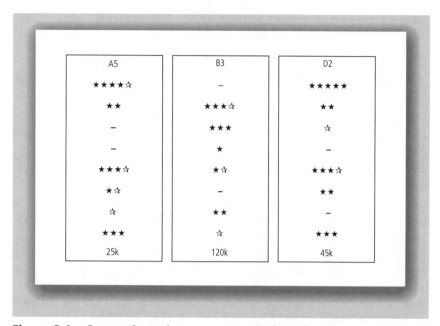

**Figure 8.4** Comparing micro-segments with each other visually (*Note:* When using symbols to indicate the importance of DBCs, as in this example, as opposed to numbers, consider transferring the details of each micro-segment onto acetates as this gives you the option of overlaying them when checking how similar they are to each other. It helps if the acetates also have white backing paper as this will make them clearer for the initial assessment of where the similarities may be found.)

As you continue to add micro-segments to your clusters and, as will eventually happen, you add clusters together, you may find it makes it easier if, at various stages, you produce a consolidated single picture for each cluster and work with these as you continue to build the segments. It helps if you label these clusters CL1, CL2 and so on, record their size and make a note of the micro-segments each of them represents. For the consolidated picture, the importance rating of each DBC should be expressed as an average (or weighted average[4]) of the ratings that have been given to them by all the micro-segments the cluster now represents.

2 Alternatively, transfer each micro-segment onto a separate piece of paper with its DBC importance ratings captured as a spider-gram, along with its size, as illustrated in Figure 8.5.

Using acetates is particularly helpful when working with spider-grams.

Follow the procedure suggested in the first option to build your segments.

3 As alternatives to spider-grams, you could consider using bar charts, as in Figure 8.6, or any other visual representation you would prefer to work with.

---

[4] Assuming the micro-segments are of different sizes, the 'weighting' is based on these sizes. Otherwise, use straight averaging. An example of how to apply weightings appears in Table 8.5 later in this chapter with a worksheet in the Exercises section of this chapter.

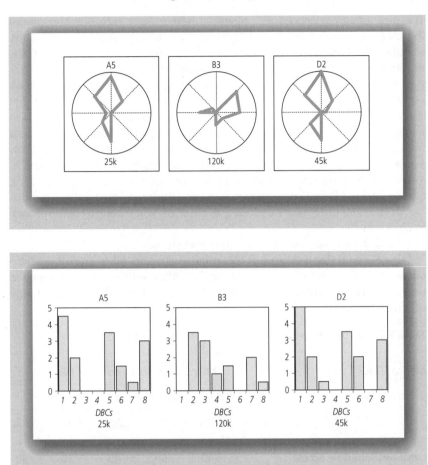

**Figure 8.5**
Comparing micro-segments with each other visually using a spider-gram (*Note:* The three micro-segments in this example are the three that appear in Figure 8.4.)

**Figure 8.6**
Comparing micro-segments with each other visually using a bar chart (*Note:* The three micro-segments in this example are the three that appear in Figure 8.4. The 'Y' axis on each bar chart is the importance rating of the DBCs.)

Once you have completed your clustering and arrived at the segments, take each one in turn, note its size and work out the segment's average (or weighted average) importance rating for each DBC across its micro-segments. To complete the picture, produce a segment profile by consolidating the profiling attributes of its constituent micro-segments. Consolidating the KDFs for each segment is optional at this stage, though it is clearly an opportune time at which to do so.

A worksheet for recording market segments, their DBCs, profiling characteristics and size appears in the Exercises section of this chapter.

## Mathematical clustering

As has already been pointed out, it is necessary to have the relative importance scores expressed numerically for this option.

The preparatory measures for mathematical clustering are exactly the same as those for visual clustering. Briefly, these were:

1  All the DBCs should appear for each micro-segment and in the same order.
2  Remove any DBCs that appear in all the micro-segments with the same, or very similar, importance ratings.
3  Consider clustering the micro-segments using only their most important DBCs.

The mathematical procedure presented here is very rigorous and one of the most frequently used in clustering programs. It also involves many calculations. How many calculations are required is governed by both the number of micro-segments you are evaluating and the number of DBCs you are including. As a first step, therefore, it is suggested that you look across the micro-segments to see if any obvious similarities appear so that some initial clusters can be formed (exactly as suggested for visual clustering). Arranging the micro-segments into groups according to their most important DBC will help here. For any clusters this produces, note their size and determine the average (or weighted average) scores of the DBCs, as these will be used in the calculations which follow. Label each resulting cluster CL1, CL2 and so on, and note which micro-segments it represents.

Additional shortcuts are included as we walk you through this approach to clustering.

An example is used to illustrate the next steps.

Table 8.2 contains a sample of five micro-segments taken from a particular market, along with their scores for the DBCs in this market. However, to help in the explanation of this procedure, only four DBCs are used, one of which is 'price'.

**Table 8.2** Micro-segment details for a clustering routine

| Market DBCs | | Micro-segments and their DBC scores | | | | |
|---|---|---|---|---|---|---|
| | | A1 | A2 | A3 | A4 | A5 |
| | Value | £30k | £20k | £20k | £20k | £30k |
| Local availability – access | | 40 | 50 | 45 | 30 | 30 |
| Eco-friendly packaging | | 30 | 25 | 30 | 20 | 15 |
| Trusted brand – reliability | | 20 | 20 | 15 | 40 | 45 |
| Price | | 10 | 5 | 10 | 10 | 10 |
| Total | | 100 | 100 | 100 | 100 | 100 |

*Note:* Although there are some obvious similarities between micro-segments in this table and the suggested 'first step' outlined earlier would see four of them merged into two separate clusters, they are put through the mathematical procedure to illustrate both how it works and how it would also conclude that these four micro-segments should merge into distinct clusters.

If you have used symbols, such as stars and half-stars, to illustrate the importance of DBCs, or scored each of them out of 10, they can be converted to scores that total 100 by following the procedure discussed later in this chapter for isolating the most important DBCs and illustrated in Table 8.7.

The difference between each of these micro-segments needs to be calculated. The method of doing this is illustrated in Table 8.3, using micro-segments A1 and A2 from Table 8.2 as the example.

The difference between A1 and A2 following the method appearing in Table 8.3 is, therefore, '12.2'.

This is then repeated for A1 and A3, then A1 and A4, followed by A1 and A5, then for A2 and A3, A2 and A4 and so on until all the micro-segments have been compared with each other (a total of ten pairings in this example).

**Table 8.3** Calculating the difference between micro-segments

| Market DBCs | Micro-segments and DBC scores | | Difference between scores | Difference squared | Square root of total difference |
|---|---|---|---|---|---|
| | A1 | A2 | (A1 − A2) | | √‾‾‾ |
| Local availability – access | 40 | 50 | −10 | 100 | − |
| Eco-friendly packaging | 30 | 25 | 5 | 25 | − |
| Trusted brand – reliability | 20 | 20 | 0 | 0 | − |
| Price | 10 | 5 | 5 | 25 | − |
| Total | 100 | 100 | − | 150 | 12.2 |

*Note:* This particular procedure is known as 'squared Euclidian distances'.

A worksheet for following this method appears in the Exercises section of this chapter.

The results of all the difference calculations required for the micro-segments appearing in Table 8.2 are summarized in Table 8.4. For ease of reference, Table 8.4 is presented along the same lines as a distance chart in an atlas.

**Table 8.4** Difference scores for five micro-segments

| | Micro-segments | | | | |
|---|---|---|---|---|---|
| | A1 | A2 | A3 | A4 | A5 |
| Micro-segments | | | | | |
| A1 | 0 | 12.2 | 7.1 | 24.5 | 30.8 |
| A2 | | 0 | 10.0 | 29.2 | 33.9 |
| A3 | | | 0 | 30.8 | 36.7 |
| A4 | | | | 0 | 7.1 |
| A5 | | | | | 0 |

The closest matching micro-segments in the example are A1 and A3, with a difference calculated at 7.1, along with A4 and A5, which also have a difference calculated at 7.1. There is very little similarity, however, between either A1 or A3 and A4 or A5 (the difference scores ranging from 24.5 for A1 versus A4, to 36.7 for A3 versus A5).

The first cluster is formed by combining the micro-segments with the least difference between them. In the example, two sets of micro-segments have the lowest scores, meaning two sets of micro-segments can be combined on this first run. Therefore, assuming a difference of 7.1 is acceptable, A1 and A3 can be combined, which will now be referred to as 'Cluster 1' (CL1), and A4 and A5 can be combined, which will now be referred to as 'Cluster 2' (CL2). The issue of 'acceptability' is discussed later in this chapter.

For the procedure to progress, a single set of DBC scores needs to be calculated for each new cluster. This can be either the average or weighted

**Table 8.5** Calculating weighted average DBC scores for a cluster

| Market DBCs | Micro-segment/Cluster A1 — Volume/value £30 000 — Weight – 60% | | | Micro-segment/Cluster A3 — Volume/value £20 000 — Weight – 40% | | | New Cluster (CL1) — Size: £50 000 — 100% |
|---|---|---|---|---|---|---|---|
| | DBC score (a) | Weight (b) | DBC score × weight (a) × (b) (e) | DBC score (c) | Weight (d) | DBC score × weight (c) × (d) (f) | DBC score (e) + (f) |
| Local availability – access | 40 | 60% | 24 | 45 | 40% | 18 | 42 |
| Eco-friendly packaging | 30 | 60% | 18 | 30 | 40% | 12 | 30 |
| Trusted brand – reliability | 20 | 60% | 12 | 15 | 40% | 6 | 18 |
| Price | 10 | 60% | 6 | 10 | 40% | 4 | 10 |
| Total | 100 | – | 60 | 100 | – | 40 | 100 |

average scores of the DBCs, with the 'weighting' based on the size of each constituent micro-segment. Weighted average scores can be calculated using either of the following two approaches:

1 in Cluster 1 (CL1), micro-segment A1 accounts for £30 000 and micro-segment A3 for £20 000, therefore the DBC scores in A1 have a weighting of 1.5 times the DBC scores in A3 (£30k/£20k = 1.5);
2 alternatively, the weighting attributed to each micro-segment can be expressed as a percentage of the total size of the new cluster. Using percentages, the DBC scores in A1 have a weighting of 60 per cent (£30k/£50k = 60 per cent), leaving A3 accounting for 40 per cent.

Calculating weighted average DBC scores for a new cluster using percentages is illustrated in Table 8.5. A worksheet for calculating DBC scores following this method appears in the Exercises section of this chapter.

The updated status for the market as originally illustrated in Table 8.2 appears in Table 8.6.

**Table 8.6** Clustering update

| Market DBCs | | Clusters, micro-segments and weighted average DBC scores | | |
| --- | --- | --- | --- | --- |
| | | CL1 (A1 and A3) | A2 | CL2 (A4 and A5) |
| | Value | £50 000 | £20 000 | £50 000 |
| Local availability – access | | 42 | 50 | 30 |
| Eco-friendly packaging | | 30 | 25 | 17 |
| Trusted brand – reliability | | 18 | 20 | 43 |
| Price | | 10 | 5 | 10 |
| Total | | 100 | 100 | 100 |

*Note:* There are more rigorous routines which do not calculate the weighted average scores for clusters, but retain the highest and lowest scores that exist for each DBC from the micro-segments in the cluster. When calculating differences, these routines work out the *maximum* difference for each DBC. This means that when comparing a DBC for two clusters, the difference score is determined by the greatest difference that exists between the highest or lowest scores in one cluster and the highest and lowest scores in the second cluster. If, therefore, we were to compare CL1 with CL2 using this approach, the difference between them on 'trusted brand – reliability' would be 45 minus 15 (the A5 score less the A3 score).

Ideally, the calculations in Table 8.3 should be repeated, in the first instance, across all the micro-segments in the project before any clustering took place. However, before conducting any calculations, all the obvious similarities between micro-segments would have been looked for and initial clusters formed for each group of like-minded micro-segments. In the example, this would have seen A1 and A3 placed in one cluster, and A4 and A5 placed in another cluster.

Once this first run of calculations has been completed, the new clusters are required to have their difference scores calculated against all the remaining micro-segments and against all the other clusters, after which the clustering sequence detailed above is repeated once again. The project continues along this path until a conclusion is reached.

| | |
|---|---|
| **Marketing insight** | As each successive run of calculations uses ever-increasing differences to build up the clusters, look across the data before starting each new sequence to see if there are any obvious similarities that would be uncovered at the next level of 'difference'. If there are, merge them together and recalculated their DBC scores along the lines already suggested.<br><br>You can also cut down the number of calculations by omitting calculations for pairs of micro-segments/clusters that are clearly dissimilar to each other.<br><br>Difference calculations can then be limited to:<br><br>● clarifying the position between micro-segments/clusters when it is visually unclear; and<br>● determining where a particular micro-segment/cluster should move to next when there is more than one contender and it is unclear where the best fit occurs. |

At some stage you may need to calculate the difference between all the remaining clusters and micro-segments to progress with forming the segments but, by following the above suggestions, the number of occasions on which you will have to do this will be limited.

After each completed cluster run, it is useful briefly to record the project's status in case you need to refer back to it later. It is particularly useful to have a record of the size of each cluster as it grows, as well as a record of the micro-segments and, as will eventually happen, the clusters it contains. Number each run in sequence and record it on a separate sheet. A suggested worksheet for recording the results of a cluster run appears in the Exercises section of this chapter.

Once you have completed your clustering and arrived at the segments, each of them sized and with a single set of DBC scores, take each segment in turn and consolidate the profiling attributes of its constituent micro-segments to produce a segment profile. Consolidating the KDFs for each segment is optional at this stage, though it is clearly an opportune time at which to do so.

A worksheet for recording market segments, their DBCs, profiling characteristics and size appears in the Exercises section of this chapter.

## Isolating the most important DBCs

The mechanics for isolating the most important DBCs by identifying those that account for 80 per cent of the decision are exactly those that were presented in Chapter 6 when we were discussing the 80/20 rule as a method of identifying the most influential features. This requires the importance ratings to be expressed in percentages. If you have been using symbols to illustrate importance, such as stars and half-stars, they need first to be converted to numbers with each 'half-star', for example, being equivalent to a single unit, thus '★★★★☆' (four and a half stars) is equivalent to 'nine'. Once all the DBCs for a micro-segment have their importance expressed numerically, the steps to follow when determining the most important 80 per cent are as follows (this also applies to micro-segments with the importance of their DBCs rated on a scale of, say, one to ten);

1 Arrange the DBCs for the micro-segment in a descending order of importance.
2 Add up the individual numbers to arrive at a total.
3 Rework the individual numbers into percentages by dividing each of them by the total and multiplying the answer by 100.
4 Build a cumulative picture by progressively adding up the reworked individual figures.
5 Determine the best position for the 80 per cent cut-off point.

The results of these calculations for micro-segments A5 and D2 in Figure 8.4 appear in Table 8.7.

**Table 8.7** Prioritizing DBCs

| | Micro-segment – A5 | | | | Micro-segment – D2 | | |
|---|---|---|---|---|---|---|---|
| DBC rating | As a number | Reworked | Cumulative | DBC rating | As a number | Reworked | Cumulative |
| ★★★★☆ | 9 | 30 | 30 | ★★★★★ | 10 | 31 | 31 |
| ★★★☆ | 7 | 23 | 53 | ★★★☆ | 7 | 22 | 53 |
| ★★★ | 6 | 20 | 73 | ★★★ | 6 | 19 | 72 |
| ★★ | 4 | 13 | 86 | ★★ | 4 | 13 | 85 |
| ★☆ | 3 | 10 | 96 | ★★ | 4 | 12 | 97 |
| ☆ | 1 | 4 | 100 | ☆ | 1 | 3 | 100 |
| Total | 30 | 100 | | Total | 32 | 100 | |

*Note:* The dotted line indicates the suggested cut-off point. When the cumulative scores do not provide an 80 per cent cut-off point, the most sensible cut-off point is selected.

Micro-segment D2 in Table 8.7 highlights a decision that you may have to make when reducing the DBCs to the most important. This micro-segment has two DBCs with the same rating competing with each other as to which of them falls above or below the cut-off point. Such situations can only be resolved in the first instance by making a judgement as to which of them is probably the more important of the two. What can be done later is a check to see whether reversing this decision would have made any difference to the segment D2 finally ends up in. If it does make a difference, it will once again have to be a matter of judgement as to which segment you leave it in.

## Acceptable differences

The most useful method of assessing 'acceptability' is your own judgement. The main consideration for this judgement concerns the effect the merger of micro-segments/clusters would have on the marketing strategy you would put together to win their business. If by merging two micro-segments/clusters the resulting scores for their DBCs would have little impact on the type of offer best suited to one or the other as they currently stand, then the level of difference between them is acceptable. If, on the other hand, the combination would weaken a good offer you could put together for one or both of them separately, the level of difference is *usually* not acceptable. The exception would be if one of the micro-segments/clusters was only quite small, while the other was quite large, as the smaller of the two would not justify a distinct offer for itself anyway. Finally, if you are only addressing this problem at the last stages of clustering and simply trying to sweep up some currently 'homeless' micro-segments/clusters, too small to form their own segments, note which cluster they would join, add their volume/value figure to that cluster, but do not change the cluster's current DBC scores. The overriding rule is, however, if in doubt do not merge them, as you can always revisit this decision later.

## What if ...

Not all projects see their micro-segments settle into a clean set of clusters that match up to what was being expected. The three most often mentioned concerns with the results at this stage are as follows:

1 A number of micro-segments do not appear to have a natural fit with any cluster.
2 The resulting clusters are fewer in number than expected or a small number of the concluding clusters account for a high proportion of the market.
3 The best result in terms of producing clusters with very clear market DBC preferences between them produces more clusters than expected, but taking the clustering routine further blurs the distinctiveness.

Each project clearly has to be looked at individually, but the following may help you through these issues if you have to address any of them.

1 'Homeless' micro-segments.
First check the size of these micro-segments, as a single micro-segment could be large enough to form a segment in its own right. If this is not the case for any of them, consider the potential future size of these micro-segments. If this would qualify any of them as a segment in the future, take advantage of that possibility *now*. Both these possibilities were covered earlier in this chapter

For any which are of a reasonable size, but not large enough to qualify as a segment, and which do not currently appear to demonstrate any possibility of future growth, revisiting them at a later stage is an option you could consider for any follow-up work.

If you are still left with a number of 'homeless' micro-segments, add up the total volume/value they account for and if this total is, say, less than 10 per cent of the market, then you can usually put them to one side without having to face any major repercussions in the market. No specific marketing strategies will be targeted at them, unless, of course, there are niche operators in the market for whom they represent a worthwhile marketing opportunity.

As a final resort, it often helps if you, or your research agency, talk with a representative sample of these micro-segments to ensure that you have a full understanding of their buying requirements. They are, after all, active in the market today and it is unlikely any supplier is putting together a bespoke offer for them. On the other hand, they may represent a group, or groups, in the market whose needs are not being satisfied by any supplier and who are currently having to compromise on what they buy. Build this understanding into the segmentation process and they may well form into a new cluster.

This same approach would be applicable if your project was ending up with homeless, small, clusters.

2 Fewer clusters than expected.

This usually means that only two or three market DBCs have attracted high scores from the micro-segments and/or a large number of micro-segments seem to want a portion of everything.

In these cases it can often mean that the prominent market DBCs require further investigation in the market in order to establish if, at the qualitative research phase, the real requirements were teased out. For example, if one of the prominent DBCs was, say, 'a large, reputable company', it would be useful to establish a clearer understanding of what exactly was meant by this. At the time of the qualitative work for the project, assuming you required such research, the DBC arrived at may have appeared to be adequate. You could not have known at that stage its true level of 'popularity'. This does not, however, prevent the segments you have arrived at from being taken through to the next step and into the second phase of the process. What can be usefully done in the meantime is to revisit this DBC with customers represented by the micro-segments giving this DBC a high rating. You can check with these customers whether or not there are some more specific requirements being delivered by this DBC which, if introduced into the segmentation project would lead to a more focused result.

---

A DBC such as 'large *reputable* company' could mean to some customers that the companies they associate with this description deliver a 'conservative' line of products or services. To others it could represent companies that are innovative, while to a further group of customers it could mean 'strong ethical business policies', and so on.

**Marketing insight**

---

A useful clue as to whether you may have overlooked more exacting requirements could be in the KDFs associated with the micro-segments. If a prominent DBC covers a range of different features, such as different brands, these different features may be delivering different benefits. A wrong assumption may have been made earlier on in the project.

3 More clusters than expected.

The first check would be on the size of each cluster to see if any qualify as a segment (including future growth, if appropriate). If a large number of them qualify by size in their own right, you may have to accept that your market splits into more than the number of segments you were anticipating, especially if each of them has quite distinctive requirements. Alternatively, it could be because the market definition is too broad.

Too many clusters may also be generated when the DBCs are not actually reflecting the real needs-based buying requirements of the market.

Finally, if only some of the clusters qualify as segments in terms of size, check the other clusters to see if any of them are, in fact, growing into the market segments of tomorrow. For the clusters which are tomorrow's new segments, these should progress to the next step in their own right. For the remaining clusters which, we can now assume, are quite small, refer back to the earlier section which looked at 'homeless micro-segments' (the second and subsequent paragraphs).

As will be clear, each particular project needs to be looked at in turn, as the range of possibilities could go beyond those summarized above. Those discussed in this section tend to be the most frequently observed.

It is worth emphasizing, however, that *most* markets tend to split into between five and ten segments.

## Computer-assisted clustering

The purpose of this section is briefly to introduce the clustering techniques you may come across and to provide some guidelines on what to look for when working with external agencies running the clustering analysis for you. For a detailed discussion of alternative clustering algorithms we would refer you to Everitt (1993).

In his review of the more traditional statistical methods used for clustering, Everitt recommends Euclidian distances, which is the technique described in the section on mathematical clustering earlier in this chapter, or Ward's hierarchical clustering method, which builds clusters based on minimizing the loss of information between data sets (customer groups). Of these two, the most frequently used appears to be Euclidian distances, and it is this approach to clustering that you will generally find your market research agency using.

A more recent development in clustering packages is the use of a neural network, or the use of a technique similar to a neural network, to analyse the data and it is the latter approach that has been built into the PC-based software package developed in association with the authors, Market Segment Master®. One of the main advantages of this approach is that it is extremely fast, which means that testing the impact of varying the data included in the analysis can be conducted very easily, thus enabling the analysis to be a more continuous process.

*It is important to involve yourself in the cluster analysis rather than leave it solely in the hands of an external agency.*

When using an external agency to conduct the clustering, we would strongly recommend that you involve yourself in the analysis, rather than have the agency present you with their analysis. This is because, more often than not, interpreting the results involves a degree of intuition along with an element of judgement as to whether or not what is being presented actually makes sense.

The most useful approach to analysing the data is to start with a series of cluster solutions and compare one with the other. Deciding on what series of cluster solutions you would like to review is based on the number of segments you are expecting to find in your market. If, for example, you were expecting the number of segments to be between five and eight, it would be in order to request separate data runs for a four-cluster solution, a five-cluster solution, a six-cluster solution, along with a seven-, eight- and nine-cluster solution, requiring a total of six separate data runs. The cluster solution producing the best result, which is a decision principally based on the solution that contains the most distinctive clusters, is then selected.

For these initial cluster runs, it is also useful to review the profiling characteristics associated with each cluster and how other key data appears for each cluster. In particular, if the data has been collected through research you have commissioned for your project, you could use this as an opportunity to look at the features that appeal to each cluster (their KDFs), which is an area of questioning we would suggest is included in the survey. A complete run of all the questions in the survey should, however, be deferred until you have selected the preferred cluster solution.

As an alternative to predetermining the cluster solutions you would like to see, there is occasionally the option of choosing to see what cluster solutions are produced at various levels of 'difference'. Depending on the outcome, you then select a higher or lower level of difference until you arrive at a cluster solution that produces the best result. Referring to the example appearing in Table 8.4, here we see difference scores ranging from just over 7 to just under 37 for a small selection of micro-segments, so in the option being discussed here, what you could request is to see the clusters that are produced when the level of difference is set at no more than 8 (which would be three clusters in the example).

Finally, as the main focus of the analysis will be the different scores given to the benefits by each cluster, it is worth giving some thought to the format you would prefer to work with. The options tend to be either a presentation of the benefit scores numerically, or as points either side of a central line to indicate how the score for a particular benefit in a cluster varies with the overall average score given to that benefit by the sample as a whole. These two options appear in Table 8.8.

A further alternative is to have the clusters positioned on a two-dimensional map which shows their overall relative positions to each other for all the benefits, as illustrated in Figure 8.7.

**Table 8.8** Standard formats for comparing clusters

| Format 1: Benefit scores as numbers | | | Format 2: Benefit scores as variations | | | |
|---|---|---|---|---|---|---|
| *Market DBCs* | *Cluster 1* | *Cluster 2* | *Market DBCs* | *Cluster 3* | | *Cluster 4* |
| Access | 6.3 | 1.6 | Access | ★★★ | | ★ |
| Eco-friendly | 2.9 | 8.3 | Eco-friendly | ★ | | ★★ |
| Reliability | 7.0 | 3.7 | Reliability | ★★ | ★★★ | |
| Price | 1.8 | 3.1 | Price | ★ | | ★ |

*Note:* The vertical line in 'Format 2' represents the average score for that benefit across the whole sample, with stars on the left of the vertical line indicating where a score for a cluster is below the average and stars on the right indicating where a score for a cluster is above the average. The number of stars indicates the extent of the difference around the average. Where a score for a particular benefit in a cluster is equal to the average score, no star appears.

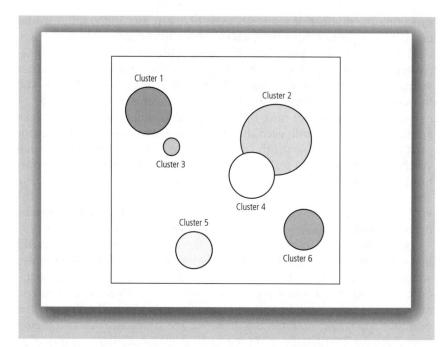

**Figure 8.7** Comparing clusters using a two-dimensional map (*Note:* In this example, a six-cluster solution, the clusters are fairly well separated from each other (using the mid-point of each circle) and therefore look quite distinctive. Other cluster solutions may improve on this separation (distinctiveness) or worsen it. The size of each circle can either represent the number of customers in each cluster or the quantity they account for.)

The distinctiveness of each cluster becomes immediately apparent using the format illustrated in Figure 8.7. It is also the format available in the software package the authors have been involved in developing.

# Segment checklist

To determine whether the clusters qualify as 'market segments', apply the checklist as follows:

*Volume/Value*  The size of each segment must be sufficient to justify the expense of developing specific offers for them and the expense of taking these offers into the market. The 'size' test for each segment should already have been cleared. Segments have to be measurable.

*Differentiated*  Is the offer required by each segment sufficiently different from that required by the other segments? This is where the marketing strategies appropriate for one segment are checked to ensure they are distinguishable from the marketing strategies developed for the other segments.

*Reachable*      This is where the different segments are checked to ensure that the marketing strategies appropriate for each of them can be directed towards them in some way. Each segment must, therefore, have some distinctive characteristics that can be used to identify the customers it represents, thereby enabling us to communicate with them and distribute our products and services to them, for example:

- distinct television viewing, radio listening, newspaper or magazine reading profiles; and/or
- distinct characteristics which can classify them by who or what they are, such as socio-economic group, type of company; and/or
- distinct characteristics which can classify them by a geographic area, such as postcodes; and/or
- distinct characteristics which can classify them by their purchasing preferences, such as purchasing patterns, distribution channels, distinct benefits looked for, distinct response to prices.

This is discussed in more detail after the final item on the checklist.

*Compatibility*      This is where you rigorously check your own company's ability to focus on the new segments by structuring itself around them organizationally, culturally, in its management information systems and in its decision-making processes. Such changes may not be possible immediately, therefore the organization's ability and willingness to evolve to the required structure should be tested.

The checklist questions appear towards the end of this section after a final look at segment profiling and reachability.

## Profiling revisited

Profiling, and its importance in segmentation, was covered in Chapter 6 when we looked at the components of a micro-segment. There we discussed standard approaches to profiling, namely demographic/firmographic, geographic, geodemographic and psychographic profiling, and the possible use of acquisition routes (outlets and channels) along with the other interests and product usage characteristics of customers to reach particular segments. Now that the segments are fully developed, there are the additional possibilities of distinguishing between them by relying on the strength of their individual propositions to self-select their target customers, by how the offer is communicated to them or even by price bands.

A financial services company in the European Union looking at how customers segmented in a particular market they specialized in, found that the standard approaches to profiling did not adequately distinguish between the segments. However, there were major differences between the segments in terms of the propositions they would respond to and they believed that these in themselves would overcome the problem. After some initial tests proved that this was the case, they moved to a regional launch using direct response advertising in the press. To further verify that the propositions were hitting their target segments, respondents who telephoned the company were asked a series of short questions, their answers to which enabled the company to check which segment the respondent was from.

The match between the segment a proposition was targeting and the segment the respondent was from proved to be extremely high, so the campaign was extended to other regions in the knowledge that the individual propositions would reach their target segments.

Whereas in the above example the company in question was using a short series of questions to verify what segment a customer was from, some companies have used this approach as their sole method of determining a customer's segment. These questions, sometimes referred to as the 'golden questions', have been used by sales representatives when with prospective clients to assess quickly what selling message they should follow, and by telephone sales staff to determine what sales line should be adopted when either prospecting or receiving enquiries.

A world-wide credit card company has developed and put into effect a 'golden question' routine for its telephone sales staff. For every prospecting call or new enquiry, the computer-generated screen-prompt starts with these golden questions. Once the customer, through their answers, has indicated the segment they are from, the screen prompt seamlessly transfers to the sales routine designed specifically for that segment.

While this has certainly increased the time required for each call, the increased success rate has more than compensated for it. Periodically, current customers have their segment re-verified through the same routine.

In other cases, companies have used a mix of current knowledge and feedback from sales calls to allocate customers progressively into their respective segments.

The ability to reach customers with their segment-specific offers is a key measure of success for a segmentation project. Addressing the issue of profiling early in the project and exploring a wide range of potential profiling attributes will make an important contribution to this success. What cannot be ignored, of course, is that any difficulties you may have with this issue are of no concern to your customers, just as it is of no concern to you as a customer of other businesses. Customers, including you, will not change their buying preferences simply to slot themselves into an administratively convenient segment for any company.

When reviewing the profiling information you have put together, it is important to remember that it is not necessary to have the identical profile for *all* the customers in a segment, as we are just looking for one distinctive, but usable, characteristic, or one particular distinctive set of 'conditional', but usable, characteristics, such as 'medium-sized companies *and* privately owned' or 'single *and* gym-club member *and* aged 30–35'. It is also not necessary for *all* the customers in a segment to have this single, or conditional set of, distinctive characteristic(s), as long as the majority have. Table 8.9 provides an example.

**Table 8.9** Segment age profiles in a market

| Micro-segments | Segment 1 (2200 units) Vol/val by age: Age ranges | | Micro-segments | Segment 2 (3050 units) Vol/val by age: Age ranges | |
| --- | --- | --- | --- | --- | --- |
| | 31–40 | 41–50 | | 31–40 | 41–50 |
| A2 | 150 | | A1 | 250 | |
| A3 | | 1250 | A4 | 350 | |
| B2 | 300 | | A5 | 200 | |
| B3 | | 500 | B1 | | 250 |
| | | | C1 | 2000 | |
| Total | 450 | 1750 | | 2800 | 250 |
| Segment (%) | 20.5 | 79.5 | | 91.8 | 8.2 |

From the above table, you could now state that 'Segment 1 was predominantly in the age group 41–50', and that 'Segment 2 was predominantly in the age group 31–40'. These distinctions could therefore be used to reach one or the other segment. If, however, the concluding segments had a less focused age structure, you would then conclude that 'age' was not a profiling discriminator between segments in the market being looked at and an alternative would have to be found. This alternative may, of course, be a 'conditional' set of profiling characteristics which could include age. For example:

Let us assume that for the market represented by Table 8.9, you were *not* satisfied with the result when using age profiles as a means of distinguishing between segments. If it was known that in this market all of the micro-segments originating from customer group 'B' did not own a car, namely 'B2' and 'B3' in Segment 1, along with 'B1' in Segment 2, then a more targeted description of customers found in Segment 1 would be, '41–50-year-olds *and* 31–40-year-olds *with no car*', which would give you a 93.2 per cent hit rate. This would, of course, have no effect on the hit rate for Segment 2, though it already stands at a very acceptable 91.8 per cent.

| Marketing insight | With the increasing sophistication of multidimensional profiling packages, many of which are capable of being run on desk-top PCs, and the extension of this technology into business marketing, the problems that have sometimes been faced with profiling segments defined by their needs are increasingly becoming problems of the past. |
|---|---|
|  | This sophistication, however, does not mean that the packages define segments. Their value is in enabling you to identify the characteristics associated with the customers in a specific segment. |

If, despite all that has been tried and tested, you still have a cluster populated by customers who are difficult to isolate and reach, and assuming they are customers you would like to do business with, first ensure that there are not some other attributes that could be used to identify them. As a last resort, you may simply have to be pragmatic and modify the ideal segmentation picture to one that can be effectively implemented.

## Checklist questions

For *every* cluster generated, check out your answers to the following questions (of the seven questions, questions 2, 3, 4, 5 and 7 are the most important; it is therefore *essential* that they each can be answered by a 'Yes'):

1  Can this segment be sized by a set of measurable parameters (for example, volume, value, number of customers)?      Yes [   ] No [   ]

2  Has the segment achieved sufficient size to make it worth being considered a significant business opportunity? (This should have been covered earlier in this chapter, which will also have ensured you have not excluded those segments with strategic potential, either because of unmet needs, or because they are at an early stage of their growth curve.)      Yes [   ] No [   ]

3  Can the customers in this segment be served by a distinctive marketing strategy that they will respond to and other segments will not be attracted to? (This should, by definition, have been built into the segment.)      Yes [   ] No [   ]

4  Can this segment be reached by sales and distribution channels you currently use, or could use?      Yes [   ] No [   ]

5  Can you identify and reach customers in this segment by means of a distinctive and cost effective communications strategy (for

example, promotion, selling, direct marketing, advertising)? Yes [   ] No [   ]

6 Can this segment be clearly identified by a set of common characteristics and can you describe it? Yes [   ] No [   ]

7 Can your company adopt a structure, information and decision-making system which will enable you to serve this segment effectively? Yes [   ] No [   ]

You may also want to consider your answer to the following question, which applies to segments that are to be served through independent intermediaries who have an important role in the marketing mix required by the segment:

8 Will your intermediaries play their part in the marketing activity required by the segment? Yes [   ] No [   ]

With your clusters successfully through the checklist, you have now not only arrived at how the customers in your market segment themselves, you also have segments you can work with, develop propositions for and profit from.

---

**Marketing insight**

Now that the internal project has completed the phase of developing segments, it is time to consider if there are any information gaps that need to be filled before you commit resources to any of the segments you have arrived at. If there are such gaps, this is the point at which to complete the research brief and look at commissioning an external market research company to provide the substantive evidence you may be challenged to provide.

Justifying the expense of a market research project may also have to depend on the strategic implications which emerge from the findings of the internal segmentation project. In this regard, you may find it useful to progress through the next phase of the segmentation process, prioritizing and selecting segments, and present these conclusions as part of your proposal for funding.

---

**Market research note**

Depending on how accurate you believe your concluding segments are in representing the market, it is possible to take account of them in the design of the sample frame for any follow-up research you commission. This would be especially appropriate for the initial, small-scale detailed study intended to provide the qualitative insights, rather than for the subsequent, larger-scale study that would use these insights to develop the quantitative conclusions. In particular, coverage of the different profiling characteristics that occur between segments and the different features they focus on could be specified in the sample frame.

However, depending on the range of specifications built into the sample frame, this could lead to an unnecessarily large sample size in terms of cost and/or in terms of the number of interviews required to capture the different buying criteria found across the market, and may need to be scaled down. Focusing on the really key differences between the concluding segments will help here.

The number of interviews for the quantitative phase should be based on a statistically valid sample size to ensure it captures all the different types of decision-makers in the defined market. However, if certain decision-makers were of particular interest to the company, quotas could be specified for them and added to the overall sample frame. For the analysis of the market as a whole, any over-represented decision-makers would then be scaled down to reflect their true position so as not to distort the final results.

# Process check

With all the details in place for identifying how the customers in your market split into segments, this, the fifth step in the segmentation process, provides guidelines on how this data can be built into segments, thereby completing the first phase of the segmentation project.

We began by summarizing the three components of a 'market segment', namely their needs, profiling attributes and a volume or value figure, all of which will already be embedded in your micro-segments. Two questions were then raised which we suggested should be considered before proceeding to build the micro-segments into market segments, and these concerned:

1 the minimum economic size a segment needed to have to justify the development of a distinct marketing strategy for it; and,
2 the number of segments, and therefore the number of different marketing strategies, it was believed the company could actually work with.

A detailed section then looked at the process of 'clustering', which is the term usually used to describe the combining of like-minded customers into segments.

We introduced this section by first highlighting the order of events in a clustering process, which starts with merging customers who are an exact match with each other, followed by finding very close matches to these customers and then progressively decreasing the level of similarity customers are required to have with each other before they are merged (more often referred to as 'increasing the difference' between customers). We made the point, however, that forcing customers together who were really quite different from each other in terms of their needs simply to achieve segment size targets and/or the preferred number of segments, should be avoided. A cluster derived this way would not qualify as a market segment because, by definition, these consist of a group of customers within a market who share a similar level of interest in the same, or comparable, set of needs.

We then moved on to highlight the possibility that in addition to building clusters using all the decisive buying criteria (DBCs), it is possible to look at building clusters with only some of the DBCs, a move that would depend on how well the micro-segments came together to form distinct segments using all the DBCs.

Guidelines were then presented on how manual clustering could be conducted for projects with a manageable number of micro-segments, a situation that would apply to most internally resourced segmentation projects. We discussed how to proceed with visual clustering using pattern analysis, along with some alternative formats to consider, and we presented the procedures to follow if building clusters from a mathematical base was preferred. Where appropriate, shortcuts were suggested to speed the clustering process along.

This was followed by a brief review of how to isolate the most important DBCs for the clustering process, which may be required for manual clustering if a large number of DBCs appear for each micro-segment, and a section with comments about 'acceptable differences'.

Because not all projects find their micro-segments coming together into a clean set of segments, some suggestions were put forward on how to approach three of the most mentioned concerns that occur with clustering. These covered 'homeless' micro-segments, fewer clusters than expected, and more clusters than expected.

The section on clustering finished with a brief review of the clustering techniques you may come across and some guidelines on what to look for when working with an external agency running the clustering analysis on your behalf.

Finally, we presented a series of key questions that each cluster must be checked against before it qualifies as a segment. These principally check on its size, its distinctiveness, its reachability and its compatibility with the company. Some final comments on segment profiling and reachability were also included here, because with the segments now fully developed there are additional possibilities for distinguishing between them.

## Case study

As will be recalled from the previous chapter, a total of ten market DBCs, with the inclusion of price, were identified in the Agrofertilizer Supplies' project, all of which were graded for each of the 34 micro-segments using the total sum approach for illustrating their relative importance. The segmentation team were now faced with sifting through these 34 micro-segments to uncover the market segments that, unbeknown to the company, had been there all along.

Manual clustering was certainly possible for the internal project, especially when the most important DBCs were identified for each micro-segment, but with access to a clustering programme the team delegated this task to technology.

A selection of micro-segments and their DBC scores appear in Table 8.10, with the selection designed to illustrate how two pairs of micro-segments could be clustered manually.

For the 34 micro-segments generated in the case study, Figure 8.8 illustrates where they started from, in terms of their preliminary segments, and how they ended up.

As can be seen from the final clusters, the preliminary segment structure, which basically distinguished between the final users according to their different application for the product, was a good starting point. Most of the final clusters are based on important differences that existed between the members of a preliminary segment. Only one of the final clusters, Segment 7, covers more than one preliminary segment, a cluster which, interestingly, is the segment that is very price sensitive – a purchase priority that will often bring together members from different preliminary segments. The final segments and their market DBC scores appear in Table 8.11.

**Table 8.10** DBCs and their scores for a selection of micro-segments in the case study

| Market DBCs | Micro-segments | | | | |
|---|---|---|---|---|---|
| | *A4* | *G4* | *G6* | *M2* | *M3* |
| Innovative/new | 18 | – | – | – | – |
| Sophisticated | 4 | – | – | – | – |
| Proven/traditional (reassurance) | – | 20 | 20 | 29 | 32 |
| Healthy-looking crop or grass | – | – | – | – | – |
| Healthy-looking animal stock | – | 25 | 25 | – | – |
| Service (qualified help) | – | – | – | 6 | 4 |
| Ease of handling | – | 8 | 10 | – | – |
| Maximum output/yield per acre | 12 | – | – | – | – |
| Convenience/easy access to supplies | – | 42 | 40 | 21 | 18 |
| Price | 66 | 5 | 5 | 44 | 46 |
| *Total* | 100 | 100 | 100 | 100 | 100 |

*Note:* 'A' identifies micro-segments originating from the Arable preliminary segment, 'G' for micro-segments from the Grassland preliminary segment and 'M' for micro-segments from the Mixed preliminary segment.

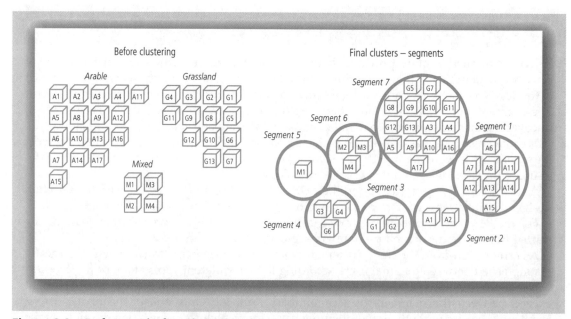

**Figure 8.8**   Before and after clustering for the case study
(*Note:* 'A' identifies micro-segments originating from the Arable preliminary segment, 'G' for micro-segments from the Grassland preliminary segment and 'M' for micro-segments from the Mixed preliminary segment.)

**Table 8.11** The concluding segments and their market DBC scores for the case study

| Market DBCs | Segments and their market DBC scores | | | | | | |
|---|---|---|---|---|---|---|---|
| | S1 | S2 | S3 | S4 | S5 | S6 | S7 |
| Innovative/new | 40 | 5 | 10 | – | – | – | 20 |
| Sophisticated | 15 | – | – | – | – | – | 5 |
| Proven/traditional (reassurance) | – | 20 | 5 | 20 | 35 | 30 | – |
| Healthy-looking crop or grass | – | 5 | 25 | – | 5 | – | – |
| Healthy-looking animal stock | – | – | – | 25 | 5 | – | – |
| Service (qualified help) | – | 25 | 10 | – | 15 | 5 | – |
| Ease of handling | – | 20 | 15 | 10 | 25 | – | – |
| Maximum output/yield per acre | 30 | – | 20 | – | – | – | 10 |
| Convenience/easy access to supplies | – | 15 | 10 | 40 | 10 | 20 | – |
| Price | 15 | 10 | 5 | 5 | 5 | 45 | 65 |
| Total | 100 | 100 | 100 | 100 | 100 | 100 | 100 |

*Note:* 'S1', 'S2' and so on represent 'Segment 1', 'Segment 2' and so on.

As you will have noticed, one of the segments consisted of only one micro-segment (Segment 5). It may well be a segment in terms of the different requirements it is looking for, but is it a big enough segment to warrant its own marketing strategy? With respect to the volume of product bought by each of the concluding segments, Figure 8.9 summarizes this as a pie chart.

Segment 5, although only consisting of a single micro-segment, is, in fact, one of the larger segments.

When assessing each of the seven segments against the four criteria on the segment checklist, it was clear that two of the criteria could be met without any further consideration.

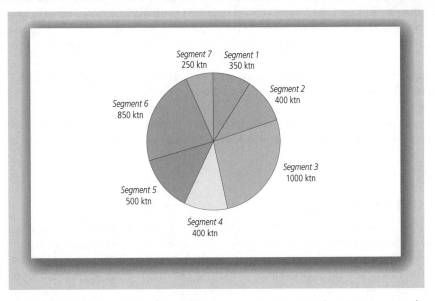

**Figure 8.9** The volume attributed to each segment for the case study (*Note:* The quantities are kilotonnes (ktn) of fertilizers.)

All the segments were large enough to justify a distinct marketing strategy, and they were all quite different from each other in terms of what they required. The difficulty, at least initially, appeared to be with the profiling characteristics of the final users in each segment, and with the company's ability to adopt this new segmented approach in its activities.

Although some profiling criteria were tracked throughout the Agrofertilizer project, the two of most interest being farm size and formal level of agricultural training, none came through as being really distinctive identifiers for the different segments. The reality was that the segmentation team had not given profiling sufficient thought and attention. Fortunately, however, most of the segments by their very nature narrowed down the possible range of farms that would be found within them. This shortfall, therefore, was easily surmountable for Agrofertilizer Supplies.

At a later date, once the findings and implications with respect to a new marketing strategy had been presented, the segmentation team, working alongside the sales force and assisted by a simple series of questions about the farm and the farmers' buying practices, began to allocate farmers to segments, concentrating first on the customers of Agrofertilizer Supplies.

The only item now remaining on the checklist was company compatibility.

Although presenting different offers in the market was not new to the company (after all, it already had two brands), rigorously following this approach for a larger number of segments looked too difficult, particularly as the company had, in fact, largely dismissed its two-brand strategy on the grounds of its ability to deliver any commercial advantage, and its belief that the farmers could see through it anyway. The reality here, however, was that the *company* did not like running with a two-brand strategy. Research for Agrofertilizer Supplies' segmentation project found that farmers clearly differentiated between the two brands, seeing them targeted at different requirements. To convince the company of this fact, tapes made during some of the group discussions were played at a sales and marketing conference, attended by senior executives from across the company. They 'heard', but it was still going to prove difficult.

The next difficulty originated from the product-focused structure of the company. What was being called for now was a segment-focused structure at the 'front end', in other words, at the customer-facing end of the business. Critically, the 'power' of the product managers looked to be under threat. Segment managers would begin to control the external marketing activity of the business and start specifying the product requirements, with the product managers focusing on the crucial link that is required between marketing and production. This was *not* acceptable! Not immediately, anyway.

The majority of staff in Agrofertilizer Supplies, however, signed up to the conclusions enthusiastically. This included staff in one of the most critical links with the marketplace, the sales force.

In a matter of only a few months, after a very successful test of the conclusions in the marketplace with a new product targeted at one of the segments, the company took its leap of faith.

The *market* had won!

## Case study conclusion

As was mentioned in Chapter 4 when first introducing the case study, although Agrofertilizer Supplies is based on a real company, certain facts have been modified for reasons of commercial confidentiality and to assist in demonstrating the process in practice. This has enabled us to bring into this case study observations made in the many other segmentation projects with which we have been involved.

The status of the project for Agrofertilizer Supplies at the end of this first phase of the segmentation process is summarized in Figure 8.10. This figure also shows the formal titles given

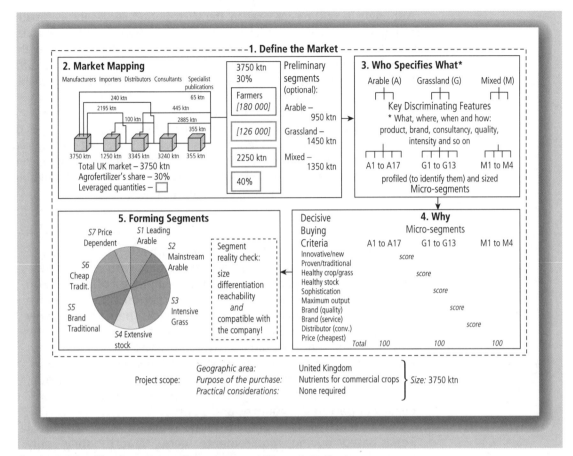

**Figure 8.10** The segmentation process – Steps 1 to 5

to each of the segments by Agrofertilizer Supplies. Each title represents the best overall description for their particular segment.

Although the segmentation team took this project through the steps featured in Chapters 9 and 10 before putting together their marketing objectives and strategies, we shall have to leave Agrofertilizer Supplies at this point. However, the output from these next steps, a segment portfolio, can be found towards the end of Chapter 10 in Figure 10.6.

A more detailed look at 'Agrofertilizer Supplies' as it really was, including how the customer insights gained from the segmentation project contributed to a new, and highly successful, marketing strategy, can be found at www.marketsegmentation.co.uk.

# Further examples

The first example for this chapter is a case study, written by a company that has applied segmentation to their business. This appears in Chapter 15.

For the next example we take a further look at profiling.

Identifying which customers are to be found in the concluding segments, along with the ability, or even willingness, of companies to structure themselves around segments, are the two most frequent problems companies have with the checklist.

Although in one recent case in the distribution sector the company carrying out the project completely overlooked the need to collect profiling information, in most instances where profiling is a problem it is because the information collected was not extensive enough. This is because it is difficult at the outset of a project to know what profiling information will enable you to distinguish between segments. The only solution when the project has reached this far in the process is to go back and investigate further.

It may, however, be the case that a segment does consist of all types of customers, from all walks of life, with absolutely nothing that can be used to distinguish them easily from any other customer, and for whom even the proposition they are looking for is unusable as a means of isolating them. Thus far, this has only been encountered once:

---

Some years ago an airline wished to investigate whether a 'segment' existed that consisted of customers with a fear of flying. It was considered at the time that an improved offer could be put together the better to meet their requirements! A research project was commissioned and reported back. There was certainly a group of customers who did have a fear of flying. The difficulty was, however, that they did not fly in any particular class, did not watch any particular programmes or read any particular papers, they did not come from any particular socio-economic group, were not of any particular age group, neither were they from any particular part of the country, and so on.

The research project did, however, establish what their real needs-based buying requirements were. Unfortunately, only Scotty on the Starship Enterprise had the technology!

---

For a more down to earth project, Table 8.12 presents a summary of demographic profiles for the concluding segments in a study of the USA's historical romance novel market.

Finally, we take a further look at the issue of company compatibility.

With respect to the difficulty companies may have in focusing onto the concluding segments, the most productive approach is to anticipate this problem at the very beginning of the project and start pre-empting it at an early stage. It is often by involving a wider audience in the project, through actively seeking their contribution and sharing with them the project's progress from the earliest stages, that difficulties associated with the 'mindset' of the business have a more than equal chance of being overcome. This should be one of the key responsibilities of the segmentation team, who should be kept regularly informed of progress by the core group conducting the detailed work (see Chapter 3).

In planning the launch of a segmentation project, a number of companies have held an opening workshop attended by a cross-section of key personnel in their company, the objective of the workshop being to obtain the enthusiasm and support of the participants for the project, as well as

**Table 8.12** Segment demographics of the historical romance novel market (USA)

| Demographic | Segment 1 (Movers and shakers) | Segment 2 (Isolated readers) | Segment 3 (Young swingers) | Segment 4 (Laggards) |
|---|---|---|---|---|
| Age | Average age: 31–40 | Average age: 41–50 | Average age: 30 and under | Average age: over 50 years |
| Children | One or no children | At least one child | Most have no children | Most have grown children |
| Education | High school education | High school education | One-third have college degree | Least education |
| Employment and income | Most employed; family income of $20 000 | Half are employed; family income of $20 000 | Most employed; income less than $20 000 | More unemployed; lowest income |

*Source:* Schnaars, S. P. and Schiffman, L. G. (1984). 'An application of segmentation design based on a hybrid of canonical correlation and simple crosstabulation'. *Journal of the Academy of Marketing Science*, 12 (Fall), 187.

preparing them for the possibility that the outcome may require some internal and external changes if the company is to become truly customer focused. Briefings beforehand have identified specific issues to be addressed in the workshop, the areas of questioning to be expected and, on some occasions, the individuals to focus on and engage during the workshop, either because they are key to the success of the project and/or they are likely to provide the stiffest resistance to it.

Other project teams have drawn up lists of key influencers in the company, attached a member of the team to each of them to 'account manage' them, and then worked out for each key influencer their strengths, weaknesses, opportunities and threats with respect to the segmentation project. This would then be followed by a plan of engagement to both obtain and retain their support.

With segmentation being such a strategically critical issue, initiatives along these lines can never be regarded as 'over the top'.

Organizational issues in market segmentation are looked at in Chapter 14.

With an enthusiastic following across the business, and, through regular feedback, no big surprises, even structural changes that may be required can be moved from the 'can't be done' box into the 'leave it with me' category.

# References

Everitt, B. S. (1993). *Cluster Analysis*. Oxford: Heinemann Educational.

Schnaars, S. P. and Schiffman, L. G. (1984). 'An application of segmentation design based on a hybrid of canonical correlation and simple crosstabulation'. *Journal of the Academy of Marketing Science*, 12 (Fall), 187.

# Exercises

**Exercise 8.1**

Considering the resource flexibility of your company, along with any technical considerations which could impact on the company's ability to tailor its propositions:

1 How large would a segment need to be for it to be seen as an economically attractive group of customers?
2 How many segment-specific strategies could your company effectively manage at any one time?

Consider the same questions with respect to your two main competitors.

If, as best as you can determine, either one or both of your two main competitors would require a lower threshold for economic viability and/or could handle a greater number of segment-specific strategies:

3 What are the factors that enable them to do this?
4 What would your company need to do in order to match or exceed their capabilities?

Involve colleagues in your deliberations on the above, especially question 4.

**Exercise 8.2**

One of the greatest challenges a company faces with an approach to segmentation that is different from the one they have been used to, is its ability to focus on these new segments structurally, culturally, in its management information systems and in its decision-making processes.

Consider what the top five challenges would be in your company to implement effectively a segment-focused approach to its business. Note them down, with the most difficult appearing first and the least difficult appearing last.

For each of these internal challenges, identify the 'owner', in other words, the key individual who controls this part of the company's operation, and develop a short series of actions that would be required to obtain their enthusiastic support for incorporating a new segmented approach into their area of responsibility.

Now add a new name at the top of the list, namely the chief executive, assuming the chief executive has not already appeared, and develop a short series of actions that would be required to win their support, as without it, there will be little progress elsewhere in the company.

**Exercise 8.3**

This chapter has principally focused on the mechanics of forming segments, and an exercise based on the mechanics requires completion of the steps that precede it in the process. The final exercise, therefore, is to apply the process to your market and then take the micro-segments you develop through the clustering sequence contained in this chapter.

There now follows a series of worksheets appropriate to this step. Make as many copies of these worksheets as you need.

**Table 8.13** Worksheet – recording clusters/segments, their DBCs, profiling characteristics and size

| | | | | | Clusters/Segments | | | | |
|---|---|---|---|---|---|---|---|---|---|
| **Market DBCs** | | | | | | | | | |
| | | | | | | | | | |
| | | | | | | | | | |
| **Profiling** | | | | | | | | | |
| Category | Group | Specification | | | | | | | |
| | | | | | | | | | |
| | | | | | | | | | |
| Acquisition routes | | | | | | | | | |
| | | | | | | | | | |
| | | Size | | | | | | | |

*Note:* The worksheet in Table 8.14 can be used for completing the profiling details in the above table. If you are also using this step as an opportunity to add KDF details to each segment, structure this information along the same lines as that for recording the profiling details, and add this to the above table. The worksheet in Table 8.15 can be used for compiling the KDF details.

**Table 8.14** Worksheet – calculating the profiling characteristics for a segment

| Segment:<br><br>Size: | | Profiling group: | | | | |
|---|---|---|---|---|---|---|
| | | Profiling specifications | | | | |
| | | | | | | |
| Micro-segments | and their size | vol/val | vol/val | vol/val | vol/val | vol/val |
| | | | | | | |
| Total | | | | | | |
| Segment % | 100% | | | | | |

*Note:* For a selected profiling group, distribute each micro-segment's volume or value total between its applicable profiling specifications and add up the total for each specification. Either enter this total on Table 8.13, or recalculate it as a percentage of the segment as a whole and enter this percentage on the table. A worked example appears in Table 8.9.

**Table 8.15** Worksheet – calculating the KDF details for a segment

| Segment:<br>Size: | | KDFs | | | | |
|---|---|---|---|---|---|---|
| | | | | | | |
| Micro-segments | and their size | vol/val | vol/val | vol/val | vol/val | vol/val |
| | | | | | | |
| Total | | | | | | |
| Segment % | 100% | | | | | |

*Note:* Enter each micro-segment's volume or value total to its applicable KDFs and add up the total for each KDF. Either enter this total on the table created to complement Table 8.13, or recalculate it as a percentage of the segment as a whole and enter this percentage on the table.

**Table 8.16** Worksheet – calculating the difference between micro-segments/clusters

| | Micro-segments and DBC scores | | Difference between scores | Difference squared | Square root of total difference |
|---|---|---|---|---|---|
| Market DBCs | (a) | (b) | (a) – (b) | | $\sqrt{\phantom{x}}$ |
| | | | | | – |
| | | | | | – |
| | | | | | – |
| | | | | | – |
| | | | | | – |
| | | | | | – |
| | | | | | – |
| | | | | | – |
| | | | | | – |
| | | | | | – |
| | | | | | – |
| | | | | | – |
| | | | | | – |
| Total | 100 | 100 | – | | |

**Table 8.17** Worksheet – calculating weighted average DBC scores for a cluster

| | Micro-segment/ cluster | Volume/ value | DBC score × weight | Micro-segment/ cluster | Volume/ value | DBC score × weight | New cluster (CL1) |
|---|---|---|---|---|---|---|---|
| | | Weight – % | | | Weight – % | | Size: |
| | | | | | | | 100% |
| Market DBCs | DBC score (a) | Weight (b) | (a) × (b) (e) | DBC score (c) | Weight (d) | (c) × (d) (f) | DBC score (e) + (f) |
| | | | | | | | |
| Total | 100 | – | | 100 | – | | 100 |

**Table 8.18** Worksheet – cluster run record

| Cluster run no: | | |
|---|---|---|
| Cluster generated CL ... | Cluster generated CL ... | Cluster generated CL ... |
| Micro-segments/clusters contained in each new cluster, and size | | |
| Micro/CL          Size | Micro/CL          Size | Micro/CL          Size |
| | | |
| Total | Total | Total |

# Chapter 9
# Determining the attractiveness of market segments

It is neither essential, nor always desirable, to serve every segment in the market. The financial and managerial resources of the company need to be focused into those segments that provide the greatest opportunities for the organization to achieve its objectives. This chapter looks at how a company determines segment attractiveness and is the sixth step in the segmentation process, as illustrated in Figure 9.1.

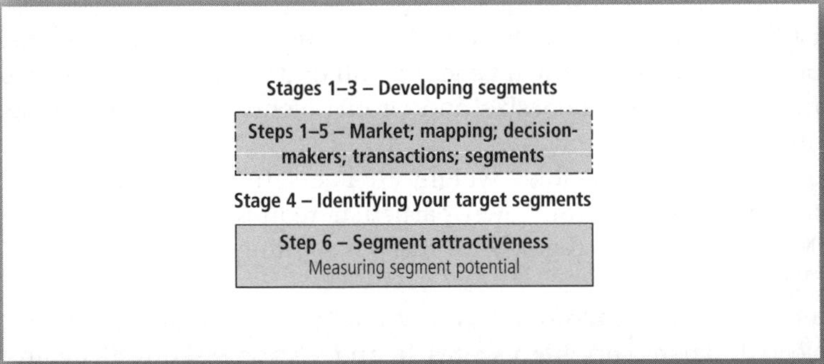

Stages 1–3 – Developing segments

Steps 1–5 – Market; mapping; decision-makers; transactions; segments

Stage 4 – Identifying your target segments

Step 6 – Segment attractiveness
Measuring segment potential

**Figure 9.1**
The segmentation process – Step 6

This step requires an objective assessment of segment attractiveness using data *external* to the organization. The criteria themselves will, of course, be determined by the organization carrying out the exercise, but it is important to remember that the criteria should be *independent* of the organization's position in its segments. As one of these criteria is likely to be the size of the segments, it is essential that you have access to up-to-date forecasts that can help you establish their size by the end of the chosen time period, which is usually three years ahead. The reason for such a lengthy period is that you are interested in *sustainable* competitive advantage, not just the short-termism that comes with looking only one year ahead.

Segment attractiveness on its own as a basis for allocating scarce resources can, however, be misleading and needs to be balanced with the company's competitive position in each segment before any segment-specific strategies are developed. Assessing the company's competitiveness by segment is looked at in the next step.

This chapter is organized as follows:

■ A 'fast track' for those looking for a quick route through the key points
■ A discussion about portfolio analysis
■ An introduction to 'segment attractiveness' and an overview of the steps it involves
■ Defining the time period for segment attractiveness
■ A brief review of the team for this phase of the project
■ Factors to consider in segment attractiveness
■ How to indicate the relative importance of each factor
■ Defining the parameters for each factor so that segment potential can be gauged
■ How to evaluate the attractiveness of segments

■ Transferring the results on to a portfolio matrix
■ A brief discussion as to why the results may not be as expected
■ A review of this step in the segmentation process
■ Examples
■ Exercises to help you further with segment attractiveness

# Fast track

● List the factors you wish to consider in comparing the attractiveness of your segments – these will generally fall under the headings of 'growth rate', 'accessible segment size' and 'profit potential' and should be agreed with key colleagues.
● For each of the factors, weight their relative importance to each other according to your own particular requirements by distributing 100 points between them, with these weightings also agreed with key colleagues.
● Define the high, medium and low parameters for each of the factors selected, where very high scores 10 and very low scores 0, again with the agreement of key colleagues.
● Take one of the segments and, based on the parameters, determine its score for each factor at the end of your planning period (usually three years), ensuring that it is an objective assessment based on data *external* to the organization, multiply these individual scores by the weight that has been given to its respective factor and divide by 100, then add all these together to arrive at a total between 0 and 10, and repeat for each segment, as illustrated in Table 9.1.

**Table 9.1** Fast track – segment attractiveness evaluation (Year 3)

| Segment attractiveness factors | Weight | Parameters | | | Segment 1 | | Segment 2 | |
|---|---|---|---|---|---|---|---|---|
| | | High 10–7 | Med 6–4 | Low 3–0 | Score | Total | Score | Total |
| Profitability | 35 | >15% | 10–15% | <10% | 8 | 2.8 | 3 | 1.05 |
| Volume growth | 25 | >10% | 5–9% | <5% | 10 | 2.5 | 2 | 0.5 |
| Size (m) | 15 | >100 | 33–100 | <33 | 1 | 0.15 | 10 | 1.5 |
| Competitiveness | 15 | Low | Med | High | 6 | 0.9 | 2 | 0.3 |
| Seasonality | 10 | Low | Med | High | 9 | 0.9 | 5 | 0.5 |
| Total | 100 | | | | | 7.25 | | 3.85 |

*Note:* The attractiveness factors, their weightings and parameters remain constant for each segment. Only the scores are specific to each segment. Parameters described as 'low', 'medium' or 'high' should be associated with a measurable definition to avoid subjective interpretation.

A worksheet for listing segment attractiveness factors, their weights and parameters, and for calculating the segment attractiveness scores, appears in the Exercises section of this chapter.

● Transpose the results on to the vertical axis of a portfolio matrix, as illustrated in Figure 9.2. Ensure the scale from the point of origin to the highest point allows a spread of segments between them rather than having the segments all grouping together at one or the other end of the scale.

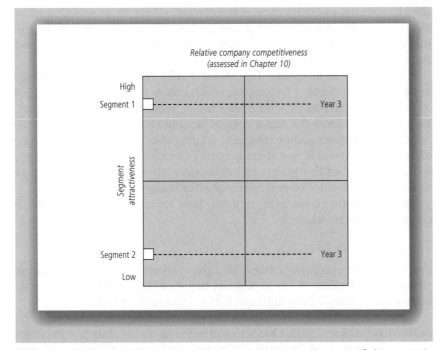

**Figure 9.2** Fast track – plotting segments on the portfolio matrix according to their attractiveness
(*Note:* To ensure a spread of segments along the attractiveness axis, the point of origin has been set to '3.0' and the highest point set to '8.0'. Segments positioned in the lower half of the matrix should *not* be treated as unattractive, they are simply less attractive than segments positioned in the top half of the matrix. The cash they generate will be an important contribution to the investment required in those segments appearing in the top half.)

A worksheet for plotting segments on the portfolio matrix appears in the Exercises section of Chapter 10. When completed, this portfolio will enable you to see the balance between sales growth, cash flow and risk for your company.

Readers who have established an agreed list of attractiveness factors, their weights and parameters, and are confident that they have made an objective assessment of segment attractiveness may go straight to Chapter 10.

This concludes the fast track for Step 6 of the segmentation process.

# Portfolio analysis

Portfolio analysis, for the purposes of this book, is simply a means of assessing a number of different segments, first of all according to the potential of each in terms of achieving an organization's objectives, and second according to the organization's ability to take advantage of the identified opportunities.

The idea of a portfolio is for a company to meet its objectives by balancing sales growth, cash flow and risk. As individual segments grow or shrink, then the overall nature of the company's portfolio will change. It is, therefore, essential that the whole portfolio is reviewed regularly and that an active policy is pursued towards the move into new segments and the exiting of old segments.

Widely referred to as the 'Directional Policy Matrix' (DPM), portfolio analysis offers a detailed framework which can be used to classify possible competitive environments and their strategy requirements. It uses several indicators to measure the dimensions of 'segment attractiveness' on the one hand, and 'company competitiveness' on the other. These indicators can be altered by management to suit the operating conditions of particular markets.

The purpose of the matrix is to diagnose an organization's strategy options in relation to the two composite dimensions outlined above.

However, before describing in detail how to use the DPM, it is worth considering its antecedents.

**Definition:** ●
A portfolio plots markets, segments or products using at least a two-dimensional matrix in order to balance growth, cash flow and risk.

## The Boston Matrix

Portfolio analysis initially came out of the work of the Boston Consulting Group, begun in the 1960s, and it has had a profound effect on the way management think about their market and their activity within it.

There are basically two parts to the thinking behind the work of the Boston Consulting Group. One is concerned with *market share* and the other with *market growth*, which we would translate into *segment share* and *segment growth*. These are brought together into a simple matrix, which has important implications for the firm, especially in respect of *cash flow*. Cash is a key determinant of a company's ability to develop its segment portfolio.

The Boston Matrix can be used to classify a firm's position in each segment found in the market according to their cash usage and their cash generation along the two dimensions described above, namely relative segment share and rate of segment growth. This is summarized in Figure 9.3.

The somewhat picturesque labels attached to each of the four categories give some indication of the prospects for the company in each quadrant. Thus, the 'question mark' is a segment in which the company does not have a dominant position and, therefore, a high cash flow, though it may have had such a position in the past. It will be a high user of cash because it is a growth segment. This is also sometimes referred to as a 'wildcat'.

The 'star' is probably a newish segment in which the company has achieved a high share and which is probably more or less self-financing in cash terms.

The 'cash cows' are segments where there is little additional growth, but a lot of stability, in which the company has a leading position. These are excellent generators of cash and tend to use little because of the state of the segment.

**Definition:** ●
The Boston Matrix classifies a firm's products according to their cash usage and their cash generation using market growth and relative market share to categorize them in the form of a box matrix. For the purposes of this book it has been adapted to classify a market's segments.

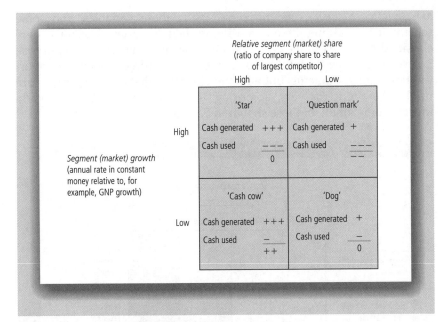

**Figure 9.3**   The Boston Matrix
(*Note:*  Although 'high' is positioned on the left of the horizontal axis it can, if you prefer, be placed on the right. The definition of high relative segment share is taken to be a ratio of one or greater than one. The cut-off point for high, as opposed to low, segment growth should be defined according to the prevailing circumstances in the defined market. As well as being a positive figure there is no reason why the dividing line on the vertical axis cannot be zero, or even a minus figure.)

'Dogs' often have little future and can be a cash drain on the company. They are probably segments the company should exit, although it is often very difficult to leave 'old friends'.

The art of managing segments as a portfolio now becomes a lot clearer. What we should be seeking to do is to use the surplus cash generated by the 'cash cows' to invest in our 'stars' and to invest in a selected number of 'question marks'.

## General Electric/McKinsey Matrix

The approach of the Boston Consulting Group is, however, fairly criticized because of its dependence on two single factors, namely relative segment share and segment growth. To overcome this difficulty, and to provide a more flexible approach, General Electric (GE) and McKinsey jointly developed a multi-factor approach using the same fundamental ideas as the Boston Consulting Group.

The GE/McKinsey approach uses *industry attractiveness* and *business strengths* as the two main axes, and builds up these dimensions from a number of variables. When applying this to segments, the first (vertical) axis is relabelled *segment attractiveness*. We have also relabelled the horizontal axis, *relative company competitiveness*. Using these variables, and some scheme for weighting them according to their importance, segments are classified into one of nine cells in a 3 × 3 matrix. Thus, the same purpose is served as in the Boston Matrix (namely, comparing investment opportunities among segments) but with the difference that multiple criteria are used. These criteria vary according to circumstances, but generally include some, or all, of those shown in Figure 9.4.

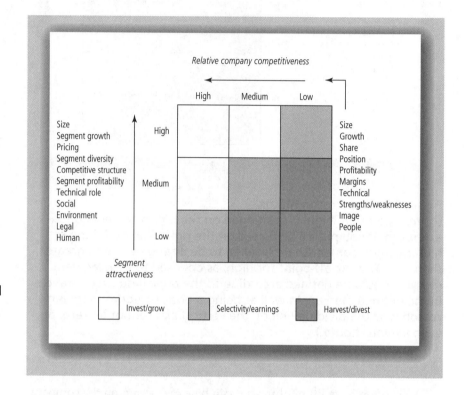

**Figure 9.4**
The GE/McKinsey Matrix
(*Note:* Although 'high' is positioned on the left of the horizontal axis it can, if you prefer, be placed on the right.)

It is not necessary, however, to use a nine-box matrix, and many managers prefer to use a four-box matrix similar to the Boston box, while using the GE/McKinsey definitions for the axes. This is the preferred methodology of the authors as it seems to be more easily understood by, and useful to, practising managers.

The four-box matrix is shown in Figure 9.5. Here, the circles represent sales into a segment, with each circle being proportional to that segment's contribution to turnover. The position of each segment on the matrix is determined by its attractiveness and the company's competitive position within it.

The difference in this case is that, rather than using only two variables, the criteria which are used for each axis are totally relevant and specific to each company using the matrix. It shows:

● segments categorized on a scale of attractiveness to the company;
● the company's relative strengths in each of these segments;
● the relative importance of each segment to the company.

An example of an actual segment portfolio directional policy matrix is presented in Figure 9.6. The procedures contained in this chapter

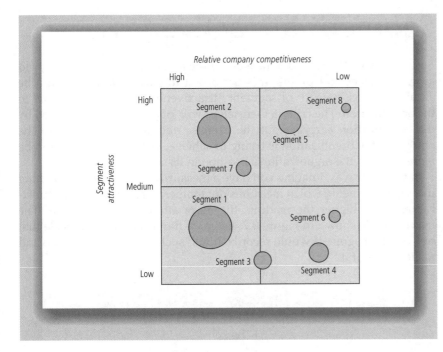

**Figure 9.5**
The McDonald
four-box DPM
(*Source:*
McDonald, M.
(2002). *Marketing
Plans: How to
Prepare Them,
How to Use Them.*
Oxford:
Butterworth-
Heinemann.)
(*Note:* Although
'high' is positioned
on the left of the
horizontal axis it
can, if you prefer, be
placed on the right.)

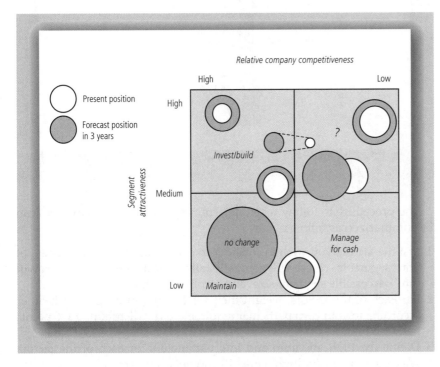

**Figure 9.6**
Directional policy
matrix for a
portfolio of
segments
(*Note:* Segment
attractiveness has
only been calculated
for the final year.
Relative company
competitiveness has
been calculated for
both the current
year and the final
year.)

and Chapter 10 will equip you to produce your own directional policy
matrix.

For a more detailed discussion of portfolio analysis, readers are referred
to McDonald (2002), Chapter 5.

# Segment attractiveness

Segment attractiveness is a measure of the *potential* of a segment to yield growth in sales and profits. It is important to stress that this should be an objective assessment of segment attractiveness using data *external* to the organization. The criteria themselves will, of course, be determined by the organization carrying out the exercise and will be relevant to the objectives the organization is trying to achieve, but the criteria should be *independent* of the organization's position in its segments.

Put another way, imagine you have a measuring instrument, something like a thermometer, which measures not temperature but segment attractiveness. The higher the reading, the more attractive the segment. The instrument is shown in Figure 9.7. Estimate the position on the scale that *each* of your segments would record (should such an instrument exist) and make a note of it.

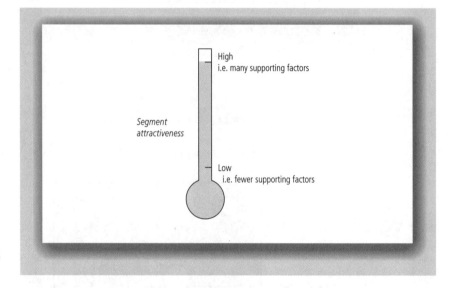

**Figure 9.7**
Measuring segment
attractiveness

The procedure to follow when determining segment attractiveness can be summarized as follows:

1 List the factors you wish to consider in comparing the attractiveness of your segments – these will generally fall under the headings of 'growth rate', 'accessible segment size' and 'profit potential'.
2 For each of the factors, weight their relative importance to each other according to your own particular requirements by distributing 100 points between them.
3 Define the high, medium and low parameters for each of the factors selected, where very high scores 10 and very low scores 0.
4 Take one of the segments and, based on the parameters, determine its score for each factor, multiply these individual scores by the weight that has been given to its respective factor and divide by 100, then add all these together to arrive at a total between 0 and 10, and repeat for each segment.

Precisely how this is done is a matter of management judgement, but it is important to follow three golden rules:

1 Never do this in isolation.
2 Make sure your key colleagues are in agreement over the factors, weightings and parameters to be used.
3 Whenever quantitative information, or techniques such as market research, is available, it should be used in preference to opinions, no matter how well founded these opinions might be.

Before looking at each of the segment attractiveness steps in turn, consideration should be given to defining the time period being scored and to the team that should be involved at this stage of your segmentation project.

## Time horizon

Prior to commencing the analysis of segment attractiveness, it is important to define the time period being scored. Three years is recommended. A segment that is attractive today will not automatically be equally attractive in the future. A particular change that can occur is the size of segments. Some segments could have shrunk in size by the end of the time period, while others, including any anticipated new segments, could have increased in size, and therefore increased their attractiveness. It is essential that you have up-to-date forecasts available to help determine both the size of the segments by the end of the time period and the size of your presence within them, which will help you in the next chapter. To this end, you will require sales forecasts for the current products/services, and for any new products/services your current policies plan to introduce during the time period.

Although it is easier and quicker to determine how attractive each segment will be at the end of the planning period only (Year 3), it can be quite useful to assess attractiveness at two points in time: today (Year 0) and in Year 3. This gives the resulting portfolio matrix a visual indication of each segment's dynamics. The directional policy matrix presented in Figure 9.6 has segment attractiveness calculated only for the final year. In such circumstances, segments can only move horizontally – that is, along the same level of attractiveness – with their direction of movement determined by your own company's activity within them (and therefore your company's changing relative business strength within each segment).

This chapter covers both options and therefore looks at determining segment attractiveness for the end of the planning period, which we will assume to be Year 3, and for today (Year 0). Segment attractiveness in Year 3 is defined as a measure of the *potential* of a segment to yield growth in sales and profits during the next three years (that is $t0$ to $t + 3$, where $t$ represents time), with Year 0 representing the current attractiveness of a segment based on the past three years (that is $t - 3$ to $t0$).

*Segment attractiveness could be calculated for both today and the end of your planning period, though it is easier and quicker to carry out only the calculations for the final year.*

## Segmentation team

To ensure that the appropriateness of the selected attractiveness criteria is high and that the scoring is realistic, it is recommended that the same cross-functional team involved in developing the segments should continue with this second phase of the segmentation project, which involves both the current step and the step that follows it. This mix will continue to encourage the challenging of traditional views during their discussions. There will also be the continuing need for a core group of two to three individuals to carry out the detailed work, the core group reporting back to the full team for consultation, comment and guidance, just as they did during the previous phase of the project.

Circumstances may also be such that the continuing presence of an outsider to act as a facilitator for the process and to continue offering an objective and alternative viewpoint to the discussion could still be warranted.

## Defining segment attractiveness factors

Here, you should list the factors you wish to consider in comparing the attractiveness of your segments. The criteria must be specific to the market and must not be changed for different segments in the same market. This will be a combination of a number of factors, though they can usually be summarized under three headings:

1 *Growth rate* – Average annual forecast growth rate of revenue in that segment (percentage growth of 2001 over 2000, *plus* percentage growth of 2002 over 2001, *plus* percentage growth of 2003 over 2002, with the total divided by three: in other words, the number of years being looked at). If preferred, compound average growth rate could be used. Clearly, in determining segment growth rates, you will need to take into account the supportiveness (or otherwise) of the overall business environment.

2 *Accessible segment size* – An attractive segment is not only large, it also has to be accessed. One way of calculating this is to estimate the total revenue of the segment during the selected time span, *less* revenue impossible to access, *regardless of investment made*. Alternatively, total segment size can be used, which is the most frequent method, as it does not involve any managerial judgement to be made that could distort the true picture. This latter method is the method advised here.

3 *Profit potential* – This is much more difficult to deal with and will vary considerably, according to segment. For example, Porter's Five Forces model (1985) could be used to estimate the profit potential of a segment, as illustrated in the example appearing in Table 9.2. Although the

**Table 9.2** Porter's Five Forces model

| Profit potential sub-factors | Sub-factor weight (Total 100) | Segment rating 10 = Low 0 = High | Weighted factor score (weight × rating) ÷ 100 |
|---|---|---|---|
| 1. Intensity of competition | 50 | | |
| 2. Threat of substitutes | 5 | | |
| 3. Threat of new entrants | 5 | | |
| 4. Power of suppliers | 10 | | |
| 5. Power of customers | 30 | | |
| | | *Profit potential factor score* | |

factors for this table are taken from Porter (1985), the table itself, and the methodology shown, were devised by the authors.

Alternatively, a combination of these and market-specific factors could be used. In the case of the market for pharmaceuticals, for example, the sub-factors could be those appearing in Table 9.3.

**Table 9.3** Profit potential sub-factors in the market for pharmaceuticals

| Sub-factors | Weight (Total 100) | Rating | | | Weighted factor score |
|---|---|---|---|---|---|
| | | High | Medium | Low | |
| • Unmet medical needs (efficacy) | 30 | | | | |
| • Unmet medical needs (safety) | 25 | | | | |
| • Unmet medical needs (convenience) | 15 | | | | |
| • Price potential | 10 | | | | |
| • Competitive intensity | 10 | | | | |
| • Cost of market entry | 10 | | | | |
| | | *Profit potential factor score* | | | |

These are clearly a proxy for profit potential. Each is weighted according to its importance. The weights add up to 100 in order to give a *profit potential factor score*, as in the Porter's Five Forces example (Table 9.2).

Naturally, growth, size and profit will not encapsulate the requirements of all organizations. For example, in the case of an orchestra, artistic satisfaction may be an important consideration. In another case, social considerations could be important. In yet another, seasonality may be crucial.

It is possible, then, to add another heading, such as 'risk' or 'other' to the three headings listed earlier. In general, however, it should be possible to reduce it to just the three main ones, with sub-factors incorporated into these, as shown.

The specific criteria to be used will require the approval of key executives, but a generalized list of possible factors contributing to segment attractiveness (from McDonald, 2002) is shown below. It is advisable to use no more than an overall total of five or six factors, otherwise the exercise becomes too complex and loses its focus.

> It is advisable to use no more than five or six factors for segment attractiveness, otherwise the calculations become too complex and lose focus.

**Segment factors**
Size (money, units or both)
Growth rate per year
Sensitivity to price, service features and external factors
Cyclicality
Seasonality
Bargaining power of upstream suppliers
Bargaining power of downstream suppliers

**Competition**
Types of competitors
Degree of concentration
Changes in type and mix
Entries and exits
Changes in share
Substitution by new technology
Degrees and types of integration

**Financial and economic factors**
Contribution margins
Leveraging factors, such as economies of scale and experience
Barriers to entry or exit (financial and non-financial)
Capacity utilization

**Technological factors**
Maturity and volatility
Complexity
Differentiation
Patents and copyrights
Manufacturing process technology required

**Socio-political factors**
Social attitudes and trends
Laws and government agency regulations
Influence with pressure groups and government representatives
Human factors, such as unionization and community acceptance

A worksheet for listing segment attractiveness factors, along with the other data required for calculating segment attractiveness scores, can be found in the Exercises section of this chapter.

## Weighting segment attractiveness factors

For each of the factors for segment attractiveness, weight their relative importance to each other according to your own particular requirements by distributing 100 points between them.

Given that the overall aim of a company is usually represented in a profit figure, and that profit is a function of:

Segment size × Margin × Growth

it would be reasonable to expect a weighting against each of the attractiveness factor headings listed earlier in this chapter to be along the lines shown in Table 9.4.

An even higher weighting for growth could be understandable in some circumstances (in which case, the corresponding weightings for the others should be reduced). These factors could then be combined with market specific factors, resulting in a table along the lines shown in Table 9.5.

It is important to note that the segment attractiveness factors and their weightings for the market being evaluated cannot change whilst constructing the DPM. Once agreed, under no circumstances should they be changed,

Segment attractiveness factors and their weightings for the market being evaluated cannot change whilst constructing the DPM.

**Table 9.4** Example weightings of segment size, margin and growth

| Factors | Example weight |
|---|---|
| Growth rate | 40 |
| Accessible segment size | 20 |
| Profit potential | 40 |
| Total | 100 |

**Table 9.5** Weighting segment attractiveness factors

| Segment attractiveness factors | Weight |
|---|---|
| 1. Volume growth potential | 25 |
| 2. Profit potential | 25 |
| 3. Potential segment size (volume/value) | 15 |
| 4. Vulnerability | 15 |
| 5. Competitive intensity | 10 |
| 6. Cyclicality | 10 |
| Total | 100 |

*Note:* The simplest way of administering the distribution of weights is first to arrange the attractiveness factors in a descending order of importance, score the most important out of 100 and then score each of the others relative to this score. Reset them back to 100 by adding up all the individual scores, divide each individual score by this total and multiply the answer by 100. The weightings given to each factor is a matter of management judgement.

otherwise the attractiveness of your segments is not being evaluated against common criteria and the matrix will become meaningless.

## Defining the parameters for each segment attractiveness factor

You now need to determine high, medium and low parameters for each of the factors selected so that the potential of each segment can be gauged, where very high scores 10 and very low scores 0. An example is given in Table 9.6.

## Scoring the segments

For each of the concluding segments arrived at in Steps 1 to 5, you can now establish how attractive each is to your business as follows: Take one of the segments and, based on the parameters, determine its score for each factor, ensuring that it is an objective assessment based on data *external* to

**Table 9.6** Parameters and their scores for the segment attractiveness factors

| Segment attractiveness factors | Parameters | | |
|---|---|---|---|
| | High (10–7) | Medium (6–4) | Low (3–0) |
| Growth | GNP + 2.5% | GNP | GNP − 2.5% |
| Profitability | >15% | 10–15% | <10% |
| Size | <£5m | £1m–£5m | <£1m |
| Vulnerability | Low | Medium | High |
| Competitive intensity | Low | Medium | High |
| Cyclicality | Low | Medium | High |

*Note:* 'GNP' refers to Gross National Product. Parameters described as 'low', 'medium' or 'high' should be associated with a measurable definition to avoid subjective interpretation. For example, the parameters for competitive intensity could be based on the number of competitors in each segment. The precise scores given to the parameters is a matter of management judgement.

the organization, multiply these individual scores by the weight that has been given to its respective factor and divide by 100, then add all these together to arrive at a total between 0 and 10, and repeat for each segment. A worked example of this quantitative approach to evaluation is given in Table 9.7.

**Table 9.7** Segment attractiveness evaluation (Year 3)

| Attractiveness factors | Weight | Segment 1 | | Segment 2 | | Segment 3 | |
|---|---|---|---|---|---|---|---|
| | | Score | Total | Score | Total | Score | Total |
| Growth | 25 | 6 | 1.5 | 5 | 1.25 | 10 | 2.5 |
| Profitability | 25 | 9 | 2.25 | 4 | 1.0 | 8 | 2.0 |
| Size | 15 | 6 | 0.9 | 5 | 0.75 | 8 | 1.2 |
| Vulnerability | 15 | 5 | 0.75 | 6 | 0.9 | 6 | 0.9 |
| Competition | 10 | 8 | 0.8 | 8 | 0.8 | 4 | 0.4 |
| Cyclicality | 10 | 2.5 | 0.25 | 3 | 0.3 | 2.5 | 0.25 |
| Total | 100 | | 6.45 | | 5.0 | | 7.25 |

In this example, an overall attractiveness score of 7.25 out of a possible maximum score of 10.0 places Segment 3 in the highly attractive category for Year 3.

A worksheet for listing segment attractiveness factors, their weights and parameters, and for calculating the segment attractiveness scores, appears in the Exercises section of this chapter.

It should be noted that if in carrying out Steps 1 to 5 you concluded your market had less than five segments, there is little point in using the DPM.

# Plotting the position of segments on the portfolio matrix

Transpose the results of your segment attractiveness evaluation on to the matrix, writing the segments on the left of the matrix. Still using the matrix, draw a dotted line horizontally across from each segment, as shown in Figure 9.8.

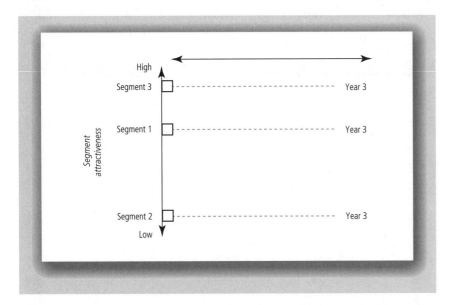

**Figure 9.8**
Plotting segments on the portfolio matrix according to their attractiveness (Year 3)

A worksheet for plotting segments on the portfolio matrix appears in the Exercises section of Chapter 10.

In considering the position of each segment on the 'attractiveness' axis at some earlier point in time (say, Year 0), it is important to remember that they can only move vertically *if* the matrix also shows their level of attractiveness for a future period. This implies carrying out one set of calculations for a future period (say, in three years' time, as in Figure 9.8) based on your forecasts using the agreed segment attractiveness factors, in order to locate segments on the vertical axis for Year 3, then carrying out another set of calculations for the present time (Year 0) using the same segment attractiveness factors. A reworked Table 9.7 illustrating the position of each segment in Year 0 appears in Table 9.8.

The present (Year 0) sees a change in the attractiveness of the three segments, with Segment 1 in the leading position, rather than second place, and Segment 3 in third position, rather than first place. Clearly, therefore, during the period of the plan, the attractiveness of Segments 1 and 2 deteriorates while the attractiveness of Segment 3 improves, and improves to such an extent that it topples Segment 1 from its leading position. By comparing Tables 9.8 and 9.7 it can be seen that the principal changes are concerned

**Table 9.8** Segment attractiveness evaluation (Year 0)

| Attractiveness factors | Weight | Segment 1 | | Segment 2 | | Segment 3 | |
|---|---|---|---|---|---|---|---|
| | | Score | Total | Score | Total | Score | Total |
| Growth | 25 | 10 | 2.5 | 7 | 1.75 | 8 | 2.0 |
| Profitability | 25 | 8 | 2.0 | 8 | 2.0 | 6 | 1.5 |
| Size | 15 | 5 | 0.75 | 7 | 1.05 | 6 | 0.9 |
| Vulnerability | 15 | 6 | 0.9 | 4 | 0.6 | 7 | 1.05 |
| Competition | 10 | 6 | 0.6 | 7 | 0.7 | 5 | 0.5 |
| Cyclicality | 10 | 2.5 | 0.25 | 3 | 0.3 | 2.5 | 0.25 |
| Total | 100 | | 7.0 | | 6.4 | | 6.2 |

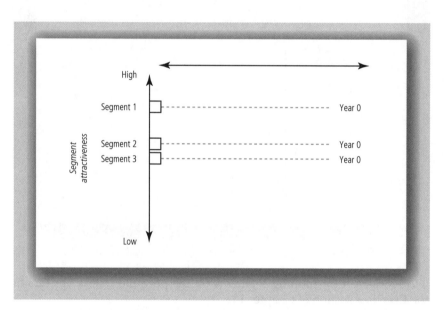

**Figure 9.9**
Plotting segments on the portfolio matrix according to their attractiveness at the beginning of the planning period (Year 0)

with 'growth' and 'profitability'. The positions of the segments for Year 0 can now be transposed on to the matrix, as in Figure 9.9.

It has to be said that, in practice, it is quicker and easier to carry out only the calculations for the final year of the planning period, in which case the circles on the DPM can only move horizontally with changes to your company's relative strength in each segment.

It is worth repeating that, once agreed, under no circumstances should segment attractiveness factors be changed, otherwise the attractiveness of your segments is not being evaluated against common criteria and the matrix becomes meaningless. Scores, however, are specific to each segment.

It is also worth stressing that segments positioned in the lower half of the matrix should *not* be treated as unattractive. All this means is that they are relatively less attractive than segments positioned in the top half of the matrix. In addition, it should not be forgotten that the cash generated from those segments in the lower half of the matrix (particularly the lower left quadrant) will be an important contribution to the investment required in those segments appearing in the top half of the matrix.

In the examples shown in Tables 9.7 and 9.8, it can be seen that for all three segments, none of them have a weighted attractiveness score lower than 5.0. If the vertical axis was scaled from 0 to 10, this would put all three segments in the 'highly attractive' zone. Should you have only three segments, which is unlikely, this would obviously be a nonsense. To overcome this problem, it is suggested that the scale on the attractiveness axis is established along the following lines:

1 Take the lowest score and round it down to the next whole number to define the point of origin (which would be 4.0 in our example).
2 Take the highest score and round it up to the next whole number to define the highest point (which would be 8.0 in our example).

This will always ensure a spread, which is, of course, the whole point of using the device in the first place. Table 9.9 shows a more likely spread of weighted attractiveness scores.

**Table 9.9** The range of weighted attractiveness scores in a market with nine segments

| Attractiveness factors | Weight | Segment 1 | | Segment 2 | | Segment 3 | |
|---|---|---|---|---|---|---|---|
| | | Score | Total | Score | Total | Score | Total |
| Profitability | 35 | 8 | 2.8 | 9 | 3.15 | 6 | 2.1 |
| Growth | 30 | 3 | 0.9 | 4 | 1.2 | 4 | 1.2 |
| Size | 20 | 3 | 0.6 | 5 | 1.0 | 5 | 1.0 |
| Competition | 15 | 9 | 1.35 | 5 | 0.75 | 7 | 1.05 |
| Total | 100 | | 5.65 | | 6.1 | | 5.35 |

| Attractiveness factors | Weight | Segment 4 | | Segment 5 | | Segment 6 | |
|---|---|---|---|---|---|---|---|
| | | Score | Total | Score | Total | Score | Total |
| Profitability | 35 | 7 | 2.45 | 7 | 2.45 | 5 | 1.75 |
| Growth | 30 | 7 | 2.1 | 8 | 2.4 | 2 | 0.6 |
| Size | 20 | 4 | 0.8 | 6 | 1.2 | 2 | 0.4 |
| Competition | 15 | 8 | 1.2 | 7 | 1.05 | 5 | 0.75 |
| Total | 100 | | 6.55 | | 7.1 | | 3.5 |

| Attractiveness factors | Weight | Segment 7 | | Segment 8 | | Segment 9 | |
|---|---|---|---|---|---|---|---|
| | | Score | Total | Score | Total | Score | Total |
| Profitability | 35 | 5 | 1.75 | 2 | 0.7 | 3 | 1.05 |
| Growth | 30 | 3 | 0.9 | 1 | 0.3 | 5 | 1.5 |
| Size | 20 | 9 | 1.8 | 2 | 0.4 | 2 | 0.4 |
| Competition | 15 | 2 | 0.3 | 2 | 0.3 | 8 | 1.2 |
| Total | 100 | | 4.75 | | 1.7 | | 4.15 |

## When the final result is not what you expected

The first time managers try using the DPM, they frequently find that the points of intersection from the two axes for their individual segments do not come out where expected. One possible reason for this is a misunderstanding concerning the use of segment attractiveness factors. Please remember, you will be most concerned about the *potential for growth in volume, growth in profit,* and so on for your company in each of your segments. For example, even if a segment is mature (or even in decline), if the *potential* is there for your company to grow in this mature segment, then it would obviously be more attractive than one in which there was little or no potential for you to grow (as would be the case, for example, if you already had a high share in a segment). Likewise, even if a segment is currently very profitable for your company, if there were little or no *potential* for profit growth, this segment might be considered less attractive than one which was currently not so profitable to your company, but which offered good *potential* for profit growth.

As a closing comment, it is worth remembering that in some markets, certain segments have to be served in order for the company to be a credible player in the market, even though the segment may be unattractive to your company. An example of this may be a large customer in an attractive segment that has a subsidiary in another, less attractive segment.

# Process check

Before committing resources to any particular segment, it is important to measure the potential of a segment to yield growth in sales and profits, and this, the sixth step in the segmentation process, provides guidelines on how to determine segment attractiveness. This on its own, however, is insufficient for making investment decisions, as it is important that the company also assesses its competitive strength in each segment before making any commitments. Company competitiveness by segment is looked at in the next chapter.

Because both the attractiveness of segments and the company's competitive position in each of them will be transposed on to a 'Directional Policy Matrix' (DPM), we began with a review of portfolio analysis. This review covered the Boston Matrix, the GE/McKinsey Matrix and the McDonald four-box DPM. The latter matrix is used in the segmentation process.

We then took a detailed look at segment attractiveness, which we opened with a brief review of the steps it involves, along with three golden rules we suggest you follow when working through these steps. Briefly these golden rules were: never do this alone; it requires agreement with key colleagues; and, whenever available, use quantitative information in preference to opinion. We also made suggestions as to the time period you should consider scoring and the team to work with.

The detailed sections for determining attractiveness began with a discussion about the factors you may wish to consider when comparing the attractiveness of your segments and pointed out that these tend to fall under three headings, namely, 'growth rate', 'accessible segment size' and 'profit potential'. We then moved on to how each of these factors should be given weightings to indicate their relative importance to each other for your company, and pointed out that the segment attractiveness factors and their weightings for the market being evaluated cannot change whilst constructing the DPM.

So that the potential of each segment can be gauged, the next step we detailed looked at giving high, medium and low parameters to each of the factors selected, with very high scoring 10 and very low scoring 0. With all the factors agreed, weighted and their parameters established, we went on to present the routine for calculating segment attractiveness scores.

We then illustrated how the segment attractiveness evaluation is transposed on to the matrix using the vertical axis and discussed the possibility of showing both the present as well as the forecast position of segments on the matrix. We pointed out that the scale of this axis should be adjusted to ensure that it allows a spread of segments between the point of origin and the highest point, but also made the point that segments located in the lower half of the matrix should *not* be treated as unattractive. They are better thought of as being relatively less attractive than segments positioned in the top half of the matrix

Finally we put forward a possible reason why the results may not be what you expected.

# Examples

The first example is of a company that preferred to consider the present, rather than forecast the future, the reason for this being the difficulties they foresaw with predicting future changes.

To arrive at the attractiveness of segments in their market, this company used growth and return on sales as the factors, weighted 35 and 65 respectively. Not surprisingly, this resulted in all the high-profit segments receiving high attractiveness scores and all the low-profit segments receiving low attractiveness scores. The chief executive, however, was not satisfied with this analysis as the company was under pressure from the financial institutions to achieve growth in business and profits because, over the last few years, these had both remained static. A look into the future was clearly essential.

The factors were therefore changed so that they now encapsulated *potential* for growth and profits over the next three years. Using their best estimates of what these might be for each of the segments, the attractiveness scores were recalculated. The result was quite dramatic in that the resulting attractiveness positions of the segments now showed most of the high-profit segments of today at the lower end of the scale in three years' time, since few of them were growth segments and the company already had a high share in most of them.

The chief executive could now see opportunities for the company to meet the demands of its shareholders.

The second example concerns a clothing manufacturer who had completed a segmentation project in one of its markets and identified five distinct segments. One of these segments stood out as being extremely attractive in that, while it accounted for approaching 20 per cent of the population in the market, it accounted for over 35 per cent of the sales. For the company in question, it did not matter how they cut the attractiveness factors, this segment always came out on top. As it was also a segment in which they had very little presence, the opportunity this presented them with was very tempting.

In just under a year, the company was ready to launch a new range of clothes targeted at this segment.

It was a disaster.

The segment had specific requirements with respect to certain style-related attributes of the clothing, as well as to the positioning associated with the brand appearing on the label. They also had a very clear preference with respect to the type of distribution outlet they felt comfortable in buying their clothes from. Although all three of these criteria had been understood by the company, the company was very entrenched in a style of clothing they were renowned for, which did not have the attributes this segment was looking for, they had a very strong brand name associated with this style which they felt compelled to associate with every garment they produced, and the company only ever dealt with a type of distribution outlet the segment in question rarely, if ever, visited.

The segment was certainly attractive, but what the company had failed to assess was their capability in meeting the needs of this segment and, therefore, be seen by the customers it represented as a potential competitor for their business. In other words, they had failed to assess their relative competitive strength for this segment.

The lesson from this example is that segment attractiveness cannot be looked at in isolation and must be seen alongside relative company competitiveness before decisions are made about which segments a company is to target. Company competitiveness is looked at in the next chapter.

# References

McDonald, M. (2002). 'Completing the marketing audit: 2 The product audit'. In *Marketing Plans: How to Prepare Them, How to Use Them*, pp. 171–254. Oxford: Butterworth-Heinemann.

Porter, M. E. (1985). *Competitive Advantage – Creating and Sustaining Superior Performance*. New York: Free Press.

# Exercises

## Exercise 9.1

Table 9.10 contains details about five segments in a particular market. The information categories are those that will be used to determine segment attractiveness.

Table 9.11 contains the importance weightings of these segment attractiveness factors along with their scores using the parameters of high, medium and low.

**Table 9.10** Segment details for Exercise 9.1

| Segments | Segment attractiveness factors | | | | |
|---|---|---|---|---|---|
| | Segment size (£ millions) | Growth (%) | Competitive intensity | Profitability (%) | Vulnerability |
| Segment 1 | 20 | 12 | Low | 17 | Low |
| Segment 2 | 120 | 2 | High | <10 | High |
| Segment 3 | 20 | 11 | Low | 20 | Medium |
| Segment 4 | 80 | 9 | Medium | 14 | Medium |
| Segment 5 | 100 | 6 | Medium | 11 | High |

**Table 9.11** Parameters and their scores for the segment attractiveness factors in Exercise 9.1

| Segment attractiveness factors | Parameters | | | |
|---|---|---|---|---|
| | Weight (Total 100) | High (10–7) | Medium (6–3) | Low (2–0) |
| Segment size | 15 | >100 | 33–100 | <33 |
| Growth | 25 | >10% | 5–9% | <5% |
| Competitive intensity | 15 | Low | Medium | High |
| Profitability | 30 | >5% | 10–15% | <10% |
| Vulnerability | 15 | Low | Medium | High |

With the above in mind, see if you can complete the segment attractiveness scoring for Segment 1 in Table 9.12. Alternatively, take a copy of the worksheet in Table 9.16 and use this for Exercise 9.1.

**Table 9.12** Attractiveness factor scores for Segment 1 in Exercise 9.1

| Segment attractiveness factors | Weight | Score | Total |
|---|---|---|---|
| Segment size | × 15 | 1 | = 0.15 |
| Growth | × 25 | | = |
| Competitive intensity | × 15 | | = |
| Profitability | × 30 | | = |
| Vulnerability | × 15 | | = |
| | | Total | |

You can check if your answer is correct by looking at Table 9.13 and comparing your result with that appearing in this table. You will note that there has to be an element of judgement in the scoring, but as long as you are consistent, the conclusions will not be affected.

As it is important to be clear about how the total segment attractiveness score is calculated, Table 9.14 presents a second opportunity to work this through, but, on this occasion, for Segment 2. You can check your answers by looking at Table 9.15.

**Table 9.13** Attractiveness factor score ranges for Segment 1 in Exercise 9.1

| Segment attractiveness factors | Weight | Score | Total |
|---|---|---|---|
| Segment size | × 15 | 1 | = 0.15 |
| Growth | × 25 | (7–10) | = (1.75–2.5) |
| Competitive intensity | × 15 | (7–10) | = (1.05–1.5) |
| Profitability | × 30 | (7–10) | = (2.10–3.0) |
| Vulnerability | × 15 | (7–10) | = (1.05–1.5) |
| | | *Total* | (6.10–8.65) |

**Table 9.14** Attractiveness factor scores for Segment 2 in Exercise 9.1

| Segment attractiveness factors | Weight | Score | Total |
|---|---|---|---|
| Segment size | × 15 | 10 | = 1.5 |
| Growth | × 25 | | = |
| Competitive intensity | × 15 | | = |
| Profitability | × 30 | | = |
| Vulnerability | × 15 | | = |
| | | *Total* | |

**Table 9.15** Attractiveness factor score ranges for Segment 2 in Exercise 9.1

| Segment attractiveness factors | Weight | Score | Total |
|---|---|---|---|
| Segment size | × 15 | (7–10) | = (1.05–1.5) |
| Growth | × 25 | (1–2) | = (0.25–0.5) |
| Competitive intensity | × 15 | (1–2) | = (0.15–0.3) |
| Profitability | × 30 | (1–2) | = (0.30–0.6) |
| Vulnerability | × 15 | (1–2) | = (0.15–0.3) |
| | | *Total* | (1.90–3.2) |

To complete the picture, the attractiveness score for Segment 3 works out at 8.05, for Segment 4 it comes to 5.55 and for Segment 5 it comes to 4.15. If you have not worked out a score for Segment 2, assume it to be 2.35.

With all the scores to hand, the segments can now be positioned on the attractiveness axis of a portfolio matrix. This has already been completed for Segments 3 and 5 in Figure 10.11 which can be found in the Exercises section of the next chapter. Alternatively, take a copy of the portfolio matrix worksheet which also appears in the Exercises section of the next chapter, establish a scale and position the segments on the vertical axis.

---

Develop a set of criteria for judging segment attractiveness in your company and develop a scoring and weighting system for these criteria. A copy of Table 9.16 can be used for this exercise. Do not forget the three golden rules: never do this alone; obtain agreement from key colleagues; and use quantitative information in preference to opinion, whenever this is available.

Now calculate the attractiveness scores for the segments in your market and locate their position on the vertical axis of a portfolio matrix. A copy of the portfolio matrix worksheet in the Exercises section of Chapter 10 can be used for this.

**Exercise 9.2**

**Table 9.16** Worksheet – calculating segment attractiveness

*Description*

Segment 1:
Segment 2:
Segment 3:

*Description*

Segment 4:
Segment 5:

| Segment attractiveness factors | Weight | Parameters | | | Segment 1 | | Segment 2 | | Segment 3 | | Segment 4 | | Segment 5 | |
| --- | --- | --- | --- | --- | --- | --- | --- | --- | --- | --- | --- | --- | --- | --- |
| | | High 10–7 | Med 6–4 | Low 3–0 | Score | Total | Score | Total | Score | Total | Score | Total | Score | Total |
| | | | | | | | | | | | | | | |
| Total | 100 | | | | | Total | | Total | | Total | | Total | | Total |

Chapter 10

# Assessing company competitiveness and the portfolio matrix

# Summary

To complement the analysis of segment attractiveness, it is essential that the company assesses how well equipped it is to deal with each segment before finally deciding where to focus its financial and managerial resources. However, no matter how 'fit' your company may be in meeting the needs of a segment, customers will make their choice based on which of the competing companies is, in their view, the 'fittest'. It is, therefore, the company's *relative* competitiveness that has to be balanced with segment attractiveness in order to determine where the greatest realizable opportunities are to be found for the organization.

Assessing relative competitiveness and balancing it with segment attractiveness is looked at in this chapter. It is the seventh and final step in the segmentation process, as illustrated in Figure 10.1.

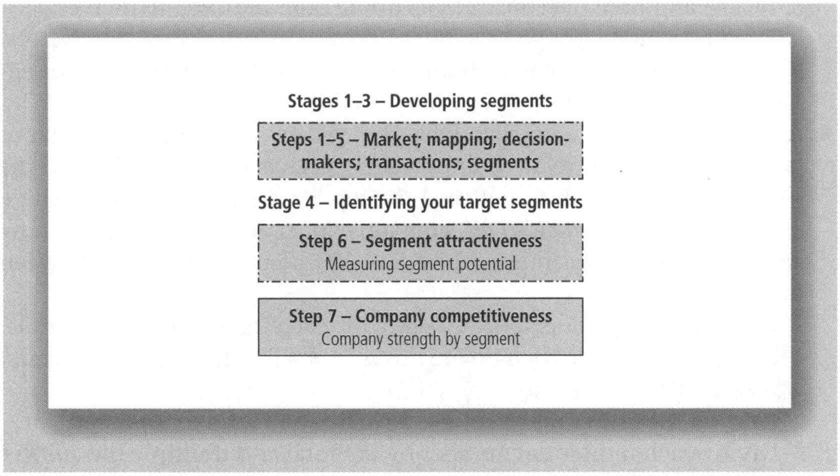

**Stages 1–3 – Developing segments**

Steps 1–5 – Market; mapping; decision-makers; transactions; segments

**Stage 4 – Identifying your target segments**

Step 6 – Segment attractiveness
Measuring segment potential

Step 7 – Company competitiveness
Company strength by segment

**Figure 10.1**
The segmentation process – Step 7

In order to arrive at a realistic assessment of company strengths, it is necessary to look at the performance of companies in terms of how it is *perceived* by customers in relation to the needs they are seeking to satisfy. This step, therefore, requires 'perceived' performance as opposed to 'true' performance to be measured.

This chapter is organized as follows:

- A 'fast track' for those looking for a quick route through the key points
- An introduction to 'company competitiveness' and an overview of the steps it involves
- Defining the time period for company competitiveness
- Factors to consider in company competitiveness for each segment
- The weightings to be allocated to these factors
- Defining the parameters for competitiveness so that company strengths can be gauged
- How to evaluate the competitiveness scores for your company and your competitors in each segment

- ■ Transferring the results on to a portfolio matrix and illustrating the size of each segment along with your share
- ■ How different time periods and different strategic assumptions for your company and your competitors can be used to produce a Directional Policy Matrix (DPM)
- ■ A review of this, the final step in the segmentation process
- ■ Examples of segment portfolios
- ■ Exercises to help you further with relative company competitiveness

# Fast track

- For each segment, list the needs they are seeking to satisfy – these, along with 'price', were identified in Step 5 as their Decisive Buying Criteria (DBCs) – and note the constituents of the offer required to deliver each DBC successfully (frequently referred to as 'Critical Success Factors' (CSFs) in a portfolio matrix, many of which will be aligned to the segment's Key Discriminating Features (KDFs)).
- Associate a weight with each DBC that reflects its relative importance (and, therefore, the relative importance of its constituent CSFs) to the segment. This was also identified in Step 5, though where the relative importance of a segment's DBCs remain expressed as symbols, they now need to be expressed numerically and 100 points distributed between them as follows;
  1. Convert the symbols to numbers with each 'half-star', for example, being equivalent to a single unit, thus '★★★☆' (three and a half stars) is equivalent to 'seven'.
  2. Add up the individual numbers to arrive at a total for the segment.
  3. Divide each individual number by the total and multiply the answer by 100.

  If required, refer to Table 10.3 later in this chapter for a worked example.
- Set the parameters for competitiveness to 'highly competitive' scoring from 10 down to 7, 'competitive' from 6 down to 4 and 'uncompetitive' from 3 down to 0 – these are fixed and do not change.
- Take one of the segments and, in considering the CSFs required to deliver each DBC, separately score your own company's and your main competitors' current (Year 0) performance for each DBC based on the parameters for competitiveness *as perceived by the customers in the segment*, multiply these individual scores by the weight that has been given to its respective DBC and divide by 100, then add all these together to arrive at a total between 0 and 10 for each company, as illustrated in Table 10.1.

  A worksheet for listing the DBCs, along with their constituent CSFs, and for calculating the competitive scores for the segments appears in the Exercises section of this chapter.
- Now assess for the segment your own company's competitiveness relative to the competition by dividing your company's total weighted score

**Table 10.1** Fast track – competitive strength evaluation (Year 0)

| | | *Segment 2* | | | | | |
|---|---|---|---|---|---|---|---|
| *DBCs & CSFs* | *Weight* | *Your company* | | *Competitor A* | | *Competitor B* | |
| | | *Score* | *Total* | *Score* | *Total* | *Score* | *Total* |
| 1. Product | 45 | 6 | 2.7 | 8 | 3.6 | 4 | 1.8 |
| 2. Service | 25 | 8 | 2.0 | 8 | 2.0 | 8 | 2.0 |
| 3. Image | 20 | 6 | 1.2 | 5 | 1.0 | 4 | 0.8 |
| 4. Price | 10 | 4 | 0.4 | 5 | 0.5 | 7 | 0.7 |
| *Total* | 100 | | 6.3 | | 7.1 | | 5.3 |

*Note:* The scores are based on the parameters for competitiveness as described in the previous bullet point and are as perceived by the segment. The DBCs and CSFs are abbreviated to a single word in this table due to limitations on space. An example of a more detailed listing can be found in Table 10.2 later in this chapter.

by the highest total weighted score of the competitors, expressing the result as a ratio (your company : best competitor). For Table 10.1 this would be 6.3 : 7.1 = 0.89 : 1.0 (0.89 being 6.3 ÷ 7.1).

● When the company's relative competitiveness scores have been calculated for each segment, transpose the results on to the horizontal axis of the portfolio matrix, as illustrated in Figure 10.2, using a logarithmic scale ranging from 3x to 0.3x (normally sufficient for most projects). At the point of intersection with the appropriate attractiveness line, draw a circle to represent the forecast size of the segment in Year 3.

A worksheet for plotting segments on the portfolio matrix appears in the Exercises section of this chapter.

● Capture your company's share of each segment as a 'cheese' in each circle. Alternatively, your company's own sales into each segment can be used to determine the size of the circle. This analysis should indicate whether your portfolio is well balanced or not, and should give a clear indication of any problems.

● Now introduce some dynamics into your matrix for it to become a Directional Policy Matrix (DPM). For example, re-score your relative competitive strength for each segment assuming that your company continues with the strategies already in place, or based on realistic assumptions about your competitor's strategies but with your company standing still, or some combination of either of these. Also consider showing the position of segments using the competitiveness of Year 0 with the attractiveness of Year 0, and then redraw these for Year 3 along with any of the competition scenarios you have developed. This will see segments moving vertically as well as horizontally in the matrix.

Readers who have established a realistic assessment of relative competitiveness and completed the portfolio matrix may go straight to Chapter 11.

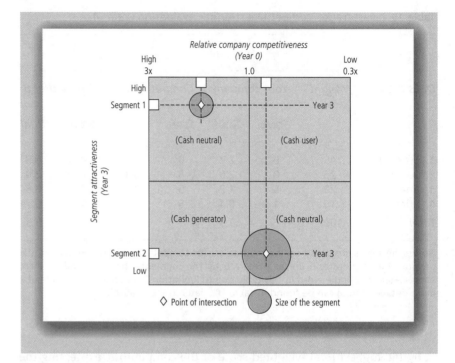

**Figure 10.2** Fast track – plotting business positions on the portfolio matrix for each segment according to their relative competitive strength (*Note:* Although 'high' is positioned on the left of the horizontal axis it can, if you prefer, be placed on the right and its scale can be extended if circumstances require it. To portray the relative size of each segment, the easiest approach is to draw each circle with the radius proportional to that segment's share of the total market.)

This concludes the fast track for Step 7 of the segmentation process.

# Company competitiveness

Definition:
Company
competitiveness is a
measure of an
organization's actual
strengths in each
segment (in other words,
the degree to which it
can take advantage of a
segment opportunity).

Company competitiveness, for the purposes of this book, is a measure of an organization's *actual* strengths in each segment, in other words, the degree to which it can take advantage of a segment opportunity. Thus, it is an objective assessment of an organization's ability to satisfy segment needs relative to competitors.

The procedure to follow when assessing company competitiveness can be summarized as follows:

1 For each segment, list the needs they are seeking to satisfy – these, along with 'price', were identified in Step 5 as their Decisive Buying Criteria (DBCs) – and note the constituents of the offer required to deliver each DBC successfully (many of which will be aligned to the segment's Key Discriminating Features (KDFs)).

2  Associate a weight with each DBC that reflects its relative importance (and, therefore, the relative importance of what is required to deliver the DBC) to the segment. This was also identified in Step 5, though where the relative importance of a segment's DBCs remain expressed as symbols, they now need to be expressed numerically and 100 points distributed between them.

3  Set the parameters for competitiveness to 'highly competitive' scoring from 10 down to 7, 'competitive' from 6 down to 4 and 'uncompetitive' from 3 down to 0 – these are fixed and do not change.

4  Take one of the segments and, in considering the constituents of the offer required to deliver each DBC, separately score your own company's and your main competitors' performance for each DBC based on the parameters for competitiveness *as perceived by the customers in the segment*, multiply these individual scores by the weight that has been given to its respective DBC and divide by 100, then add all these together to arrive at a total between 0 and 10 for each company.

5  Now assess for the segment your own company's competitiveness relative to the competition by dividing your company's total weighted score by the highest total weighted score of the competitors, expressing the result as a ratio (your company : best competitor).

Repeat the above steps until the company's relative competitiveness scores have been calculated for each segment.

A key emphasis in the above summary, and a golden rule for assessing company competitiveness, is that the performance of each company included in the analysis is *as perceived by the segment*. Therefore, 'perceived' performance should be used in preference to 'true' performance, even when there are discrepancies between them, and whenever market research information is available, it should be used in preference to opinions, no matter how well founded these opinions might be.

## Time horizon

The choice of time period to be scored is clearly linked to the decisions on time periods made in the previous chapter, this being either today (Year 0) or at the end of the planning period, with three years being the recommended time horizon.

It is suggested that the calculations for company competitiveness should first be carried out for the start of the planning period (Year 0). This enables you to establish a fixed position on the portfolio matrix for your company in each segment against which the forecast outcome of alternative strategies and assumptions for the planning period can be seen when plotted on to the Directional Policy Matrix (DPM). If you have only calculated segment attractiveness for a single year, the impact of any changes in your company's activities will only move segments horizontally – that is, along the same level of attractiveness. However, if you have determined segment attractiveness for both the start and end of the planning period, any changes to your company's relative competitive strength will see segments move both horizontally as their attractiveness changes and vertically as your relative competitive strength changes. This is shown on Figure 10.7 which appears later in this chapter.

## Competitiveness factors

These factors will be principally a combination of an organization's relative strengths versus competitors in connection with *customer-facing* needs in each segment, namely those that are required by the customer. These were identified in Step 5 as their DBCs, with each concluding segment having its own importance rating of the market's DBCs, which, you will recall, also included 'price'. To win the business in any particular segment, therefore, the company has to be relatively more *successful* than its competitors in matching up to the segment's DBCs.

Competitive 'success' is in relation to the constituents of the offer required to deliver each DBC; frequently referred to as 'Critical Success Factors' (CSFs).

This 'success' is in relation to the constituents of the offer required to deliver each DBC and these are frequently referred to as 'Critical Success Factors' (CSFs); this is the term most often found in marketing text books and papers when describing the business strengths/competitiveness axis of a portfolio matrix. For example, delivering to the customers in a segment the perception that they are being 'innovative' may require a company to be seen at the forefront of product development, for its outlets and channels to be the most modern and for its promotional activity to adopt, if not pioneer, the latest techniques and so on. Assessing competitiveness related to the DBC of being 'innovative', therefore, will require an assessment of a company's performance with respect to all the appropriate constituents of 'innovation' as perceived by the segment. There may, of course, be only a single CSF required to deliver a DBC rather than several.

As will be apparent from the preceding paragraph, many of the CSFs will be aligned to each segment's KDFs. Therefore, if you have not already consolidated the KDFs for each segment, now is the time to do so. A worksheet to help calculate these details appeared in the Exercises section of Chapter 8.

The CSFs can often be summarized under the following headings:[1]

- product requirements;
- price requirements;
- promotion requirements;
- place (distribution and service) requirements.

In the same way that 'profit' on the segment attractiveness axis can be broken down into a number of sub-headings, so can each of the above be broken down further and analysed, with the sub-headings based on those that are relevant to the segment. For example, in the case of pharmaceuticals, product strengths could be represented by:

- relative product safety;
- relative product convenience;
- relative cost effectiveness.

In your review of how well your company can meet the requirements of each segment, you may well need to consider questions such as:

- Do we have the right products?
- How large is our segment share?

---

[1] As mentioned in Chapter 7, the traditional four Ps of the marketing mix, namely product, price, promotion and place, are sometimes extended into a number of other 'Ps' such as people and processes.

- How well are we known in this segment?
- What image do we have?
- Do we have the right technical skills?
- Can we adapt to change?
- Do we have enough capacity?
- Can we grow?
- How close are we to this segment?

It should be stressed, however, that the answers to these questions should not be confused with customer-facing CSFs. They will only tell you in what ways you have to change to satisfy your customer's needs.

It will be clear that a company's relative strengths in meeting customer-facing needs will be a function of its capabilities in connection with the CSFs relative to the capabilities of the best competitor. For example, if a depot is necessary in each major town/city for any organization to succeed in any segment, and the company carrying out the analysis does not have this, yet the competition does, then it is likely that this will account for its poor performance under 'customer service'. Likewise, if a major component of 'price' is the cost of feedstock, and it is necessary in some segments to have low prices in order to succeed, any company carrying out the analysis which does not have low feedstock costs, while competitors do, will find that it is this which accounts for its poor performance under 'price'.

Clearly, this type of assessment of a company's capabilities in respect of CSFs could be made in order to understand what has to be done in the organization in order to satisfy customer needs better. This assessment, however, is quite separate from the quantification of the competitive strengths/position axis, and its purpose is to translate the analysis into actionable propositions for other functions within the organization, such as purchasing, production, distribution and so on.

## Weighting the factors

The weightings allocated to the competitiveness factors, namely the DBCs and their constituent CSFs, will, of course, be specific to each segment and will reflect the relative importance of the DBCs to each other as observed for the segment in Step 5. An example is shown in Table 10.2.

**Table 10.2** Weighting DBCs and their constituent CSFs

| Segment 4 | |
|---|---|
| *DBCs and their Critical Success Factors* | *Weight* |
| 1. Delivery reliability: ≥95% within 30 minutes of the agreed time | 50 |
| 2. Product technical performance: temperature range tolerance | 25 |
| 3. Leading edge image: e-business, product materials pioneer | 15 |
| 4. Price | 10 |
| *Total* | 100 |

In those cases where the relative importance of a segment's DBCs remain expressed as symbols, such as stars and half-stars, they now need to be expressed numerically and 100 points distributed between them. This requires the following steps to be carried out for each segment;

1 Convert the symbols to numbers with each 'half-star', for example, being equivalent to a single unit, thus '★ ★ ★ ☆' (three and a half stars) is equivalent to 'seven'.
2 Add up the individual numbers to arrive at a total for the segment.
3 Divide each individual number by the total and multiply the answer by 100.

A worked example appears in Table 10.3.

**Table 10.3** Expressing the relative importance of DBCs numerically

| | Segment 2 | | |
| --- | --- | --- | --- |
| DBCs | DBC rating | As a number | Reworked |
| 1. Product technical performance | ★ ★ ★ ★ ☆ | 9 | 41 |
| 2. Leading edge image | ★ ★ ★ | 6 | 27 |
| 3. Delivery reliability | ★ ★ ☆ | 5 | 23 |
| 4. Price | ★ | 2 | 9 |
| | Total | 22 | 100 |

If a segment's DBCs have each had their importance rated on a scale of, say, 1 to 10, these can be reworked so that they total 100 by following steps 2 and 3.

## Defining the parameters for competitiveness

The parameters for competitiveness are very straightforward, as they are common to all the CSFs. They consist of:

- highly competitive (which has a score range of 10 down to 7),
- competitive (with a score range of 6 down to 4),
- uncompetitive (scoring from 3 down to 0).

While we would recommend the above scoring structure for the parameters, they are, however, a matter of management judgement.

## Scoring your company and your competitors

*Competitiveness scores are as perceived by the customers in the segment.*

For each individual segment, refer to the parameters for competitiveness and score your own company and each of your main competitors out of 10 on each of the DBCs based on the *customer's perceived assessment* of your and their performance with respect to the CSFs, multiply the individual scores by their respective weight and divide by 100, then add these together for each company to arrive at a total between 0 and 10 as shown in Table 10.4. This calculation should first be carried out for the start of the planning period, namely Year 0. This enables you to establish a fixed position on the portfolio matrix for your company in each segment against which the forecast outcome of alternative strategies and assumptions for the planning period can be seen when plotted on to the DPM.

**Table 10.4** Competitive strength evaluation (Year 0)

| | | Segment 3 | | | | | |
|---|---|---|---|---|---|---|---|
| DBCs & CSFs | Weight | Your company | | Competitor A | | Competitor B | |
| | | Score | Total | Score | Total | Score | Total |
| 1. Delivery | 50 | 6 | 3.0 | 9 | 4.5 | 4 | 2.0 |
| 2. Product | 25 | 8 | 2.0 | 6 | 1.5 | 10 | 2.5 |
| 3. Image | 15 | 8 | 1.2 | 8 | 1.2 | 6 | 0.9 |
| 4. Price | 10 | 5 | 0.5 | 6 | 0.6 | 3 | 0.3 |
| Total | 100 | | 6.7 | | 7.8 | | 5.7 |

*Note:* The scores are based on the parameters described in the previous section and are as perceived by the segment.

From this table it can be seen that:

1 this company is not the segment leader;
2 all competitors score above 5.0.

The problem with this and many similar calculations is that rarely will this method discriminate sufficiently well to indicate the relative strengths of a number of segments in a particular company's market portfolio, and many of the SBU's segments would appear on the left of the matrix.

Some method is required to prevent all segments appearing on the left of the matrix. This can be achieved by using a ratio, as in the Boston Matrix, which is calculated for each segment by dividing your company's total weighted score by the highest total weighted score of the competitors. This will indicate a company's position relative to the best in the segment.

In the example provided, Competitor A has most strengths in the segment so our organization needs to make some improvements. To reflect this, our total weighted score should be expressed as a ratio of Competitor A (the highest total weighted score). Thus,

$$6.7:7.8 = 0.86:1.0 \ (0.86 \ being \ 6.7 \div 7.8)$$

If we were to plot this on a logarithmic scale on the horizontal axis, this would place our organization to the right of the dividing line as shown in

Figure 10.3 (we should make the left hand extreme point '3x' and start the scale on the right at '0.3x').

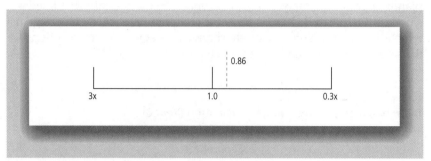

**Figure 10.3**  Plotting a relative competitive strength score of 0.86 (*Note:* If our company had scored 7.8 and the highest competitor's score had been 6.7 the ratio would work out at 1.16 : 1.0 and place our organization to the left of the dividing line.)

A scale of '3x' to '0.3x' has been chosen because such a band is likely to encapsulate most extremes of competitive advantage. If it does not, just change it to suit your own circumstances, for example, 10x to 0.1x.

A worksheet which can be used for these various calculations appears in the Exercises section of this chapter.

# Producing the portfolio matrix

Once you have completed the competitive evaluation for Year 0, you can plot your position for each segment by drawing a vertical line from the relevant point on the horizontal scale, as shown on Figure 10.4, so that it intersects with the appropriate segment's horizontal line (initially from the Year 3 calculations).

A worksheet for plotting segments on the portfolio matrix appears in the Exercises section of this chapter.

Now, at the point of intersection for each segment, draw a circle with the radius of each circle proportional to that segment's share of the total market, which will be based on your forecasts of size if the attractiveness is for Year 3. (Please note that to be technically correct, the radius of the circle should be the square root of the area occupied by the circle: that is, segment size divided by *pi*, namely 3.14.[2]) This can then be transferred to a four-box matrix with your company's share put as a 'cheese' in each circle, as on Figure 10.5.

[2] We suggest to only two decimal points!

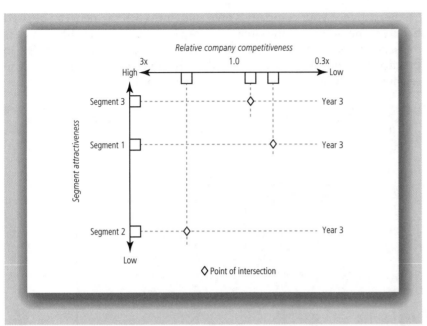

**Figure 10.4**
Plotting business positions on the portfolio matrix for each segment according to their relative competitive strength
(*Note:* Although 'high' is positioned on the left of the horizontal axis it can, if you prefer, be placed on the right. The three segments on the vertical axis are as they appeared in Figure 9.8 in the previous chapter.)

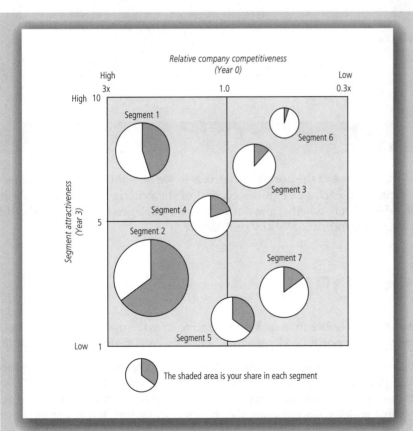

**Figure 10.5**
The initial segment portfolio matrix

Alternatively, your company's own sales into each segment can be used to determine the size of the circle. This can be seen on Figure 10.6 which is the segment portfolio matrix for the case study, Agrofertilizer Supplies. In practice, however, it is advisable to do both and compare them in order to see how closely actual sales match the opportunities.

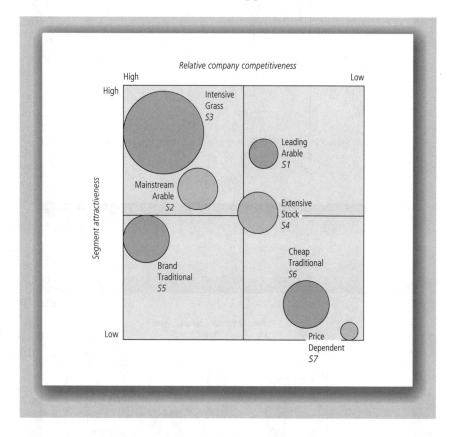

**Figure 10.6**
The segment portfolio matrix for the case study (*Note:* 'S5', 'S3' and so on represent 'Segment 5', 'Segment 3' and so on as listed in Chapter 8.)

The purpose of the portfolio matrix is to see how the segments in a market relate to each other in the context of the criteria used. This analysis should indicate whether the portfolio is well balanced or not, and should give a clear indication of any problems.

# The DPM

It is now possible to start being creative in your use of the matrix and redraw your portfolio along a number of alternative lines by, for example:

1 re-scoring your relative competitive strength for each segment assuming the company continues with the strategies already in place;
2 re-scoring your relative competitive strength for each segment based on some realistic assumptions about your competitors, but assuming your company just stood still;
3 a combination of the above.

By including these new locations of the segments on the original portfolio matrix, the resulting matrix will indicate whether your own position is getting worse or better. With the attractiveness scores being kept at Year 3, then it will be clear that the circles can only move horizontally along the axis as all that will change is your competitive strength. Alternatively, you could show the position of the segments on the portfolio matrix as they are today, using segment attractiveness for Year 0 and the relative company competitiveness for Year 0, and then redraw the segments to show their attractiveness position in Year 3 along with any of the competition scenarios you have developed for Year 3. In such a case, the circles can move both vertically and horizontally, as is the case in Figure 10.7.

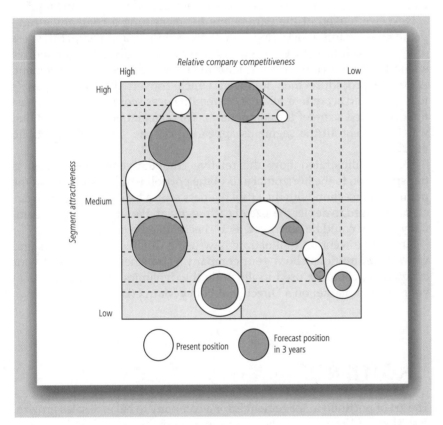

**Figure 10.7**
The DPM

# Process check

This, the seventh and final step in the segmentation process, provides guidelines on how to assess relative company competitiveness in each segment. The outcome of this analysis, when balanced with segment attractiveness, can then be used to determine which segments provide the greatest opportunities for the company to achieve its objectives.

We began with a brief review of the steps involved in assessing company competitiveness for each segment. Here we highlighted the point that the assessment of your company's performance and that of your competitors is based on how it is perceived by the customers in a segment, even if this is at odds with what you know to be the 'true' performance.

After a brief review of the time period you should consider, we turned to the competitiveness factors to be included in the evaluation and pointed out that these were directly linked to the DBCs identified for each segment in Step 5. Here we emphasized that what was actually measured was each company's performance in relation to the constituents of the offer required to deliver each DBC, frequently referred to as 'Critical Success Factors' (CSFs). We then pointed out that the weightings allocated to the competitiveness factors were those recorded for each segment's DBCs in Step 5.

Next, we looked at the parameters for measuring a company's competitiveness before illustrating how the weightings and competitiveness scores for each factor were used to calculate the individual competitive strengths of your company and your main competitors in each segment. A simple procedure then followed which converted your company's total weighted score to a relative competitiveness score using the highest total weighted score of the competitors. This calculation, we pointed out, was to prevent all the segments appearing on one side of the portfolio matrix.

We then illustrated how the relative competitiveness evaluation is transposed on to the horizontal axis of the portfolio matrix and how, at the point of intersection with the attractiveness scores for each segment, a circle can be used to depict the size of each segment. We suggested your company's share could be portrayed as a 'cheese' in each circle.

Finally, we went on to illustrate how using different time periods and various assumptions about your company's strategies and those of your competitors could be used to illustrate the dynamics of the segments in your defined market on a Directional Policy Matrix (DPM).

# Examples

The art of portfolio management is for a company to balance sales growth, cash flow and risk. Using the picturesque labels associated with the four quadrants of the Boston Matrix (Figure 9.3 in the previous chapter), we should be seeking to use surplus cash generated by 'cash cows' to invest in 'stars' and a selected number of 'question marks'.

Figure 10.8 shows a well-balanced portfolio. There is one large 'cash cow', two sizeable 'stars', and three emerging segments presenting growth opportunities for the future. There are only two small 'dogs'.

Figure 10.9 shows a poorly balanced portfolio. The company has no 'cash cows'. There is only one small 'star'. It has three 'question marks' and three 'dogs', one of which is a sizeable segment. There could be cash flow problems with this company.

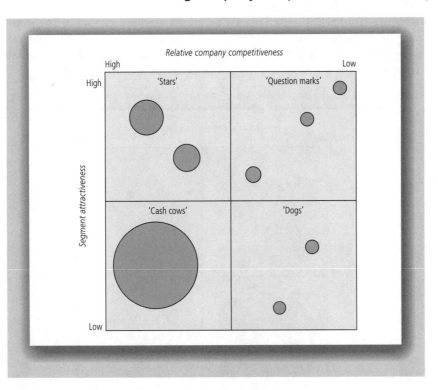

**Figure 10.8**
Well-balanced
portfolio

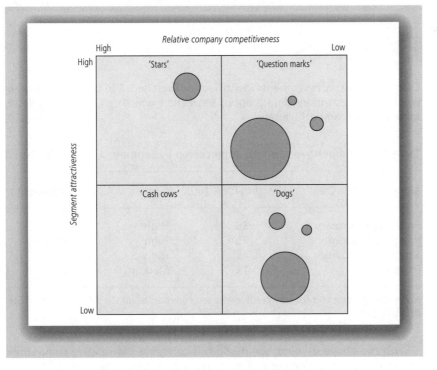

**Figure 10.9**
Poorly balanced
portfolio (1)

Figure 10.10 also shows a poorly balanced segment portfolio. This company is probably cash rich, with three sizeable 'cash cows'. However, all the danger signs are evident. There is only one small 'star' and one small 'question mark' presenting growth opportunities for the future.

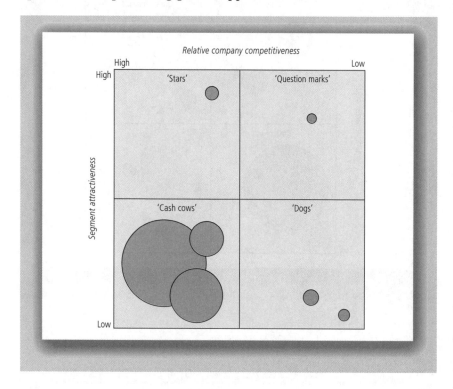

**Figure 10.10**
Poorly balanced
portfolio (2)

# Exercises

**Exercise 10.1**

Continuing with the segments identified for Exercise 9.1 in the previous chapter, Table 10.5 contains details about Segment 1 which can be used to determine relative competitiveness.

**Table 10.5** Competitive strength as perceived by Segment 1 in Exercise 10.1

| Market DBCs & CSFs | Weight (Total 100) | Company A | Best competitor |
|---|---|---|---|
| Product performance | 35 | High | Medium |
| Image with segment | 25 | High | Medium |
| Service availability | 25 | High | Low |
| Price | 15 | Medium | High |

*Note:* The parameters for competitiveness are common to all the DBCs and their constituent CSFs.

With the above in mind, see if you can complete the relative competitive strength score for Company A with respect to Segment 1 in Table 10.6.

Alternatively, take a copy of the worksheet in Table 10.11 and use this for Exercise 10.1. Assume that the parameters being used for competitiveness correspond to the following scores:

- 'High', 10 down to 7;
- 'Medium', 6 down to 4;
- 'Low', 3 down to 0.

**Table 10.6** Relative competitive strength evaluation for Segment 1 in Exercise 10.1

| DBCs | Weight | Company A | | Best competitor | |
|------|--------|-----------|-----|-----------------|-----|
| | | *Score* | *Total* | *Score* | *Total* |
| Product | × 35 | 8 | = 2.8 | 5 | = 1.75 |
| Image | × 25 | | = | | = |
| Service | × 25 | | = | | = |
| Price | × 15 | | = | | = |
| | | | *Total* | | *Total* |
| *Relative competitive strength of Company A:* | | | : 1.0 | | |

You can check if your answer is correct by looking at Table 10.7.

**Table 10.7** Relative competitive strength score ranges for Segment 1 in Exercise 10.1

| DBCs | Weight | Company A | | Best competitor | |
|------|--------|-----------|-----|-----------------|-----|
| | | *Score* | *Total* | *Score* | *Total* |
| Product | × 35 | 8 | = 2.8 | 5 | = 1.75 |
| Image | × 25 | (7–10) | = (1.75–2.5) | (4–6) | = (1.0–1.5) |
| Service | × 25 | (7–10) | = (1.75–2.5) | (0–3) | = (0.0–0.75) |
| Price | × 15 | (4–6) | = (0.6–0.9) | (7–10) | = (1.05–1.5) |
| | | | *Total* (6.9–8.7) | | *Total* (3.8–5.5) |
| *Relative competitive strength of Company A:* (2.29 : 1.0–1.25 : 1.0) | | | | | |

If you would like the practice, Table 10.8 contains details about Segment 2 which can be used to determine relative competitiveness in Table 10.9. You can check your answers by looking at Table 10.10.

With similar information to hand about the other segments, the relative competitiveness score for Segment 3 works out at 0.49, for Segment 4 it comes to 1.08 and for Segment 5 it comes to 2.02. If you have not worked out a score for Segment 2, assume it to be 0.62.

With all the scores to hand, the company can now be positioned on the competitiveness axis of a portfolio matrix for each segment. The location of each segment in the matrix can then be established by drawing a vertical line

**Table 10.8** Competitive strength as perceived by Segment 2 in Exercise 10.1

| Market DBCs & CSFs | Weight (Total 100) | Company A | Best competitor |
|---|---|---|---|
| Product performance | 25 | High | Medium |
| Image with segment | 15 | Medium | High |
| Service availability | 20 | Medium | Medium |
| Price | 40 | Low | High |

**Table 10.9** Relative competitive strength evaluation for Segment 2 in Exercise 10.1

| DBCs | Weight | Company A | | Best competitor | |
|---|---|---|---|---|---|
| | | Score | Total | Score | Total |
| Product | × 25 | 8 | = 2.0 | 5 | = 1.25 |
| Image | × 15 | | = | | = |
| Service | × 20 | | = | | = |
| Price | × 40 | | = | | = |
| | | | Total | | Total |

Relative competitive strength of Company A:        : 1.0

**Table 10.10** Relative competitive strength score ranges for Segment 2 in Exercise 10.1

| DBCs | Weight | Company A | | Best competitor | |
|---|---|---|---|---|---|
| | | Score | Total | Score | Total |
| Product | × 25 | (7–10) | = (1.75–2.5) | (4–6) | = (1.0–1.5) |
| Image | × 15 | (4–6) | = (0.6–0.9) | (7–10) | = (1.05–1.5) |
| Service | × 20 | (4–6) | = (0.8–1.2) | (4–6) | = (0.8–1.2) |
| Price | × 40 | (0–3) | = (0.0–1.2) | (7–10) | = (2.8–4.0) |
| | | Total | (3.15–5.8) | Total | (5.65–8.2) |

Relative competitive strength of Company A: (1.03 : 1.0–0.38 : 1.0)

from the relevant point on the competitiveness axis so that it intersects with the appropriate segment's horizontal line drawn from its position on the attractiveness axis. A partially completed portfolio matrix for this exercise showing the positions of Segments 3 and 5 appears in Figure 10.11 to which you can add the remaining segments. Alternatively, take a copy of the worksheet in Figure 10.12 and use this to complete the exercise.

You will note in Figure 10.11 that, because of the attractiveness scores established in the previous chapter, the scale ranges from 2.0 to 9.0 to ensure a spread of segments on this axis. The range of attractiveness scores is from

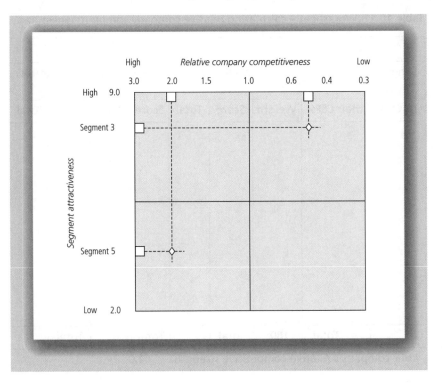

**Figure 10.11**
Portfolio matrix
for Exercises 9.1
and 10.1

2.35 (the assumed score for Segment 2) to a possible maximum score of 8.65 for Segment 1.

The portfolio matrix is almost complete. What remains to be done is to indicate the sales quantity for each of these segments. This is achieved by drawing a circle proportional to the sales quantity at each segment's point of intersection. It is often a matter of trial and error to establish the best basis for drawing these circles. If, for example, the range was from twenty units to sixty units, you may decide that every twenty units is equivalent to 5.0 mm of diameter. This would mean, for example, that thirty units would be shown as 7.5 mm and fifty units as 12.5 mm. If this proved to be too large or too small, then change it to suit the diagram.

---

**Exercise 10.2**

For each of the segments in your market, assess your performance and that of your main competitor for their DBCs, preferably as perceived by the segment. This, however, may need to be an informed judgement at this stage.

Position your company for each segment on the competitiveness axis of the portfolio matrix you developed for Exercise 9.2 and locate the point of intersection with the appropriate attractiveness score. Now, indicate your current sales for each segment with a circle using an approximate scale of your own choice, making the circle diameter proportional to the sales quantity.

Comment on the current portfolio.

Indicate approximately the size and position of the segments in three years time and outline the strategies you would pursue to achieve these objectives.

**Table 10.11** Worksheet – calculating relative company competitiveness

| Market: | | | | | | | |
| --- | --- | --- | --- | --- | --- | --- | --- |
| Segment: | | Your company | | Competitor: | | Competitor: | |
| DBCs and their CSFs | Weight | Score | Total | Score | Total | Score | Total |
| | | | | | | | |
| | | | | | | | |
| | | | | | | | |
| | | | | | | | |
| Total | 100 | Total | | Total | | Total | |
| Your company's relative competitive strength: :1.0 | | | | | | | |

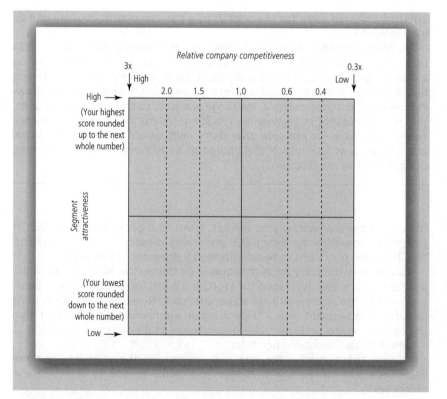

**Figure 10.12**
Worksheet –
portfolio matrix

# Chapter 11
# Realizing the full potential of market mapping

# Summary

In Chapter 5 when we looked at using a market map both to illustrate how a market works and to identify decision-makers, it was pointed out that 'market mapping' as defined and developed by the authors has become an increasingly important part of the toolkit for marketers. Not only can it be used to provide an informative picture of the distribution and value-added chain that exists between final users and suppliers, it can also be used to present your own company's performance on these routes to market and illustrate where your sales and marketing resources are allocated. This provides a useful check when evaluating your sales and marketing strategies, especially when looking at predicted changes to the market's structure and when comparing yourself with your key competitors on where resources are committed.

> A reminder:
> This book refers to those who produce the products or services supplied to a market as 'suppliers'.

This chapter looks at how to capture the above refinements on a market map. You are also at the stage where you can plot your selected segments onto the market map and consider what changes may occur in the market's distribution and value added chain during your chosen planning period. A more detailed discussion about the future shape of markets, with particular reference to IT-enabled channels, occurs in the next chapter.

We recommend that Chapters 11 and 12 be read before proceeding to set marketing objectives and strategies, although it is an option to go straight to Chapter 13 if preferred.

This chapter is organized as follows:

- A brief review of market mapping in Chapter 5
- Time period for projecting market maps into the future
- Adding company share and quantities to the map, along with the number of companies/customers found at each junction
- Extending the detail to junction types and introducing segments on to the map
- Noting the quantities decided at each junction type (market leverage)
- Detailed market maps in the tabular form
- A review of the chapter
- Examples of market maps

# Enhancing the information on your market map

A 'market map', you may recall from Chapter 5, defines the distribution and value added chain between final users and suppliers of the products or services included within the scope of your segmentation project. It was also pointed out that this should take into account the various buying mechanisms found in your market, including the part played by 'influencers', even though they may not actually feature in a transaction themselves.

> ● Definition reminder:
> A market map defines the distribution and value added chain between final users and suppliers, which takes into account the various buying mechanisms found in a market, including the part played by 'influencers'.

As in Chapter 5, we will focus on the use of diagrams to illustrate the various points made in the text about market maps, but if you find that the diagrammatic approach to market mapping is not to your liking, we also include guidelines for constructing a market map in the tabular form.

## Market mapping reviewed

We began by plotting the various stages that occur along the distribution and value added chain between the final users and all the suppliers of the products and services competing with each other in the defined market. These stages we referred to as 'junctions' and they were represented as cubes on the diagrammatic form of the market map. We then added the particular routes to market the products were sourced through. Then, to ensure that your map presented a complete picture of the market, we covered the inclusion of:

A reminder: We use the word 'product' to avoid unnecessary references to 'services', 'not-for-profit services, 'capital goods' and 'retail'. The text is equally relevant to these.

1 contractors or agencies who carry out the work on behalf of the final users and, therefore, appear to 'consume' the product on their behalf;
2 third parties who make the purchase on behalf of the final user, such as parents on behalf of their children or company purchasing departments on behalf of employees;
3 purchasing procedures, such as those seen in business-to-business markets;
4 influencers and sources of advice, such as consultants, specialist reports and websites set up to provide user feedback.

Next, we looked at quantifying the market map by initially marking at each junction on the market map and along each route between these junctions a volume or value dealt with by each of them. The market map this resulted in appears in Figure 11.1, a repeat of Figure 5.10 in Chapter 5, with the equivalent map in the tabular form appearing in Table 11.1, a repeat of Table 5.2 in Chapter 5.

It is at this point we pick up market mapping for this chapter. For the diagrammatic form we will, however, revert to using the horizontal format, an option introduced in Chapter 5, and Figure 11.2 re-presents Figure 11.1 using this format.

## Looking to the future

Before enhancing the detail contained in your market map, this is an opportune point at which to consider how the market may change in the future and redraw the market map as it currently stands to reflect these changes. The end of the time period selected for your portfolio matrix is clearly the most appropriate time horizon for this projection.

## Further quantification of the market map

In addition to showing at each junction and along each route the volumes or values dealt with by each of them, note your company's share and, if you choose to, also show what this means in terms of the number of units for your company, as illustrated in Figure 11.3. It is usually easier to do this for the current year in the first instance. As suggested in previous chapters, where figures are not available, guesstimates should be made.

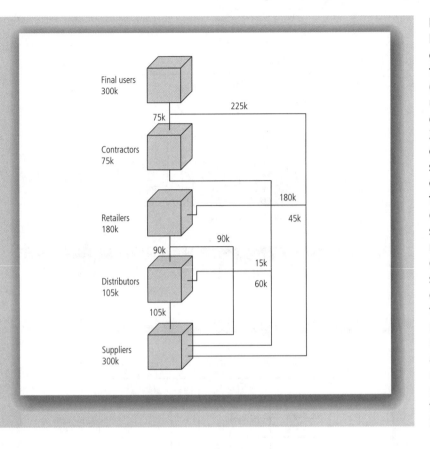

**Figure 11.1**
Initial quantification of a market map – figures
(*Note:* Using 'Final users' as an example: of the 300k units they consume, 75k are sourced through contractors, and of the 225k sourced elsewhere, 180k are sourced through retailers and 45k direct from the suppliers. In most cases the annual figures for the market would be used. The quantities are thousands (k) of units. The total number of units in this market is 300 000 (300k).)

**Table 11.1** Initial quantification of a market map in tabular form

| Market size: 300k | A Final users | Sourced through | | | |
| | | B Contractors | C Retailers | D Distributors | E Suppliers |
|---|---|---|---|---|---|
| A Final users | **300k** | 75k | 180k | X | 45k |
| B Contractors | | **75k** | X | 15k | 60k |
| C Retailers | | | **180k** | 90k | 90k |
| D Distributors | | | | **105k** | 105k |
| E Suppliers | | | | | **300k** |

*Note:* Using 'Retailers' (junction 'C') as an example and reading across the table (left to right); 180k units are sourced through retailers by final users and the retailers in turn source 90k of this 180k through distributors (junction 'D') and the remaining 90k direct from suppliers (junction 'E').

**Figure 11.2**
Market map in the horizontal format (*Note:* A reminder: The number of units 'consumed' by the final users usually equates to the number of units entering the market. If you follow the routes through the map you will observe that, like the work of an accountant, it all 'balances'.)

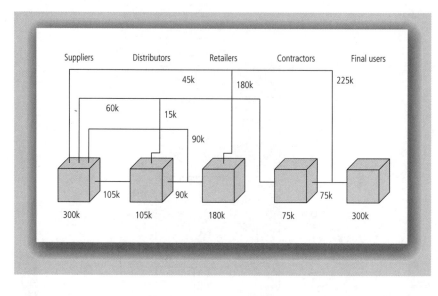

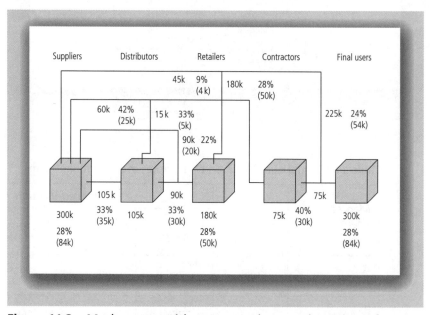

**Figure 11.3** Market map with company share and number of units (*Key:* Using the transaction between 'Retailers' and 'Distributors' as an example; the total number of units that retailers acquire from distributors is 90k, of which your company's share is 33%, which equates to (30k) units.)
(*Note:* Of the 84k units produced by the company, 4k go direct to the final users, 25k direct to contractors, 20k direct to retailers and 35k to distributors. Because the company knows that they have around 40 per cent of the units sold through contractors, a total of 30k, of which they supply 25k directly, they have deduced that the remaining 5k must come to the contractors through distributors (the only other source of product for the contractors).)

As a further addition to the market map, you could also note the number of companies/customers that exist at each junction. For the map in Figure 11.3, this is 23 500 final users, 90 contractors, 434 retailers, 66 distributors and 9 suppliers (these details appear later in Figure 11.5).

From the picture presented in Figure 11.3, we can immediately see that the company in question has a very poor share of direct sales to final users (9 per cent, compared with the company's overall market share of 28 per cent) but clearly has a very good relationship with the contractors, where the company has an overall share of 40 per cent. The company has an even better relationship with contractors when it comes to direct supplies as the company's share of this route to market is 42 per cent. The poor share of direct sales to final users may be nothing to be too concerned about as these purchases only represent 15 per cent of the total market. However, if the redrawn map for the end of the planning period shows that direct purchases by final users were forecast to grow at the expense of purchases through retailers, and this trend was expected to continue, then the company in question could have a serious strategic issue to address.

An initial look at how your company currently allocates its sales and marketing resources between the various junctions and routes to market can be useful at this point. With the picture portrayed in Figure 11.3, it would be interesting to see if this allocation could possibly be related to the company's success with direct supplies to contractors (42 per cent share) compared with its poor performance in direct supplies to retailers (22 per cent share) and its very poor performance in direct supplies to final users (9 per cent share), or if it could be related in any way to the company's better performance with distributors (33 per cent share) compared to its market average share with retailers (28 per cent share). Access to information about the sales and marketing activities of your key competitors would help in this analysis. It would enable you to determine whether, for example, the poor performance of your company was due to the intense activity of competitors or simply down to the allocation of your own resources not matching up to the importance of certain junctions or routes to market.

## Extending the detail to junction types

In Chapter 5 we listed for various junctions the different types of companies/customers found there. What has now been developed for the 'top line' picture of the market can be extended to the junction types. Once again, it is usually easier to do this for the current year in the first instance.

The first stage for adding this detail is to redraw the market map so that it now shows the various routes to market between the junction types. However, for the junction you have segmented, you can now replace the original junction types with segments and introduce into the map all the outlet and channel details you have pulled together for each of them. But rather than having each segment as a separate junction type, we suggest you list the segments on which you intend to focus your financial and managerial resources as separate junction types and group together the other segments found at this junction.

**Marketing insight**

You may find that for particularly critical and/or complex parts of your map it often helps if the detail for these areas is captured in a separate diagram or table away from the composite map in order to emphasize their importance and/or portray them more clearly.

Figure 11.4 illustrates this first stage in extending the detail to junction types and has replaced the original junction types listed for the final users in Chapter 5 (Figure 5.11) with three individual segments and one which covers all the other segments identified among the final users.

If it improves the clarity of your market map you could, of course, produce separate maps for each of your target segments.

The information already contained in the map appearing in Figure 11.4 is much more helpful than the 'top line' picture appearing in Figure 11.3. We can now see where the various segments source their product from and

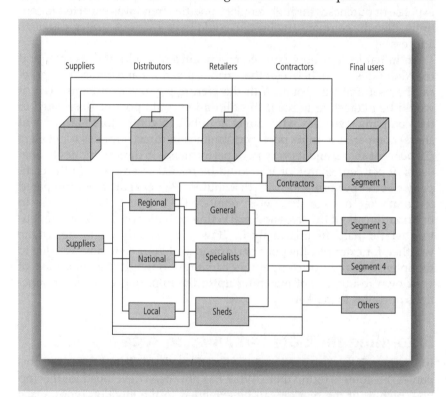

**Figure 11.4**  Market map with the routes between junction types (*Note:* Segments 1, 3 and 4 represent the segments on which the company intends to focus its resources. The remaining segments are represented by 'Others'. The junction types for retailers and distributors are those that were listed in Chapter 5 (Figure 5.11). Further details could be included in this map such as listing the suppliers individually or by their junction types, as appears in Table 11.4 later in this chapter, or just separating out your company, and adding the different methods used by the segments to contact the businesses they source their product from (though this may benefit from being presented as a separate diagram or table).)

it is a useful visual presentation of the distribution relationship between retailers, distributors and the suppliers of the product.

Your market map is now at the stage where the details added to the top line picture in Figure 11.3 can be extended to the map appearing in Figure 11.4 by including the quantities dealt with by each junction type, your company's share and what this means in terms of the number of units for your company. This detail could also be added to the various routes to market appearing on your market map. This is illustrated in Figure 11.5, again using guesstimates if necessary. The number of companies/customers at each junction type is also included in this figure.

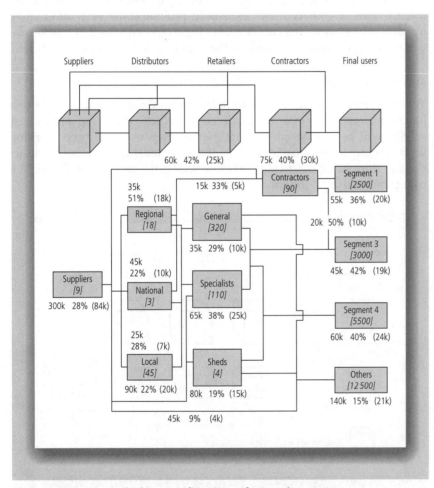

**Figure 11.5**  Detailed quantification of a market map
(*Key:* Using 'Specialists' as an example; the total number of companies/customers found here is *[110]* and the total quantity of units they handle is 65k of which your company's share is 38% which equates to (25k) units.)
(*Note:* Figures for the routes to market between each of the segments and the retailer junction taken as a whole appear in Table 11.3 later in this chapter, with figures for all the routes to market, such as between Segment 4 and all three retailers, appearing in Table 11.4.)

**Marketing insight**

At this level of detail, using separate diagrams for particularly critical parts of the map and/or for each of your target segments could prove helpful. You could also consider focusing this level of detail in the first instance on the junction you have segmented and their immediate sources of the product. The detail for the other junctions would then be developed later when considering your plans for these companies/customers.

Redrawing the map in Figure 11.5 for the end of the planning period and taking a more detailed look at how your company currently allocates its sales and marketing resources between the various junction types and routes to market, along with any equivalent information (or informed guesses) about the activities of your competitors, would provide some very informative insights at this point. Even more interesting would be to look at this in relation to where decisions are made in the market, which we look at next.

## Adding market leverage to junction types

You will recall that we use the term 'market leverage point' to refer to a junction where decisions are made about which competing product or service will be purchased. For the market map we have been working with in this chapter, the distribution of market leverage between the junctions as it appeared in Chapter 5 (Figure 5.13) is re-presented in Figure 11.6 using the horizontal format.

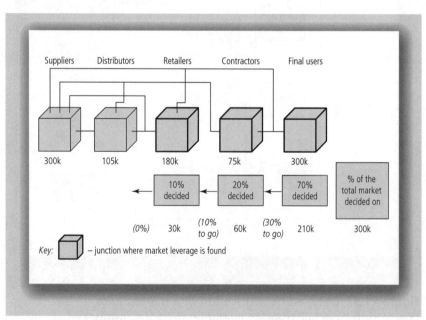

**Figure 11.6**
Market leverage points on a market map

This information could now be usefully extended to the junction types (where they have been identified) along with an indication of your company's share of the quantities decided on at each market leverage point, as illustrated in Figure 11.7. As before, guesstimate these figures if they are not known. You should be able to refine these figures from any follow-up work generated by your segmentation project.

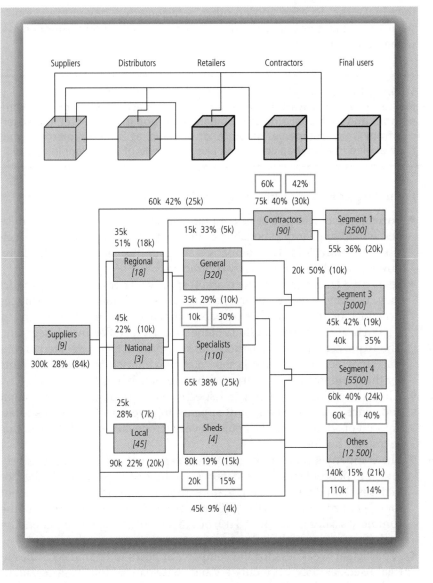

**Figure 11.7**
Detailed
quantification of a
market map with
leverage points
(*Key:* Using 'Segment
3' as an example;
the quantity
decided on by the
companies/customers
found at this
junction type is 40k
and your company's
share of this
quantity is 35% .)

In addition to showing the amounts decided on at each junction type you may also wish to note the amounts influenced by various junction types. Your market map would then illustrate the full role of each junction type in the market.

**Marketing insight**

As a further refinement to the market map presented in Figure 11.7, you could also note the number of companies/customers with leverage in each of the segments that have been listed. This could, of course, be extended to other junction types where there is leverage but, as is likely to be the case for contractors and retailers in Figure 11.7, on some occasions they make the decision and on other occasions they have to respond to what their customers specify. In such instances only a total number as a whole can be recorded.

| **Marketing insight** | Showing the current allocation of the company's resources on this detailed market map, along with the sales and marketing activities of your key competitors, and then analysing the company's position in the market, is an exercise from which companies obtain a lot of value, as is then projecting what this detailed market map could look like at the end of your planning period. |
|---|---|

From the picture appearing in Figure 11.7 we could conclude that:

- Focusing resources into Segment 1 (accounting for 18 per cent of the market) would appear questionable, as this segment delegates all their decisions to contractors. The company's share in this segment is, therefore, down to the decisions made by contractors.
- Segment 3 (15 per cent of the market) specify 90 per cent of the product they use and clearly justify having sales and marketing resources expended on them, which is probably what the company does, seeing as it has a healthy 35 per cent share of the product specified by this segment. The 10 per cent this segment does not specify is, in fact, delegated to contractors which, given what is shown about contractors, clearly accounts for the company's overall share of this segment being 42 per cent.
- All the customers in Segment 4 specify what product is to be bought and, once again, the company appears to give these customers a fair amount of attention, as they enjoy a very strong 40 per cent share of this segment's business.
- The company's share in the remaining segments is, however, relatively low at 15 per cent compared to its overall share of 28 per cent. On the face of it this should be of concern to the company as these segments account for 47 per cent of the market (140k out of 300k) and for 25 per cent of the company's sales (21k out of 84k), but this would very much depend on such items as profitability and future growth.
- A particular weakness for the company appears to be in direct sales to final users, as they have only a 9 per cent share of this business, all of which will be specified by these final users. This may be because the company has a poor infrastructure for direct sales because it is a very weak performance compared to what the company appears capable of achieving. As pointed out earlier in this chapter, how concerned the company should be with this situation would depend on whether direct purchases by final users were expected to grow in the future.
- The company's position with contractors is very healthy, as noted earlier, and it is interesting that when the contractors are specifying what product is to be bought, the company's share actually increases. Committing resources to contractors clearly makes sense as they are responsible for 20 per cent of what is bought (60k units), and it is a strategy the company appears to be pursuing.
- Turning to the retailers, it is clear that the company has a generally good relationship with the general retailers (they give the company 30 per cent

of what they specify) but something is not quite right with the Sheds (their equivalent percentage is down to 15) but, fortunately, the Sheds specify only 7 per cent of what is bought in the market. But that is the position of the Sheds today. Whether this is a concern or not would really depend on what was forecast to happen in the future.

When reviewing the allocation of resources with respect to Figure 11.7, it should clearly be borne in mind that, despite the retailers accounting for only 10 per cent of what is specified in this market, it would clearly be wrong to assess the resources expended on them purely on this basis as they provide an important role in distributing the product to the final users (handling 60 per cent of the total product in the market). The question to consider is how much inconvenience would, for example, Segment 4 tolerate before abandoning their preferred brand? Likewise, the distributors play an important role in the market as they handle 35 per cent of the total.

Considering all of the above with respect to the future structure of the market would make a critical contribution to the company's thinking while developing their sales and marketing strategies for the next few years.

## Detailed market maps in the tabular form

If you prefer to present your market maps in the tabular form, Table 11.2 presents the market map in Figure 11.3 using this format.

**Table 11.2** Market map with company share and number of units in tabular form

| Market size: 300k | A Final users | B Contractors | C Retailers | D Distributors | E Suppliers |
|---|---|---|---|---|---|
| | | Sourced through | | | |
| A Final users | **300k** **28% (84k)** | 75k 40% (30k) | 180k 28% (50k) | X | 45k 9% (4k) |
| B Contractors | | **75k** **40% (30k)** | X | 15k 33% (5k) | 60k 42% (25k) |
| C Retailers | | | 180k 28% (50k) | 90k 33% (30k) | 90k 22% (20k) |
| D Distributors | | | | 105k 33% (35k) | 105k 33% (35k) |
| E Suppliers | | | | | **300k** **28% (84k)** |

*Key:* Using 'Contractors' as an example; the number of units that are sourced through them is 75k of which your company's share is 40%, which equates to (30k) units.
*Note:* As a further addition, you could also note the number of customers that exist at each junction – 23 500 final users, 90 contractors, 434 retailers, 66 distributors and 9 suppliers.

To extend the detail to junction types along the lines appearing in Figure 11.5 requires all the junctions that need to source the product to have a row for each of their junction types. This would result in, for example, a total of three rows appearing for retailers with 'General' retailers coded 'CA', 'Specialists' coded 'CB' and 'Sheds' coded as 'CC'. This expanded table could then accommodate the details appearing in Figure 11.5 as illustrated in Table 11.3 (which, as you will notice, contains more details on the routes to market for the individual segments than appears in Figure 11.5).

**Table 11.3** Detailed quantification of a market map in tabular form

| Market size: 300k | A Segments | Sourced through | | | |
| | | B Contractors | C Retailers | D Distributors | E Suppliers |
|---|---|---|---|---|---|
| AA Segment 1 | **55k 36% (20k)** | 55k 36% (20k) | X | X | X |
| AB Segment 3 | **45k 42% (19k)** | 20k 50% (10k) | 25k 36% (9k) | X | X |
| AC Segment 4 | **60k 40% (24k)** | X | 60k 40% (24k) | X | X |
| AD Others | **140k 15% (21k)** | X | 95k 18% (17k) | X | 45k 9% (4k) |
| BA Contractors | | **75k 40% (30k)** | X | 15k 33% (5k) | 60k 42% (25k) |
| CA General | | | 35k 29% (10k) | 35k 29% (10k) | X |
| CB Specialists | | | 65k 38% (25k) | 55k 36% (20k) | 10k 50% (5k) |
| CC Sheds | | | 80k 19% (15k) | X | 80k 19% (15k) |
| DA Regional | | | | 35k 51% (18k) | 35k 51% (18k) |
| DB National | | | | 45k 22% (10k) | 45k 22% (10k) |
| DC Local | | | | 25k 28% (7k) | 25k 28% (7k) |
| EA – EC Suppliers | | | | | 300k 28% (84k) |

*Note*: Details on the product sourced by each of the segments from the retailer junction appears in this table. This was not included in Figure 11.5, though it could quite easily have been. Additional rows are not required at the supplier junction because this junction is the final source of the product.

The leverage information contained in Figure 11.7 can be added to the 'grid squares' in Table 11.3 containing the totals for each junction type. Alternatively, insert an extra column for market leverage next to the list of junction types and use this for recording the leverage information.

To extend the detail further so that it covers all the routes to market, such as between Segment 3 and the two types of retailers they source product through and between general retailers and all three distributors, requires all the junctions the product is sourced through to have a column for each of their junction types, including the suppliers if you choose to extend the detail to them. This would result in, for example, a total of three columns appearing for distributors, with each distributor type coded the same as it was in Table 11.3. This fully detailed quantification of a market map in the tabular form appears in Table 11.4.

Leverage information can be added to Table 11.4 in the 'grid squares' as for Table 11.3 or by adding an extra column along the lines already described.

# Chapter 11 review

This chapter provides guidelines on how the information on the market map developed as part of the segmentation process can be enhanced, as market maps are a very strong visual device for illustrating your own company's performance and resource allocation in the market. They can also be used to illustrate the activities of competitors in the market and be redrawn to present the predicted structure of the market at the end of your planning period.

We began with a brief review of the market maps developed in Chapter 5 and suggested that the first enhancement could be the inclusion of your company's share of business at each of the various stages ('junctions') and routes along the map, with a further addition at each junction being the number of companies/customers that are found there.

Next, we moved on to extending this detail to the different types of companies/customers found at each of these junctions, pointing out that it would now be appropriate to introduce segments into the map and include all the outlet and channel details that have been pulled together for each segment.

The final enhancement we put forward was the addition of decision-making information ('market leverage') to the different types of companies/customers on the map. We also pointed out that showing the company's allocation of resources on this detailed market map, along with those of your competitors, and projecting this picture into the future was an extremely valuable exercise.

Throughout the chapter we noted that guesstimates would probably be required for a number of these enhancements, though many could probably be refined at a later date using insights gained from any follow-up work generated by the segmentation project.

**Table 11.4** Fully detailed quantification of a market map in tabular form

Sourced through

| Market size: 300k | A Final users — AA–AD Segments | B Contractors — BA Contractors | C Retailers — CA General | C Retailers — CB Specialist | C Retailers — CC Sheds | D Distributors — DA Regional | D Distributors — DB National | D Distributors — DC Local | E Suppliers — EA 'Big 3' | E Suppliers — EB Regional | E Suppliers — EC Other |
|---|---|---|---|---|---|---|---|---|---|---|---|
| AA Segment 1 | 55k 36% (20k) | 55k 36% (20k) | X | X | X | X | X | X | X | X | X |
| AB Segment 3 | 45k 42% (19k) | 20k 50% (10k) | 3k 67% (2k) | 22k 32% (7k) | X | X | X | X | X | X | X |
| AC Segment 4 | 60k 40% (24k) | X | 7k 29% (2k) | 43k 42% (18k) | 10k 40% (4k) | X | X | X | X | X | X |
| AD Others | 140k 15% (21k) | X | 25k 24% (6k) | X | 70k 16% (11k) | X | X | X | 25k 16% (4k) | 20k – | X |
| BA Contractors | | 75k 40% (30k) | X | X | X | 5k 60% (3k) | 10k 20% (2k) | X | 45k 56% (25k) | 15k – | X |
| CA General | | | 35k 29% (10k) | | | 7k 71% (5k) | 10k 30% (3k) | 18k 11% (2k) | X | X | X |
| CB Specialist | | | | 65k 38% (25k) | | 23k 43% (10k) | 25k 20% (5k) | 7k 71% (5k) | 10k 50% (5k) | X | X |
| CC Sheds | | | | | 80k 19% (15k) | X | X | X | 65k 23% (15k) | 15k – | X |
| DA Regional | | | | | | 35k 51% (18k) | | | 25k 72% (18k) | 5k – | 5k – |
| DB National | | | | | | | 45k 22% (10k) | | 40k 25% (10k) | X | 5k – |
| DC Local | | | | | | | | 25k 28% (7k) | 15k 47% (7k) | 5k – | 5k – |
| EA – EC Suppliers | 300k 28% (84k) | | | | | | | | 225k 37% (84k) | 60k – | 15k – |

*Note:* The company whose share is being measured on this map is one of the 'Big 3' who, between them, supply 75 per cent of the market.

# Examples

The following is a selection of market maps pulled together by various companies as part of their segmentation projects. The level of information they contain is varied. All have been edited for reasons of commercial confidentiality.

The example in Figure 11.8 is for the case study, Agrofertilizer Supplies.

Figure 11.9 is for a market whose needs are currently met through the use of very expensive, specialized technical equipment. This equipment is found both in large companies and in smaller, specialist companies. It is a development of the map in Chapter 5, Figure 5.21, and now has the technicians and final users separated into two distinct junctions whereas they were originally combined into one junction.

The next example, Figure 11.10, is an extract from the market map developed by a company supplying a particular type of equipment for use in offices. The purpose of this extract was to illustrate the discrepancy between the company's established routes to market and the routes to market used by the final users.

The final example in Table 11.5 is for a company manufacturing items that are installed both in commercial and domestic premises. This company preferred to use the tabular format and their first look at the map for their market appeared in Chapter 5, Table 5.3. The two percentages shown in each grid square relate to the market shares held by the company's two brands sold in this particular market. The first of these percentages relate to their premium brand which had an overall share in the market of 41 per cent. The company's second and less expensive brand had a further 17 per cent share of the market.

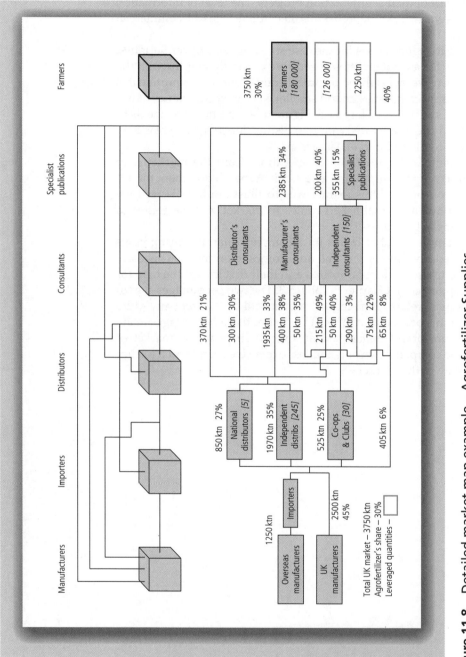

**Figure 11.8**  Detailed market map example – Agrofertilizer Supplies

(*Note*: Only the leverage figures for the final users are illustrated on this market map, which also includes an estimate of the number of farmers who decide on which fertilizer will be bought *[126 000]*. The quantities are kilotonnes (ktn) of fertilizers.)

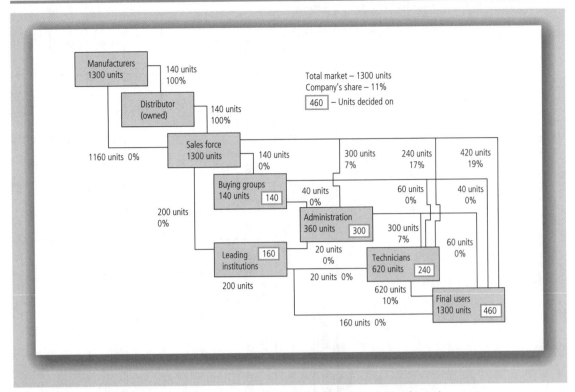

**Figure 11.9** Detailed market map example – specialized technical equipment
(*Note:* The quantities, expressed as units, are pieces of equipment bought.)

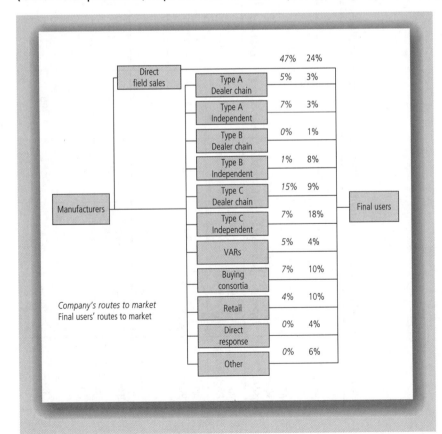

**Figure 11.10**
Detailed market map example – comparing a company's routes to market with the routes used by the final users
(*Note:* The impact of this finding on the company's distribution policy was substantial, with a major switch of resources from direct field sales to a number of other routes to market, with a particular emphasis given to direct purchases which were forecast to grow rapidly.)

**Table 11.5** Detailed market map example in tabular form – items installed in premises

| | A Final users | B Consultants | C Installers | | | | D Distributors | | | | E Suppliers | |
| Market size: 3275 | AA – AC Types | BA Consultants | CA In-house | CB National f. | CC Local ind. | CD Contract. | DA National | DB Large ind. | DC Small ind. | DD Sheds | EA Domestic | EB Importers |
|---|---|---|---|---|---|---|---|---|---|---|---|---|
| AA Residential | 2015 40% 18% | X | X | 220 | 1235 | 515 | X | X | X | 45 | X | X |
| AB Public | 720 43% 16% | 30 | 125 | 30 | 235 | 300 | X | X | X | X | X | X |
| AC Comm'l | 540 44% 16% | 300 | X | 30 | 180 | 30 | X | X | X | X | X | X |
| BA Consult. | | 330 44% 16% | X | 20 | 100 | 180 | X | X | X | X | X | X |
| CA In-house | | | 155 42% 17% | | | | 75 | 80 | X | X | X | X |
| CB National f. | | | | 300 50% 18% | | | 190 | 110 | X | X | X | X |

Sourced through

| | | | | | | | | |
|---|---|---|---|---|---|---|---|---|
| **CC** *Local ind.* | 1750 37% 15% | | 670 | 855 | 225 | X | X | X |
| **CD** *Contract.* | | 1025 48% 17% | 610 | 290 | 125 | X | X | X |
| **DA** *National* | | | 1545 70% 21% | | | | 1545 | X |
| **DB** *Large ind.* | | | | 1335 18% 13% | | | 995 | 340 |
| **DC** *Small ind.* | | | | | 350 11% 4% | | 175 | 175 |
| **DD** *Sheds* | | | | | | 45 0% 0% | X | 45 |
| **EA – EB** *Suppliers* | 3275 41% 17% | | | | | | 2715 49% 21% | 560 / – |

Key: 'Comm'l' – Commercial; 'In-house' – In-house engineering; 'National f.' – National fitters; 'Local ind.' – Local independents; 'Contract.' – Contractors; 'Large ind.' – Large independent; 'Small ind.' – Small independent; 'Domestic' – Domestic manufacturers.

Note: In addition to information about their own brands, the company also had information about the brands of their domestic competitors, though this information was limited to transactions by the distributors. This, however, enabled them to draw up a further table which illustrated sales by brand through the different types of distributors. The quantities are in thousands of units.

# Chapter 12
# Predicting market transformation

# Summary

We live in a time of rapid innovation. The FMCG companies which have long been held up as examples of marketing excellence are themselves privately admitting that they have yet to learn how to move beyond the continuous, minor innovations at which they are expert towards the step-change innovations now demanded by the business environment.

While product innovation continues apace, with the internet giving many opportunities for providing digitizable products and surrounding services remotely, we believe that a dominant business theme of the next ten years will be innovation in the route to market – the channels by which the customer is communicated with the product delivered. Companies such as Direct Line, First Direct, easyJet, eBay and Amazon all compete by exploiting IT-enabled remote channels to add value, reduce costs, or both.

A reminder: Because there is not a general consensus on the distinction between customers and consumers, this book subsumes both under the title of 'customer'.

How organizations should respond to the opportunities and threats of these IT-enabled channels and use them to build profitable customer relationships, is the subject of this chapter.[1] Having segmented the market and understood customer needs, we now need to consider such questions as which channels to use for what segments, and how different channels should work together to meet customer needs.

This chapter is organized as follows:

- An overview of the process for multi-channel strategy formulation
- A discussion about the possible configurations of future market maps
- Matching channels to the different stages of the customer's purchasing process
- How to assess the value of alternative channels against the needs of different segments
- Channel options and selecting between channel possibilities
- A review of some of the issues that may need to be addressed for the successful implementation of new channel tactics
- A review of the chapter
- Exercises to help you with future market mapping

# Multi-channel strategy formulation

The dotcom stock market bubble of the twentieth century could not carry on indefinitely, and it duly burst early in 2000. With it, the prevailing attitude towards channel innovations using this high-profile channel also seemed to change.

---

[1] The authors are grateful for the substantial contributions of Liz Daniel, Dr Hugh Wilson, Professor John Ward and Professor Adrian Payne to this thinking on planning for IT-enabled channels.

Marketing
insight

The 'just do it' rhetoric of first-mover advantage, internet years and the new economy in 1999 was supplemented by a rediscovery of the language of profit, customer satisfaction and return on investment, and a recognition of the need to safeguard hard-won brand values from being diluted by rushed channel initiatives.

If the stagnating dangers of planning based on extrapolation of the past are not to be replaced by fashion-led, highly expensive channel experiments, some kind of synthesis is needed, in a process which endeavours to allow for channel creativity and which is applied flexibly and without dogmatism.

In this chapter, we will address this need by working through a process for multi-channel strategy formulation, shown in Figure 12.1. The following sections describe each stage in the process, and present diagnostic tools for performing the stage.

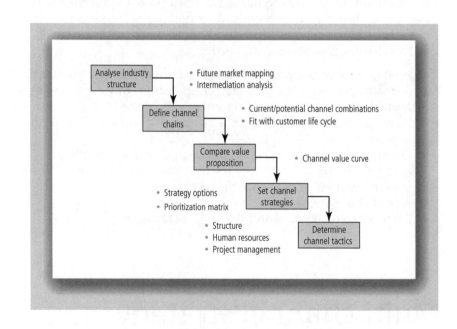

**Figure 12.1**
A process for multi-channel strategy formulation

The process outlined in Figure 12.1 draws extensively on existing planning processes and tools, but differs from them particularly in the following respects:

1 *The emphasis on evolving industry structures:* Many planning methods skip from an understanding of the industry's current structure, perhaps supplemented with PEST analysis (political, economic, sociological and technological) and lists of opportunities and threats, to the issue of how the organization should position itself within that structure. Our industry structure analysis stage adds the important step of predicting how the industry structure itself is likely to be changed as a result of channel

initiatives, quite independently of what position the planning organization takes towards potential new channels.

2 *The analysis of how channels combine to serve customers through their life cycle:* Rather than simply looking up the relevant chapter of a marketing textbook corresponding to 'the channels we use in our industry', we advocate a creative analysis of how channels might be combined to add customer value, via the channel chain technique.

3 *The adaptation of competitive strength analysis to the problem of channel choice:* Our 'channel value curve' provides an intuitively sensible 'acid test' as to whether a channel innovation will, in fact, succeed.

4 *The adaptation of the directional policy matrix to the evaluation of business models:* Often it is not competitors who compete, but business models. Yet talk about business models can become an excuse for woolly thinking and endless losses. The variant on traditional prioritization matrices we outline allows the right business model to be chosen to best meet the channel needs of customers as well as the organization's objectives.

# Future market mapping: analysing industry structure

There is clearly little point in making decisions on what channels to use until the future shape of the whole industry has been considered. Therefore, once a market map of the current market structure has been developed, it is necessary to consider what factors are likely to change the flow of goods and services through this map. E-commerce is clearly one such major factor.

> There is little point in making decisions on what channels to use until the future shape of the whole industry has been considered.

Any analysis of forces affecting industry competition often proves very useful for generating ideas on what changes might occur. These ideas can be fed into a redrawn future market map.

We saw in Chapter 5 how to annotate a current market map with flows of goods and services and made the point that one of the four principal components of a market map is the inclusion of information sources. As Evans and Wurster (1997) pointed out, physical and information flows together represent the value added by each step in the chain. We can then consider whether these components of value can be better provided by a different configuration of the map.

> A reminder: The four principal components of a market map are final users, the channel, suppliers and sources of information.

One possible way in which the car dealer's role might become unbundled in future, for example, is shown in Figure 12.2.

Recent innovations such as direct car sales by manufacturers, or sales by web-based intermediaries such as Autobytel, have begun to experiment with these kinds of changes. Which of these experiments proves permanent is, of course, another issue; but drawing market maps of this sort can help a management team flesh out the possible options and identify the relevant opportunities and threats.

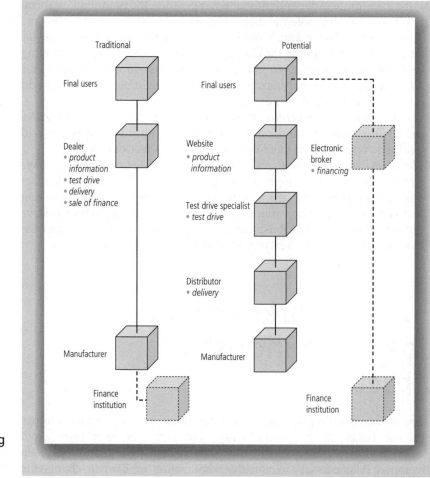

**Figure 12.2**
Traditional and
potential market
maps in car retailing
and related
financing

## New channels

There are five main ways in which the market map can be reconfigured:

1 *Substitute/reconfigured products.* A new channel may enable the underlying customer need to be satisfied in a different way ('substitute products'). E-mail, for example, can substitute for physical post, providing a
threat to paper manufacturers, stationers and post offices, while online
distance learning provides a challenge to book publishers. Or customer
needs may be bundled into different product configurations ('reconfigured products'). To illustrate, the newspaper is a bundled product providing job advertisements, weather information, news, person-to-person
advertisements and so on for a bundled price. It is now competing with
internet services which either simply offer one of these components –
such as customer auction sites – or in other cases, combine some aspect
of the value provided by newspapers with other types of value – an
example being portals. A portal such as Yahoo! meets some of the needs
met by a newspaper, such as the day's news, and acts as a gateway to
others, such as weather and auction sites, while also satisfying further

needs not covered by the newspaper through the ability to search the Web. It can be seen that reconfigured products add complexity to the planning process, as two market maps from different industries may 'collide' and need to be considered together.

2 *Disintermediation.* As with other IT-enabled channels such as call centres, the internet can sometimes enable a link to be removed from the market map, by removing intermediaries whose primary function of information transfer can be more effectively performed by other means. Examples are telephone and internet banking; direct purchase from clothes manufacturers via websites; and the bypassing of sales agents and distributors by some consumer goods manufacturers who are selling direct to retailers.

● Definition: Disintermediation is the bypassing of an agent, distributor, or other intermediary with a direct sales channel.

3 *Reintermediation.* In some cases, a previous intermediary is replaced by a new online intermediary, rather than bypassed. Online sites which automatically search for the cheapest car insurance are competing with telephone-based brokers, which in turn caused the demise of the Automobile Association's high-street shops in the UK. General Electric's TPN Register provided an early successful example of an online marketplace between suppliers on the one hand, and GE and its partners on the other.

● Definition: Reintermediation is the introduction of an electronic marketplace or other intermediary between customers and suppliers who previously traded directly.

4 *Partial channel substitution.* This forms a halfway house towards disintermediation, in which an intermediary's role is reduced but not eliminated, through some of its value being provided remotely by the supplier to the intermediary's customer. Websites such as those of car manufacturers may build a brand and provide customer information while pointing customers to traditional outlets for actual purchase. This is the model adopted by a card manufacturer we studied in its relationship with retailers, where its website is supplementing its agent network rather than replacing it.

5 *Media switching/addition.* Finally, the organizations which form the various steps in the chain to the final user may remain the same, but communication between them may be partially or fully switched from one medium to another. The many examples of this, the simplest type of transformation of the market map, include Dell's addition of the internet to its other means of communicating with customers, and electronic components distributor RS Components, which has similarly added a Web channel to its dominant telephone sales model, while still selling to the same customers.

Predicting what reintermediation will occur is particularly difficult, as the possibilities are numerous. Will a given relationship – say, between CTN (confectioners, tobacconists and newsagents) stores and the manufacturers of the goods they sell – be a direct one? If so, will the shops buy from a range of suppliers' websites, or will the suppliers respond to tender requests provided electronically by shops? Or will there be a new intermediary acting as a marketplace between the two? As shown in Table 12.1, the various possibilities can be placed in an approximate order, from a supplier's website (such as Japan Airlines, which puts out open invitations to tender to suppliers), at one extreme, to a vendor's websites (such as *Harvard Business Review*, which provides an electronic version at a cost) at the other.

Neutral marketplaces are midway between the two. An example is an auction site, which is tied neither to the buyer nor the seller. Somewhat

**Table 12.1** Types of intermediaries

| Website ownership | Intermediary type | Examples |
| --- | --- | --- |
| Vendor controlled | Vendor website | Ernst & Young, HBR |
| Vendor orientated | Vendor-run community | Cambridge Information Net |
| | Consortium Distributor | thetrainline |
| | Vendor's agent | Chemdex |
| | Lead generator | Autobytel |
| | Audience broker | DoubleClick |
| Neutral | Market maker | eBay, FastParts, priceline |
| | Shop | RS Components, Blackwells |
| | Mall | msn.com |
| Buyer orientated | Purchaser's agent | Comparenet |
| | Purchasing aggregator | TPN Register, Covisint |
| Buyer controlled | Buyer website | Japan Airlines |

closer to the vendors are intermediaries such as Autobytel, which passes on leads to a local dealer (though it has also more recently added a direct sales operation). A more buyer-orientated intermediary we have already referred to is TPN Register: set up by a consortium of buyers, it acts to ensure that they gain low prices through economies of scale, as well as gaining efficiencies in processing costs.

Which of these possibilities becomes the dominant trading mechanism in a given relationship depends on the number of vendors and buyers, and their relative power.

*Which type of intermediary becomes the dominant trading mechanism depends on the number of vendors and buyers, and their relative power.*

**Marketing insight**

Where there are few buyers and many suppliers, or buyer power is great, the market will tend towards either individual buyer websites or buyer-orientated intermediaries such as the Covisint exchange set up by several car manufacturers. Conversely, a small number of suppliers selling to large numbers of customers will have the power to control the market through their own websites, or through supplier-orientated consortia.

Large numbers of both suppliers and buyers will tend to use a neutral marketplace to reduce the search and transaction costs of both parties, though a supplier with a particularly strong brand and/or product differentiation, such as *Harvard Business Review* or the medical journal *The Lancet*, may choose not to participate in such marketplaces.

## Reconfiguring the market map

To reconfigure the market map, therefore, we need to consider the potential effect of each of our five broad changes in turn. In each case, we need to:

1 sketch the effect of the change on the market map, indicating who will now provide the various aspects of value previously received by the end customer;

2 consider whether the value received by the end customer, in benefits minus costs, is greater with the new structure (for each segment);
3 if the effect is positive for some segments, incorporate the transformation in a revised market map.

Whether we regard the effect on customer value as positive depends on the organization's positioning within the relevant market. In terms of Michael Porter's (1985) three generic strategies (low cost, differentiation or niche), this will imply:

- for low-cost strategies, an approximate parity needs to be ensured on non-price buying criteria, while beating the competition on price;
- for differentiation strategies, excellence needs to be ensured on one or more value-related criteria, while ensuring approximate parity on others;
- for niche strategies, strength needs to be high on criteria important to the target niches.

Table 12.2 contains some additional questions for disintermediation, partial channel substitution and media switching/addition.

**Table 12.2** Evaluating potential changes to the market map/value chain

| Type of reconfiguration | Additional questions |
| --- | --- |
| Disintermediation | Does the removal of an intermediary improve physical flows? If so, can information flows or other value-adding services provided by the intermediary be as effectively handled by others in the chain? Can the flow improvements be translated into enhanced value for the final users? |
| Partial channel substitution | Does the addition of an internet communication channel improve information flows (for example, cheaper communication with the customer)? Can the relationship with the intermediary be redefined to deliver mutual benefit? |
| Media switching/ addition | Within the current structure, can the internet reduce costs or add value for some communications? |

This process may seem complicated, but in practice it is possible to develop a good enough future market map in a couple of workshops. A summarized example from a UK groceries company is shown in Figure 12.3.

The current market structure, represented by the unshaded boxes, involves manufacturers reaching customers via a combination of the major multiple supermarkets, independent stores and CTN stores. Our analysis suggests that because the major multiples are few in number and hold considerable buying power, their relationship with manufacturers will either continue to be a direct one, using purchasing systems dictated by

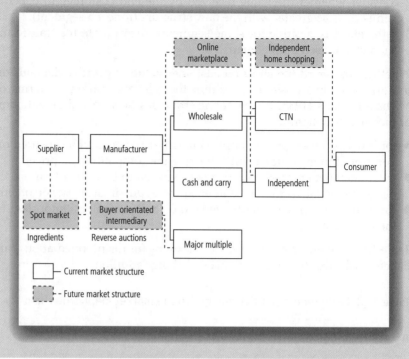

**Figure 12.3**
Reconfiguring the
value map –
groceries

the multiples, or will be mediated by a buyer-orientated intermediary, as shown in the potential future structure represented by the shaded boxes.

The many-to-many relationship between manufacturers and independents or CTNs, though, needs a more neutral intermediary, such as is provided currently by wholesalers. We predict a similarly neutral online intermediary succeeding here, either through a new entrant start-up or through media addition by a wholesaler. Likewise, the relationship between manufacturers and suppliers is likely to include a neutral spot market for commodity ingredients. These predictions appear consistent with industry developments to date.

## Towards a future market map in financial services

An example of a possible reconfigured market map is given for retail financial services in Figure 12.4. Although this does not go as far as a fully completed future market map, the shaded annotations suggest ways in which the map might change in the future as a result of e-commerce.

Predicted changes include:

1 *Fund managers go direct.* Fund managers may find that e-commerce makes it easier to sell their products directly to customers. The simplification and transparency of pricing being encouraged throughout the industry should help customers feel more comfortable buying products direct: in fact they may prefer this route since they will not be swayed by an agent who is receiving a large commission for their advice. The

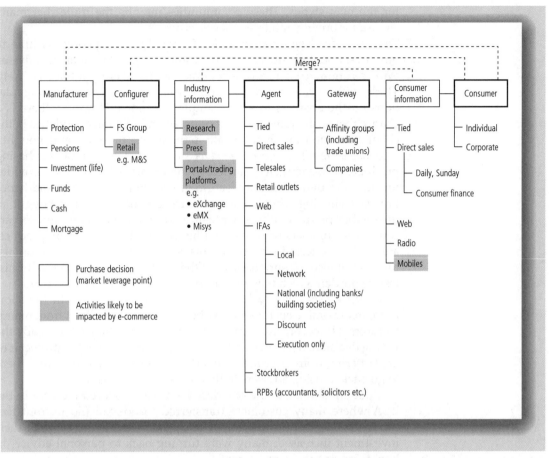

**Figure 12.4**
Long-term investment: future market

ability of fund managers to present clear and easy-to-understand information online about their products and their performance should encourage such direct sales.

2 *The customer becomes the configurer.* Using e-commerce, customers may be able to configure their own investment products from suppliers. Currently this would be time-consuming and configurers have the significant amount of regulatory knowledge which is necessary to undertake this function. However, e-commerce applications that contain this regulatory knowledge as 'rules' could allow customers to undertake this function themselves.

3 *There is a blurring of industry and customer information.* Currently information provided to agents and other professional advisers in the market is quite distinct from that provided to customers. The former is more detailed and may require specialist knowledge to understand. However, there are already signs of the distinction blurring, with insurance exchanges, such as eXchange, eMX and Misys, that have traditionally been wholesale or trade exchanges now providing e-commerce routes to the final users.

4 *Affinity groups may become trusted portals.* Customers in the online world may 'join' communities of interest, such as ThirdAge.com, a community

for the over-sixties. These communities may be the route that many choose for buying goods and services online.

5 *There is a 'dumbing down' of advice.* Currently many people wishing to buy investment products turn to a trained, regulated financial adviser. With e-commerce a rise of electronic agents offering advice is likely. These will be rule-based algorithms that base product recommendations on the answers to a few simple questions. However, there is a chance that such systems are over-simple and will miss subtleties in the client's situation, and hence result in the wrong product being bought.

6 *E-commerce results in greater product switching.* The ease of purchasing products via e-commerce, particularly with interactive TV that provides for flow-through sales, may lead to greater impulse buying and hence greater switching when a customer realizes that they have bought an unsuitable product. While sophisticated customers may gain, others could lose financially if they withdraw prematurely from products aimed at long-term investment. This is not only unsatisfactory for customers but also for suppliers since they will face a significant administrative burden which they will need to streamline in order to cope.

7 *E-commerce may cause cycles in customers' buying patterns.* In the short term, many online customers may be tempted to buy direct from manufacturers. However, after time they may find that they either made the wrong decision, have made a lot of money and now want to protect it or are suffering from information overload. These factors will cause them to go back to using advisers in their investment decisions.

A pattern similar to the one described was observed recently in the USA where many customers transferred to no-load (no upfront fee) funds via telephone and internet sales channels. As the value of their investment increased, many were turning back to personal advice on how to protect their investment.

Another factor resulting in a cyclic approach to financial advice is that of market conditions. Advice is often seen as less important in a rapidly growing bull market, since anyone can invest and make money. However, as markets begin to slow down, customers' confidence is reduced and they return to sound sources of advice.

8 *Smaller players are more nimble.* Evidence of this in the investments market is already being seen with small IFAs (Independent Financial Advisers) adopting e-commerce services ahead of larger chains.

9 *E-commerce encourages customers to serve themselves, but does not remove face-to-face contact.* By encouraging customers to use online services that require them to register changes of address or premium amounts, the agent or manufacturer is outsourcing some of the administrative burden to the customer. However, many customers will continue to wish to combine electronic communication with face-to-face contact with advisers, particularly for more complex products.

Similar effects of e-commerce can be expected to occur in other markets.

Whatever the specifics for your own industry, it is clearly sensible to come to a view on the future shape of the market before taking decisions on which channels to use for what purposes. Exercise 12.1 at the end of this chapter suggests some steps for doing this in your own organization.

# Multi-channel integration: channel chains

Once the future shape of the industry structure has been predicted, we can combine this with what we already know about each segment and the channels they currently use. Here, though, there is a complicating factor. In many markets, customers do not use a single channel. Rather, they use a number of channels in combination to meet their needs at different stages of their relationship with the supplier. To represent the current channel use, we therefore suggest the use of a new tool, channel chain analysis, which we illustrate in Figure 12.5.

Channel chain analysis involves describing which channels are used at which stages of the purchasing process. We have suggested what these stages might be on the left of the diagram, but you can use whatever stages

*In many markets, customers do not use a single channel. Rather, they use a number of channels in combination to meet their needs at different stages of their relationship with the supplier.*

*Channel chain analysis involves describing which channels are used at which stages of the purchasing process.*

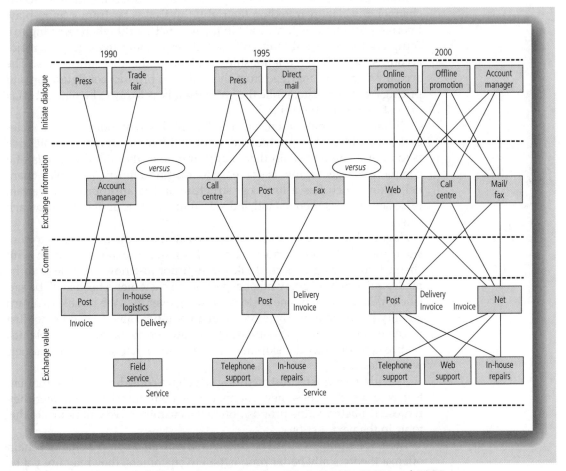

**Figure 12.5**    Channel chains – the market for PCs in 1990, 1995 and 2000

make most sense in your industry. The channels used to accomplish the stage are listed against each stage. The channel used for one stage will often affect which channel is likely to be used at the next stage, so the relevant boxes are joined with a line.

In this example from the business-to-business PC market, three of the common channel combinations being offered by the various competitors are illustrated. The channel chain on the left shows the traditional account management approach, as used by most of the large computer companies until the start of the 1990s, when most of the sales process was handled face-to-face by account managers. Still a model used for larger computers or major contracts, it has tended, though, to be supplanted by other channel chains which offer better channel economics for smaller deals.

The first of these new channel chains was the direct model pioneered by Dell, illustrated in the middle of the figure. Here, press advertising formed the dominant marketing tool, with further information provided by product brochures and call centre staff. The actual order could be placed by a number of means – often a traditional fax or order sent by post by the accounts department.

More recently, Dell and its competitors have added the internet to the channel mix, as illustrated on the right. But Dell is far from a 'pure-play' internet provider (the term used in the internet world when referring to a company that uses only this channel). It has account managers for major accounts, who build relationships and negotiate discount levels. The account managers are freed from the details of product configuration and pricing by the website, while the order itself is as likely to be placed by fax or post as it is on the Web.

Different channels, then, are needed at different points in the sales cycle, and different competitors may adopt different approaches. The trick is to offer a channel chain that is appropriate to the differing needs of a company's target segments. It is easy to imagine a fourth, pure-play channel chain which has a low cost structure and is appropriate to certain price-sensitive segments – and, indeed, competitors adopting this approach exist.

> The trick is to offer a channel chain that is appropriate to the differing needs of a company's target segments.

Having drawn the channel chains in current use, the next step is to consider possible future channel chains. This requires experimentation with channel chain diagrams to think through not just how the sale is to be made, but also how every other aspect of the customer's needs will be satisfied. Will a mobile phone customer buying over the Web be able to return a faulty phone to a nearby store? Will an e-hub be able to handle not just price negotiations, but also information flows on stock levels, complaints, returns and product development – and if not, what additional channels will be needed?

As with the industry restructuring which we considered earlier, the acid test as to whether these new channel chains will flourish is whether they represent a better value proposition to the customer. We will return to this topic in the next section.

There is a timing issue to be considered as well. Even if a channel chain offers a theoretically better proposition to customers, they may not yet be ready for it.

A channel chain innovation, like a product innovation, is likely to proceed along the lines of Rogers' (1962) bell-shaped diffusion of innovation curve.

Marketing
insight

If one hopes to convert customers to the internet, for example, it is clearly necessary to consider what proportion of the customer base has internet access and how mature their use of it is. We recall one department store which wasted millions on an aborted Web service in the mid-1990s because it was simply too far ahead of its market.

As a slightly different approach, Exercise 12.2 at the end of this chapter suggests some steps for considering how channels combine to meet customer needs in your own organization.

# Channel choice: the channel value curve

Channel chain analysis may generate numerous possible bases of channel competition.

In a reasonably pure market, in other words, one which is not too skewed by regulation or monopolistic dominance, successful channel chains will be those which offer the best value proposition to the customer.

Marketing
insight

At this stage, we need to compare the value proposition across the various potential channel combinations we have identified.

For this purpose, we recommend drawing up a chart as shown in Figure 12.6, which we call a 'channel value curve'. For each segment, the Decisive Buying Criteria (DBCs) and weights indicating their relative importance to the customer are listed. The ability of each channel, or channel chain, to deliver against each DBC is then assessed judgementally on a scale of 1 to 10: the higher the score, the better this channel meets this DBC.

In this hypothetical example, the various means by which a book can be purchased are compared. It can be seen that taking all the criteria together, the internet best matches the needs of this particular segment. In reality, different segments of the book market are clearly best matched to different channels, which would show up clearly if the channel value curve was drawn for each segment's differing buying criteria.

Another simplification of this example is that, as we have seen, it is often channel chains which compete rather than individual channels. In these cases, the various possible channel chains would each be compared against the buying criteria – so the channel chains would be listed in the key at the top, rather than individual channels.

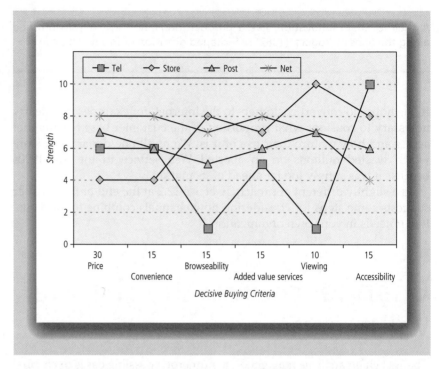

**Figure 12.6**
The channel value
curve – books
example
(*Note:* The
weightings for the
DBCs are out of 100.)

Other than looking at the lines by eye to decide which offers the best
match to customer needs, how can one determine which channel 'wins'? An
alternative way of presenting the same information makes this clearer. In
Figure 12.7, the same underlying data – shown in Table 12.3 – is presented
as a stacked bar chart. The height of each section of the bar is proportional
to the score of a DBC multiplied by its weight, divided by 100. So the overall height of the bar gives an approximate measure of how well, taking one
thing with another, the channel meets customer needs. As with all analyses,
though, management judgement should be exercised in its interpretation.

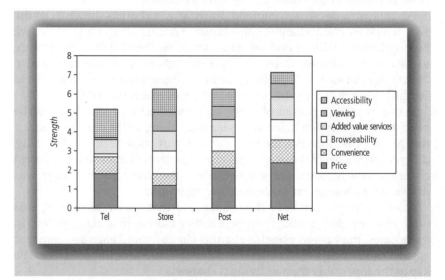

**Figure 12.7**
The channel value
curve – an
alternative
presentation

**Table 12.3** The channel value curve – calculations for the alternative presentation

| | | *Segment 5* | | | | | | | |
|---|---|---|---|---|---|---|---|---|---|
| *DBC* | *Weight* | *Tel* | | *Store* | | *Post* | | *Net* | |
| | | *Score* | *Total* | *Score* | *Total* | *Score* | *Total* | *Score* | *Total* |
| Price | 30 | 6 | 1.8 | 4 | 1.2 | 7 | 2.1 | 8 | 2.4 |
| Convenience | 15 | 6 | 0.9 | 4 | 0.6 | 6 | 0.9 | 8 | 1.2 |
| Browseability | 15 | 1 | 0.15 | 8 | 1.2 | 5 | 0.75 | 7 | 1.05 |
| Added value services | 15 | 5 | 0.75 | 7 | 1.05 | 6 | 0.9 | 8 | 1.2 |
| Viewing | 10 | 1 | 0.1 | 10 | 1.0 | 7 | 0.7 | 7 | 0.7 |
| Accessibility | 15 | 10 | 1.5 | 8 | 1.2 | 6 | 0.9 | 4 | 0.6 |
| *Total* | 100 | | 5.2 | | 6.25 | | 6.25 | | 7.15 |

Both forms of presentation in Figures 12.6 and 12.7 have their advantages, and you can use either or both. The main point is, one way or another, to assess channels not against whether we, as a company, happen to like them, but against which will ultimately win out in the eyes of customers.

The main point is, one way or another, to assess channels not against whether we, as a company, happen to like them, but against which will ultimately win out in the eyes of customers.

Our interests do, though, come into the analysis when it comes to price. The score of a channel chain against price-related factors, such as the total cost including delivery, will be affected by the channel economics, which will determine the price which any competitor using the channel chain will be able to offer. One factor in assessing the channel economics is the transaction cost involved. The TPN Register business-to-business exchange set up by General Electric, the first significant e-hub, saves GE 50–90 per cent on processing costs for each order. But acquisition and retention costs should not be forgotten. The dotcom arm of one retail chain recently discovered that customer acquisition through banner advertising was costing £700 per customer, when the average sale was only £50 – good news for the bricks-and-clicks retailer in its competition with pure-play dotcoms, as it could leverage its physical stores for customer acquisition at a cost of just £13 per customer. Conversely, the overall advantage of the channel value curve compared with other channel chains will affect the rate of diffusion of a new channel chain, and therefore the revenues included in the channel economics analysis. So you will need to estimate how much higher, or lower, your costs will be if you use a new channel combination, before you can complete this chart.

**Marketing insight**

The ideal way to do this is to work out the 'Current Lifetime Value' (CLV) for customers in each segment – that is, the value of future revenues minus costs, discounted to the present using an appropriate cost of capital. You can then use the CLV model to work out how the customer lifetime value would be affected by use of a new channel, by changing inputs such as transaction costs appropriately.

Whether or not you yet have customer lifetime value figures in your organization, some rough calculations leading to a channel value curve chart will help you to check whether you are proposing the right channel for the right purpose.

# The prioritization matrix: defining channel strategy

As a result of the previous stages, the organization will have a list of possible channel innovations, and an assessment of the strength of each potential channel combination's value proposition to customers. All sorts of exciting possible strategies typically emerge by this point. But as one always has a limited budget and limited management time, it is now necessary to prioritize between the options available.

Our research suggests that companies can select from the following broad channel strategy options:

- A *single channel provider* provides at least the bulk of its customer interaction through one channel. Direct Line and First Direct both started as primarily telephone operations, while in the internet world the single channel approach (pure-play) is represented by Amazon, eBay and so on.
- A *channel migrator* starts with one single channel, but attempts to migrate its customer base onto another channel on the grounds of increased value or reduced cost. EasyJet initially sold tickets by telephone, but now provides financial incentives to its price-sensitive customers to buy online, where the great majority of its tickets are now purchased.
- An *activity-based strategy* uses different channels in combination to perform different tasks in the customer experience – that is, a channel chain involving different channels at different points in the buying cycle. For example, Thomas Cook's corporate foreign exchange business uses the internet to generate leads, a direct sales force to sign up new clients, and a call centre or the internet to take orders.
- An *integrated multi-channel approach* involves offering different channels to the customer without attempting to influence which the customer uses. First Direct provides both telephone and internet banking as an integrated service. While the internet service has much lower unit costs and also has proved better for cross-selling, First Direct chooses to position itself on customer service and accept the higher costs from those customers who primarily use the telephone without penalizing them or rewarding internet users.
- A *needs-based segmentation strategy* involves offering different channels to different customer groups to meet their varying needs. Each of these routes to market may use the same brand name, or different names. The insurer Zurich's multiple brands, including Allied Dunbar, Zurich and Eagle Star, tend to concentrate on different routes to market where they

have different strengths – direct sales force, IFAs, company pension schemes – in order to serve customer groups with differing needs and attitudes. Zurich has begun to rationalize this set of brands, though, to achieve economies of scale across Europe and concentrate on the brands with the best brand values.

- A *graduated customer value strategy* uses channels selectively according to the financial value of the customers, with high-cost channels, such as account managers, for high-value customers, and lower-value customers steered toward the lower-cost channels such as the internet, call centres or value-added resellers. The IT industry has long made use of this approach. The UK's clearing banks, though, are in danger of doing the precise opposite, offering the high-cost branch network to the lower-value customers who prefer not to bank by telephone or internet.

How are we to choose between these approaches? Although the channel value curve will determine which approaches are likely to succeed in the market as a whole, an organization will typically not have the resources to pursue all viable options – some of which may, in any case, deliver little value to shareholders, despite being accepted by the market. It is this dimension of attractiveness to the organization which we have not yet considered fully. The answer is to use a variant of the directional policy matrix, the tool we used when looking at prioritizing and selecting segments.

The variant we have developed, termed the 'prioritization matrix', is explained in full in Exercise 12.3 at the end of this chapter. It is summarized in Figure 12.8.

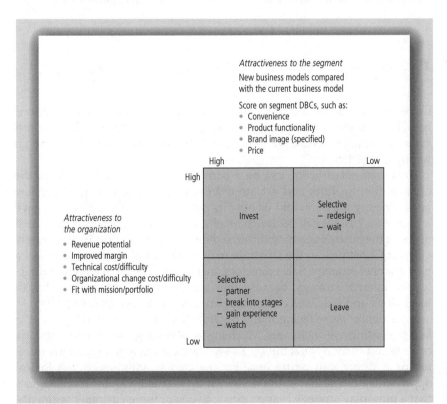

**Figure 12.8**
The prioritization matrix
(*Note:* Although 'high' is positioned on the left of the horizontal axis it can, if you prefer, be placed on the right.)

In brief, this approach compares opportunities such as e-commerce projects against two dimensions: attractiveness to us and attractiveness to the segment. In many ways it is just like the directional policy matrix. But in assessing the horizontal axis, attractiveness to the segment, we compare not rival competitors but rival business models. In other words, if we are considering selling via a Web/call centre combination rather than a direct sales force, how would this business model compare in the customer's eyes with their current way of doing business?

You may have spotted that we have already done much of the work to fill in this matrix in previous tools. The rival business models are often different channels, or channel combinations, which we have identified in the 'channel chains' tool. We have compared these against customer needs using the 'channel value curve'. So the horizontal axis simply corresponds to the position of each proposed way of doing business on the channel value curve compared with the current model. A better value curve than the current business model will correspond to a position well to the left of the matrix. In fact, using the alternative presentation shown in Figure 12.7, the position on the horizontal axis can be determined mathematically by comparing the height of the bar chart for each proposed channel, or channel combination, with the height of the bar chart for the current model.

We have found that using this tool provides a welcome structure to the board's decision-making debate and rapidly sorts out which projects are the top priorities. It also forces the proponents of a project to ask the right questions early on, increasing the quality of proposals put to the board. Exercise 12.3 explains exactly how to use the tool for your own organization.

> The prioritization matrix rapidly sorts out which projects are the top priorities.

# Determining channel tactics

Once strategic decisions about channel choice and channel combinations have been made, the work is of course only just beginning. Here are just some of the areas where we have found that channel innovations can go wrong in practice.

*Organizational structure* can be a barrier to change if it encourages the organization to think and act around existing channels rather than new ones. One organization told us how its powerful sales force directors gave a highly successful call centre channel a decidedly mixed reception, as it reduced the business coming through their direct sales force. Turkeys rarely vote for Christmas, so the structure may need radical overhaul to reflect a new channel strategy. Sales directors, incidentally, often make good directors of internet strategy, because they are thoroughly unimpressed with technology and fads, and concentrate on serving customers profitably.

> Organizational structure can be a barrier to change if it encourages the organization to think and act around existing channels rather than new ones.

A particular issue facing many organizations is whether to 'spin out' a business using a new channel. Much in vogue during the internet euphoria of 1999 and early 2000, setting up a separate company to exploit the internet or a 'direct' call centre business has had varying success. A logical approach is to consider spin-outs when the channel value curve suggests that a pure-play strategy is appropriate to one or more customer segments.

Where the customer need is for a hybrid model, though, innovation needs to be wedded with integration.

> Just as IBM initially set up its PC division with considerable autonomy, later 'roping it in' to exploit synergies with the rest of the business, so Gap initially set up its Web operations with highly independent departments which, however, were kept within the company in order to integrate them as time went on. Another successful example of melding independence with synergy is Thomas Cook, which has reintegrated ThomasCook.com Ltd back into the business.

This hybrid, semi-detached approach seems appropriate for the many companies requiring a multi-channel model, particularly in the cases of an integrated multi-channel strategy or activity-based strategy which we discussed earlier.

As with organizational structure, *reward systems* can become tied to a particular channel, hence distorting behaviour in favour of maximizing returns from that channel. As profits ultimately come from satisfied customers, a more beneficial approach is to provide rewards based on customer profits or, ideally, customer lifetime value.

> Reward systems can become tied to a particular channel, hence distorting behaviour in favour of maximizing returns from that channel.

> The chief executive of a major retailer's Web service found that store managers were not encouraging customers to visit a low-cost Web channel because they feared it would reduce their annual bonuses. The chief executive therefore worked with the store managers to define metrics which would estimate how much trade was generated by each store for the website, as well as measuring business passed in the other direction from the website to local stores. These metrics could then be used to reward managers to act in the best interests of the business.

Finally, *project management* for large IT-enabled projects is never easy. Evidence from an in-depth study of numerous projects suggests that the use of software packages, where these are available, not only reduces risk, but also acts to embed and encourage best practice. Channel innovators may well find, as with innovators in other IT-enabled areas, that packages are not yet sufficiently mature to meet the whole of their needs; but it is certainly worth making a thorough exploration of what is available. A staged approach to project management is also likely to reduce business and technical risk, as well as being more likely to keep the board on side through delivery of quick wins.

Implementation is never easy, but those organizations which develop their channel strategy by focusing on their customers, not their products or their cost base, will reap the rewards of high loyalty and high customer lifetime value.

# Chapter 12 review

This chapter provides a structured process for multi-channel strategy formulation. This is to ensure that the most appropriate channels structure is put together for each of your selected segments, with a particular reference to IT-enabled channels.

We began with a brief summary of the complete process and then took a detailed look at the first of the five stages it involves. For this first stage we considered the future shape of the whole industry and put forward five main ways in which the current market map may be reconfigured. These covered substitute/reconfigured products, disintermediation, reintermediation, partial channel substitution and media switching/addition. We made the point, however, that predicting what reintermediation will occur is particularly difficult given the numerous possibilities, but provided some guidelines on which of the possibilities may become the dominant trading mechanism. Possibilities for the future were then discussed using two reconfigured market maps.

The second stage then looked at the use of channel chain analysis to describe which channels were used by each segment at the different stages of the purchasing process. This was to recognize the fact that in many markets customers use more than one channel to meet their needs at different stages of their relationship with suppliers.

Next, we looked at the basis for selecting which of the new channel chains will flourish. We pointed out that the only arbiters here were the customers themselves and that they will assess the alternatives based on which offers each segment the best value proposition. We recommended using a channel value curve to help with this stage of the process and suggested how you could determine which channel chain would be the 'winner'.

We introduced the fourth stage of the process by highlighting a number of broad channel options that companies were able to select from and suggested using a variant of the directional policy matrix to assess which option would be the most attractive to the company. This prioritization matrix rapidly sorts out which projects are the top priorities.

Finally, we discussed some of the issues that may need to be addressed by companies for their new channel tactics to be implemented successfully.

# References

Evans, P. B. and Wurster, T. S. (1997). 'Strategy and the new economics of information'. *Harvard Business Review*, September–October, 71–82.

Porter, M. E. (1985). *Competitive Advantage – Creating and Sustaining Superior Performance*. New York: Free Press.

Rogers, E. M. (1962). *Diffusion of Innovation*. New York: Free Press.

# Exercises[2]

**Exercise 12.1**  Take one of the segments in your market that you propose to serve and, using your earlier analysis, note the ways in which their needs can/will be better met by e-commerce. Repeat this for each of your selected segments.

[2] Adapted from McDonald, M. and Wilson, H. (2002). *The New Marketing: Transforming the Corporate Future*. Oxford: Butterworth-Heinemann. Used with kind permission.

Redraw the market map as it will be at the end of your planning period, say, in three years' time, given your knowledge about likely developments in the market such as new entrants, new channels, industry consolidation, and so on. The worksheet for market mapping in the Exercises section of Chapter 5 can be used for this part of the exercise. Make as many copies as you need.

Now draw up a list of e-opportunities for your organization under the headings of 'cost reduction' and 'value creation'.

---

For each segment you propose to serve, consider what different means of communication customers use, leading to the purchase they make. The worksheet in Table 12.4, which you can copy for this exercise, indicates (as column headings) the major steps in any purchase process as they were presented in Chapter 2 when we re-described the process of communicating value. Against each step, indicate what means is used by the decision-maker to perform the step. Thus, in each vertical column, what percentage of this task is currently completed using this medium?

How, from the customer's point of view, could this sales process be improved? Re-assess the percentages in these columns as they will be at the end of your planning period taking account of e-commerce or other new media.

**Exercise 12.2**

**Table 12.4** Worksheet – the communications mix

| Channel/Medium | Purchase phase | | | | |
| | Initiate dialogue | Exchange information | Negotiate/ tailor | Commit | Exchange value |
| --- | --- | --- | --- | --- | --- |
| Offline advertising (TV, press, etc.) | | | | | |
| Direct mail | | | | | |
| Sales force/ face-to-face contact | | | | | |
| Telephone | | | | | |
| Electronic | | | | | |
| Other (state:) | | | | | |

A completed example of the worksheet for this exercise is illustrated in Table 12.5 and shows figures for the current year along with figures for the end of the planning period.

In any rows where you envisage the percentage changing, list the opportunities for your organization under the headings of 'cost reduction' and 'value creation'.

**Table 12.5** The communications mix

| Channel/Medium | Purchase phase | | | | |
|---|---|---|---|---|---|
| | Initiate dialogue (%) | Exchange information (%) | Negotiate/ tailor (%) | Commit (%) | Exchange value (%) |
| Direct mail | 85 | 60 | 20 | 20 | None |
| | 60 | 40 | 10 | 10 | |
| Sales force/ | None | 5 | 10 | None | 95 |
| face to face | | 5 | 10 | | 90 |
| Telephone | 5 | 10 | 40 | 80 | None |
| | 5 | 10 | 20 | 70 | |
| E-mail | 5 | 5 | 30 | None | None |
| | 20 | 10 | 35 | | |
| Website | 5 | 20 | 0 | 0 | 5 |
| | 15 | 35 | 25 | 20 | 10 |

*Note:* The figures indicate what percentage of each purchase phase is completed using the listed communication channel/medium with the first figure relating to the current year and the second figure relating to the end of the planning period.

## Exercise 12.3

This exercise is based on the prioritization matrix which can be used:

1 to decide on the relative importance of a number of possible channel initiatives, such as, for example, e-commerce projects;
2 as a first-cut prioritization to decide which potential opportunities should be developed into a full proposal;
3 as a second-cut prioritization to help the board prioritize limited resources, taking into account 'soft' issues such as strategic fit as well as 'hard' financial issues;
4 to help depoliticize debates about prioritization, and to sell the conclusions reached.

The tool is, though, no substitute for the development of carefully researched financials such as return on investment calculations, which should be done in parallel and used to inform the vertical axis, particularly for a second-cut prioritization.

First, select a business unit the opportunities for which you wish to prioritize. This may be the organization as a whole, or one of the markets it serves.

Using a copy of the worksheet in Table 12.6, list the channel-related opportunities, such as e-commerce projects, which you wish to prioritize. These may be projects in development, projects which have gone live or possible future projects.

Now, using the same worksheet, determine the attractiveness of each opportunity to the organization as follows:

1 List the opportunity attractiveness factors for your organization, in other words, the factors that attract you to one opportunity rather than another.

**Table 12.6** Worksheet – calculating channel-related opportunity attractiveness to the organization

Opportunity 1:                 *Name and description*
Opportunity 2:
Opportunity 3:

Opportunity 4:                 *Name and description*
Opportunity 5:

| Opportunity attractiveness factors | Weight | Parameters | | | Opportunity 1 | | Opportunity 2 | | Opportunity 3 | | Opportunity 4 | | Opportunity 5 | |
| | | High 10–7 | Med 6–4 | Low 3–0 | Score | Total | Score | Total | Score | Total | Score | Total | Score | Total |
|---|---|---|---|---|---|---|---|---|---|---|---|---|---|---|---|
| | | | | | | | | | | | | | | | |
| Total | 100 | | | | | Total | | Total | | Total | | Total | | Total | |

*Note*: The attractiveness factors, their weightings and parameters remain constant for each opportunity. Only the scores are specific to each opportunity. Parameters described as 'low', 'medium' or 'high' should be associated with a measurable definition to avoid subjective interpretation.

For example: impact on revenue; impact on margins; fit with the organization's mission; fit with the organization's skills; IT difficulty; business change difficulty and so on.

2 For each of the factors, weight their relative importance to each other according to your own particular requirements when comparing opportunities by distributing 100 points between them.

3 Define the high, medium and low parameters for each of the factors selected, where very high scores 10 and very low scores 0.

4 Take one of the opportunities and, based on the parameters, determine its score for each factor at the end of your planning period (usually three years), multiply these individual scores by the weight that has been given to its respective factor and divide by 100, then add all these together to arrive at a total between 0 and 10, and repeat for each opportunity.

Examples of completed attractiveness evaluations following the above procedure can be found in Chapter 9 where it was used to calculate segment attractiveness.

When determining attractiveness to the organization:

1 Keep the factors to between three and six if possible for simplicity. Consider deleting factors with a weighting of less than 10, or combining them with other factors.

2 The factors should have nothing to do with customer take-up, which is dealt with in the following analysis. Therefore, assume project success, from the point of view of the customers, in your scoring. For example, in assessing the 'impact on revenue' of a new website, assume that customers will like it and use it.

3 Clear factors, weights and parameters on this axis with key colleagues before proceeding.

4 Keep factors separate from each other.

5 Research your financial scores as carefully as you can, particularly for a second-cut prioritization.

6 If the results do not match your intuitive feelings, consider whether you need to iterate, or whether your intuition needs updating!

Now determine the attractiveness of your proposed new business models to each of your selected segments as follows:

1 From the competitive strength evaluation conducted in Chapter 10, transfer to a copy of the worksheet in Table 12.7 the Decisive Buying Criteria (DBCs) and constituent Critical Success Factors (CSFs) for one of the segments you propose to serve. Also transfer to the worksheet the weighted importance of each DBC for this segment.

2 In the column headed 'Current model', enter the competitiveness scores and totals for your company as they appeared when evaluating your competitive strength for Year 0. 'Current' refers to your company's 'traditional' way of doing business, such as selling via a direct sales force, or selling over the Web with your current site.

3 In each of the columns headed 'New model', list the new channel-related opportunities you are considering for this segment.

4 Take one of the new opportunities and score its attractiveness to the segment out of 10 for each DBC initially for Year 0, with 'highly attractive' scoring from 10 down to 7, 'attractive' from 6 down to 4 and 'unattractive' from 3 down to 0 (these are fixed and do not change). These scores are as perceived by the customers in the segment. Enter the scores for each new opportunity you have listed.

**Table 12.7** Worksheet – calculating channel-related opportunity attractiveness to a segment

| Segment | | Current model | | New model | | New model | |
| --- | --- | --- | --- | --- | --- | --- | --- |
| DBCs and their CSFs | Weight | Score | Total | Score | Total | Score | Total |
| | | | | | | | |
| | | | | | | | |
| | | | | | | | |
| | | | | | | | |
| | | | | | | | |
| Total | 100 | Total | | Total | | Total | |
| Attractiveness *(new model total minus current model total)* | | | | | | | |

5 For each opportunity listed, multiply the individual scores by the weight that has been given to its respective DBC and divide by 100, then add all these together to arrive at a total between 0 and 10.

6 To arrive at a number representing the 'attractiveness to customers', subtract the 'Current model' total from each 'New model' total and enter these at the bottom of the worksheet.

Once the calculations for Year 0 are complete, a further copy of the worksheet can be used to determine attractiveness for the end of the planning period. When determining attractiveness to a segment:

1 It should be approached from the customer's perspective. Whenever possible, therefore, customers should be asked for their views. Alternatively, involve a small cross-functional team of those in your organization who are close to the customer.

2 Include all the segment's DBCs, even if they are unaffected by the new business model(s) you are proposing.

3 If the opportunity is targeted at a different stakeholder group, such as the supply-side, modify these instructions to assess the attractiveness factors (as opposed to DBCs) for this group. These could include: margin achieved; transaction costs; fit with the organization's procedures; scope for building a long-term relationship and so on. A recruitment site might be assessed on, for example, range of vacancies, ease of obtaining information and so on.

The attractiveness scores can now be plotted on a prioritization matrix:

1 Transpose the organization's attractiveness scores for each opportunity on to the vertical axis of the prioritization matrix in Figure 12.9 and label each intersection on the vertical axis with the opportunity number and/or name. Ensure the scale from the point of origin to the highest point allows a spread of opportunities between them rather than having the opportunities all grouping together at one or other end of the scale (a suggestion as to how to obtain a spread appears in Figure 12.9).

2 Now transpose the segment's attractiveness scores for the opportunities evaluated for it on to the horizontal axis of the prioritization matrix in Figure 12.9 using a scale ranging from +2 to −2 (normally sufficient for most exercises).

3 Locate the points of intersection as illustrated in Figure 12.10.

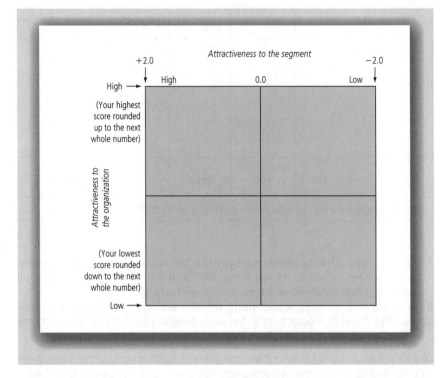

**Figure 12.9**
Worksheet – the prioritization matrix (*Note:* Although 'high' is positioned on the left of the horizontal axis it can, if you prefer, be placed on the right.)

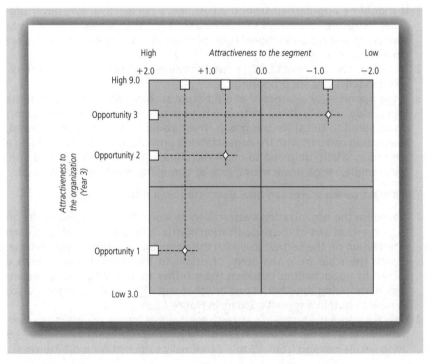

**Figure 12.10**
The prioritization matrix

In addition to producing a separate prioritization matrix for each segment, consider transferring all the segment attractiveness scores on to a single prioritization matrix to produce a consolidated picture of the new opportunities being evaluated. Identify the applicable segment for each intersection on the horizontal axis.

When you have completed the prioritization matrix, consider the implications for the organization's resource allocation:

● Where should the investment in, for example, money and management time go?
● For these high-priority opportunities, what needs to be done to ensure that your envisaged scores on the segments' DBCs are reached?

Finally, with respect to the prioritization matrix:

1 Do not take the cross-lines too literally! What matters is the relative position of your opportunities, not their absolute position on your grid.
2 Consider interactions between opportunities. If you invest in one opportunity, such as a direct sales channel, will that affect your revenue or profits through another, such as an agent's network?
3 However, you cannot hold back the tide! If customers wish to switch to a new way of doing business (represented by a position towards the left of the prioritization matrix), 'cannibalization' of your traditional business may be necessary if you are not to leave a competitor to fill the gap.

# Chapter 13
# Setting marketing objectives and strategies for identified segments

# Summary

It will by now be clear that, following the analysis that takes place as part of the segmentation process, realistic and achievable objectives, along with their associated strategies, should be set for the company's key segments. As it is the setting of objectives that forms a key step in the marketing planning process, it is at this point that segmentation becomes directly linked with marketing planning which, in turn, means that the objectives have to be developed within the framework of the overall corporate plan.

Once agreement has been reached on the broad marketing objectives and strategies, those responsible for the programmes of marketing activity can then proceed to the detailed planning stage, developing the overall strategy statements into sub-objectives.

Unless the setting of marketing objectives and strategies is carried out well, everything that follows will lack focus and cohesion. In previous chapters, you have gone to a lot of trouble to develop an in-depth understanding of your market and to select the right targets. The purpose of this chapter is to ensure that you score a bull's-eye on your selected targets!

This chapter is organized as follows:

- A discussion about what marketing objectives are and how they relate to corporate objectives
- How to set marketing objectives
- What competitive strategies are and how they can be used to gain competitive advantage
- How to start the process of marketing planning
- A brief review of product development as a growth strategy
- An introduction to marketing strategies and how to set them
- A review of the chapter
- Exercises further to help you analyse the gap between sales and financial objectives and long-term forecasts

# Marketing objectives: what they are and how they relate to corporate objectives

There are no works on marketing which do not include at least one paragraph on the need for setting objectives. Setting objectives is a mandatory step in the planning process. The literature on the subject, though, is not very explicit, which is surprising when it is considered how vital the setting of marketing objectives is.

An objective will ensure that a company knows what its strategies are expected to accomplish and when a particular strategy has accomplished its purpose. In other words, without objectives, strategy decisions and all that follows will take place in a vacuum.

Following the identification of opportunities and the explicit statement of assumptions about conditions affecting the business, the process of

> ● Definition:
> A marketing objective is the quantification of what an organization sells (its products) and to whom (its segments).

> A reminder: We use the word 'product' to avoid unnecessary references to 'services', 'not-for-profit services', 'capital goods' and 'retail'. The text is equally relevant to these.

setting objectives should, in theory, be comparatively easy, the actual objectives themselves being a realistic statement of what the company desires to achieve as a result of market-centred analysis, rather than generalized statements born of top management's desire to 'do better next year'. However, objective-setting is more complex than at first it would appear to be.

Most experts agree that the logical approach to the difficult task of setting marketing objectives is to proceed from the broad to the specific. Thus, the starting point would be a statement of the nature of the business, from which would flow the broad company objectives. Next, the broad company objectives would be translated into key result areas, which would be those areas in which success is vital to the firm. At one level, key result areas would include, for example, market penetration and the overall growth rate of sales. At a lower level, 'market penetration' could well be stepped down to 'segment penetration'. The third step would be the creation of the sub-objectives necessary to accomplish the broad objectives, such as sales volume goals, geographical expansion, segment extension, product line extension, and so on.

The end result of this process should be objectives which are consistent with the strategic plan, attainable within budget limitations, and compatible with the strengths, limitations and economics of other functions within the organization.

At the top level, management is concerned with long-run profitability which may well extend into market-related objectives; at the next level in the management hierarchy, the concern is for objectives that are defined more specifically and in greater detail, such as increasing sales and segment share, moving into new segments, and so on. These objectives are merely a part of the hierarchy of objectives, in that corporate objectives will only be accomplished if these and other objectives are achieved. At the next level, management is concerned with objectives that are defined even more tightly, such as to create awareness among a specific target segment about a new product, to change a particular customer attitude, and so on. Again, the general marketing objectives will only be accomplished if these and other sub-objectives are achieved. It is clear that sub-objectives per se, unless they are an integral part of a broader framework of objectives, are likely to lead to a wasteful misdirection of resources.

For example, a sales increase in itself may be possible, but only at an undue cost, so that such a marketing objective is only appropriate within the framework of corporate objectives. In such a case, it may well be that an increase in sales in a particular segment will entail additional capital expenditure ahead of the time for which it is planned. If this were the case, it may make more sense to allocate available production capacity to more profitable segments in the short term, allowing sales to decline in another segment. Decisions such as this are likely to be more easily made against a backcloth of explicitly stated broad company objectives relating to all the major disciplines.

Likewise, objectives should be set for advertising, for example, which are wholly consistent with the wider marketing objectives. Objectives set in this way integrate the advertising effort with the other elements in the marketing mix and this leads to a consistent, logical marketing plan.

# So what is a corporate objective and what is a marketing objective?

A business starts at some time with resources and wants to use those resources to achieve something. What the business wants to achieve is a corporate objective, which describes a desired destination or result. Most often this is expressed in terms of profit, since profit is the means of satisfying shareholders or owners, and because it is the one universally accepted criterion by which efficiency can be evaluated, which will, in turn, lead to efficient resource allocation, economic and technological progressiveness and stability. How it is to be achieved is a strategy. In a sense, this means that the only true objective of a company is, by definition, what is stated in the corporate plan as being the principal purpose of its existence.

This means that stated desires, such as to expand segment share, to create a new image, to achieve an *x* per cent increase in sales, and so on, are in fact strategies at the corporate level, since they are the means by which a company will achieve its profit objectives. In practice, however, companies tend to operate by means of functional divisions, each with a separate identity, so that what is a strategy in the corporate plan becomes an objective within each department.

For example, marketing strategies within the corporate plan become operating objectives within the marketing department, and strategies at the general level within the marketing department themselves become operating objectives at the next level down, so that an intricate web of inter-related objectives and strategies is built up at all levels within the framework of the overall company plan.

The really important point, however, apart from clarifying the difference between objectives and strategies, is that the further down the hierarchical chain one goes, the less likely it is that a stated objective will make a cost-effective contribution to company profits, unless it derives logically and directly from an objective at a higher level.

Corporate objectives and strategies can be simplified in the following way:

*Corporate objective*

- desired level of profitability

*Corporate strategies*

- which segments and which products (marketing)
- what kind of facilities (operations, distribution, IT)
- size and character of the staff/labour force (personnel)
- funding (finance)
- other corporate strategies such as social responsibility, corporate image, stock market image, employee image and so on

It is now clear that at the next level down in the organization (in other words, at the functional level) what products are to be sold into what segments become *marketing objectives*, while the means of achieving these objectives using the marketing mix are *marketing strategies*. At the next level down there would be, say, *advertising objectives* and *advertising strategies*, with the subsequent *programmes* and *budgets* for achieving the objectives. In this way, a hierarchy of objectives and strategies can be traced back to the initial corporate objective. Figure 13.1 illustrates this point.

> **Definition:**
> A corporate objective describes a desired destination or result. Most often this is expressed in terms of profit.

> The only true objective of a company is, by definition, what is stated in the corporate plan as being the principal purpose of its existence.

> **Definition:**
> Corporate strategies define how corporate objectives are to be achieved through the use of its resources.

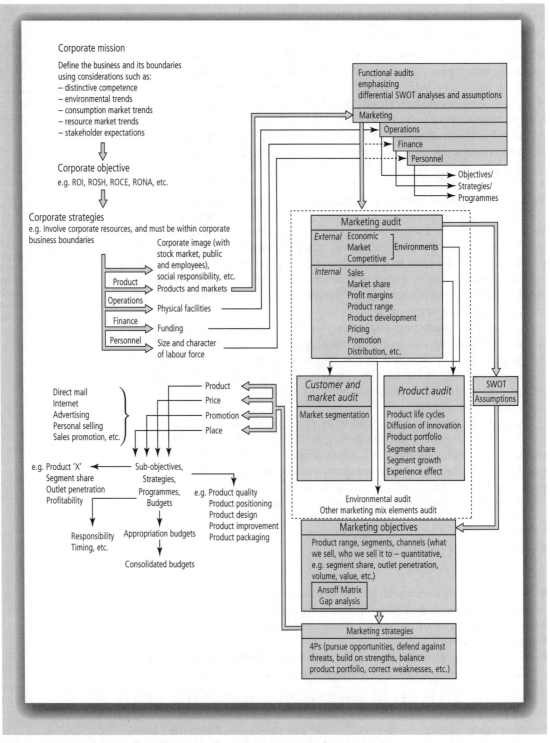

**Figure 13.1**  Objectives and strategies in a corporate framework
(*Source:*  McDonald, M. (2002). *Marketing Plans: How to Prepare Them, How to Use Them.*
Oxford: Butterworth-Heinemann.)

# How to set marketing objectives

The <u>Ansoff</u> Matrix (1957) can be introduced here as a useful tool for thinking about marketing objectives. It is a concept normally written in terms of 'markets', but for the purposes of this book we will substitute (where appropriate) 'segment' for 'market'.

A firm's competitive situation can be simplified to two dimensions only, products and segments. To put it even more simply, Ansoff's framework is about what is sold (the 'product') and to whom it is sold (the 'segment'). Within this framework, Ansoff identifies four possible courses of action for the firm:

1  Selling existing products to existing segments.
2  Extending existing products to new segments.
3  Developing new products for existing segments.
4  Developing new products for new segments.

The matrix in Figure 13.2 depicts these concepts.

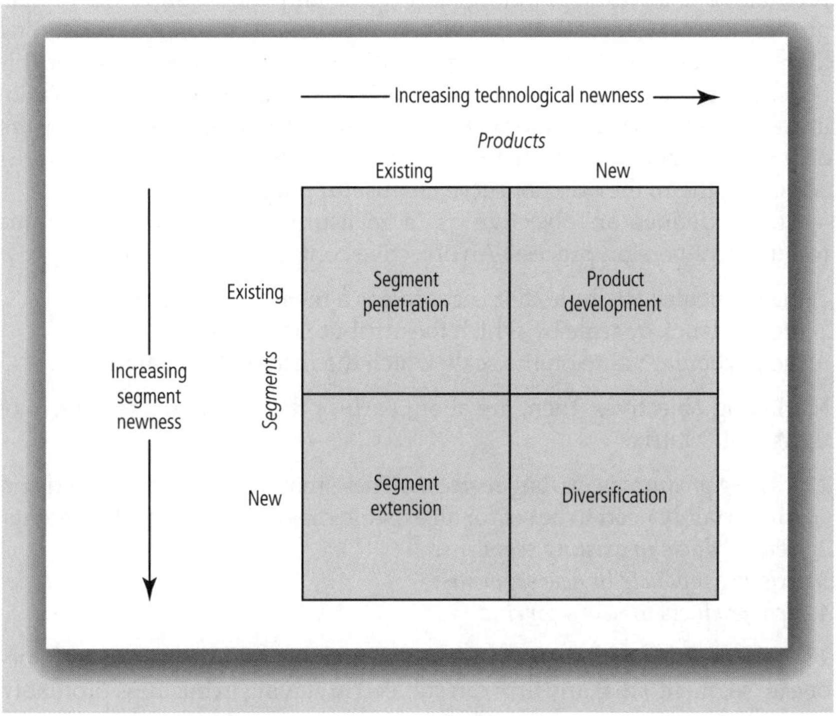

● Definition:
Igor Ansoff is a famous American planning guru who constructed a matrix known as the Ansoff Matrix, which had two dimensions and four boxes – existing products, new products, existing markets, new markets.

**Figure 13.2**
The Ansoff Matrix

It is clear that the range of possible marketing objectives is very wide, since there will be degrees of technological newness and degrees of segment newness. Nevertheless, Ansoff's Matrix provides a logical framework in which marketing objectives can be developed under each of the four main headings above. In other words, *marketing objectives are about products and segments only*.

Commonsense will confirm that it is only by selling something to someone that the company's financial goals can be achieved, and that advertising, pricing, service levels and so on, are the means (or strategies) by which it might succeed in doing this. Thus, pricing objectives, sales promotion objectives, advertising objectives, and so on should not be confused with marketing objectives.

Marketing objectives are generally accepted as being quantitative commitments, usually stated either in standards of performance for a given operating period, or conditions to be achieved by given dates. Performance standards are usually stated in terms of sales volume and various measures of profitability. The conditions to be attained are usually a percentage of segment share and various other commitments, such as a percentage of the total number of a given type of distribution outlet.

There is also broad agreement that objectives must be specific enough to enable subordinates to derive from them the general character of action required and the yardstick by which performance is to be judged. Objectives are the core of managerial action, providing direction to the plans. By asking where the operation should be at some future date, objectives are determined. Vague objectives, however emotionally appealing, are counterproductive to sensible planning, and are usually the result of the human propensity for wishful thinking, which often smacks more of cheerleading than of serious marketing leadership. What this really means is that it is unacceptable to use directional terms such as 'decrease', 'optimize' or 'minimize' as objectives, because it is logical that, unless there is some measure or yardstick against which to measure a sense of locomotion towards achieving them, they do not serve any useful purpose.

Ansoff defines an objective as 'a measure of the efficiency of the resource-conversion process. An objective contains three elements:

1 the particular attribute that is chosen as a measure of efficiency;
2 the yardstick or scale by which the attribute is measured;
3 the particular value on the scale which the firm seeks to attain.'

Marketing objectives, then, are about each of the four main categories of the Ansoff Matrix:

1 *Existing products in existing segments*. These may be many and varied and will certainly need to be set for all existing major products and segments.
2 *New products in existing segments*.
3 *Existing products in new segments*.
4 *New products in new segments*.

Thus, in the long run, it is only by selling something (a 'product') to someone (a 'segment') that any firm can succeed in staying in business profitably.

**Marketing insight**

A two-year study of the top 35 industrial companies by McKinsey and Company revealed that leader companies agreed that product/segment strategy is the key to the task of keeping shareholders' equity rising. Clearly, then, setting objectives and strategies in relation to products and segments is a most important step in the marketing planning process.

Simply defined, product/segment strategy means the route chosen to achieve company goals through the range of products it offers to its chosen segments. Thus, the product/segment strategy represents a commitment to a future direction for the firm. Marketing objectives, then, are concerned solely with products and segments.

> Marketing objectives are concerned solely with products and segments.

The general marketing *directions* which lead to the above objectives flow, of course, from a product life cycle and portfolio analysis. However, when drawing up the objectives, we must concern ourselves with both the life cycles and portfolio analysis of our segments *and* the life cycles and portfolio analysis of our products *in* our chosen segments. The link between these two concepts is illustrated in Figure 13.3. For a full explanation, please refer to McDonald (2002).

> ● Definition:
> A product life cycle plots the volume or value of sales of a product from its launch to its decline and withdrawal.

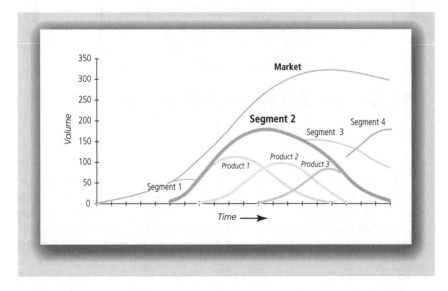

**Figure 13.3**
Product life cycles within segments

The marketing directions which come out of life cycle and portfolio analysis revolve around the following logical decisions, with a brief guide to the appropriate strategies also listed. Please note that, although we refer to the labels invented by the Boston Consulting Group (for example, 'cash cow'), such labels should not generally be used in connection with the directional policy matrix and are used here only for the purpose of explanation. We have suggested more appropriate labels for the directional policy matrix in Figure 13.5 and Table 13.1, both of which appear after the following review.

● *Maintain* – This usually refers to the 'cash cow' type of product/segment (segments that fall in the bottom left-hand box of the Boston Matrix which we first discussed in Chapter 9 and summarized in Figure 9.3 which, for ease of reference, is repeated in a simplified format in Figure 13.4) in which the company enjoys a competitive position, and reflects the desire to maintain a competitive and profitable position, even though it is acknowledged that these products/segments are not as attractive as other products/segments in terms of achieving the organization's objectives.

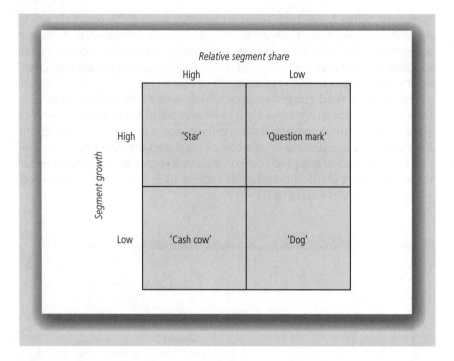

*Relative segment share*

**Figure 13.4**
The Boston Matrix
(basic outline)

The emphasis will be on maintaining present earnings in the most profitable products/segments, rather than aggressive growth, while activity in those that are less profitable should be considered for cutting back. Marketing effort should be focused on differentiating products to maintain share of key segments. Discretionary marketing expenditure should be limited, especially when unchallenged by competitors, or when products have matured. Comparative prices should be stabilized, except when a temporary aggressive stance is necessary to defend segment share.

● *Improve* – This usually refers to the 'star' type of product/segment (segments that appear in the top left-hand box) and reflects the desire to improve the competitive position in attractive segments which look as if their attractiveness will continue, or even improve. The obvious objective for such segments is to maintain your sales/volume growth rates at least at the segment growth rate, thus maintaining segment share, or to grow faster than the segment, thus increasing segment share.

Three principal factors should be considered:

1 Possible geographic expansion.
2 Possible product line expansion.
3 Possible product line differentiation.

These could be achieved by internal development, joint ventures or acquisition.

The main point is that, in attractive segments, an *aggressive marketing posture is required*, together with a very tight budgeting and control process to ensure that capital resources are efficiently utilized.

- *Harvest* – This usually refers to a particular category of 'dog' type product/segment (segments that appear in the bottom right-hand box, but towards the mid-point vertical line of the matrix) where the company has a moderately good to poor position (as opposed to an unquestionably poor position) and reflects the desire to relinquish competitive position in favour of short-term profit and cash flow, but not necessarily at the risk of losing the business in the short term. These are sometimes referred to as 'cash dogs'.

    The reality of low growth should be acknowledged and the temptation to grow sales into these segments or grow sales of those products at the previous high rates of growth should be resisted. They should not be viewed as a 'marketing problem', which will be likely to lead to high advertising, promotion, product development and inventory costs, and therefore to lower profitability. Some of the 'maintain' policies may still be appropriate, but with more of an eye on profit and cash flow.

    Finally, the attention of talented managers should be focused on these 'cash dogs'.

- *Exit* – This usually refers to the genuine 'dog' type of product/segment (segments that appear in the bottom right-hand box, but well to the right of the mid-point vertical axis), also sometimes to the 'question mark', and reflects a desire to divest because of a very weak competitive position or because the cost of staying in it is prohibitive and the risk associated with improving its position is too high. Generally, immediate divestment is the preferred course of action, unless there is still the opportunity to generate some cash with minimal marketing expenditure.

- *Enter* – This usually refers to the new and most promising emerging products/segments where it has been decided to invest for future product/segment leadership (selected segments that appear in the top right-hand box).

As already stated, however, great care should be taken not to follow slavishly any set of 'rules' or guidelines related to the above. It should be stressed that there can be no *automatic* policy for a particular segment or product, and SBU managers should consider three or more options before deciding on 'the best' for recommendation. Above all, SBU managers must evaluate the most attractive opportunities and assess the chances of success in the most realistic manner possible. This applies particularly to new business opportunities. New business opportunities would normally be expected to build on existing strengths, particularly in marketing, which can be subsequently expanded or supplemented.

In addition, the use of pejorative labels like 'dog', 'cash cow' and so on should be avoided.

A full list of marketing guidelines as a precursor to objective setting is given in Figure 13.5. A fuller list is set out in Table 13.1 which includes guidelines for functions other than marketing. One word of warning, however: such general guidelines should not be followed unquestioningly. They are included more as checklists of questions that should be asked about each major product in each major segment *before* setting marketing objectives and strategies.

> The use of pejorative labels like 'dog', 'cash cow' and so on should be avoided.

> General guidelines should not be followed unquestioningly.

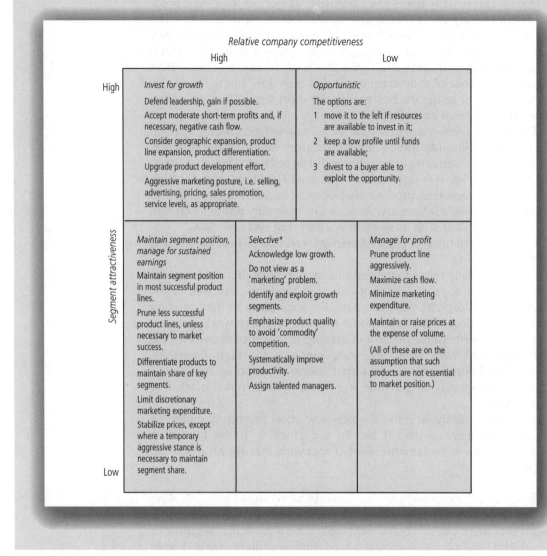

**Figure 13.5**  Strategies suggested by portfolio matrix analysis
(*Note:* 'Selective*' refers to those segments or products which fall on or near the vertical dividing line in a directional policy matrix.)

It is at this stage that the circles in the directional policy matrix can be moved to show their relative size and position in three years' time. You can do this to show, first, where they will be if the company takes no action and, second, where you would ideally prefer them to be. These latter positions will, of course, become the marketing objectives. Precisely how this is done was shown in Chapter 10. It is, however, the key stage in the marketing planning process.

**Table 13.1** Guidelines suggested for different positioning on the directional policy matrix

| |  |  |  |  | |
|---|---|---|---|---|---|
| *Main thrust* | Invest for growth | Maintain segment position, manage for earnings | Maintain selectively | Manage for cash | Opportunistic development |
| *Segment share* | Maintain or increase dominance | Maintain or slightly milk for earnings | Maintain selectively | Forgo share for profit | Invest selectively in share |
| *Products* | Differentiation – line expansion | Prune less successful. Differentiate for key segments | Emphasize product quality. Differentiate | Aggressively prune | Differentiation – line expansion |
| *Price* | Lead – aggressive pricing for share | Stabilize prices/raise | Maintain or raise | Raise | Aggressive – price for share |
| *Promotion* | Aggressive promotion | Limit | Maintain selectively | Minimize | Aggressive promotion |
| *Distribution* | Broaden distribution | Hold wide distribution pattern | Maintain selectively | Gradually withdraw distribution | Limited coverage |
| *Cost control* | Tight control – go for scale economies | Emphasize cost reduction, viz. variable costs | Tight control | Aggressively reduce both fixed and variable | Tight, but not at expense of entrepreneurship |
| *Production* | Expand, invest (organic, acquisition, joint venture) | Maximize capacity utilization | Increase productivity, for example, specialization/automation | Free up capacity | Invest |
| *R&D* | Expand – invest | Focus on specific projects | Invest selectively | None | Invest |
| *Personnel* | Upgrade management in key functional areas | Maintain. Reward efficiency, tighten organization | Allocate key managers | Cut back organization | Invest |
| *Investment* | Fund growth | Limit fixed investment | Invest selectively | Minimize and divest opportunistically | Fund growth |
| *Working capital* | Reduce in process – extend credit | Tighten credit – reduce accounts receivable, increase inventory turn | Reduce | Aggressively reduce | Invest |

# Competitive strategies

At this stage of the planning process, it would be helpful to explain developments in the field of competitive strategies, since an understanding of the subject is an essential prerequisite to setting appropriate marketing objectives.

One of the principal purposes of marketing strategy is for you to be able to choose the customers, and hence the segments, you wish to deal with. In this respect, the directional policy matrix discussed in Chapter 9 is particularly useful. The main components of competitive strategy are:

- the company;
- customers;
- products/services;
- competitors.

If we are to succeed, we need to work hard at developing a sustainable competitive advantage.

So far, we have said very little about competitors although, clearly, if we are to succeed we need to work hard at developing a sustainable competitive advantage. The important word here is 'sustainable', as temporary advantages can be gained in numerous ways, such as, for example, a price reduction or a clever sales promotion.

Most business people would agree that as segments mature, the only way to grow the business without diversifying is at the expense of competitors, which implies the need to understand in depth the characteristics of each important segment to the company and of the main competitors in it. We briefly referred to the leading thinker in this field in Chapter 9, namely Michael Porter of the Harvard Business School, and any reader wishing to explore this vital subject in more depth should refer to his book, *Competitive Strategy* (1980).

Perhaps the best way to summarize this complex subject would be to tell a story.

Imagine three tribes on a small island fighting each other because resources are scarce. One tribe decides to move to a larger adjacent island, sets up camp, and is followed eventually by the other two, who also set up their own separate camps. At first it is a struggle to establish themselves, but eventually they begin to occupy increasing parts of the island; eventually, many years later, they begin to fight again over adjacent land. The more innovative tribal chief – that is, the one who was first to move to the new island – sits down with his senior warriors and ponders what to do, since none are very keen to move to yet another island. They decide that the only two options are:

1 Attack and go relentlessly for the enemy's territory.
2 Settle for a smaller part of the island and build in it an impregnable fortress.

These two options, namely terrain or impregnable fortress (or both), are, in fact, the same options that face business people as they contemplate competitive strategy. Let us look in turn at each of these options, continuing for a moment longer with the military analogy, and starting with terrain.

Imagine two armies facing each other on a field of battle. One army has 15 soldiers in it, the other 12 (depicted by circles). Imagine also that they face each other with rifles and all fire one shot at the other at the same time, but they don't all aim at the same soldier! Figure 13.6 depicts the progress of each side in disposing of the other. It will be seen that after only three volleys, the army on the right has only one soldier remaining, while the army on the left, with eight soldiers remaining, is still a viable fighting unit.

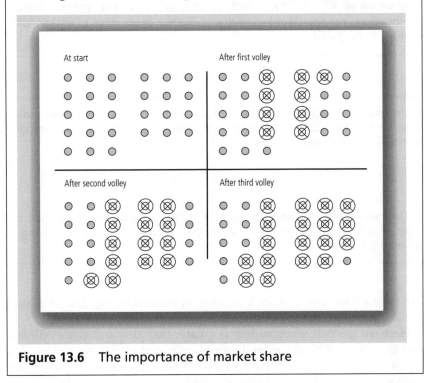

**Figure 13.6** The importance of market share

One interesting fact about this story is that the effect observed here is *geometric* rather than *arithmetic*, and is a perfect demonstration of the effect of size and what happens when all things are equal, except size. The parallel in industry, of course, is segment share.

Just look at what used to happen in the computer industry when GE, Rank Xerox, RCA, ICL and others attacked the giant IBM in its core segments. The larger competitor was able to win the battle. So, all things being equal, a company with a larger segment share than another should win in the long term over a smaller competitor. Or *should* they? Clearly, this is not inevitable, providing the smaller companies take evasive action. Staying with the computer industry, just look at how successful NCR have been with their 'global fortress' strategy (for example, Automatic Teller Machines (ATMs) for the financial market) and, more recently, Dell Computers, each of whom focused on particular segments in the overall market *not* dominated by the likes of IBM.

In 1992 and 1993, IBM got caught unawares, with disastrous financial results, by quicker-moving, smarter, smaller competitors. They have now recovered by regrouping and re-segmenting their market, just as Rank Xerox did in the 1970s to recover from the successful entry of the Japanese with smaller photocopiers. IBM have also used their enormous market power and reach to take advantage of the new but substantial markets for services. However, recent developments at Xerox leave the question of their future wide open.

| Marketing insight | In the market for banking services, First Direct in the UK took a commanding position by means of a differentiated product, dispensing with all the paraphernalia of expensive branches. |
|---|---|

| Marketing insight | In the market for insurance, Direct Line in the UK completely changed the rules of warfare by dispensing with brokers, with a consequential saving in premiums for customers. |
|---|---|

Put yet another way, look for a moment at the economists' model of supply and demand shown in Figure 13.7.

Here we see that when supply is greater than demand, price will fall, and that when demand exceeds supply, the price will tend to rise. The equilibrium point is when supply matches demand. The only way a competitor can avoid the worst effects of such a situation is by taking one of the following actions:

1 being the lowest cost supplier;
2 differentiating the product in some way so as to be able to command a higher price.

Michael Porter (1985) combined these two options into a simple matrix, as shown in Figure 13.8.

It can be seen that Box 1 represents a sound strategy, particularly in commodity-type markets such as bulk chemicals, where differentiation is harder to achieve because of the identical nature of the chemical make-up of the product. In such cases, it is wise to recognize the reality and pursue

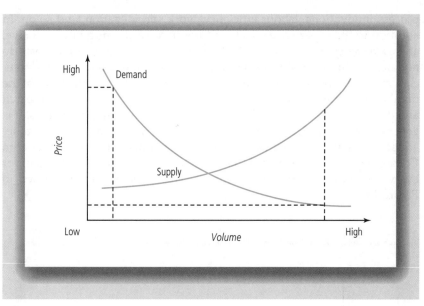

**Figure 13.7**
Supply and demand curves

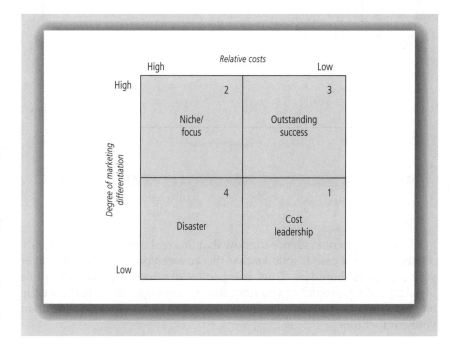

**Figure 13.8**
Cost versus differentiation matrix
(*Source:* based on Porter, M. E. (1985). *Competitive Advantage – Creating and Sustaining Superior Performance.* New York: Free Press.)

a productivity drive with the aim of becoming the lowest cost producer. It is here that the experience effect becomes especially important.

Very briefly, the experience effect, which also includes the 'learning curve', is recognition of the fact that the more we do something, the better we are at doing it. Included in the experience effect are such items as better productivity from plant and equipment, product design improvements,

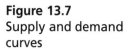

Definition: The experience effect, which also includes the 'learning curve', reflects the improvements (usually resulting in lower costs) that result from economies of scale, learning and improved productivity over time.

process innovations, labour efficiency, work specialization, and so on. In addition to the experience effect, and not necessarily mutually exclusive, are *economies of scale* that come with growth. For example, capital costs do not increase in direct proportion to capacity, which results in lower depreciation charges per unit of output, lower operating costs in the form of the number of operatives, lower marketing, sales, administration, and research and development costs, and lower raw materials and shipping costs. It is generally recognized, however, that cost decline applies more to the value-added elements of cost than to bought-in supplies. In fact, the Boston Consulting Group discovered that costs declined by up to 30 per cent for every cumulative doubling of output. This phenomenon is shown in Figure 13.9.

> Cost decline applies more to the value-added elements of cost than to bought-in supplies.

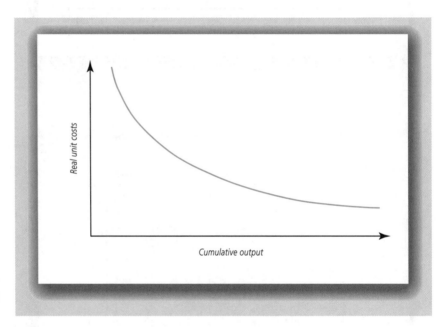

**Figure 13.9**
The impact on unit costs of the learning curve

There is sufficient evidence to show that this real cost reduction actually occurs, in which case it follows that the greater your volume, the lower your unit costs should be. Thus, irrespective of what happens to the price of your product, providing you have the highest segment share (hence the biggest volume), you should always be relatively more profitable than your competitors.

Many companies, however, such as Jaguar and BMW, could not hope to be low cost producers. Consequently, their whole corporate philosophy is geared to differentiation and what we have called 'added value'. Clearly, this represents a sensible strategy for any company that cannot hope to be a world cost leader and, indeed, many of the world's great companies succeed by means of such a focus and locate themselves in Box 2 (in Figure 13.8). Many of these companies also succeed in pushing themselves into Box 3, the outstanding success box, by occupying what can be called 'global fortresses'. A good example of this is NCR, who dominate the world's banking and retail markets with their focused technological and marketing approach. American Express is another.

Companies like IBM, McDonald's and General Electric, however, typify Box 3, where low costs, differentiation and world leadership are combined in their corporate strategies.

Only Box 4 remains. Here we can see that a combination of commodity-type markets and high relative costs will result in disaster sooner or later. A position here is tenable only while demand exceeds supply. When, however, segments in these markets mature, there is little hope for companies who find themselves in this unenviable position.

An important point to remember when thinking about differentiation as a strategy is that you must still be *cost-effective*. It is a myth to assume that sloppy management and high costs are acceptable as long as the product has a good image and lots of added value. Also, in thinking about differentiation, please refer back to the section on benefit analysis in Chapter 7, for it is here that the route to differentiation will be found. It is also clear that there is not much point in offering benefits that are costly for you to provide but which are not highly regarded by customers: in other words, benefits which are not their important DBCs. So consider using a matrix like the one given in Figure 13.10 to classify your benefits. Clearly, you will succeed best by providing as many benefits as possible that fall into the top right-hand box.

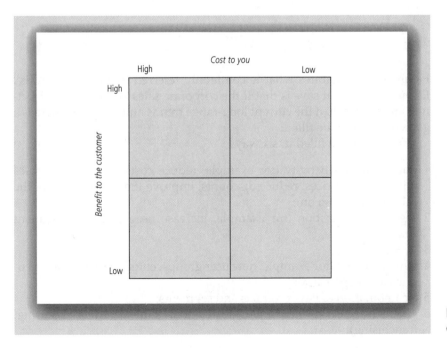

**Figure 13.10**
Cost/benefit matrix

ICI is an example of a company that is proactively changing its global strategy by systematically moving away from bulk chemicals in Box 1 (in Figure 13.8) towards speciality chemicals in Box 2 and then going on to occupy a 'global fortress' position in these specialities (Box 3). This, however, is proving very difficult in this mature market.

The main point here, however, is that when setting marketing objectives, it is essential for you to have a sound grasp of the position in your segments of yourself and your competitors and to adopt appropriate postures for the several elements of your business, all of which *may* be different. It may be necessary, for example, to accept that part of your product portfolio is in the 'Disaster' box (Box 4). You may well be forced to have some products here, for example, to complete your product range to enable you to offer your more profitable products into your chosen segment(s). The point is that you must adopt an appropriate stance towards these products and set your marketing objectives accordingly, using where appropriate the guidelines given in Figure 13.5 and Table 13.1.

Finally, here are some very general guidelines to help you think about competitive strategies.

1 Know the terrain on which you are fighting (the market and its segments).
2 Know the resources of your enemies (competitive analysis).
3 Do something with determination that the enemy is not expecting.

# Where to start – gap analysis

Figure 13.11 illustrates what is commonly referred to as 'gap analysis'. Essentially, what it says is that if the corporate sales and financial objectives are greater than the current long-range trends and forecasts, there is a gap which has to be filled.

This gap can be filled in six ways:

1 improved productivity (for example, reduce costs, improve the sales mix, increase prices, reduce discounts, improve the productivity of the sales force and so on);
2 segment penetration (for example, increase usage, increase segment share);
3 new products;
4 new segments (for example, new user groups, enter new segments, geographical expansion);
5 a combination of new products and segments;
6 new strategies (for example, acquisition, joint ventures, licensing, franchising).

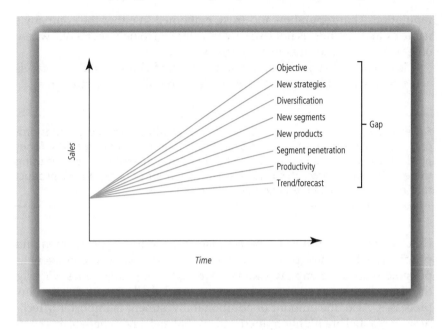

**Figure 13.11**
Gap analysis

Another option, of course, is to reduce the objectives!

Gap analysis is best done in two separate steps. Step 1 should be done for sales revenue only so, under the gap, in Figure 13.11, reducing costs is not relevant as we are only interested in revenue growth. Step 2 should then go through the same stages, but this time looking at the profit and costs implications of achieving the sales growth.

A detailed methodology for completing both steps is given in the Exercises section of this chapter.

If improved productivity is one method by which the profit gap is to be filled, care must be taken not to use measures such as 'to reduce marketing costs by 20 per cent overall'. The portfolio analysis undertaken earlier will indicate that this would be totally inappropriate for some segments (although it may be applicable to some of the products at the later stages of their life cycle sold into these segments) for which increased marketing expenditure may be needed, while for others a 20 per cent reduction in marketing costs may not be sufficient.

As for sales growth options, it is clear that segment penetration should always be a company's first option, since it makes far more sense to attempt to increase profits and cash flow from *existing* products and segments initially, because this is usually the least costly and the least risky. This is so because, for its present products and segments, a company has developed knowledge and skills which it can use competitively. Associated with this is the growing interest in customer retention and there is now much evidence to show that keeping existing customers can be a source of ever-increasing profits.

For the same reason, it makes more sense in many cases to move along the horizontal axis of the Ansoff Matrix for further growth before attempting to find new segments. The reason for this is that it normally takes many years for a company to get to know its segments and to build up a

As for sales growth options, it is clear that segment penetration should always be a company's first option.

reputation. That reputation and trust, embodied in either the company's name or in its brands, is not so easily transferable to new segments, where other companies are already entrenched.

It is essential that you ensure that the method chosen to fill the gap is consistent with the company's capabilities and builds on its strengths.

## Marketing insight

For example, it would normally prove far less profitable for a dry goods grocery manufacturer to introduce frozen foods than to add another dry foods product. Likewise, if a product could be sold through existing channels using the existing sales force, this is far less risky than introducing a new product that requires new channels and new selling skills.

New products should be consistent with the company's known strengths and capabilities. Diversification is the riskiest strategy of all.

Exactly the same applies to the company's operations, distribution and people. Whatever new products are developed should be as consistent as possible with the company's known strengths and capabilities. Clearly, the use of existing operations capacity is generally preferable to new processes. Also, the amount of additional investment is important. Technical personnel are highly trained and specialized, and whether this competence can be transferred to a new field must be considered. A product requiring new raw materials may also require new handling and storage techniques, which could prove expensive.

## Marketing insight

It can now be appreciated why going into new segments with new products (diversification) is the riskiest strategy of all, because *new* resources and *new* management skills have to be developed. This is why the history of commerce is replete with examples of companies that went bankrupt through moving into areas where they had little or no distinctive competence.

This is also why many companies that diversified through acquisition during periods of high economic growth have since divested themselves of businesses that were not basically compatible with their own distinctive competence.

The Ansoff Matrix, of course, is not a simple four-box matrix, for it will be obvious that there are degrees of technological newness, as well as degrees of segment newness. Figure 13.12 illustrates the point. It also demonstrates more easily why any movement should generally aim to keep a company as close as possible to its present position, rather than moving it to a totally unrelated position, except in the most unusual circumstances.

Nevertheless, the life-cycle phenomenon will inevitably *force* companies to move along one or more of the Ansoff Matrix axes if they are to continue to increase their sales and profits. A key question to be asked, then, is *how* this important decision is to be taken, given the risks involved.

A full list of the possible methods involved in the process of gap analysis is given in Figure 13.13. An even more detailed list, including what needs to be measured, is given in Figure 13.14. This also suggests that

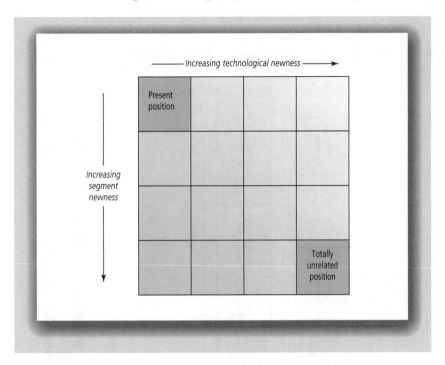

**Figure 13.12**
Technological and segment newness

executives should try to discriminate between marketing expenditure which is essential to maintain the business (maintenance) and marketing expenditure to develop the business (development). From this it will be seen that there is nothing an executive can do to fill the gap that is not included in the list. The precise methodology to implement this concept can be found in McDonald (2002).

At this point, it is important to stress that the 'objectives' point in gap analysis should *not* be an extrapolation, but your own view of what revenue would make this into an excellent business.

Marketing insight

The word 'excellent' must, of course, be relative only to comparable businesses. If all the executives in a company responsible for SBUs were to do this, and then work out what needed to be done to fill any gaps, it is easy to understand why this would result in an excellent overall business performance. Instead, what often happens is that executives wait until there is a crisis before doing any strategic planning. For many such organizations, alas, during the late 1980s and early 1990s, it was all left too late and many went bankrupt. In the late 1990s and at the dawn of the new century, countless dotcom businesses jumped on the internet bandwagon with no properly thought-out strategies, and their demise was inevitable.

One final point to make about gap analysis based on the Ansoff Matrix is that, when completed, the details of exactly *how* to achieve the objectives still needs to be worked out. This is the purpose of the strategic marketing

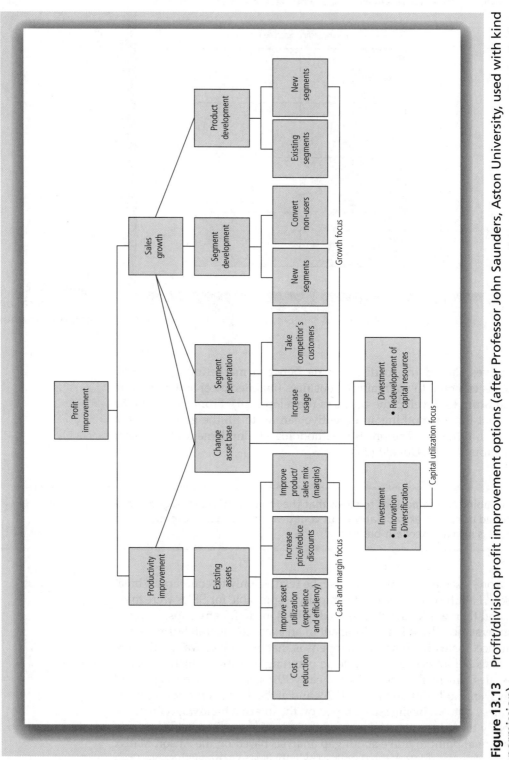

**Figure 13.13** Profit/division profit improvement options (after Professor John Saunders, Aston University, used with kind permission)

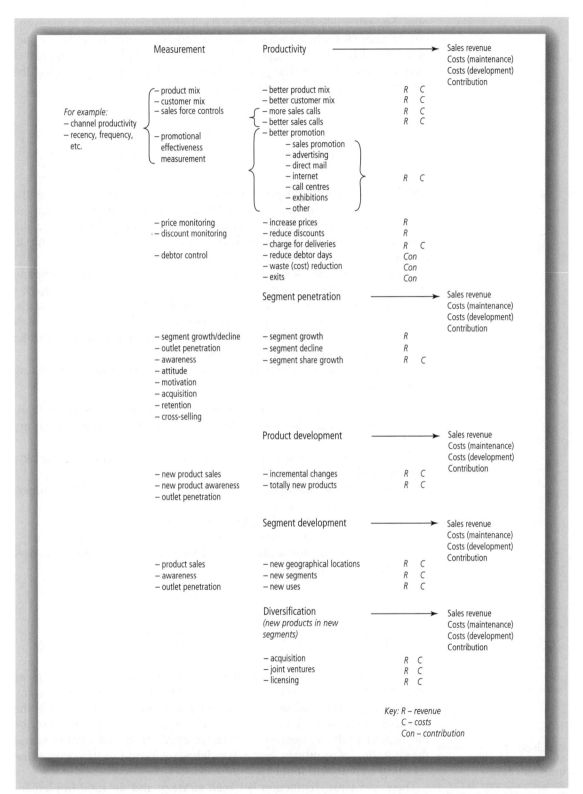

**Figure 13.14** Comprehensive list of options for filling the 'gap' and suggested measurements

plan. So, gap analysis represents a very useful starting point in mapping out the general route, which is why we suggest you start here, rather than going to all the trouble of preparing a strategic marketing plan only to have to change it later. The point is, however, that gap analysis using the Ansoff Matrix is *not* a marketing plan.

# New product development

Although it is not the purpose of this book to explore in detail any of the sub-sets of marketing, such as market research, new product development and diversification and so on, it would nonetheless be quite useful briefly to outline the process of new product development and its relationship to the gap analysis described earlier.

After new product development has been placed in a broad company context through the company understanding how it relates to its market and gap analysis, the organization must understand the micro considerations. These involve the range of factors that must be taken into account when a product is assessed in terms of its fit within the product portfolio and its contribution towards objectives.

New product development can usefully be seen as a process consisting of the following seven steps:

1 *Idea generation* – the search for product ideas to meet company objectives.
2 *Screening* – a quick analysis of the ideas to establish those which are relevant.
3 *Concept testing* – checking with the appropriate segments that the new product ideas are acceptable.
4 *Business analysis* – the idea is examined in detail in terms of its commercial fit with the business.
5 *Product development* – making the idea 'tangible'.
6 *Testing* – market tests necessary to verify early business assessment.
7 *Commercialization* – full-scale product launch, committing the company's reputation and resources.

# Marketing strategies

Strategy is the route to achievement of specific objectives and describes how objectives will be reached.

Definition: ●
Marketing strategies are the means by which a company achieves its marketing objectives and are usually concerned with the four Ps.

What a company wants to accomplish, then, in terms of such things as segment share and volume is a 'marketing objective'. How the company intends to go about achieving its objectives is 'strategy'. Strategy is the overall route to the achievement of specific objectives and should describe the means by which objectives are to be reached, the time programme and the allocation of resources. It does not delineate the individual courses the resulting activity will follow.

There is a clear distinction between strategy and detailed implementation, or tactics. Marketing strategy reflects the company's best opinion as to how it can most profitably apply its skills and resources to the marketplace. It is inevitably broad in scope. The plan which stems from it will spell out action and timings and will contain the detailed contribution expected from each department.

There is a similarity between strategy in business and strategic military development. One looks at the enemy, the terrain, the resources under command, and then decides whether to attack the whole front, an area of enemy weakness, to feint in one direction while attacking in another, or to attempt an encirclement of the enemy's position. The policy and mix, the ways in which they are to be used, and the criteria for judging success, all come under the heading of strategy. The action steps are tactics.

Similarly, in marketing, the commitment, mix and type of resources as well as guidelines and criteria that must be met, all come under the heading of strategy. For example, the decision to use distributors in all but the three largest segments, in which company salespeople will be used, is a strategic decision. The selection of particular distributors is a tactical decision.

The following headings indicate the general content of strategy statements in the area of marketing which emerge from marketing literature:

1 Policies and procedures relating to the products to be offered, such as number, quality, design, branding, packaging, positioning, labelling, and so on.
2 Pricing levels to be adopted, margins and discount policies for product groups in particular segments.
3 Advertising, sales promotion, direct mail, call centres and the internet, along with the creative approach, the type of media, type of displays, the amount to spend, and so on.
4 What emphasis is to be placed on personal selling, the sales approach, sales training, and so on.
5 The distribution channels to be used and the relative importance of each.
6 Service levels, and so on, in relation to different segments.

Thus, marketing strategies are the means by which marketing objectives will be achieved and are generally concerned with the four major elements of the marketing mix as follows:

| | |
|---|---|
| *Product* | The general policies for product branding, positioning, deletions, modifications, additions, design, packaging, and so on. |
| *Price* | The general pricing policies to be followed for product groups in market segments. |
| *Promotion* | The general policies for communicating with customers under the relevant headings, such as advertising, sales force, sales promotion, public relations, exhibitions, direct mail, call centres, the internet and so on. |
| *Place* | The general policies for channels and customer service levels. |

The following list of marketing strategies (in summary form) covers the majority of options open under the headings of the four Ps:

1 *Product*
   - expand the line
   - change performance, quality or features
   - consolidate the line

- standardize design
- positioning
- change the product portfolio
- branding

2 *Price*
- change price, terms or conditions
- skimming policies
- penetration policies

3 *Promotion*
- change advertising or promotion
- change the mix between direct mail, call centres, the internet
- change selling

4 *Place*
- change delivery or distribution
- change service levels
- change channels
- change the degree of forward or backward integration

You should refer to McDonald (2002), Chapters 7–10, for a much more detailed consideration of promotion, pricing, service and distribution. These chapters describe what should appear in advertising and sales promotion, sales, pricing and place plans. This detail is intended for those whose principal concern is the preparation of a detailed one-year operational or tactical plan. The relationship between this detail and the strategic plan is in the provision of information to enable the planner to delineate broad strategies under the headings outlined above. In Chapter 5 of the same book, all the product options are covered.

Formulating marketing strategies is one of the most critical and difficult parts of the entire marketing process. It sets the limit of success. Communicated to all management levels, it indicates what strengths are to be developed, what weaknesses are to be remedied, and in what manner. Marketing strategies enable operating decisions to bring the company into the right relationship with the emerging pattern of market opportunities, which previous analysis has shown to offer the highest prospect of success.

> Formulating marketing strategies is one of the most critical and difficult parts of the entire marketing process.

# Marketing objectives, strategies and profitability – valuing key market segments

Finally, guidelines follow on the *profitability* aspects of setting marketing objectives and strategies for your key market segments.

It is strongly advised, however, that you consult your accountant when considering this section, as the methodology described is quite complex and the implications are very profound for the total organization.

## Background/facts

- Risk and required return are positively correlated, in other words, as risk increases, investors expect a higher return.
- Risk is measured by the volatility in expected returns, in other words, the likelihood of making a very good return or losing money. This can be described as the quality of returns.
- All assets are defined as having future value to the organization. Hence, assets to be valued include not only tangible assets like plant and machinery, but intangible assets, such as key market segments.
- The present value of future cash flows is one of the most acceptable methods to value assets including key market segments.
- The present value is increased by:
  - increasing the future cash flows
  - making the future cash flows 'happen' earlier
  - reducing the risk in these cash flows, in other words, improving the certainty of these cash flows (hence the required return).

## Suggested approach

- Identify your key market segments according to their attractiveness to your company, as suggested in Chapter 9.
- Based on your current experience and planning horizon that you are confident with, make a projection of future cash flows.
- Identify the key factors that are likely to either increase or decrease these future cash flows. We suggest identifying the top five factors.
- Use your judgement to rank your segments according to the likelihood of the events leading to those factors occurring. This will help you to identify the relative risk of your key market segments.
- Ask your accountant to provide you with the overall required return for your company: this is often referred to as the weighted average cost of capital (WACC), or cost of capital.
- Now identify the required rate of return for each of your key segments based on the WACC. (WACC is the return required from the average segment.) A higher required rate will apply for more risky segments and a lower rate for less risky segments. Your ranking of segments above will help you to decide the required return based on your understanding of the risk of each of these key segments.
- We recommend a range of plus or minus 30 per cent of WACC provided by your accountant.
- Thus (assuming your WACC is, say, 10 per cent) in your portfolio matrix drawn up in Chapter 10, such as the one shown in Figure 13.15, you and your financial adviser may decide to use, say, 8.5 per cent for segments in Box 1 (in other words, a 15 per cent reduction on the WACC), 11.5 per cent for those in Box 2 (in other words, a 15 per cent premium over the WACC), 13 per cent for segments in Box 3 (in other words, a 30 per cent premium over the WACC) and 10 per cent for segments in Box 4.
- Discount the future cash flows identified above using the risk-adjusted rates to arrive at a value for your segments.

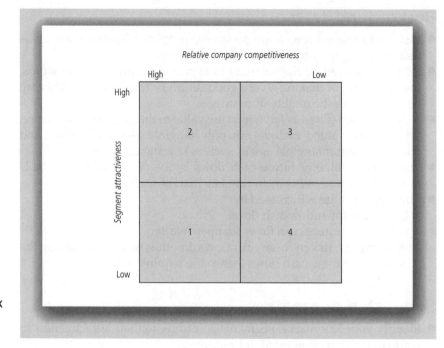

**Figure 13.15**
The portfolio matrix and valuing key market segments

- An aggregate positive net present value indicates that you are creating shareholder value, in other words, achieving actual overall returns greater than the weighted average cost of capital, having taken into account the risk associated with future cash flows.

# Chapter 13 review

This chapter has confirmed the need for setting clear, definitive objectives for all aspects of marketing, and that marketing objectives themselves have to derive logically from corporate objectives. The advantages of this practice are that it allows all concerned with marketing activities to concentrate their particular contribution on achieving the overall marketing objectives, as well as facilitating meaningful and constructive evaluation of all marketing activity.

Because marketing objectives have to be set within the framework of the corporate plan, we began by discussing the relationship between corporate objectives and marketing objectives. In doing so we identified that a hierarchy of objectives existed within organizations and that corporate objectives would only be accomplished if all these levels of objectives were achieved. We used this as the opportunity to explain the difference between an objective and a strategy because at whatever level you are in an organization, what you want to achieve at that level is an objective, how you plan to achieve it is your strategy. For those responsible for implementing the strategies, they set the required outcomes as their objectives and how they plan to achieve them become, in turn, their strategies. The result is an intricate web of interrelated objectives and strategies built up at all levels within the framework of the overall company plan. By breaking down the overall objectives in this way, the problem of strategy development becomes more manageable, hence easier.

Next, we discussed how to set marketing objectives and introduced the Ansoff Matrix (Ansoff, 1957) as a useful tool for thinking about these objectives. Here we pointed out that because it is only by selling something (a 'product') to someone (a 'segment') that any firm can succeed in staying in business, this means that marketing objectives are concerned solely with products and segments. We also introduced into the discussion the need to relate the general marketing direction of these objectives to the life cycles and portfolio analyses of both your products and your chosen segments and, while doing so, provided some guidelines for appropriate strategies.

We then considered developments in the field of competitive strategies as it is only by developing a sustainable competitive advantage that a company can hope to succeed. Here we introduced a simple matrix for competitive advantage developed by Michael Porter (1985) and briefly ran through its implications for companies.

With all the tools for objective-setting in place, we then looked at using 'gap analysis' as a start to the process of marketing planning. Here we identified six ways of filling the gap between corporate sales and financial objectives and the current long-range trends and forecasts when the latter were predicted to fall short of the former, and used the Ansoff Matrix to identify where the least and most risky strategies were to be found. Considerations with respect to the portfolio and life-cycle analysis were also discussed.

After a brief review of new product development we took a look at marketing strategies and how these were the means by which a company achieved its objectives and were usually concerned with the four Ps. Here we emphasized that formulating marketing strategies was one of the most critical and difficult parts of the marketing process.

Finally, we provided guidelines on the profitability aspects of setting marketing objectives and strategies and how the location of segments on your portfolio matrix could be used to distinguish between different rates of return required from each of them.

Here it is worth stressing that the vital phase of setting objectives and strategies is a highly complex process which, if done badly, will probably result in the considerable misdirection of resources. For more detailed insights into this key aspect of marketing and a practical guide to marketing planning, readers are recommended to refer to McDonald (2002).

# References

Ansoff, H. I. (1957). 'Strategies for diversification'. *Harvard Business Review*, September–October, 113–24.

McDonald, M. (2002). *Marketing Plans: How to Prepare Them, How to Use Them.* Oxford: Butterworth-Heinemann.

Porter, M. E. (1980). *Competitive Strategy: Techniques for Analysing Industries and Competitors.* New York: Free Press.

Porter, M. E. (1985). *Competitive Advantage – Creating and Sustaining Superior Performance.* New York: Free Press.

# Exercises

The Exercise shown here, concerned with carrying out a gap analysis, is in two parts. The first part considers *revenue* and the second part considers *profit*.

A series of worksheets accompany this exercise. Make as many copies of these worksheets as you need.

## Exercise 13.1
### Part 1 – Revenue

Objective – start by plotting the sales position you wish to achieve at the end of your planning period, illustrated by point 'E' in Figure 13.16.

Next, plot the forecast position, point 'A' in Figure 13.16.

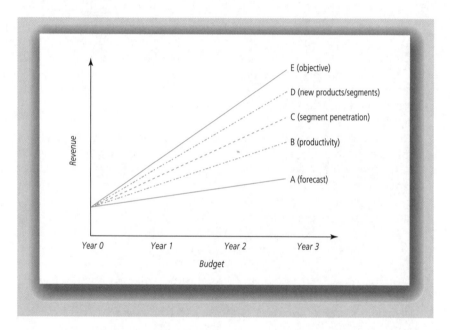

**Figure 13.16**
Gap analysis – plotting the revenue positions for Exercise 13.1

**Table 13.2** Worksheet – productivity actions to close the sales gap

| Productivity (NB Not all factors are mutually exclusive) | Revenue |
|---|---|
| Better product mix (1) | |
| Better customer mix (2) | |
| More sales calls (3) | |
| Better sales calls (4) | |
| Increase price | |
| Reduce discounts | |
| Charge for deliveries | |
| Total | |

Productivity – are there any actions you can take to close the gap under the headings in Table 13.2? Plot the total revenue value of these actions, point 'B' in Figure 13.16. (These represent cash and margin focus.)

Existing products/existing segments (segment penetration) – list your principal products on the horizontal axis of Figure 13.17 and principal segments on the vertical axis. In each smaller square, write in current sales (top left) and achievable sales during the planning period (bottom right). Figure 13.17 represents the top right quadrant of the Ansoff Matrix (see Figure 13.2).

Now, plot the segment penetration position, point 'C' in Figure 13.16. This point will be the addition of all the values in the bottom right of the small boxes in the Ansoff Matrix (Figure 13.17). Please note, revenue from productivity actions (1), (2), (3) and (4) in Table 13.2 should be deducted from the segment penetration total before plotting point 'C'.

New products/existing segments and existing products/new segments – next, list the value of any new products you might develop for existing segments (Figure 13.18). Alternatively, or in addition, if necessary, list the value of any existing products that you might sell to new segments (Figure 13.19). Figures 13.18 and 13.19 represent the top right and bottom left quadrants respectively of the Ansoff Matrix. Plot the total value of these, point 'D' in Figure 13.16.

New products/new segments (diversification) – list the value of any new products you might develop for new segments until point 'E' is reached. (This step, along with the previous two steps, represents a sales growth focus.)

Capital utilization – if none of this gives you the required return on investment, consider changing the asset base. This could be:

1 acquisition;
2 joint venture.

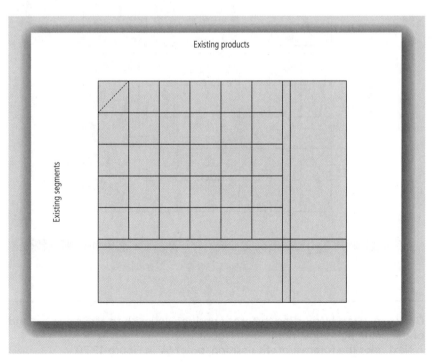

**Figure 13.17**
Worksheet – current and achievable sales revenue of existing products in existing segments

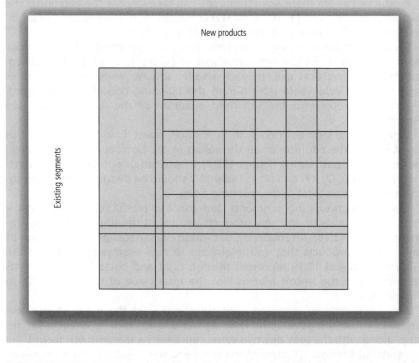

**Figure 13.18**
Worksheet – sales revenue of new products in existing segments

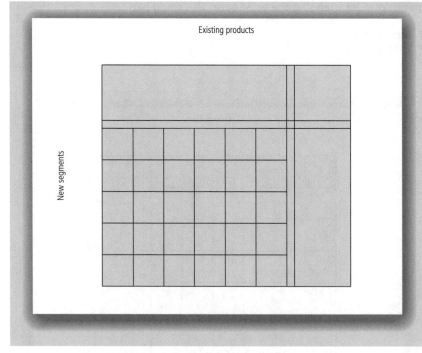

**Figure 13.19**
Worksheet – sales revenue of existing products in new segments

## Exercise 13.1
Part 2 – Profit

Objective – start by plotting the profit position you wish to achieve at the end of the planning period, point 'E' in Figure 13.20.

Next, plot the forecast profit position, point 'A' in Figure 13.20.

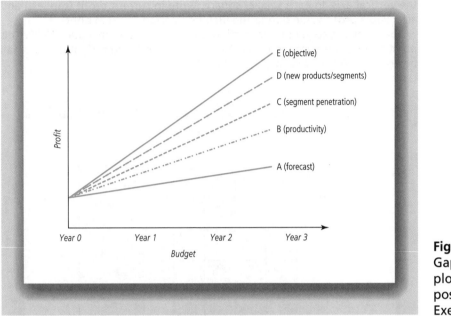

**Figure 13.20**
Gap analysis –
plotting the profit
positions for
Exercise 13.1

Productivity – are there any actions you can take to close the gap under the headings in Table 13.3? Plot the total profit value of these actions, point 'B' in Figure 13.20. (These represent cash and margin focus.)

**Table 13.3** Worksheet – productivity actions to close the profit gap

| Productivity (NB Not all factors are mutually exclusive) | Profit |
|---|---|
| Better product mix | |
| Better customer mix | |
| More sales calls | |
| Better sales calls | |
| Increase price | |
| Reduce discounts | |
| Charge for deliveries | |
| Reduce debtor days | |
| Cost reduction | |
| Others (specify) | |
| Total | |

Existing products/existing segments (segment penetration) – list your principal products on the horizontal axis of Figure 13.21 and principal segments on the vertical axis. In each smaller square, write in current profit (top left) and achievable profit value during the planning period (bottom right).

Now, plot the segment penetration position, point 'C' in Figure 13.20. This point will be the addition of all the values in the bottom right of the small boxes in the Ansoff Matrix (Figure 13.21).

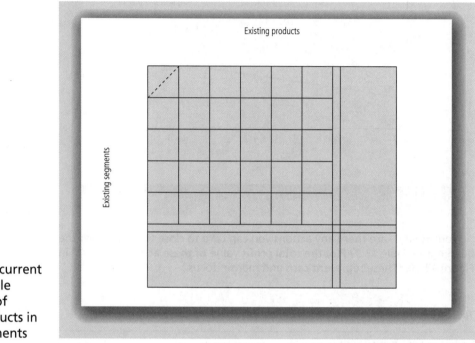

**Figure 13.21**
Worksheet – current and achievable profit value of existing products in existing segments

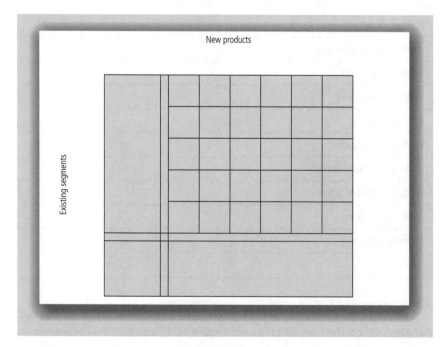

**Figure 13.22**
Worksheet – profit value of new products in existing segments

New products/existing segments and existing products/new segments –
next, list the profit value of any new products you might develop for existing
segments (Figure 13.22). Alternatively, or in addition, if necessary, list the
profit value of any existing products that you might sell to new segments
(Figure 13.23). Plot the total value of these, point 'D' in Figure 13.20.

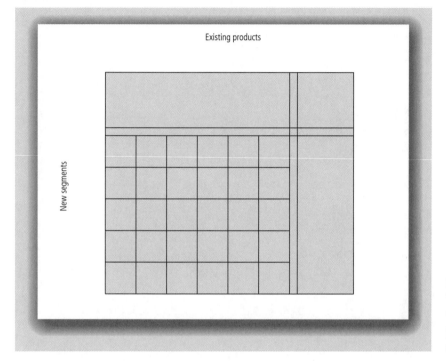

**Figure 13.23**
Worksheet – profit
value of existing
products in new
segments

New products/new segments (diversification) – list the profit value of any
new products you might develop for new segments until point 'E' is reached.
(This step, along with the previous two steps, represents a sales growth focus.)

Capital utilization – if none of this gives you the required return on investment, consider changing the asset base. This could be:

1 acquisition;
2 joint venture.

# Chapter 14
# Organizational issues in market segmentation

# Summary

The structuring of markets into clearly defined segments is undoubtedly a key input into the company's marketing plan. Segmentation not only identifies the customer groups your company should focus its resources into, but also, through the detailed analysis required in a professionally conducted segmentation process, identifies vitally important elements of a successful marketing strategy. Having an organization which is both supportive of the process and supportive of carrying through the findings into the marketplace is therefore crucial.

The purpose of this chapter is to raise and discuss the organizational issues associated with segmentation, many of which need to be addressed at the very early stages of a segmentation project.

This chapter is organized as follows:

- The vital role of the chief executive and top management
- How the need for formalized marketing procedures are related to company size and diversity of operations
- Issues to take account of when planning for the segmentation process
- A further look at the issues relating to line management and gaining their support
- The importance of integrating the segmentation process into a marketing planning system and, in turn, into a total corporate planning system
- Why an inclusive, cross-functional approach to segmentation produces the best results
- The importance of organizing the company's activities around segments
- Further considerations with respect to integrating the selected segments into the organization at the strategic level
- A brief discussion about management information systems and their support for the selected segments
- Supporting a segmentation strategy with effective marketing tactics
- A suggestion on how to bring segments to life within the organization and help win the support and enthusiasm of staff
- A review of this chapter

# Segmentation as a company exercise

Marketing's contribution to business success in manufacturing, the provision of services, distribution or retailing activities lies in its commitment to detailed analysis of future opportunities to meet customer needs and a wholly professional approach to selling to well-defined market segments those products or services that deliver the sought-after benefits. Achieving revenue budgets and sales forecasts are a function of how good our intelligence services are, how well suited our strategies are, and how well we are led.

## Support from the chief executive and top management

| | |
|---|---|
| **Marketing insight** | There can be no doubt that unless the chief executive sees the need for a segmentation review, understands the process, and shows an active interest in it, it is virtually impossible for a senior functional marketing executive to implement the conclusions in a meaningful way. |

This is particularly so in companies that are organized on the basis of divisional management, for which the marketing executive has no profit responsibility and in which he or she has no line management authority. In such cases, it is comparatively easy for senior operational managers to create 'political' difficulties, the most serious of which is just to ignore the new segments and their requirements entirely.

The vital role that the chief executive and top management *must* play in segmentation underlines one of the key points in this chapter: that it is *people* who make systems work, and that system design and implementation have to take account of the 'personality' of both the organization and the people involved, and that these are different in all organizations.

One of the most striking features we have observed is the difference in 'personalities' between companies, and the fact that within any one company there is a marked similarity between the attitudes of executives. These attitudes vary from the impersonal, autocratic kind at one extreme to the highly personal, participative kind at the other.

Any system, therefore, has to be designed around the people who have to make it work, and has to take account of the prevailing traditions, attitudes, skills, resource availability and organizational constraints. Since the chief executive and top management are the key influencers of these factors, without their active support and participation any formalized approach to segmentation is unlikely to work. The worst outcome can be a chief executive and top management ignoring the plans built out of the segmentation review and continuing to make decisions which appear illogical to those who have participated in the segmentation process and in producing the resulting marketing plan. This very quickly destroys any credibility that the emerging plans might have had, leading to the demise of the procedures and to serious levels of frustration throughout the organization.

Indeed, there is some evidence leading to the belief that chief executives who fail, first, to understand the essential role of marketing in generating profitable revenue in a business and, second, to understand how marketing can be integrated into the other functional areas of the business through marketing planning procedures, are a key contributory factor to poor economic performance.

There is a depressing preponderance of executives who live by the rule of 'the bottom line' and who apply universal financial criteria indiscriminately to all products and segments, irrespective of the long-term consequences. There is a similar preponderance of executives with a utilitarian mentality who see marketing as an unworthy activity that is something to do with activities such as television advertising, and who think of their

> The active interest of the chief executive and top management is vital if any formalized approach to segmentation is to be successful.

products only in terms of their technical features and functional characteristics, in spite of the evidence that exists that these are only a part of what a customer buys. Not surprisingly, in companies headed by people like this, market-based segmentation reviews and marketing planning are either non-existent, or where they are tried, they fail. This is the most frequently encountered barrier to effective marketing.

## Size and diversity

In a large diversified company operating in many markets, a complex combination of market, segment, product and financial plans is possible. For example, what is required at the individual segment level will be different from what is required at headquarters level, while it is clear that the total corporate plan has to be constructed from the individual building blocks. Furthermore, the function of marketing itself may be further functionalized for the purpose of marketing planning, such as market research, advertising, selling, distribution, and so on, while different markets and different segments may need to have separate plans drawn up.

*In a large diversified company operating in many markets, a complex combination of market, segment, product and financial plans is possible.*

Let us be dogmatic about requisite planning levels:

- First, in a large diversified group, irrespective of such organizational issues, anything other than a systematic approach to the issues addressed in marketing is unlikely to enable the necessary control to be exercised over the corporate identity.
- Second, unnecessary planning, or overplanning, could easily result from an inadequate or indiscriminate consideration of the real planning needs at the different levels in the hierarchical chain.
- Third, as size and diversity grow, so the degree of formalization in its marketing processes must also increase. This can be simplified in the form of a matrix as shown in Figure 14.1.

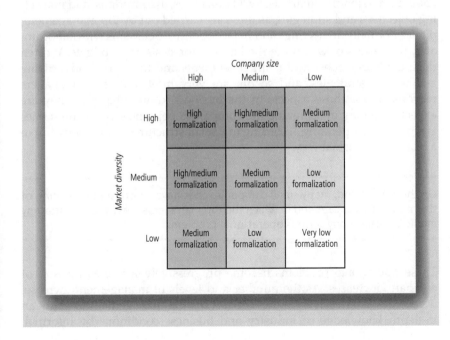

**Figure 14.1**
The influence of size and diversity on the need for formalization in marketing

The degree of formalization must increase with the evolving size and diversity of operations. However, while the degree of formalization will change, the need for a complete marketing planning system, along with all its inherent processes, does not. The problem that companies suffer, then, are a function of either the degree to which they have a requisite marketing planning system or the degree to which the formalization of their system grows with the situational complexities attendant upon the size and diversity of operations.

### Size

Size of operations is, without doubt, the biggest determinant of the two in the type of marketing systems required.

In small companies, there is rarely much diversity of markets or products, and top management has an in-depth knowledge of the key determinants of success and failure. There is usually a high level of knowledge of both the technology and the market. While in such companies the central control mechanism is the sales forecast and budget, top managers are able to explain the rationale lying behind the numbers, have a very clear view of their comparative strengths and weaknesses, and they are able to explain the company's marketing strategy without difficulty. This understanding and familiarity with the strategy is shared with key operating subordinates by means of personal, face-to-face dialogue throughout the year. Subordinates are operating within a logical framework of ideas, which they understand. There is a shared understanding between top and middle management of the industry and prevailing business conditions. In such cases, since either the owner or a director is usually also deeply involved in the day-to-day management of the business, the need to rely on informational inputs from subordinates is considerably less than in larger companies. Consequently, there is less need for written procedures about understanding markets, SWOT analyses, assumptions, and marketing objectives and strategies, as these are carried out by top management, often informally at meetings and in face-to-face discussions with subordinates, the results of which are the basis of forecasts and budgets. Written documents in respect of the target segments and their price, advertising and selling strategies, and so on, are very brief, but those managers responsible for those aspects of the business know what part they are expected to play in achieving the company's objectives. Such companies are, therefore, operating according to a set of structured procedures, but in a relatively informal way.

In small companies, there is rarely much diversity of markets or products, and top management has an in-depth knowledge of the key determinants of success and failure.

*valuable section*

**Marketing insight**

On the other hand, many small companies that have a poor understanding of the marketing concept and in which the top manager leaves his or her strategy implicit, suffer many serious operational problems.

These operational problems become progressively worse as the size of company increases. As the number and levels of management increase, it becomes progressively more difficult for top management to enjoy an in-depth knowledge of industry and business conditions by informal, face-to-face means. In the absence of written procedures and a structured framework, the different levels of operating management become increasingly less able to react in a rational way to day-to-day pressures.

In general, the bigger the company, the greater is the incidence of standardized, formalized procedures in their marketing processes.

## Diversity of operations

From the point of view of management control, the least complex environment in which to work is an undiversified company.

For the purposes of this discussion, 'undiversified' is taken to mean companies with homogeneous customer groups or limited product lines. For example, a diverse range of products could be sold into only one sector such as, say, the motor industry, with this being the only 'market' in which segmentation is required. Alternatively, hydraulic hoses could be sold to many diverse sectors, but it is only the benefits being sought from hydraulic hoses the segmentation work is required to consider. Both could be classified as 'undiversified'.

In such cases, the need for institutionalized marketing processes increases with the size of the operation, and there is a strong relationship between size and the complexity of the management task, irrespective of any apparent diversity.

---

For example, an oil company will operate in many diverse markets around the world, through many different kinds of marketing systems, and with varying levels of segment growth and segment share. In most respects, therefore, the control function for headquarters management is just as difficult and complex as that in a major diversified conglomerate. The major difference is the greater level of in-depth knowledge which top management has about the key determinants of success and failure underlying the market or product world-wide, because of its homogeneity.

**Marketing insight**

---

Because of this homogeneity of market or product, it is usually possible for headquarters to impose world-wide policies on operating units in respect of things such as certain aspects of advertising, public relations, packaging, pricing, trade marks, product development and so on, whereas in the headquarters of a diversified conglomerate, overall policies of this kind tend to be impracticable and meaningless.

The view is often expressed that common marketing processes in companies comprising many heterogeneous units is less helpful and confuses rather than improves understanding between operating units and headquarters. However, the truth is that conglomerates often consist of several smaller multinationals, some diversified and some not, and that the actual task of marketing rests on the lowest level in an organization at which there is general management profit responsibility. Forecasting and budgeting systems by themselves rarely encourage anything but a short-term, parochial view of the business at these levels, and in the absence of the kind of procedures described in this book, and found in books devoted to the process of marketing planning, higher levels of management do not have a sufficiently rational basis on which to set long-term marketing objectives.

Exactly the same principles apply at the several levels of control in a diversified multinational conglomerate, in that at the highest level of control there has to be some rational basis on which to make decisions about the portfolio of investments, and research has shown that the most successful companies are those with standard marketing procedures to aid this process. In such companies there is a hierarchy of market audits, SWOT analyses, assumptions, objectives, strategies and marketing programmes, with increasingly more detail required in the procedures at the lowest levels in the organization. The precise details of each step vary according to circumstances, but the eventual output of the process is in a universally consistent form.

The basis on which the whole system rests is the information input requirements at the highest level of command. Marketing objectives and strategies necessary to exploit the chosen segments are frequently synthesized into a multi-disciplinary corporate plan at the next general management profit-responsible level, until at the highest level of command the corporate plan consists largely of financial information and summaries of the major operational activities. This is an important point, for there is rarely a consolidated operational marketing plan at conglomerate headquarters. This often exists only at the lowest level of general management profit responsibility, and even here it is sometimes incorporated into the corporate plan, particularly in capital goods companies, where engineering, manufacturing and technical services are major factors in commercial success.

Here it is necessary to distinguish between short-term operational plans and long-term strategic plans, both products of the same process. Conglomerate headquarters are particularly interested in the progress of, and prospects for, the major areas of operational activities, and while obviously concerned to ensure a satisfactory current level of profitability, are less interested in the detailed short-term scheduling and costing-out of the activities necessary to achieve these objectives. This, however, is a major concern at the lowest level of general management profit responsibility.

To summarize, the smaller the company, the more informal and personal the procedures for segmentation and marketing planning. As company size and diversity increase, so the need for institutionalized procedures increases.

The really important issue in any system is the degree to which it enables *control* to be exercised over the key determinants of success and failure. A formally designed system seeks to find the right balance between the flexibility of operating units to react to changes in local market conditions and centralized control. The main role of headquarters is to harness the company's strengths on a world-wide basis and to ensure that lower-level decisions do not cause problems in other areas and lead to wasteful duplication. At the same time, however, it must not stifle creativity.

There would be little disagreement that in today's abrasive, turbulent and highly competitive environment, it is those firms that succeed in extracting entrepreneurial ideas and creative marketing programmes from systems that are necessarily yet acceptably formalized, that will succeed in the long run. Much innovative flair can so easily get stifled by systems.

> The really important issue in any system is the degree to which it enables control to be exercised over the key determinants of success and failure.

There is clearly a need, therefore, to find a way of injecting new enthusiasm into the periodic reviews of the market. Inertia must never set in. In companies with effective marketing processes, whether these are formalized or informal, this renewal of enthusiasm is often best achieved by the involvement of senior managers, from the chief executive down through the hierarchy. Essentially what takes place is a personalized presentation of the findings in the review of the market and its segments, together with the proposed marketing objectives and strategies and outline budgets for the strategic planning period. These are discussed, and amended where necessary, and agreed in various synthesized formats at the hierarchical levels in the organization *before* any detailed operational planning takes place. It is at such meetings that managers are called upon to justify their views, which tends to force them to be more bold and creative than they would have been had they been allowed merely to send in their proposals. Obviously, however, even here much depends on the degree to which managers take a critical stance, which will be much greater when the chief executive takes an active part in the process. *Every hour of time devoted at this stage by the chief executive has a multiplier effect throughout the remainder of the process.* And let it be remembered that we are not, repeat not, talking about budgets at this juncture in anything other than outline form.

While the segmentation task and the development of the findings into marketing objectives and strategies is less complicated in small, undiversified companies, and there is less need for formalized procedures than in large, diversified companies, the fact is that exactly the same framework should be used in all circumstances, and that this approach brings similar benefits to all.

In a multinational conglomerate, headquarters management is able to assess major trends in markets and products around the world, and is thus able to develop strategies for investment, expansion, diversification and divestment on a global basis. For their part, subsidiary management can develop appropriate strategies with a sense of locomotion towards the achievement of coherent overall goals.

This is achieved by means of synthesized information flows from the bottom upwards, which facilitates useful comparison of performance around the world, and the diffusion of valuable information, skills, experiences and systems from the top downwards. The particular benefits which accrue to companies using such systems can be classified under the major headings of the marketing mix elements as follows:

- *Product* – control is exercised over the product range. Maximum effectiveness is gained by concentrating on certain products in certain markets, based on experience gained throughout the world.
- *Price* – pricing policies are sufficiently flexible to enable local management to trade effectively, while the damaging effects of interaction are considerably mitigated.
- *Promotion* – duplication of effort and a multitude of different platforms and company images are ameliorated. Efforts in one part of the world reinforce those in another.
- *Place* – substantial gains are made by rationalization of the logistics function.

To which should be added the particular benefits which accrue from the exchange of marketing information: there is a transfer of knowledge, a sharing of expertise and an optimization of effort around the world.

The procedures which facilitate the provision of such information and knowledge transfers also encourage operational management to think strategically about their own areas of responsibility, instead of managing only for the short term.

It is abundantly clear that it is through the complete process of segmentation, marketing planning and planning skills that such benefits are achieved, and that discussions such as those about the standardization process are largely irrelevant. Any standardization that may be possible will become clear only if a company can successfully develop a system for identifying the needs of each market and each segment in which it operates, and for organizing resources to satisfy those needs in such a way that it results in the best utilization of resources worldwide.

> It is through the complete process of segmentation, marketing planning and planning skills that major benefits are achieved.

## Planning for the segmentation process

A recipe for the failure or partial failure of segmentation is to assume that the process appearing in this book can be implemented immediately and taken all the way through to its conclusions in a matter of days, or even weeks.

If the outcome of the review is best put into effect by incorporating it into a complete marketing planning system, then we are talking about years, with the evidence indicating that a period of around three years is required in a major company before a complete marketing planning system can be implemented according to its design.

Failure, or partial failure, then, is often the result of not developing a timetable for introducing a new system, to take account of the following:

1 The need to communicate why segmentation and reviews of segmentation are necessary.
2 The need to recruit top management support and participation.
3 The need to test the process out on a limited basis to demonstrate its effectiveness and value.
4 The need for training programmes, or workshops, to train line management in its use.
5 Complete lack of data and information in some parts of the world, or data and information built either around products or around past 'segments'.
6 Shortage of resources in some parts of the world.

Above all, a resolute sense of purpose and dedication is required, tempered by patience and a willingness to appreciate the inevitable problems which will be encountered in implementing the conclusions.

This is all closely linked to the next issue companies need to get right in the segmentation process: line management support.

## Line management support

Hostility, lack of skills, lack of data and information, lack of resources, and an inadequate organizational structure, all add up to a failure to obtain the willing participation of operational managers. The reasons for this are not hard to find and are related to the initiator's lack of a plan for segmentation.

New processes inevitably require considerable explanation of the procedures involved and the accompanying proformas, flow charts and so on. Often these devices are most conveniently presented in the form of a manual. When such a document arrives on the desks of busy line managers, unheralded by any previous explanation or discussion, the immediate reaction often appears to be fear of their possible inability to understand it, let alone comply with it, followed by anger and finally rejection. They begin to picture a headquarters as a remote 'ivory tower', divorced from the reality of the marketplace.

This is often exacerbated by line management's absorption in the current operating and reward system, which is geared to the achievement of *current* results, while the segmentation process, and its translation into operational requirements through the marketing planning process, is geared towards establishing the future revenue sources for the company. Also, because of the trend in recent years towards the frequent movement of executives around organizations, there is less interest in spending time on future business gains from which someone else is likely to benefit.

Line management is often absorbed in the achievement of current results, while the segmentation process, and its translation into operational requirements through the marketing planning process, is geared towards establishing the future revenue sources for the company.

Allied to this is the fact that many line managers are ignorant of basic marketing principles, have never been used to breaking up their markets into strategically relevant segments, nor of collecting meaningful information about them.

This lack of skill is compounded by the fact that there are many countries in the world which cannot match the wealth of useful information and data available in, for example, Europe and the USA. This applies particularly to rapidly-growing economies, where the limited aggregate statistics are not only unreliable and incomplete, but also quickly out of date. The seriousness of this problem is highlighted by the often rigid list of corporate headquarters' information requirements, which is based totally on the home market.

The solution to this particular problem requires a good deal of patience, common sense, ingenuity and flexibility on the part of both headquarters and operating management. This is closely connected with the need to consider resource availability and the prevailing organization structure. The problem of lack of reliable data and information can only be solved by devoting time and money to its solution and, where available resources are scarce, it is unlikely that the information demands of headquarters can be met.

It is for this reason that some kind of appropriate headquarters organization has to be found for the collection and dissemination of valuable information, and that training has to be provided on ways of solving this problem.

Again, these issues are complicated by the varying degrees of size and complexity of companies. It is surprising to see the extent to which organizational structures cater inadequately for marketing as a function. In small companies, there is often no one other than the sales manager who spends all their time engaged either in personal selling or in managing the sales force. Unless the chief executive is marketing-orientated, detailed studies of markets to determine the most appropriate segments for the business are just not made.

Unless the chief executive is marketing-orientated, detailed studies of markets to determine the most appropriate segments for the business are just not made.

In medium-sized and large companies, particularly those that are divisionalized, there is rarely any provision at board level for marketing as a discipline. Sometimes there is a commercial director with line management responsibility for the operating divisions, but apart from sales managers at divisional level, or a marketing manager at head office level, marketing as a function is not particularly well catered for. Where there is a marketing manager, that person tends to be somewhat isolated from the mainstream activities.

| Marketing insight | The most successful organizations are those with a fully integrated marketing function, whether it is line management responsible for sales, or a staff function, with operating units being a microcosm of the head office organization. |
|---|---|

However, it is clear that without a suitable organizational structure, any attempt to implement a marketing process such as segmentation which requires the collection, analysis and synthesis of market-related information is unlikely to be successful.

## Integrating the segmentation process into a marketing planning system and into a total corporate planning system

| Marketing insight | Segmentation as a stand-alone process will end up being an intellectually challenging, but theoretical, exercise if the process and conclusions are not incorporated into a marketing planning system. |
|---|---|

While effective segmentation requires there to be a marketing planning system, in turn it is difficult to initiate an effective marketing planning system in the absence of a parallel corporate planning system. This is yet another facet of the separation of operational planning from strategic planning. For unless similar processes and timescales to those being used in the marketing planning system are also being used by other major functions, such as distribution, operations, finance and personnel, the sort of trade-offs and compromises that have to be made in any company between what is wanted and what is practicable and affordable will not take place in a rational way. These trade-offs have to be made on the basis of the fullest possible understanding of the reality of the company's multifunctional strengths and weaknesses, and opportunities and threats.

One of the problems of systems in which there is either a separation of the strategic corporate planning process, or in which marketing planning is the only formalized system, is the lack of participation by key functions of the company, such as research and development, information technology or production. Where these are key determinants of success, as is frequently the case, a separate marketing planning system is virtually ineffective.

Where marketing, however, is a major activity, as in fast-moving industrial goods companies, it is possible to initiate a separate marketing planning system. The indications are that when this happens successfully, similar systems for other functional areas of the business quickly follow suit because of the benefits which are observed by the chief executive.

## Cross-functional involvement

The very nature of the segmentation process brings with it the temptation to delegate the process in its entirety to the market research manager, or to the marketing planning manager or, in the absence of a marketing planning manager, to the corporate planning function. This divorcing of the process from operations is likely to result in a strong reluctance by line management to accept the conclusions, especially if they represent a change from current thinking, as well as resentment of the rigorous process it involves and of the people who follow it.

> Divorcing the segmentation process from operations is likely to result in a strong reluctance by line management to accept the conclusions.

It also has to be said that such an approach is unlikely to produce the best results. Those staff in contact with the marketplace bring practical experience to the process. Staff from other areas of the company bring a different perspective to the issues addressed in the process, as well as a further resource for creative thinking.

The detailed work required for segmentation does not, however, suit a committee environment. As suggested in Chapter 3, 'Preparing for segmentation – avoiding the big mistakes', a core team of two or three individuals needs to be established, whose job it is to carry out the detailed work, commission externally contracted agencies as required or agree such briefs with the relevant section of the company, use the cross-functional steering group as a sounding board, and raise topics with other members of staff as appropriate.

This raises the question again of the key role of the chief executive in both the segmentation process and marketing planning as a whole. Without both the chief executive's support and understanding of the very serious implications of initiating an effective segmentation review, everyone else's efforts will largely be ineffective.

> Without both the chief executive's support and understanding of the very serious implications of initiating an effective segmentation review, everyone else's efforts will largely be ineffective.

# Successful implementation of segmented marketing

As was pointed out at the beginning of this chapter, it is impossible to divorce implementation from the process of arriving at the concluding segments. Of critical importance here are:

1 the support of the chief executive and top management;
2 a feeling of 'ownership' of the conclusions by the company's key operating units engendered by their involvement in the process;
3 an institutionalized marketing planning process which can take the results of the segmentation review and develop it into both a strategic three-year plan and a one-year marketing programme.

The world's leading
companies now
organize themselves
around segments and
processes rather than
around products.

In addition, to operate effectively in the selected segments, the company's activities should, wherever practicable, be organized around them, rather than around products, functions or geography. If this cannot be achieved, the company's market share goals and financial objectives are unlikely to be reached. Increasingly, companies are organizing themselves around customers and processes, such as product development, rather than solely around products.

## Marketing insight

Many a company has been caught out by subtle changes in their several markets causing a product to become practically redundant. In consumer goods, for example, many companies are beginning to admit that their rigid product/brand management system has allowed their major intermediaries to take the initiative, and many are now changing belatedly to a system where the focus of marketing activity revolves around major segments rather than individual products.

> Computer firms, such as AT&T for example, organize around end-use markets and appoint multi-disciplinary teams to focus their attention on their specific needs. The result is personnel, accounting, production, distribution and sales policies that are tailored specifically to a unique set of market needs.

This consideration of 'internal compatibility' is so important that it should be borne in mind whilst following the segmentation process. It is also one of the criteria used to assess the suitability of a concluding segment, along with size, differentiation and reachability.

Marketing departments can, of course, operate within the new segmentation structure on their own and develop advertising and promotional programmes accordingly: which is an implementation strategy referred to as 'bolt-on segmentation' because of its high level of customer focus but low level of organizational integration (see 'Segmentation archetypes in companies' in Chapter 3). This approach will not, however, be as successful as one which has both a high level of customer focus *and* a high level of organizational integration, or 'effective segmentation' as this particular archetype is called (Jenkins and McDonald, 1997).

Organizational integration can be looked at on three levels: the strategic, the managerial and the tactical.

### Strategic integration through the mission statement

Many organizations find their different departments, and sometimes even different groups in the same department, pulling in different directions. This often has disastrous results, simply because the organization has not defined the boundaries of the business and the way it wishes to do business in its mission or purpose statement.

Take the example of a high-technology company. One group of directors felt the company should be emphasizing technology, while another group felt technology was less important than marketing. With such confusion at the top of the company, it is not hard to imagine the chaos further down.

Marketing insight

A different example concerns a hosiery buyer for a department store group. She believed her mission was to maximize profit, whereas research showed that women shopped in department stores for items other than hosiery. They did, however, expect hosiery to be on sale, even though that was rarely the purpose of their visit. This buyer, in trying to maximize profit, limited the number of brands, colours and sizes on sale, with the result that many women visitors to the store were disappointed and did not return. So it can be seen that in this case, by maximizing her own profit, she was sub-optimizing the total profit of the group. In this case, the role of her section was more of a *service* role than a profit-maximizing role.

Marketing insight

Here, we can see two levels of mission. One is a *corporate* mission statement, the other is a lower level, or *purpose*, statement. But there is yet another level, as shown in the following summary:

*Type 1* 'Motherhood', usually found inside annual reports designed to 'stroke' shareholders. Otherwise of no practical use.

*Type 2* The real thing. A meaningful statement, unique to the organization concerned, which 'impacts' on the behaviour of the executives at all levels.

*Type 3* This is a 'purpose' statement (or lower level mission statement). It is appropriate at the strategic business unit, departmental or product group level of the organization.

The mission statement should in itself consist of brief statements, which should normally run to no more than one page and cover the following points:

1 *Role or contribution of the unit* – for example, profit generator, service department, opportunity seeker.

2 *Definition of business* – preferably in terms of the *needs* you satisfy or the *benefits* you provide, rather than in terms of what you make. Do not be too specific (for example, 'we sell milking machinery') or too general (for example, 'we are in the engineering business').

3 *Distinctive competence* – these are the essential skills/capabilities/resources that underpin whatever success has been achieved to date. This statement should be brief, consisting of one particular item or the possession of a number of skills that apply only to your organization or specific SBU. A statement that could equally apply to any competitor cannot, by definition, be a *distinctive* competence and is therefore unsatisfactory.

4 *Indications for future direction* – a brief statement of the principal things you will do, and those you would give serious consideration to (for example, move into a new segment). In some instances it may also be appropriate to cover what you will *never* do.

It is particularly in the 'business definition' and 'indications for the future' areas that the conclusions drawn from the segmentation review will have an influence.

## Managerial integration

In addition to adopting an organizational structure built around segments, as discussed earlier, it will be necessary to provide management information in a form that supports the new segmentation focus. It has to be said, however, that changing organizational structures and management information systems are not tasks that can be achieved overnight. Both will take time, and it may take a great deal of determination to prevent the difficulties that will be encountered becoming a justification for throwing out the segmentation conclusions. Evolution, as opposed to revolution, may need to be the order of the day, and the process of evolution will be slower the more the 'new order' challenges the status quo and the distribution of power.

## Tactical integration

Here we are concerned with the ability of the organization at the operational level to be effective in the segment.

The advertising and promotions department needs to be able to target their activities into the selected segments. Single approach solutions will have to be dropped in favour of differentiated solutions, some of which may need to employ techniques currently unfamiliar to the department.

The sales force will need to be trained both in distinguishing between the different segments, and in the appropriate benefits to be highlighted during sales meetings. Alternatively, of course, it may be possible to reorganize the sales group around the segments.

Differential pricing will need to be supported and understood within the organization, as the days of the single pricing policy will most likely have disappeared. This will be particularly difficult for the sales force, but they will be helped by being given carefully targeted products/services, supported by clear and distinctive promotional campaigns.

Distribution will also need to adapt, both in terms of the availability levels and channels required by the segments.

# The human face in segmentation

The personal dimension in segmentation is clearly very important: without the belief and commitment of the employees to this method of looking at the market, the segmentation process is all but sunk. But the 'personal' side of the segments themselves can help win the support and enthusiasm of staff and, in doing so, encourage them to change any previously entrenched ways.

Marketing
insight

A number of companies have turned to cartoonists in order to give a human face to their segments and put their segments on first name terms. This has the additional advantage of emphasizing that each segment is, in fact, a collection of living, breathing human beings who, just like the company's employees, look for the proposition that best meets their needs at a price they perceive as providing superior value for money. If in doing this they find themselves having to switch brands, then that is exactly what the segments will do.

This 'personalizing' of segments was certainly put to good effect in ICI Fertilizers when a new marketing plan was rolled out at the end of their extensive segmentation project. After internally researching the needs of the target market (the company's employees) and testing alternative 'offers', the seven segments which emerged from the project were named, Martin, David, Oliver, Brian, George, Arthur and Joe. All seven of them were captured as cartoon characters, with each drawing carefully tested amongst the target market in terms of its ability to portray the profile of the segment it was meant to represent. The cartoon depictions of Brian, George and Joe appear in Figure 14.2.

**Figure 14.2**
Personalizing segments using cartoon characters (Drawings by Arthur Shell)

# Chapter 14 review

A successful segmentation project is one which results in a company implementing the conclusions drawn from it. However, the degree of commitment to implementation is directly related to the extent of an organization's commitment to, and involvement in its segmentation review. In this chapter we looked at the organizational issues associated with a company's approach to segmentation and their approach to implementing the conclusions.

We first highlighted the vital role of the chief executive and top management and emphasized that it was essential to obtain their active support and participation. Without it, any formalized approach to segmentation is unlikely to work. Their commitment will not only make it far easier for the project to obtain the resources it requires but will also help surmount any internal barriers to implementation.

Next, we discussed the parameters which drive the level of formalization a company requires in its marketing processes. Here we identified company size and the extent of a company's diversity with respect to customer groups or products as the key determinants of how formalized the marketing processes needed to be, with increases in formalization being directly related to increases in size and/or diversity. Of these two, we suggested that company size had the greatest influence. The point was made, however, that when operating a formalized system, a careful balance was required between the flexibility of operating units to react to changes in local market conditions and centralized control. It is particularly important not to stifle creativity.

We then moved on to discuss the importance of planning for the segmentation process and putting together a timetable for introducing it into the company. A number of issues to be taken account of were identified, including the recruitment of top management support and participation, training, and the difficulty some areas will have in obtaining the information a *market*-based segmentation approach requires. We linked this to the next consideration, namely, obtaining line management support and their willing participation both in the process itself and in the implementation of its conclusions. This was also an opportunity to point out that the most successful organizations were those with the marketing function fully integrated into its organizational structure.

Integrating the segmentation process and its conclusions into a marketing planning system was discussed next because, if left on its own, segmentation becomes a sterile exercise. We also pointed out that it was difficult to initiate an effective marketing planning system in the absence of a parallel corporate planning system.

To conclude the discussion of segmentation as a company exercise we looked at the need to involve a number of functions from across the business in the project. However, we emphasized that the detailed work required by the project was not suited to a committee environment and that this needed to reside with a core team of two to three individuals.

We then moved on to discuss the implementation issues and began by emphasizing the critical importance, once again, of the chief executive and top management, involving the key operating units in the process, and having an institutionalized marketing planning process to ensure that the segmentation findings are embedded in the company's strategic marketing plan and one-year marketing programme.

Our discussion on implementation then looked at the need to integrate the segmentation conclusions into the company by ensuring that the company's activities were organized around them. To develop this theme, we first discussed the importance of a company having a clear mission statement and pointed out that the conclusions drawn from the segmentation review would influence some of the key statements in the mission statement. We then highlighted the importance of supporting an organizational structure built around segments with appropriate management information, and suggested that evolution rather than revolution was required here as such a change often presents a major challenge to the company.

We completed our discussion on implementation issues at the tactical level of a company's operations and emphasized that to be effective in each segment, each element of the marketing mix had to have a segment focus.

To conclude the chapter we suggested that as part of winning the support and enthusiasm of staff for the new segments, engaging the skills of a cartoonist to capture each of them as a memorable character has worked well for many companies.

# Reference

Jenkins, M. and McDonald, M. (1997). 'Market segmentation: Organisational archetypes and research agendas'. *European Journal of Marketing*, Vol. 31, No. 1, 17–32.

# Chapter 15
# Using segmentation to improve performance – a case study

# Summary

This chapter contains a case study written by a company that has applied segmentation to their business. Although the case is based on the supply of services to business customers, it contains insights that are of interest to all companies, regardless of what they supply or to whom they supply it.

   This chapter is organized as follows:

■ GlobalTech – developing service support for high-tech products

The real identity of the company has been disguised and, where necessary, the company has modified any commercially sensitive data.

   Additional case studies can be found at www.marketsegmentation.co.uk.

# GlobalTech

This case study describes the use of market segmentation to assist in the development of a service product. Customer requirements were captured via qualitative research and the segmentation was completed through the use of quantitative research. The result was a set of segments that enabled the development of a new approach to delivering service whilst improving customer satisfaction.

   *GlobalTech* is the fictitious name of a real company marketing high-tech and service products globally. Customers are counted in hundreds of thousands. The markets are mainly business-to-business with a very few large customers buying thousands of items. Service is a major revenue stream measured in billions of dollars. The lessons learnt from this case study could be of interest to any organization having to care for large numbers of customers.

## Background

### A failed segmentation

An internal GlobalTech team tried to complete a marketing audit in 2000. This included market definition, market segmentation and quantification. Each product division conducted their audit separately. They used mainly brainstorming techniques to define their markets and to produce the data required.

---

Markets transcend your internally-defined product divisions. Therefore, it is best to understand the markets and monitor your overall performance in those markets. To reshape market information to meet the needs of internal reporting will lead to misinformation.

**Company insight 1**

---

On completion, the results were compared across the divisions. It rapidly became apparent that each division addressed almost all the markets. However, the market definitions they produced were different with significant bias to just the products they offered. Similarly the segments each division identified where in conflict with the outputs from the other divisions.

On reflection it was agreed that the results were unreliable. They could not be used to help shape future strategies or marketing investments.

GlobalTech was now in the uncomfortable situation of being in a market information vacuum. Any confidence they had in their understanding of the market had been destroyed. Consequently the decision was taken that all future market analysis and understanding tasks would be supported by appropriate investments in market research.

| | |
|---|---|
| **Company insight 2** | Do not rely on the internally gathered opinions of your sales and marketing staffs to define markets and identify customer requirements and attitudes. Do invest in the necessary market research to provide a reliable segmentation and support for strategy and product development. |

### First market segmentation

The following year the segmentation was redone supported by extensive qualitative and quantitative market research. The objective was to understand and group into segments the product buyers in the overall market.

The qualitative study produced a very clear picture and definition of the markets addressed by GlobalTech. It also provided the customers' view of the benefits they sought from the products and the differences in their attitudes towards their suppliers. The questionnaire for the quantitative study was based on the results of the qualitative study. The result was seven clearly defined segments.

This enhanced understanding of the market assisted the marketing of hardware and software products but did not address service products or customer satisfaction and loyalty issues.

### The internal need

At the dawn of the twenty-first century the market life cycle had matured. All but the more sophisticated products were perceived as 'commodities'. Consequently, the opportunities for effective product differentiation had diminished. GlobalTech, in common with its competitors, was finding that customers were becoming increasingly disloyal.

For many years, product churns and upgrades from existing customers had accounted for some 70 per cent of GlobalTech's product revenues. Service and exhaust revenues[1] almost equalled total product revenues. Service was perceived to be a key influencer of loyalty. But the costs of delivering service were becoming unacceptable to customers. Concurrently, service pricing was coming under increasing competitive pressures.

[1] Exhaust revenues are those revenues that follow on, almost automatically, from an initial product sale. These would normally include service plus training, consultancy, consumables, supplies, add-ons and so on.

The challenge was to increase loyalty whilst achieving a step function improvement in margins. Thus, it was decided to invest in a better understanding of the service market as an enabler to delivering cost-effective differentiation and loyalty.

This case history covers the project from inception to implementation.

## The segmentation project

### Buy-in

The GlobalTech main board director responsible for customer service sponsored the project. This was a critical prerequisite, as the outcome would have a significant impact on the organization, its processes and behaviours.

Similarly, the project team included key members of service, marketing and finance to ensure buy-in. However, at that time, it was deemed inappropriate to include representatives from all but two of the countries due to travel implications, costs, and resource impacts. In retrospect this was not a good decision.

---

Try and anticipate the scale of organizational change that may result from a major segmentation project. Then ensure the buy-in planned from the start of the project embraces all those who will eventually have a say in the final implementation.

Company insight 3

---

### Business objectives

The project team agreed the overall business objectives as:

1 To develop strategies for profitable increase in market share and sustainable competitive advantage in the service markets for GlobalTech's products.
2 To identify opportunities for new service products and for improving customer satisfaction within the context of a robust customer needs segmentation, which can be readily applied in the marketplace.
3 To identify the key drivers of loyalty so that GlobalTech may take actions to increase customer loyalty significantly.
4 To provide the information required to help develop a new and innovative set of service products designed and tailored to meet differing customer requirements while significantly reducing internal business process costs.

### Results from the qualitative study

The output from the qualitative study was a thorough report documenting the results, in line with the desired research objectives. Some of the more surprising aspects were supported by verbatims. A key output was the polarization of very different attitudes towards service requirements that some buyers had in comparison with others. For example:

● Some wanted a response within a few hours, whereas many others would be equally happy with next day.

- Some wanted their staff thoroughly trained to take remedial actions supported by a specialist on the telephone. Others did not want to know and would just wait for the service provider to fix the problem.
- Some wanted regular proactive communications and being kept up to date. Others wanted to be left alone.
- Some would willingly pay for a premium service, under a regular contract, whilst others would prefer to take the risk.
- The attitudes of professional buyers, procuring on behalf of user departments, were consistently different from those of the user departments.

## Results from the quantitative study

The output from the quantitative study was extensive. Much of the output was detailed demographic data, opportunities information and competitive positioning comparisons. However, the focus was on a fairly extensive executive summary for internal communications within GlobalTech. What follows are summarized extracts from those outputs.

## The segments

Six market segments were identified as a result of iterative computer clustering. Initially the clustering routines had identified more segments but by careful analysis these were reduced to what was decided to be the most manageable level. Some previously very small segments were merged with very similar larger segments. A summary of the six concluding segments appears in Table 15.1.

## Polarizations in attitude

The computer clustering generated the segments by grouping customers with similar attitudes and requirements. This resulted in some marked differences in attitude between segments. As illustrated in Figure 15.1, the Koalas really did not want to know about being trained and having a go, but the Teddies, Polars and Yogis had an almost opposite attitude.

## Satisfaction and loyalty

GlobalTech was measuring customer satisfaction for use both locally, as a business process diagnostic tool, and globally, as a management performance metric. These satisfaction metrics were averaged across all customers, both by geographic business unit and by product division to meet internal management reporting requirements.

However, the outputs from the quantitative study clearly showed that these traditionally well-accepted metrics were, in fact, almost meaningless. What delighted customers in one market segment would annoy customers in another, and vice versa. To make the metrics meaningful, they had to be split by key criteria and the market segments.

Loyalty was obviously highest where GlobalTech's 'one size fits all' service deliverable coincidentally best matched a segment's requirements, as illustrated in Figure 15.2.

**Table 15.1** GlobalTech's segments

| Segment | Description |
|---|---|
| Koala bears | Preserve their assets (however small) and use, for example an extended warranty to give them cover. Won't do anything themselves, prefer to curl-up and wait for someone to come and fix it.<br><br>Small offices (in small and big companies). *28% of the market* |
| Teddy bears | Lots of account management and love required from a single preferred supplier. Will pay a premium for training and attention. If multi-site, will require supplier to effectively cover these sites. (Protect me.)<br><br>Larger companies. *17% of the market* |
| Polar bears | Like Teddy bears except colder! Will shop around for cheapest service supplier, whoever that may be. Full third party approach. Train me but don't expect to be paid. Will review annually (seriously). If multi-site, will require supplier to effectively cover these sites.<br><br>Larger companies. *29% of the market* |
| Yogi bears | A 'wise' Teddy or Polar bear working long hours. Will use trained staff to fix problems if possible. Needs skilled product specialist at end of phone, not a clerk who books appointments. Wants different service levels to match the criticality of the product to their business process.<br><br>Large and small companies. *11% of the market* |
| Grizzly bears | Trash them! Cheaper to replace than maintain. Besides, they are so reliable that they are probably obsolete when they bust. Expensive items will be fixed on a pay-as-when basis, if worth it. Won't pay for training.<br><br>Not small companies. *6% of the market* |
| Andropov big bears | My business is totally dependent on your products. I know more about your products than you do! You will do as you are told. You will be here now! I will pay for the extra cover but you will . . .!<br><br>Not small or very large companies. *9% of the market* |

## Correlation between loyalty and customer satisfaction

The life cycle for many of GlobalTech's products in the market was moving into the 'commodity' phase. Therefore, not surprisingly, customers were becoming less loyal.

Each percentage point increase in loyalty translated into almost the same increase in market share. Each percentage point in market share added many millions of dollars of gross revenues. The cost of reselling to a loyal customer was about one-sixth the cost of winning a new customer. Consequently, each percentage point increase in loyalty had a significant impact on the bottom line.

Because of this, the quantitative study included correlating the key drivers of satisfaction and loyalty within each market segment. The qualitative study

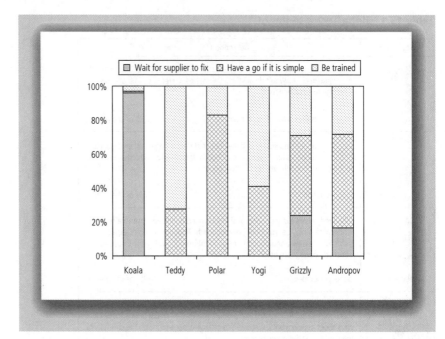

**Figure 15.1**
Differences in
attitude between
segments

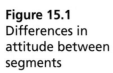

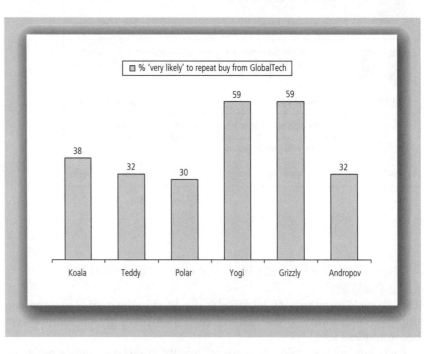

**Figure 15.2**
Loyalty to
GlobalTech by
segment

identified some 28 key customer requirements of their service provider. The quantitative study prioritized these to provide a shorter list of 17 common requirements. The correlation exercise reduced this to only two requirements that drew a significant correlation between satisfaction and loyalty:

- Providing service levels that meet your needs.
- Providing consistent performance over time.

Although GlobalTech was achieving the second, it was really only delivering the first in two of the market segments.

## Segment attractiveness

As an aid to deciding where best to invest, a chart of segment attractiveness was produced using attractiveness factors determined by GlobalTech. Demographic data from the quantitative study was combined with internal GlobalTech financial data. Each factor was weighed to reflect the relative importance to GlobalTech. This highlighted quite a few issues and some opportunities. For instance, the highest margins were coming from some of the least loyal segments. The resulting attractiveness chart appears in Figure 15.3.

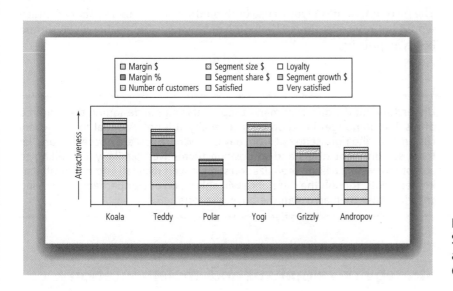

**Figure 15.3**
Segment attractiveness for GlobalTech

## Competitive positioning

Fortunately for GlobalTech, its competitors did not appear to have an appreciation of the market segments or the different requirements of their customers. They were also mainly delivering a 'one size fits all' service offering. However, there were some noticeable differences in their offerings. These resulted in each major competitor being significantly stronger in just one or two segments where their deliverables best matched the segment's needs.

The quantitative study provided detailed rankings of the decisive buying criteria (DBCs) and their constituent critical success factors (CSFs) for each market segment. These were to prove invaluable during the phase of designing the service products and developing the strategy to achieve competitive advantage.

## Reachability

Key to GlobalTech successfully implementing any strategies or communications that were to be segment-based would be the ability to identify each customer by segment. As part of the quantitative study, two statistical reachability tasks were conducted. The results were as follows:

1 A sampling of internal GlobalTech databases showed that there was sufficient relevant data to achieve better than 70 per cent accuracy, using computer imputation methods, to code each customer with its market segment. This was considered to be good enough to enhance marketing communications measurably, but might not be sufficiently accurate to ensure that the most appropriate offer was always made.
2 Statistical analysis identified four 'golden questions' that would provide acceptable accuracy in segment identification. These questions could then be used during both inbound and outbound call centre conversations until all customers had been coded.

The recommendation was to use both methods in parallel so that accuracy would improve over time. The coding of larger customers, however, should be given priority.

| Company insight 4 | Understanding the different market segments helps in designing the required offers. But do not get hung-up on reachability. It is not essential to code every customer to the right segment from day one. Where you are not really sure, let them see different offers and so position themselves. Similarly, be willing to accept that within a large organization some buyers may fall into different market segments, though the difference will only be on one or perhaps two buying criteria rather than across all the buying criteria. |
|---|---|

## Strategy development and implementation

### Market understanding and strategy development

The challenge now was for the project team to absorb and understand all the findings from the two research studies. The team then had to turn that understanding into realizable strategies. To achieve this, a workshop process covering opportunities, threats and issues (OTIs) was used.

Briefly, the process involved an extensive, but controlled, brainstorming session followed by a series of innovative strategy development workshops.

- A facilitator took the team systematically through every piece of relevant information available.
- Using brainstorming, the team tried to identify every conceivable opportunity, threat or internal issue associated with each item of information.
- The information was also then tested against a predetermined list of business behaviours and processes in an endeavour to entice additional and creative ideas out of the brainstorming.
- Using the DBCs and CSFs from the market model, strengths and weaknesses were added, thus turning the process into a SWOT.
- Similar ideas were merged and de-duplicated.

- Each idea was given two scores in the range of 1 to 9. The first ranked the probable financial impact, the second ranked the probability of success.
- The ideas were then grouped by the similarity of activity and where they had the same or an overlapping financial impact. This ensured that double counting was eliminated and that opportunities and threats were offset as appropriate. Any one group of ideas would take on the highest single financial impact score and a reassessed probability of success score.
- If the resolution of an internal issue was a prerequisite for capturing an opportunity or overcoming a threat, then the issue plus associated costs and resources was included in the same group as the opportunity or threat. The norm was for a single issue to be attached to many groups.
- The groups were named and then ranked both by financial impact and probability of success. This provided a prioritized short list of imperatives that should deliver the maximum realizable benefits to both GlobalTech and its customers.
- Iterative discussions developed this into an overall strategy with a number of prioritized sub-strategies.
- Each sub-strategy was supported by a documented description of the opportunity. At this stage encouragement was given to creating innovative, yet simple, implementation options that would maximize the chances of success. Each implementation option was supported by market, revenue and organizational impact data, associated issues, resources, costs, and required control metrics.
- Board members were involved in an option selections and investment approvals process.
- Finally, the implementation programmes and project plans were created.

## The strategy

The overall recommendation was to create a set of service deliverables tailored to the individual needs of each segment. These would be complemented by a set of premium add-ons that could be offered to the appropriate segments. By focusing on business process simplification during the design of the offering for each segment, redundancy was eliminated.

The objective of each offering was to increase customer satisfaction significantly with an emphasis on those items that would most positively impact loyalty. Some offerings were quite different from others, both in terms of the deliverable and the internal processes that made it possible. This differentiation was also intended to create a measurable competitive advantage in a number of the market segments.

A key to the implementation of the project was a recommended change to the customer satisfaction metrics, so that they became an effective diagnostic tool for tuning the ongoing deliverables for each market segment.

## Implementation

Throughout the project, the same core team had been intimately involved with each stage of the project. They guided the work and took on board the results. They delved deeply into the analysis and did their best to understand the markets, their customer requirements and likely competitive impacts. Finally they worked hard at developing the proposed strategies.

They thought buy-in had been achieved by being sponsored by a main board director.

The implementation roll-out across country boundaries became difficult. Each country wanted their say. They had different views of their customer needs and how things should be done in their country. They did not easily understand or even accept the findings of the research and the meaning of the outputs.

The majority of these internal barriers were eventually overcome. Inevitably there were compromises. These led the project team into believing that not all the market segments would be fully satisfied with the new offerings in all countries.

# Index